RESOURCES

OF

WEST VIRGINIA,

BY

M. F. MAURY,

FELLOW OF THE GEOLOGICAL SOCIETY OF LONDON; MEMBER OF THE AMERICAN INSTITUTE OF MINING ENGINEERS; ASSOCIATE OF THE ROYAL SCHOOL OF MINERS, ENGLAND.

AND

WM. M. FONTAINE, A. M.,

PROFESSOR OF NATURAL HISTORY &C., AT THE UNIVERSITY OF WEST VIRGINIA.

PREPARED UNDER THE DIRECTION OF

THE STATE BOARD OF CENTENNIAL MANAGERS.

WHEELING:
THE REGISTER COMPANY, PRINTERS.
1876

STATE BOARD OF CENTENNIAL MANAGERS OF WEST VIRGINIA.

To the Honorable Members of the Senate and House of Delegates, and to His Excellency J. J. Jacob, Governor of the State of West Virginia:

GENTLEMEN: The act appropriating $20,000 for the purpose of exhibiting, at the Centennial International Exhibition, of 1876, in Philadelphia, the resources of West Virginia, and confirming the appointment, by the Governor, of the State Board of Centennial Managers previously made, and then in active service, passed both Houses on the 10th of December, and was approved by the Governor on the 14th of December, and by resolution took effect from its passage. The time left for the collection, preparation, and arrangement of the various subjects of exhibition, was so very short, the field so extensive, usual information so entirely wanting, and the people so apathetic, and so unappreciative of the real importance and value of the undertaking, that the Board found it necessary to use extraordinary exertions, and incur many expenses in prosecuting the work, and in endeavoring to realize their hope of a creditable and remunerative display of the Minerals, Timber, etc., really possessed by the State, and as yet almost entirely unknown and undeveloped. Local Boards were appointed in every county in the State, circulars were prepared and distributed, urgent personal letters were written to citizens, and competent and active young men were engaged, and at once employed in the several departments of the work. Prof. M. F. Maury, of Charleston, Kanawha county, was entrusted with the classification and arrangement of all exhibits, and assisted by Prof. Wm. M. Fontaine, of the University of West Virginia, instructed to prepare for publication, all the information collected by the Board, relating to the objects contemplated by the law. The result of their labors is herewith submitted. Mr. A. R. Guerard, of South Carolina, and Messrs. J. W. C. Davis, St. Geo. Bryan, and Major R. J. Echols, of Virginia, were sent—Mr. Guerard to the East, Mr. Davis to the Southwest, Mr. Bryan to the West, or Ohio River Division, and Major Echols to the Kanawha Valley. Each of these gentlemen discharged the duties confided to him, with the utmost diligence, and to the entire satisfaction of the Board. It was difficult to have her citizens anticipate the value of the material results expected to be hereafter realized from exhibiting to the capitalists and people of the world, the wonderful natural wealth lying, and yet undeveloped, within the borders of

West Virginia, and, while from this cause, the efforts of our agents were sometimes fruitless in obtaining satisfactory specimens and information in many of the counties, yet, in others they were greatly assisted by the active aid and co-operation of citizens, sufficiently alive to the importance of the occasion, to whom the Board desires generally to tender its hearty thanks. It was deemed necessary by the Board, after due consideration, to erect for West Virginia an exhibition building, attached to the "Headquarters," previously determined upon, in order that she might present her collection as a whole, rather than to have it in so many separate places and buildings, as it would have been, under the arrangements made by the United States Commissioners. Accordingly, a site was selected, drawings and plans prepared by C. C. Kemble, Esq., architect, of Wheeling, and after due advertisement, contracts made with H. S. White, of Belton, for the completion of the buildings on the grounds. The "Headquarters" are built entirely of the woods of the State, finished in their natural colors.

Profs. Maury and Fontaine have been untiring and devoted in the discharge of their duties, and have manifested a zeal and energy which the Board fully appreciates. The Board regrets that (while not half has been told) the accompanying book has grown to nearly three times the size originally intended, but accepts the statement of its compilers and authors, that it is terse and concise, and that nothing can be eliminated from it, without injury to some important interest.

The Board will present to the Legislature (at its next meeting), as required by law, a full report of its proceedings and expenditures. No one can now certainly determine whether the $20,000, so generously appropriated by the Legislature, will be a dead loss and a useless investment, or whether it will pay back to the State, millions, by inducing capital and immigration, and so developing the valuable minerals and the natural wealth, with which she is so lavishly endowed by nature. Let us hope that the latter may be the result.

Very respectfully,

A. J. SWEENEY,

Chairman State Board of Centennial Managers.

O. C. Dewey, *Secretary.*

Hon. A. J. Sweeney, Chairman of the State Board of Centennial Managers for West Virginia:

SIR: I herewith submit the Report on the Resources of West Virginia, the preparation of which was made one of my duties as Director in Charge of the Centennial collection of West Virginia.

As soon as the appropriation was made by the Legislature for the purpose of having our resources represented at the International Exhibition of 1876, I at once began to take active steps to collect information from all portions of the State for the compilation of this work. To this end I prepared a set of fifty-one questions, on the agricultural, stock-raising, timber, mineral, and industrial interests, leaving blanks for the answers. These, to the amount of four thousand copies, were distributed in every county, but I am sorry to say that our people generally took so little interest in, and seemed to have so slight an appreciation of, the importance of the work undertaken by the Board, that out of that number only two hundred and fifteen were filled up and returned, and very many of those had the questions answered so carelessly as to be of no value. In the initiatory steps in setting the Centennial "ball in motion," the duties connected with my position, that claimed immediate attention, were so many and so varied, that it was not until the 26th of January, 1876, that I was able to begin writing this report, although it had to be completed by the 1st of April. But it could not have been finished then, or, in fact, for several months afterward, had it not been for the untiring energy and invaluable assistance of Prof. Wm. M. Fontaine, of the University of West Virginia, who was specially detailed, on the 1st of February, by the Board of Regents of that Institution, to the service of your Board. The many admirable chapters that appear under his name give most ample evidence of the value of his services, whilst his accurate knowledge concerning the State, contributes largely to whatever effectiveness this volume may possess.

The resources of West Virginia are so many and so varied that it is impossible, in a work of this size, or in the time that was at my disposal, to make anything more than a mere outline sketch of what we possess. It was my aim to give every industry a fair and impartial exhibition. To this end, not only were the circulars of questions sent out broadcast, but letters were written to representatives in each industry, asking for certain specified points of information that were of importance. I am sorry to say that a large majority of these elicited but very few of the facts that were wanted, so that if any district of the State, or any branch of natural wealth has not received its due consideration, it must be ascribed to those persons and corporations that were too apathetic to their sectional interests to furnish the necessary points. To this, and to the shortness of the time in which the book had to be completed, I hope you will ascribe all the imperfections that may appear in it.

Besides to Prof. Fontaine, I beg to tender my especial thanks to the other gentlemen, whose names appear as the authors of various chapters, for the kind assistance they have rendered. I have also to acknowledge a great deal of help derived from the Hand Book of West Virginia, by J. H. Diss Debar.

Hitherto, the people of one section of West Virginia knew but little of what was in the others, and had no fair conception of what our borders contained. For they, themselves, to be schooled in this, is as important as for the world at large to have authentic information concerning our young State, and I consider that the wise step that the Board took in disbursing a portion of the Centennial appropriation in this way, will be of more solid, permanent, and substantial benefit than any other that could have been devised, and if this report is productive of a more careful and complete investigation of, and a livelier interest in, the innumerable advantages that West Virginia presents to the successful prosecution of all kinds of industries, I shall be glad to have been able to render any aid toward developing my adopted State and a former portion of my native one.

Very respectfully,

M. F. MAURY.

Director in Charge of the Centennial Collection.

1st April, 1876.

TABLE OF CONTENTS.

CHAPTER I.

TOPOGRAPHY.

CHAPTER II.

CLIMATOLOGY.

CHAPTER III.

AGRICULTURAL GEOLOGY.

CHAPTER IV.

FARM PRODUCTS.

CHAPTER V.

CATTLE AND GRASSES.

CHAPTER VI.

SHEEP AND WOOL.

CHAPTER VII.

FOREST TREES, SHRUBS AND MEDICINAL PLANTS.

CHAPTER VIII.

TIMBER—ITS DEVELOPMENT AND DISTRIBUTION.

CHAPTER IX.

THE COAL FIELD.

CHAPTER X.

THE QUALITY AND VARIETY OF COAL AND THE MINING ADVANTAGES.

CHAPTER XI.

IRON.

CHAPTER XII.

SALT AND PETROLEUM.

CHAPTER XIII.

MISCELLANEOUS MINERALS.

CHAPTER XIV.

MINERAL WATERS.

CHAPTER XV.

TRANSPORTATION.

CHAPTER XVI.

EDUCATIONAL INTERESTS.

CHAPTER VII.

DESCRIPTION OF INDIVIDUAL COUNTIES.

NOTICE.

Owing to the shortness of time in which this volume had to be published, the following errors unfortunately appear in the text, and the reader is requested to kindly correct them before reading:

Page 78, line 3, for *add to this* read *add to* 10,800,000 *pounds, the production N. of the Little Kanawha.*

Page 78, line 5, for 13,000,500 read 13,500,000.
" 114, " 28, for *Fagus fermginea* read *Fagus Ferruginea.*
" 163, " 4, for 12,049,505 read 13,049,505.
" 163, " 7, for 5 *per cent* read 4.66 *per cent.*
" 164, " 17, for *series rocks* read *series of rocks.*
" 171, " 22, for *first of* read *first seam of.*
" 178, " 10, for *protoxide* read *peroxide.*
" 181, " 3, for *does pay* read *does not pay.*
" 199, table, for *Black Flint Ridge* read *Black Flint Ledge.*
" 200, table, for 54 *ft.* 3 *in.* read 56 *ft.* 3 *in.*
" 209, line 14, for *one* read *on.*
" 225, analyses, for *Ash* 18.73 read *Ash* 1.873.
" 226, analyses for *Quinnimont No.* 1, *Ash* 6.15 read *Ash* 5 85.
" 226, " for *Quinnimont No.* 2, *Ash* 5.57 read *Ash* 5 09.
" 237, line 14, for *J. M. St. John* read *I. M. St. John.*
" 252, " 26, for *cacareous* read *calcareous.*
" 260, " 20, for *iron ore* read *iron ore in workable quantities.*
" 264, " 29, for *Nov.* 25 read *No.* 25.
" 267, " 9, for *mined* read *mixed.*
" 294, " 1, for 1.200 read 1200.
" 318, " 7, for *frequently* read *apparently.*
" 318, " last for *is* read *are.*
" 323, " 16, for *Aeidulous* read *Acidulous.*
" 343, " 14, for *Marae* read *Marea.*
" 343, " 30, for *connecting* read *collecting.*
" 351, " 1, for *thereafter* read *thereof.*
" 372, " 8, for *in* read *into.*
" 373, " 33, for 12 *months* read 10 *months.*
" 383, " 36, for *Shepherdstown* read *Charlestown.*
" 385, " 33, for *exports* read *markets.*
" 389, " 15 and 16, for *Tin* read *Fire.*
" 389, " 24, for *fine* read *Fire.*
" 390, " 20, for $1000 to $1500 read $250 to $300.
" 392, " 2, for *I. W. C. Davis* read *J. W. C. Davis,*
" 394, " 30, for *it* read *coal.*

CHAPTER I.

TOPOGRAPHY.

BY WM. M. FONTAINE.

In dealing with the topography of West Virginia, we can give little more than general statements. Few measurements of altitudes are in existence, and the limited time allowed for the preparation of this hand-book, will not permit even these to be procured and digested.

It will, perhaps, give a better general idea of the topography of the country, if we select for examination one of the streams which rise on the eastern edge of the State, near the Alleghany mountains, and flow westward into the Ohio. Such a stream, when followed from its mouth to its source, will take us across the entire width of all the various surface features to be seen in that region. For it must be noted, that areas with similar topographical features, have their greatest dimensions along lines running N. E. and S. W., here as elsewhere in the Appalachian region.

In this connection we must call attention to the fact, that north of the Little Kanawha no considerable stream flows directly into the Ohio, after taking its rise in, or near, the Alleghanies. In this part of the State, the streams rising near the mountains flow N.W.,N., and N.E., and go into the Monongahela and Potomac. South of the Little Kanawha, all the streams go more or less directly west, into the Ohio, passing entirely across the State.

If we draw a N. W. line from Pocahontas to Tyler county, on the Ohio, this would nearly separate the streams flowing westward from those flowing northward. Along this line an important change in the geological structure takes place. This is more fully noted elsewhere. It is sufficient to say here, that south of this line we may consider the country as tilted towards the northwest, while north of it the surface is thrown into folds, lying closer together on the east, and opening out on the west, when at the same time a general northward slope is determined. This causes the important change seen in the direction of the rivers.

We may now describe the changes of surface to be seen along one of the east and west flowing rivers. For our present purpose no stream is better suitable than the Kanawha, and its continuation in the New and Greenbrier rivers. The features seen along this line are to be found on any of the streams which pursue a similar course. Such are the Big Sandy, Guyandotte, Gauley, Elk, and Little Kanawha.

Commencing then on the Ohio, and proceeding eastward, we note the following facts:

In the vicinity of the Ohio, as we enter the Kanawha, we are accompanied by hills of moderate height (200—300 feet), with gentle slopes, and placed more or less widely apart, having extensive bottoms along the river, and other indications of a surface composed of soft and easily worn-down material. These features accompany us for a long distance, until we approach Charleston. As we near this point, the hills become higher and higher, with more precipitous slopes and narrower valleys. At the same time they close down on the river nearer and nearer.

Passing Charleston, the same features continue, the hills gaining in height along the river until they reach, in the vicinity of Coalsburg, the altitude of 800 feet above the stream. They continue to rise gradually, until near the Falls they attain the height of 1,100 feet. At the Falls the river passes into that part of its course marked by canon features, and from this point takes the name of New river. A little back from the immediate banks, the hills rise into quite lofty mountains, attaining in Gauley mountain the height of 1,800 to 1,900 feet above the river.

The canon features attend New river to beyond Quinnimont, a distance of more than 40 miles. These are caused by the rise, above the water level, of the massive sandstones of the conglomerate series, which will be more fully described in another connection. Wherever the rivers are flowing through, and over, this series, especially its upper portion, they present much the same character. In such cases they are walled in by high hills, or precipitous cliffs, which rise almost immediately from the water's edge, leaving no bottoms or low grounds. The beds of the streams are rugged, and choked with great masses of stone, fallen from the cliffs above, while continual rapids and falls combine to give them still more of the character of mountain torrents. Such a conformation has given to New river its well-known reputation for wildness and ruggedness. But in these features it is even surpassed by its southern neighbors, the Guyandotte and Big Sandy.

While such wild and rugged scenery is presented along the immediate banks of the streams in this area occupied by the conglomerate, the case is very different when we ascend the the inclosing hills. It is thus seen that the rivers are really flowing in deep trenches, far below the general plane of the country. This general plane is determined by the upper surface of the conglomerate series, which continues to rise to the east, at an average rate of 50 feet to the mile. As a consequence of this state of things, the conglomerate rising faster than the rivers fall, the cliffs which border them become higher and higher, and the general surface more elevated, as we proceed east, until the upper surface of the conglomerate series is carried so high in the air, that it has been broken down and removed by the action of the elements.

This plane, determined by the upper surface of the conglomerate, is dotted over with hills, which do uot, in their general aspects, differ from those seen elsewhere over most of the State. Many of them rise to a considerable height, owing to special agencies, which have acted to preserve them. Where their conglomerate base has risen to a considerable height, they attain above tide an elevation which would by no means be suspected by an inspection of their altitude above their bases. Such elevations are those of Big Sewell, Cherry Pond, and Guyandotte mountains, &c.

The conglomerate base continues to rise as above described, until it makes its last appearance on the east in the Great Flat

Top, and White Oak mountains. Here it has attained the elevation of 2,800 to 3,000 feet.

Passing beyond the line of these mountains, near Hinton, and following the Greenbrier river eastward, we find the general plane of the country greatly lowered, the canon features lost, and the surface presenting general features like those seen below Charleston. This continues until we approach the White Sulphur, on the eastern border of Greenbrier, when we meet for the first time the long parallel folds of the Alleghany mountains.

If now we take a similar course from west to east in the northern part of the State, we will find a different topography. There is no rise of the general plane of the country to the east in this quarter, for the conglomerate is too deeply buried, and its thickness has become too much diminished. Commencing on the Ohio in the northern part of Wetzel, and proceeding east across Monongalia, to the west border of Preston, we find no essential difference. On the Ohio, the hills are higher here than at the mouth of the Kanawha, since they reach the height of 500 and 600 feet above the river. In Wetzel they rise still higher above their valleys, but in Monongalia they again show the same altitude as on the Onio. On the west border of Preston, we meet in Laurel Hill, the most westerly of the parallel folds of the Alleghany system, and thence these are continued, growing closer and higher, as we proceed eastward.

A bird's-eye view of the Ohio river, would show it, throughout much of its course, flowing between high, sharp-backed hills. These are higher in the north, lower in the middle, and higher again in the southern part of its course.

In order to understand the topography of a country, we must know its geology. For the rocks which underlie the soil, form the materials out of which the surface features have been carved, and their varying hardness, and proneness to disintegration, will determine the shapes finally assumed. We will then, in this connection, briefly describe some of the more important geological formations, solely in their topographical relations. The formations which have had by their presence, the most influence on the topography of our State are the following, beginning with the highest and latest formed. 1. The Upper

Barren Measures, and Productive Coals. 2. The Lower Barren Measures, and Productive Coals. 3. The Conglomerate Series. 4. The Umbral Shales and Limestone. 5. The Vespertine Shales. We may omit, in this connection, the consideration of the other formations, reserving their description for another topic, since they compose a comparatively small portion of our area.

The Upper Barren Measures, and Productive Coals, are everywhere in the state, mainly soft crumbling rocks, such as shales, and shaly sandstones, which are easily worn down and removed by rains and running streams. They are greatly thickened in the northern part of the State, but in passing South, become comparatively unimportant. Whenever they are present, owing to the readiness with which they are worn away, they produce high, conical, or rounded hills, with deep, narrow valleys, forming an irregular net-work of streams. These streams rarely have much bottom land, but it is not uncommon to find the hills with broad, flat summits.

The Lower Barren Measures, and Productive Coals, in the northern part of the State, are comparatively thin, and do not differ materially in their structure and topography from the overlying series first described. But in the south, there is a very material change. The series becomes greatly thickened, and there is a much larger proportion of firm, massive sandstones in it, especially towards the lower portion. As the topographical effects of these sandstones are in general, the same with those of the conglomerate series, we need not consider them separately. It will be sufficient to say that the change in the topography, described above, as seen in approaching Charleston from the Ohio river, is due to the rise of these rocks above water level. The conglomerate series, in the northern portion of the State, is comparatively quite thin, and is so deeply buried under the productive coal measures, that it has no effect on the topography. It is first seen in Laurel Hill, rising above the surface, and from that point eastward, it has an important influence on the surface contours, entering mainly into the mountain ridges. It is here principally massive sandstone.

In the south, on the contrary, we find it greatly thickened, and elevated to the surface over broad areas. Along New river, and southward, it has a threefold structure, being massive sandstone at bottom, more shaly and easily eroded strata in the center, and on top, again massive sandstone of great thickness. Throughout the series massive sandstones predominate. The influence of this series combined with that of the more massive portions of the Lower Productive Coals, has had an exceedingly important effect on the topography of the central and eastern portions of the State. This is in large part due to the highly siliceous character of many of these sandstones, which has enabled them to resist in a remarkable manner, degradation and removal by running streams. Such sandstones are indestructible, except by undermining and throwing down the ledges, and this process of undermining, is what has filled the streams flowing in this formation, with the huge masses of stone which we see. Especially is this true of the uppermost ledge, which is usually over 150 feet thick.

Underlying the conglomerate series, we have the umbral shales and sandstones, followed below by the umbral limestone. These shales and sandstones are generally soft and easily cut away, while much of the limestone beneath is more resistent. Hence the country having these rocks on the surface, is usually much lower than that occupied by the conglomerate, they having been cut away much more rapidly. We find these strata over much of the country lying to the east of the conglomerate, which as stated above, makes its last appearance in White Oak, Elk Knob, and Flat Top mountains.

The last formation to be mentioned here, is the upper member of the Vespertine, which is formed of crumbling red shales, and these even more readily than the shales of the umbral, are broken down and removed. These form the only other rock composing the surface of Mercer, Monroe, and Greenbrier, besides the above named.

For the purpose of topographical description, we may divide the State into two Regions, in which the surface features present important differences, and are due to the action of essentially different causes. Our dividing line must be somewhat arbitrarily selected. It may be taken as follows:

Beginning in the north, it commences in Laurel Hill, on the west border of Preston, and is thence continued south, in the mountain of that name, on the western border of Barbour;

thence in Rich mountain in Randolph; Gauley and Greenbrier mountains in Pocahontas; the Main Alleghany near the White Sulphur; and lastly Peter's mountain in the southern part of the State. The country between this line and the Ohio river may be styled *The Hilly Region*, and that lying to the east of it, *The Mountain Region.*

It must be borne in mind that this division is not founded on altitude, alone, but also on considerations which will be presently given. Indeed, contrary to what the titles might suggest, the elevation of much of the hilly region, is above that of a portion of the mountain region.

In that section which we have styled the *Hilly Region*, and which comprises much the larger part of the State, are to be found those peculiar topographical features, which have given our State considerable celebrity. Leaving out of view, for the present, the special features which mark the canon portions of the streams in the south, and the country wherever the conglomerate has attained a considerable height above the rivers, we may briefly describe them as follows: First, we note a vast multitude of hills, sometimes closely placed, and rising immediately from the V shaped depressions, in which the streams flow; again, sloping more gently, with considerable bottoms at their base, spreading out into flat-topped, gently undulating plains on their summits; or again, expanding into elevations attaining the dignity of mountains. Looking across such a region, it often presents nothing but a succession of such hills and valleys. As a rule, these succeed each other in no particular order, but occur just as the streams, turning hither and thither, to avoid some harder rock, carved them out. Occasionally the out-crop of some more indestructible stratum, has determined the direction of a line of elevations, or a remnant of a harder overlying mass, has along certain-determinate lines, preserved the underlying softer material from erosion, and so left more or less connected ridges and mountains. These are the general features presented by the elevations in the softer strata of the productive coals, and in the similar rocks underlying the conglomerate series. The special modifications produced by this latter series, will be noted further on.

Again, as might be inferred, the streams in the above described districts, are marked by the great irregularity of their courses.

They flow to every quarter of the compass, but all finally make their way westward, or northwestward into the Ohio. These, as well as all the streams in the State, are remarkable for the great depth to which they have cut their channels. Here, however, although the valleys are deep, and narrow, they have none of the canon features, but the bordering hills may be cultivated to their tops, though often too steep, and with a soil too light, to render frequent ploughing advisable.

In all this hilly region, the surface features are entirely the work of erosion. The rains and running streams have cut lofty hills and veritable mountains out of the gently sloping, and often almost horizontal strata, having removed a truly astounding mass of material by their slow, ever-wearing flow. Indeed, when one thinks over the vast amount of wear that the surface of our state exhibits, he is tempted to speculate about a period when the rains were far heavier, and the streams more powerful, than at present; a period when the land, newly raised from the carboniferous seas, was exposed as a lofty barrier to the sweep of westerly winds, laden with moisture from extensive seas penetrating into the land, far beyond the present Gulf of Mexico.

THE MOUNTAIN REGION.

We will now turn to the inspection of the topography of the mountain region. Omitting the counties of Berkeley (in part) and Jefferson; this region includes all east of the line described as the eastern boundary of the hilly region. Here, also, we find stupendous monuments of the levelling powers of the atmospheric agencies, but these have not been the only forces at work in this district in modelling the hills and valleys, as was the case in the hilly region.

The surface of this part of the State, when first upheaved and exposed to denuding forces, was thrown into long parallel elevations and depressions, running in a N. E. and S. W. direction. These folds, on the the east border of the State, are comparatively close together and narrow. Going west, they widen out, and become more distant, until before reaching the Ohio they become imperceptible. As will be noted under the head of Agricultural Geology, the strata which compose these folds, are alternations of soft yielding rocks and massive sandstones, among which latter, the conglomerate series above described, plays no unimportant part.

In the easternmost, and more sharply folded flexures, the stiff, unyielding sandstones, were along the crest lines of the ridges, where the strain was greatest, burst asunder, and broken to fragments, exposing the next succeeding soft strata below.

When now these elevated ridges, or anticlinals, were exposed to the wearing action of rains and torrents, these stripped off all softer material from the summits, and left bare the arches of massive standstone, with their fractured crowns. The surface waters working their way along these fractures, soon reached the softer material below. Here their progress was more rapid, and by cutting down, and undermining the walls on either side, they have finally excavated channels of greater or less width.

Such has been the history of the formation of many of the narrow parallel valleys in the northeastern counties of the State, and more particularly in Randolph, and Pendleton. Where the process above described, has been carried on, on an extensive scale, we see the river now flowing in a narrow valley between two mountain walls. This is the case with Tygart's Valley river in Randolph. Where less complete, we find the stream flowing on the top of a mountain, and still cutting its way down in the massive standstone, as in the case of the some of the Forks of Cheat.

Again, in the originally depressed portions, or synclinal valleys, which being less elevated have suffered less from erosion, we find streams flowing in like manner, between mountain chains, and it is easy to see how the waters would have gathered in such valleys. *Synclinal valleys* may be distinguished by the fact that the rocks dip from both sides towards them, while in the case of valleys of the former class, or anticlinal valleys, they dip away from them on both sides.

It often happens in the mountain region which we are describing, that that the arches and folds are too broad to be cracked along their crest lines. Then they often afford on their summits, flat, or gently undulating surfaces, which are called *Glades* by the inhabitants, but which are simply table lands of

2

greater or less extent. This feature is more common when the huge unyielding masses of the conglomerate series enter into the structure of the country. We also find the anticlinal valleys, with their cañon-like features, more commonly where the conglomerate is present. This rock is extensively exposed in the mountain region.

Such are the general features presented in the two regions into which we have divided the State, and such were some of the special circumstances which modified erosions in the mountain district, and which had to be first described, before any general view could be taken of the effects of erosion over the State elsewhere.

We are now prepared to take such a view. In order to do this, let us, in imagination, travel back to that remote period at the close of the carboniferous age, when the land which now forms our State, was first elevated above the waters. The elevating force was a lateral one, acting from the S. E. It seems to have, in the county north of Pocahontas, thrown the strata into ridges and depressions, as above described. While the mountain ranges in the east, no doubt, rose to great heights, there is no reason to suppose that the country westward partook of a corresponding elevation. The disturbing force seems to have exhausted itself in producing the folds.

South of Pocahontas, the case was different. Here the entire country from the east border of the State to the Ohio river, seems to have been elevated in one mass, pivoting on that river, as a hinge-line, and causing a surface sloping to the N. W. towards that stream.

This mass of elevated country was composed in the main of the strata we have previously described. While now the rocks in the folded mountain region, were undergoing the change described above, let us see what would take place in the country to the W. and S. of this section. In the northern part of the State, as we have seen, we have a thick mass of crumbling shales, and argillaceous sandstones, of the Upper Barrens, and Productive Coals. These being but comparatively little elevated, remain still in great force, not having been so extensively exposed to the denuding effects of the elements. In these strata the streams are still flowing, and in their great thickness and comparative softness, we find the origin of the topographical features seen in this part of the country.

In the description of the topography along the New River, we have seen that the conglomerate series rose as we passed eastward, at the average rate of 50 feet to the mile. We are now able to see why this is so. This, with the over and underlying series, were all carried up, and given a slope N. W. in the central and southern portions of the State.

Hence all these rocks, followed from west to east, rise in succession above water level.

In our description of the several series, the fact was noted that the lower portions of the Lower Barren measures, and Lower Coals, contained much massive sandstone, and that these produced much the same topographical effects as the conglomerate. These rise above the level of the streams near Charleston. Drawing a N. E. and S. W. line through this point, all the country between that and the Ohio river, is formed out of strata, which, in their topographical effects, resemble those in the north of the State, and hence along the Ohio river, we have a pretty wide belt, occupied by high hills and narrow valleys, which have lost comparatively little of their original height.

The case is different as we go east of Charleston. We have seen how the topography changes as the massive sandstones of the lower coals and conglomerate occupy the country. Let us now see how these rocks have modified the topography in this portion of the State.

When first raised above the waters, the central and southern portions of the State, formed a great plane sloping from the east to the northwest. This was covered with the comparatively incoherent strata of the higher members of the carboniferous system, supported on the massive plates of sandstone, forming the lower portions. In the east this complex system was lifted high in the air, and exposed to the full effects of the elements. In these higher, and more easterly portions, the softer overlying portions were soon stripped off, the harder conglomerate, was reached and this, too, was broken down and removed. Now the work of erosion going on in the soft underlying umbral strata, was carried on with comparative rapidity.

This was the extreme stage reached, and up to this, we have all the graduations of degradation.

Thus, in some parts of our eastern border, the country has been worn down through the umbral sandstones and shales until the more resistent umbral limestone has been reached. This has caused the exposure of this limestone over parts of Greenbrier and Monroe. Again, the red umbral rocks have not been removed in other parts, and we find them alongside the limestone, overspreading much of the two counties named above, as well as of Summers and Mercer. Scattered here and there in these counties, portions of the conglomerate have escaped destruction, and by their presence, have preserved from removal the umbral strata which lay under them. Hence we find these remnants standing out as mountains, capped by sandstone, in a region of limestone and red shales. Of this character are many of the mountains in the counties above named, such as Elk Knob, Muddy Creek, Meadow, Yew Mountains, &c. These usually contain in their summits only the lowest strata of the comglomerate, the middle coal bearing portions having been carried off. The degree of erosion described above as having taken place in this region, accounts for the comparatively small altitude of the district, which does not exceed 2,000 feet.

In some parts, along the west border of this region, the erosion has been less complete. The base of the conglomerate, and even the central coal bearing portions, remains. In consequence of this state of things, we find along the Blue Stone River, and in the east face of Flat Top Mountain, on the west border of Mercer, workable beds of coal.

From this point, looking westward, we are confronted by the eastern outcrop of the conglomerate series, which is here all present, and rises in an unbroken wall, forming the level topped mountains which bear in our state the names of White Oak, and Flat Top, and in Tennessee that of the Cumberland. The tops of these mountains are formed by the massive plates of the highest strata of the conglomerate, and from this point westward, these continue unbroken, inclining towards the Ohio as before stated, with the average dip of 50 feet per mile.

In the crests of these mountains, which rise to the height of 2,800 to 3,000 feet, all the softer overlying strata have been removed, and the basal conglomerate is exposed; but as this sinks towards the Ohio, we find a thicker and thicker covering of productive coal strata, until at last the conglomerate series sinks below the water level a short distance east of the Falls of the Kanawha. Throughout this area the presence of this massive system, in the hills, has exerted a predominant influence on the topography. We have seen that so long as the rivers are flowing in this series, they possess canon features. We have described these features, and noted the peculiar relations which the channels bear to the general level of the country.

The region of country now underlaid by the conglomerate, when first exposed to the elements, lost rapidly its upper softer strata, and this loss was in direct ratio to the elevation of the strata. Accordingly, as stated above, along the eastern outcrops we find them more or less removed, and a greater amount remaining in the lower western portions.

The descending waters in cutting down through the productive coal strata, produced in this region, as everywhere else, where these rocks are present, that system of hills and valleys, already described, and hence wherever these coal measures remain on the conglomerate, they give the surface that undulating character mentioned as found in the country along the canon portions of the rivers. But when once the upper surface of the conglomerate was reached, the general degradation of the surface ceased, since the eroding power of the rains, and smaller streams, was too feeble to effect it. As a consequence, the upper massive beds of this series, determine the general plane of the country. The larger streams when once they had cut their channels into these beds, deep enough to confine their waters, had their eroding power immensely increased. Enclosed by walls of massive rock, their entire force was exerted in scouring out their bottoms. Thus they cut their narrow channels deeper, and deeper, while the general level of the country remained unaltered. While this was going on, the surface drainage from either side, over the enclosing walls, unlike what occurs in ordinary streams, could not plane down the hard sandstones which compose them, and hence they usually stand up in cliffs close to the channel. The usual methods by which these sandstones were thrown down, seems to have been by undermining them. The streams that enter the rivers, almost always do so at the water level, and almost never by cascades. But if we follow them a short distance up their gorge-like passage ways, we soon find them passing into rapids and cascades. The low level of their mouths seems due to the undermining action of the river, aiding the erosion of the tributary.

It is somewhat singular to find that the larger streams, as a rule, have exerted but little action in widening their channels, even when they reached the softer central portions of the conglomerate. They have generally cut their way straight down. This, however, is not always the case. In some cases the streams, on reaching their central portions, which are occupied largely by shaly rocks, have ceased almost entirely their downward action, but have cut laterally on each side, throwing down the massive ledges, and forming wide and beautiful valleys in which the fall of the stream is almost imperceptible. Of this character are the so-called marshes of Coal river, in the southern part of Raleigh county. This is a deep valley, 10 to 12 miles wide, excavated in the central portion of the conglomerate series, and lying between the Guyandotte mountains and the Raleigh plateau. Here the water is almost stagnant, having no very perceptible flow. Of a similar character are the *Flats* along the Meadow river, to which the name of this stream is due. These remarkable flats lie in the western edge of Greenbrier county, near Big Sewell mountain. They are more than 2500 feet above tide, or more than two hundred feet higher than the summit of the Alleghany near the White sulphur Springs in Greenbrier county. Major Chas. Ellett says of these meadows, "Within the space enclos-"ed by several mountains, such as Big Sewell, Little Sewell, "Laurel mountain, Meadow mountain, Keeney's Knob, &c.; "are found the "Meadows" of Meadow river, one of the prin-"cipal tributaries of the Gauley. These meadows are exten-"sive "Glades," through which flow the waters of numerous "streams which descend from the neighboring mountains and "which, passing through portions of the meadows, one by one, "unite to form the Meadow river, which name, however, is "borne by one of these smaller streams. These extensive "flats present the appearance of the bottom of an exhausted "lake. They are as level as a graded lawn, so level, indeed, "that it is found difficult to drain them. The width of these "glades is extremely irregular, sometimes not over 500 yards, "and again opening out to two miles."

In this region, Major Ellett proposed putting his reservoir lake, to supply the Kanawha and Ohio rivers with water in their low stages. The surveys made here in connection with that scheme, showed the great elevation above tide of these flats, viz: 2,548 feet.

Such are the features occasionally presented, caused by the action of erosion on the middle members of the conglomerate. They are, however, exceptions.

From what has been said above, concerning the effectual resistance opposed by the upper surface of the conglomerate, to the wearing down of the general plane of the country, it is easy to see that wherever this has attained a considerable altitude above tide, it will give to the country the character of an elevated plateau. The eastern border of this elevated plateau is in the White Oak and Flat Top mountains, and in a line drawn in their prolongation in a N. E. direction. Here, the level has risen to the altitude of 2,800 to 3,000 feet, and more. To the east, the country falls off into the lower plateau of Greenbrier and Monroe, which has the height of 2,000 to 2,200 feet, owing to causes above explained.

On the western side, we may assume as the limit, a N. E. and S. W. line, drawn through the Hawk's Nest on New river. Here the upper surface of the conglomerate is 521 feet above the river, or 1,272 feet above tide. All the country between these lines, i. e. the eastern parts of McDowell, Wyoming, Raleigh, Fayette, Nicholas, and Webster, may be styled the *Plateau Region.* Much of it is flat or gently undulating, giving rise to the so-called *Glades.* Along the principal rivers, the general level falls off by precipitous slopes, until their beds are reached. This high belt of country is studded over by hills and mountains, which, owing to the great height of the plane from which they rise, attain an altitude above the sea, which, as we have before stated, one would by no means suspect. As an illustration of this fact, we may mention here the heights of a few points in this region, and for comparison the height of the Alleghany, in the vicinity of the White Sulphur. This latter, is, according to Ellett, 2,325 feet above tide.

The surface of the conglomerate, which, as we have before stated, determines the plane of the country, is at Quinnimont on New river, in the vicinity of Big Sewell, according to Mr. S. F. Morris, 2,610 feet above tide. Big Sewell, according to Mr. S. C. McCorkle, of the coast survey, is 3,500 feet above tide.

No reliable measurements have been made of the lofty Cherry Pond, and Guyandotte mountains, between Raleigh and Wyoming, but estimates on which some reliance may be placed, make them fully 4,000 feet high, and shows them to be among the very highest.

There is a remarkable elevated region near the junction of Randolph, Pocahontas, Pendleton, and Highland counties, which merits a particular description. Unfortunately, measurements of the altitudes in this quarter are rare.

An inspection of the map will show that in this comparatively limited area, nearly all the important rivers of the State take their rise, as well as the James and Potomac, of Virginia. These rivers flow to every quarter of the compass, except directly east. Owing to this fact, it might be suppposed, without measurements, that here we should find some of the highest land west of the Alleghanies. This supposition is confirmed by such measurements as we have, which give in Panther Knob, Pendleton county, the highest point in the State, which has been actually measured. For this, Mr. McCorkle gives 4,000 feet. This, as will be noticed, does not surpass the estimated height of Cherry Pond, or Pond mountain, in Raleigh. The height of the stream beds in this section is put at 2400 to 2600 feet. If we were to pass planes through the level of the headwaters of these streams, and continue them at water level, until they issue from the State, they would cut out the greater part of the circumference of a cone, whose apex would be 2500 feet above tide, and its base from 500 to 600 feet.

Having given the above general description of the surface features of our State, with the explanation of some of the causes producing them, we may now turn our attention to the altitudes of different points so far as these have been measured. The farthest points south, for which we have measurements, are situated on the line of the Kanawha river, and the Ches. & O. R. R., these follow below.

The level of the Ohio river, at the mouth of the Kanawha, according to the latest and most reliable measurements, obtained by combining the measurements of the U. S. Engineer Dep't, for the height of the Kanawha at Charleston, with the known fall of the river to its mouth, is 509 feet above mean tide. The Kanawha, at Charleston, according to the the U. S. Eng. Corps measurements, is 556 feet high. Vineyard hill, 6 miles above Charleston, is 1236 feet. The river at the mouth of Paint creek, 570 feet. Hills at that point, 1550 feet. River at Hawk's Nest, 751 feet. Hawk's Nest Cliff, 1272 feet. Gauley mountain near Hawk's Nest, 2600 feet. New river at Quinnimont 1165 feet. Cliffs at that point, 2610 feet. New river at Hinton, 1364 feet. White Oak mountain near that point, 2800 to 3,000 feet, (estimated.) Big Sewell, according to McCorkle 3500 feet. Meadow mountain 2719, (Ellett.) Greenbrier river, at Greenbrier bridge, 1584. Plateau of Meadow river, according to Ellett, 2548. White Sulphur Springs 2,000 feet. Alleghany mountains, between Crow's and White Sulphur, 2320 feet.

For the elevations in the northern part of the State, along the line of the Wash. & O. R. R., see list furnished by Mr. McKenzie, Pres't of that road; for those along the line of the Balt. & O. R. R., see list furnished by Mr. Randolph, Chief Eng'r of that road. Measurements on the line of the W. & O. R. R. were only given as far as Cheat river, in the list furnished.

On the western border of the State, along the Ohio river, we may note the following. The height of the river at Wheeling is 645.4 feet. In the vicinity of Wheeling, and for a considerable distance down, the hills are high, being 500 and 600 feet above the river, and 1200 to 1300 feet above tide. They decline in altitude as we approach Parkersburg, and from that point to Point Pleasant, where they are not more than 100 to 200 feet above the river, and 600 to 700 feet above tide. In the south, where the river leaves the State, its elevation is less than 500 feet, as it is, at the mouth of the Kanawha, only 509 feet. The hills here are higher, being formed out of the more massive strata of the lower coals. They are 200 to 300 feet above the river, and 700 to 800 feet above tide.

The approximate elevation of different parts of the State, may be given as follows:

A N.E. and S.W. line parallel to the general course of the Ohio river, and drawn through a point about 6 miles east of Charleston, would pass over a region having an elevation of 1200 to 1300 feet above tide.

A second line, having a similar direction to the first, and drawn through the western part of Fayette, would pass over a region having a general altitude of 1600 to 1700 feet. A third line, having the same general direction, and drawn through the eastern part of Raleigh, would pass over a district having the elevation of 2600 to 2700 feet.

A fourth line, passing through the plateau of Monroe and Greenbrier, and thence through the longitudinal valleys, in the eastern part of Randolph, wonld have an altitude of 2,000 to 2,200 feet.

The following are the heights on the line of the Washington and Ohio Railroad as far west as the Forks of Cheat:

ELEVATIONS ON THE LINE OF THE W. & O. R. R.

Winchester	726 feet
Lockhart's Gap	896 feet
Capon Spring's Divide	1,325 feet
Lost River	1,240 feet
Baker's Run Divide	I,938 feet
South Branch Mountain	2,148 feet
Moorfield	806 feet
N. Fork of the Potomac	1,600 feet
Summit of the Alleghanies	3,227 feet
Dry Fork of Cheat	2,166 feet

The following elevations were determined on the Paddy's Gap line of survey for this road. This line lies considerably south of the line on which the measurements above given were determined:

Paddy's Dlvide, the dividing ridge between Frederick and Hardy	2,009 feet
Ore Bank	1,780 feet
Rocky Ridge	1,840 feet
Thorn Bottom	1,470 feet
Sandy Ridge	2,636 feet
Lost River	1,100 feet
South Branch Mountain	3,114 feet
Moorfield	806 feet

The following is the list of elevations along the line of the Baltimore and Ohio Railroad, in W. Virginia:

Stations, &c.	*Elevations. A. M. T.*
Mill's Creek Viaduct, at Cumberland, Md........	639.0
Rowling's Station...........	698.0
Black Oak Bottom Station	735.9
Crossing of Potomac (2 spans of 156 feet each)..	786.
West abutment of New Creek Bridge, at Keyser..............................	797.71
Piedmont.........................	919.39
Crossing Potomac (3 spans of 56 feet each...........	999.
Opposite Church, at Bloomington	1,037.05
Frankville Station..........	1.699.22
Swanton Water Station....	2,282.21
Altamont........................	2,620.
Deer Park.......................	2,441.8
Little Youghiogheny River Bridge......................	2,397.67
Oakland.........................	2,372.
Cassidy's Summit...........	1,855.27
E. portal Kingwood Tunnel, (length, 4,132 ft.)...	1,819.
W. portal Kingwood Tunnel..........	1,778.7
E. portal Murray's Tunnel........	1,554.
Newburg.........................	1,215.3
Hook's Run.....................	1,164.
Road to Morgantown at Independence	1,157.9
Helvitia Station..............	1,109.7
Bridge over Raccoon Cr'k (5 spans, 25 ft.)............	1,105.4
Thornton Station............	1,037.9
Water Station, No. 59, at Thorn's Run...............	1,032.4
Three Fork Creek bridge, (2 spans of 50, and 1 of 25 ft.).........................	1,020.2
Grafton..........................	987.2
Fetterman	984.2
Plum Run Bridge..........	978.2
Valley River Falls Station (water station 61)........	969.2
Nuzum's Mill Station......	936.2
Texas Station.................	883.2
Benton's Ferry...............	883.2
Monongahela Bridge.......	877.2
Fairmont	877.2
Water Station, No. 63, at Barnesville..................	871.2
Bridge over Buffalo Cr'k..	890.9
Barracksville....................	901.
Little Youghiogheny River Bridge.....................	2,370.8
Great Yonghiogheny River Bridge.....................	2,371.66
Summit above Chisholm's	2,486.6
Hutton's Switch..............	2,477.
Marysville Station..........	2,428.
Bridge across N. Fork of Snowy Creek................	2,469.2
Cranberry Summit Station	2,548.7
Cranberry Suumit..........	2,550.687
E. Portal of McGuire's Tunnel........................	2,382.4
Rodemer's Tunnel..........	2,083.3
Bridge over Salt Lick Creek at Amblersburg..	1,619.1
Cheat River Bridge.........	1.392,4
Rowlesburg	1,392.4
Buckeye Run Viaduct.....	1,515.5
Tray Run Viaduct..........	1,572.
Buckhorn Run...............	1,720.4
Davis Run.....................	916.5
Dunkard's Mill Run........	922.5
Farmington.....................	927.2
Wood's Run	956.67
Mannington....................	966.9
Glover's Gap Station......	1,047.2
Burton's Station............	1,060.37
E. portal of upper Eaton's Tunnel........................	993.2
E. portal of Lower Eaton's Tuunel	962.
Littleton Station............	936.
W. portal of Board Tree Tuunel	1,077.
Belton Station................	886.5
E. portal of Welling Tunnel..........	1,201.8
W. portal of Welling Tunnel	1,193.
Opposite engine house at Cameron Station	1,049.2
E. portal of Shepard's Tunnel......	838.5
Rosby's Rock Station......	773.2
Opposite Rosby's Rock....	786.7
Moundsville....................	640.06
Opposite Kate's Rock......	664.3
McMicken's Run...........	664.8
Opposite station house at Benwood....................	648.6
Wheeling Creek at Wheeling	645.4
Fourth and John's Sts.....	656.2

The above are the elevations along the line from Cumberland, Maryland, to Wheeling, West Virginia. The following are those on the line from Harper's Ferry to Cumberland:

ELEVATIONS FROM HARPER'S FERRY TO CUMBERLAND, MARYLAND.

Stations, &c.	*Elevations, A. M. T.*	*Stations, &c.*	*Elevations, A. M. T.*
Harper's Ferry	277.	Cacapon	449.5
Snyder's Summit	600.9	Doe Gully Tunnel	518.
Opecquan River	403.75	Little Cacapon	531.
Tuscarora Creek Bridge	392.	South Branch	550.
Martinsburg	425.	Green Spring Run	548.8
Tabb's Summit	547.5	Dan's Run Bridge	563.
Tabler's Summit	546.	Patterson's Creek	568.
Cherry Run	398.9	Potomac River	604.5
Sleepy Creek Bridge	410.5	Evitt's Creek	615.7
Warren Spring Run oppisite Hancock	428.5	West side of Baltimore Street at Cumberland, Md	639.
Sir John's Run	434.5		

The following extracts from a report addressed to the Superintendent of the Coast Survey, by S. C. McCorkle, assistant on the Coast Survey, were kindly furnished, and are here presented. They will explain themselves.

"FEBRUARY 14th, 1876.

"*C. P. Patterson, Superintendent United States Coast Survey:—*

"SIR: * * * * Beginning with Pendleton county in West Virginia, "near the headwaters of the North Fork of the Potomac, is Panther Knob, "said to be the highest point in the vicinity. In about the same latitude "on the Alleghany range, is Paddy's Knob, in the corner of Bath and "Highland counties, Virginia, and Pocahontas, West Virginia. From "here the mountain falls gradually to the south and west, some thirty "miles, rising again at the Salt Pond Mt., in Giles county. Hay Stack "Knob, near the line of Pocahontas and Randolph counties, on the south "end of the Cheat Mountain Range, and near its junction with the Great "Greenbrier mountains, is said to be the highest point west of the Alle-"ghanies, and north of the Greenbrier river. South and west of this "we have the Great Greenbrier, the Yew, Big and Little Sewell moun-"tains, including Cold Knob, and Job's Knob, and ending with Keeney's "Knob, which is about two miles north of the Greenbrier river, in Sum-"mers and Greenbrier counties.

"From these mountains north of the river, there is a gradual decline "from 3,500 feet above tide to 700 feet on the Ohio river.

"Powell's mountain, in the northern part of Nicholas county, falls off "to the Elk river, and from thence to the Ohio, in a succession of hills "and plains, the average height of the hills being 1,200 to 1,500 feet.

"The highest elevations (in this vicinity, author,) will be found in "Jack's Bend of the Elk river, and between the Forks of the Big Sandy "creek.

"South of the Kanawha river, in the counties of Fayette, Raleigh, "Wyoming, Boone, and Logan, are some very high mountains, the prin- "cipal of which is called the Great Flat Top mountains, near the head "waters of the Coal river, and I believe, in the Guyandotte range, (this "is wrong, they meet at right angles—Author), but I have not explored "south of Coal river.

"In the vicinity of the headwaters of Loup and Paint creeks, the ele- "vation is near 2,700 feet above tide. West of this will be found a suc- "cession of sharp peaks, varying but little in height, the highest being "1,700 feet, and the lowest on the Ohio 600 to 700 feet.

"I append some elevations obtained with compensating aneroid barom- "eter, and give them for what they are worth. Good enough for recon- "naisance, but not entirely reliable.

"Signed, "SPENCER C. MCCORKLE."

APPROXIMATE ELEVATIONS ABOVE SEA LEVEL, IN WEST VIRGINIA, OBTAINED WITH CONPENSATING ANEROID BAROMETER, IN 1874-1875.

Pendleton County, Panther Knob	4,000 feet
Bath and Highland, Va., and Pocahontas, W.Va., Paddy's Knob	3,300 "
Randolph and Pocahontas, Hay Stack Knob	3,800 "
Pocahontas and Greenbrier, Briery Knob	3,600 "
Summers and Greenbrier, Keeney's Knob	3,700 "
Fayette, Big Sewell	3,500 "
Greenbrier, Lewisburg	2,200 "
Fayette, Payne's Mountain	2,700 "
Nicholas, Summersville Mountain	2,600 "
Kanawha (south), Table Rock Mountain	1,700 "
Kanawha (north), Gibson's	1,200 "
Lincoln, Mud Creek Mountain	1,700 "
Cabell, back of Huntington	700 "

The county of Morgan, and the western part of Berkley, belong to the mountain region, but the eastern part of Berkley, and all of Jefferson, can be included in neither of the grand divisions which we have made in the State. They partake of the character of the Great Valley, extending S. W. into Virginia, and have a rolling, or gently undulating surface, with an altitude of 700 to 800 feet above tide. The following heights, given by Mr. McKenzie, may be added here.

Wilson's Gap, on the Blue Ridge, between Jefferson and Loudoun	1,445 feet
Keyes' Gap, in the same range	960 "

For the convenience of surveyors and civil engineers in different parts of the State, the following table of Magnetic Declinations, is appended.

Magnetic Declinations for different points in the State, determined in 1864, by Assistant Mosman, of the Coast Survey :

	Lat.	*Long.*	*Decl'n.*
Clarksburg, W. Va.	39° 16′.9	80° 20′.4	—0° 30′.3 in J.
Wheeling	40° 04′.1	80° 43′.6	—2° 00′.5 "
Parkersburg	39° 16′.0	81° 34′2.	—1° 17′.6 "
Mt. Pleasant	38° 50′.5	82° 08′.8	—1° 34′.9 "
South Point, Ohio	38° 25′.2	82° 35′.4	—1° 52′.9 in F.
Grafton, W. Va.	39° 20′.6	80° 01′.7	+1° 52′4. in J.
Charleston, W. Va	38° 21′.3	81° 38′.0	—0° 37′.3 in M.
Cumberland, Md.	39° 39′.2	78° 45′.4	+1° 31′.9 "
Cameron, W. Va.	39° 49′.8	80° 34′.4	—0° 24′.0 in J.

The sign —, denotes East; the sign +, denotes West; J., F. and M., denote January, February and March, 1864. The annual change is 3′.5, increasing West and diminishing East.

CHAPTER II.

CLIMATOLOGY.

BY WM. M. FONTAINE.

In considering the climate of the State, we may divide it into three belts, running in a northeast and southwest direction.

The first belt comprises the counties along the Ohio river and may be taken to coincide with our first topographical belt. This comprises the lowest land in the State. The second climatic belt may be taken to include all the rest of the State, except the mountain region. The third half includes the mountain district. It will be convenient to designate the first belt, as the "Ohio counties;" the second belt, as the "plateau district;" and the third, as the "mountain district;" inasmuch as these names suggest the position, and altitude of the areas which they designate.

For all of these, there is a great lack of data connected with the climate; but in the Ohio counties, records have been kept for a much longer time than elsewhere. For the plateau district, we have a few details, and for the mountain district none at all.

The Ohio River Valley is often spoken of, as possessing features of climate, distinct from those shown in other parts of the State. This, taken without qualification, would lead to erroneous ideas of the topography of the stream. The valley proper, is a narrow trench, cut out in high hills for most of the way.

It attains at most, the width of only a mile or two, and cannot exert any important influence on the climate of the country in general. In summer it may influence to some extent the formation and course of showers, or it may facilitate the passage of bodies of warm, moist air from the southwest. Apart from minor and local influence, it is to be considered merely as *one* of the factors influencing the climate of the belt of country along its banks.

If, however, we apply the term "Ohio Valley," to the belt of comparatively low country along the west border of our State, then, no doubt, climatic features somewhat different from those of the rest of the State, do exist here.

Leaving out of consideration the influence of altitude, the most important general causes controling our climate, are the character of the exposure of the surface, the direction assumed by the principal elevations, and the prevailing winds. The State forms a sloping surface, inclining in a northwesterly direction, from the highest ridges of the Alleghany, to the hills along the Ohio river. The principal elevations, even in the hilly region, run in a northeast and southwest direction.

When now we take into consideration the winds which prevail along the Appalachian belt of the United States, we can easily see that these topographical features, assume great importance. In our latitude, even east of the Blue Ridge, easterly winds are not the predominant ones. But in Virginia, especially in winter, they often blow for a considerable space of time, bringing with them, when from the northeast, the longest spells of wet weather. Owing to our protection by the Blue Ridge and Alleghanies, such winds do not reach us, and hence in West Virginia, winds with an easterly element are extremely rare. If they do reach us, they are usually drying and clearing winds, having been deprived of their moisture by passing over the mountain tops.

Our winds are almost exclusively those with a westerly element, such as S.W., W., and N.W. When these enter our State, the N.E and S.W. direction of our elevations, exert such a guiding influence on them, that instead of passing directly across the State, they are forced to traverse it longitudinally. The consequence is, that we feel the full effects of such winds, whatever they may be. S.W. winds enter freely, and are guided unchecked in their original direction. Hence such winds the year round, predominate, at least in influence. Westerly, and northwestlerly winds, are partly deflected, so as to preserve a S.E. or N.E. direction. The inclination of the face ot the country also, exerts an important influence.

Such winds enter the State on its lowest side, and in working their way over it, they rise higher and higher. The consequence is, that they become cooled, and their moisture is condensed, if they be moist, warm winds. Thus an abundant rain fall is secured. The country never suffers from the prolonged dry spells, which sometimes occur east of the Alleghanies. A mere inspection of the map of this region will show, by the enormous number of perennial streams possessed by it, that this precipitation is not only abundant, but that it is uniformly distributed throughout the year. Our State contributes no small proportion of the volume of water carried by the Ohio into the Mississippi. It is well known that this surpasses that of any other tributary of that great stream. After these general considerations, we may turn to the examination of the individual factors which constitute the climate of a country.

TEMPERATURE.

Temperature is influenced both by latitude and elevation. The main body of the State of West Virginia lies between the parallel of 37 deg. and 40 deg. For points at the same elevation, this would give a difference of about 3 deg., in the mean annual temperature of the southern, and northern portions of the State. According to Dodge, the State is embraced between the isothermals of 50 deg. and 54 deg. The isothermal of 52 deg. passes nearly through the centre of it. The general elevation of the surface, renders the mean temperature somewhat lower than that of points on the same parallel of latitude, in the States further west. Within the State itself, the greater altitude of the plateau, and mountainous portions, renders the mean temperature of these belts, lower than that of the Ohio counties. This difference of altitude, may be taken on an average, to be about 1500 feet, causing a lowering of the mean annual temperature of about 4½ deg., on the same parallel of latitude. Hence such elevated counties as Fayette, Nicholas, Raleigh, &c.; do not possess that higher mean temperature, which they should have, in consequence of their more southerly position. The isothermals passing through the mountain, and plateau districts, bend strongly up northward. The mean annual temperature of the State may be taken as 52 deg.

The following means of temperature, are taken from Dr. E.

A. Hildreth's reports, based on records kept at Wheeling for 18 years, ending 1867. Wheeling may be taken as representing in climate, the northern half of the Ohio belt of counties. For these then we have:

January	28°.97
February	33 .05
March	38 .43
April	49 .75
May	60 .06
June	69 .77
July	73 .91
August	73 .41
September	65 .56
October	50 .95
November	41 .96
December	34 .01
Annual mean	51 .64

The same author gives for Wheeling, the following means for the seasons, based on observations for twenty-three years and seven months:

Spring	51°.00
Summer	71 .54
Autumn	52 .72
Winter	32 .08
Year	52 .08

Highest temperature, 104° (July, 1854.
Lowest temperature, —15° (January, 1856.
Extreme range, 119°.

For the southern part of the the State, in the Ohio belt, we have no records south of Kanawha county. At Kanawha Salines, records were kept for 4 years and 4 months, from June, 1856, to January, 1861, for the Smithsonian Institution, with the following results:

January	34.92°
February	38 .98
March	44 .28
April	52 .88
May	64 .15
June	70 .35
July	75 .76
August	72 .70
September	65 .82
October	55 .05

November	43 .75
December	37 .97
Spring	53 .77
Summer	72 .94
Autumn	54 .87
Winter	37 .29
Year	54 .72

Records have been kept for the Smithsonian Institution at Lewisburg, for 7 years and 1 month, from January, 1854 to March 1861. The climate of the eastern part of Greenbrier and Monroe is remarkably mild. The Lewisburg records cannot be taken to represent the climate of the plateau districts, which they might be supposed to do, from the position of that town. Two causes render the climate of the Greenbrier valley milder than that of the eastern portion of the plateau district. First, This region (see topography) is much lower than the belt of country to the W., N. W. and S. W. of it. In the second place, It is sheltered by the high country from the cold N. W. and W. winds of winter.

The following is the record referred to above:

January	30°.64
February	34 .12
March	40 .79
April	51 .59
May	62 .98
June	69 .35
July	74 .05
August	71 .95
September	64 .03
October	52 .01
November	41 .68
December	33 .49
Spring	51 .79
Summer	71 .78
Autumn	52 .57
Winter	32 .75
Year	52 .22

The table given on page 34, represents the mean temperature and other climatic features, at Morgantown, and may be taken to represent the north central part of the State. The other tables are taken from Dr. Hildreth's report. As no records exist for the mountainous portions of the State, we can say nothing of their climate with any definiteness.

PREVAILING WINDS.

Concerning these, it has already been stated that they contain almost always a westerly element. The southwesterly and southerly winds prevail during the summer months, and influence the climate largely in the other seasons also. The northwesterly, westerly and northerly winds are more frequent in winter, but cannot even then be said to be the prevailing ones.

Owing to its latitude, our State is the battle ground of the S. W. and N. W. winds. The S. and S. W. winds come to us from the Gulf of Mexico, creeping around the southern foot, and along the western slopes of the Appalachian belt. Hence they are warm and moist. Passing over the elevated surface of our State, they part with much of their heat and moisture. As has been shown, the topography of our section of country specially favors the free passage of these winds.

The westerly and northwesterly winds come to us from cooler regions. being deflected from the ranges of the Rocky Mountains. Hence their effect is cooling and drying. The effects of these classes of winds on our climate is best illustrated by our winter weather. Their influence in other seasons is essentially the same, but this is modified by the varying dryness and heat of the areas over which they pass.

In winter the S. W. winds, which may be taken as the normal ones outside of the mountain district, so long as they blow, bring a higher temperature, cloudiness and gentle rains. These are soon met by N. W. and N. winds, and in the struggle of these for the mastery, we have the cause of our heaviest rains, wind storms, and snow storms. Should the N. W. winds prevail, a season of clearing up and cold weather occurs, and continues so long as such winds predominate. This is usually not long. The S. W. winds again push back the cold air and prevail, causing a rapid melting of the snow, a rise of temperature, and a fall of rain, or a cloudiness of the atmosphere. Such is essentially the course of events in winter. Extreme weather at at any season, whether stormy, hot, or cold, rarely lasts more than three days, in consequence of this alternate swing of the winds. Accordingly our climate, especially in winter, is marked by great variability. The extreme ranges, however, are not correspondingly great. Our considerable altitude causes us never to have the extreme summer heats felt on the Atlantic slope. The prevalence of the S. W. winds, besides giving us a uniform abundant rainfall at all seasons, acts as a shield to protect us against these extreme and sudden falls of temperature which are felt to the N. and N. E. of us. Those waves of cold, which in winter, are generated in the Rocky Mountains, move east, and invade the Middle and Eastern States, generally expend much of their severity in overcoming and cooling the S. W. winds. It is true that when they are of extraordinary violence, and move in more southerly tracts, they press upon us with sufficient force to cause, at long intervals, the extreme range of —10 deg. to —15 deg. As an illustration of this fact, Dr. Hildreth, from observations during 23 years and 7 months at Wheeling, gives —15 deg. as the lowest temperature reached. The annexed table, gives the prevalent winds at Morgantown:

STATION MORGANTOWN, W. VA.

Records Kept by United States Signal Service from Jan. 27, 1873, to Dec. 31, 1875—Monthly Means for the Entire Period.

MONTH.	Mean barometer.	Mean thermometer.	Prevailing wind.	Rain and melted snow. inches	Mean relative humidity.	Maximum velocity of wind. miles.	Days of rain and snow.
January	30.16	33.1	S. W.	3.14	71.4	38	18
February	30.07	31.5	W.	3.44	68.2	42	14
March	30.00	40.1	W.	4.29	64.7	48	16
April	29.97	47.9	S. W to N. W.	4.07	66.6	48	18
May	29.93	62.7	S. W.	2.35	60.2	48	13
June	29.98	71.4	S. W.	4.78	69.9	24	13
July	29.97	73.1	S. W.	7.08	75.2	35	15
August	29.99	69.8	N. W.	4.11	75.9	30	12
September	30.03	63.7	S. W.	4.56	74.6	24	14
October	30.05	51.38	S. W.	3.19	69.5	37	9
November	30.06	41.0	S. W to N. W.	4.11	69.4	51	14
December	30.09	39.3	S. W.	4.10	72 4	40	18
Annual Mean for period	30.02	52.7	S. W.	49.22	69 8	....	13⅜

In the above results deduced, from observations for thirty-five months, the wind prevailed from the S. W. during twenty-one months, from the West five months, from the South three months, from the N. W. four months, from the North two months. The rain fall in July, 1875, was exceptionally great. The maximum velocity of the wind is given in miles per hour. This record is, no doubt, representative of the northern central belt of counties in the State. Morgantown is about 800 feet above tide, and the hills around it about 1,300 feet. For Wheeling, according to the observations of Dr. E. A. Hildreth, continued for 16 years and 7 months, in 15,173 cases of winds, the distribution according to the quarters of the compass, is as follows:

South, 438 days; *North*, 2,093; *West*, 1,022; *East*, 61; *Southwest*, 5,306; *Northeast*, 15; *Northwest*, 3,571; *Southeast*, 292.

From this list, the great predominance of S. W. winds, so far north as Wheeling, can be seen. This predominance increases in the more southern districts; but how much, there are no observations to show.

RAINFALL AND MELTED SNOW.

From what has been already said, a pretty good idea of the precipitation over the state may be gained. The following statistics, though scanty in amount, are offered. For Wheeling observations for 17 years ending 1871, made by Dr. E. A. Hildreth, give us the following:

Spring	10. 9	inches
Summer	12.93	"
Autumn	9.57	"
Winter	9.36	"
Year	41.95	"

By the same observer at the same place, the following annual average of rainy, snowy, &c., days are given, during a period of 27 years.

For each year	Rainy and snowy days	119.81
"	Clear and fair	170.16
"	Cloudy	76.28

He also deduces the mean annual rainfall for the state from observations amounting in the aggregate to 103 years to be 39.89 inches. While the above estimates for Wheeling may represent fairly the precipitation along the Ohio in the north, it cannot be doubted that for the plateau and mountain sections, the precipitation is greater, but unfortunately details from these elevated parts of the state are mostly wanting. The rainfall deduced from the records at Morgantown a point more inland, and near the foot of Laurel Hill, show an unusual average of 49.22 inches. As the year 1874 was noted for the heavy summer rains no doubt this is too high, and a mean annual precipitation of 45 inches may be taken as near the mark, for the more elevated districts.

The following record from Kanawha Salines, was taken for 3 years and 3 months, from April 1857 to February 1861.

Spring	12.92 inches	Autumn	16.18 inches
Summer	12 03 "	Winter	14.71 "
Year			35.75 inches

This without donbt is above the average, but it would seem that the Kanawha river valley, has usually, an exceptionally high rainfall.

For Lewisburg records kept during 6 years, for the Smithsonian Institution, show the following results.

Spring	7.39 inches	Autumn	9 60 inches
Summer	9.21 "	Winter	9.55 "
Year			35 75 inches

Records kept at the White Sulpher Springs, for 5 years and 6 months, shows a mean annual rainfall of 37.54 inches. Both of these results are below the average of places of the height of Lewisburg and the White Sulphur, which are each about 2,000 feet above tide. This is due to the position of these localities. They are situated between the Alleghany mountains on the east, and the high country of the eastern part of Fayette and Raleigh, on the southwest. These latter highlands lie in the direct path of the S. W. winds which bring moisture into the country, and in passing over them, these winds are deprived of much of their temperature and vapor. But beside records from weather observations, we may get an excellent idea of the climate of a country from the usual times of seeding and harvesting crops &c. The following calendar is taken, with considerable alterations, from the former Handbook of this state, compiled by J. H. Diss Debar. It applies especially to the Ohio belt.

FARMING CALENDAR.

February 28th—Break up soil. *March 1st*—Plant early potatoes; sow Timothy, Blue Grass and Clover; sow early garden vegetables. Manufacture Maple Sugar. *March 15th*—Turn out cattle on Blue Grass. *April 1st*—Sow early oats. *April 15th*—Sow main crop of garden vegetables. *April 20th*—Cherry, Plum, Apple and Peach trees are in bloom: Poplar and Maple are leafing. Turn Cattle on Timothy and Clover. *April 25th*—Sow late Oats and Flax. Plant late Potatoes. *May 1st*—Set out Fruit trees. Plant early corn. Turn out cattle in the woods to range. Timber generally begins to leaf out. Plant Sorghum. Light white frosts may be still looked for in the 1st week. *May 7th*—Plant Beans and Cucumbers &c. *May 10th—20th*—Plant and sow all late garden vegetables, Sweet Potatoes, and Watermelons. Dogwoods in bloom. Plant main crop of Corn, also Pumpkins and late Beans. *May 31st*—Corn and Potatoes planted on fresh cleared land. Grapes are in bloom. *June 1st*—Shear sheep. *June 8th*—Plant Tobacco, Corn may still be planted on fresh cleared land Clover is in bloom. *June 15th*—Harvest Clover, plant late Cucumbers. Beans, Melons and even Potatoes. Send early grass-fed cattle to market. *July 1st—4th*—Plough corn for the last time. Early Potatoes are ripe. *July 10th*—Harvest Wheat and Rye. *July 15th*—Commence cutting Timothy, Sow Buck wheat. *July 25th*—Harvest Oats. Early Apples are ripe. *August 10th—September 1st*—Sow turnips. *August 15th*—Finish hay harvest. Plough for wheat and rye. *August 25th—September 10th* Peaches and Melons ripening. Isabella, Hartford, Prolific, and Concord grapes ripening. *September 10th—20th*—Cut Tobacco, sow Wheat, Timothy, and Rye. Catawba, and Norton's Virginia seedling grapes, are maturing. *Sept 25th—Oct 1st*—Cut corn, harvest Buck wheat. *Oct. 1st—15th*—First white frosts occur. Cut late corn. Sow Wheat and Rye on corn ground. Cut Sorghum and make Syrup. *Oct. 25th* Dig late Potatoes. Leaves fall fast. Send late fat stock to market. *Nov. 1st—15th* Gather Turnips and other root crops. Commence husking corn. Commence winter feeding of young stock, and milch cows. *Nov. 31st*—Winter feeding in general.

Dates for the higher plateaus and mountains are 10—15 days later in spring and earlier in Autumn.

While within the State itself records of long periods are lacking, we are fortunate in being able to avail ourselves of a series of observations, made for a considerable term of years, at Marietta, Ohio.

Marietta is situated on the Ohio river, opposite the center of the State. From its position, it is better fitted than any other single point, to furnish data from which conclusions can be drawn concerning the general climate of our State. The records, of which we speak, were kept from 1817 to 1823, inclusive, by Mr. Wood, and from 1826 to 1859, both inclusive, by S. P. Hildreth. These were presented to the Smithsonian Institution, where they were given in charge to Mr. Schott, and by him were discussed on the general plan adopted by the Institution for other observations of the same kind. The results of this discussion were published in the "Smithsonian Contributions to Knowledge," No. 120. Extracts from this valuable publication, are here given. The annexed table A. page 34, will explain itself.

In this, the observed monthly means, are referred to the mean, resulting from hourly observations.

TABLE A.

Resulting Mean Monthly Temperature Observed at Marietta Between 1818 and 1859, Inclusive.

Year.	Jan.	Feb.	Mar.	Apr.	May	Jun.	July	Aug.	Sep.	Oct.	Nov.	Dec.
1818	....	....	....	....	....	72°.62	77°.19	74°.56	64°.02	51°.42	46°.26	32°.54
1819	40°.28	38°.11	38°.58	52°.82	63.°19	72 .53	74 .50	75 .95	63 .40	49 .98	46 .23	33 .28
1820	27 .10	42 .14	40 .44	57 .96	61 .75	72 .18	76 .72	72 .86	66 .87	48 .21	38 .36	32 .29
1821	24 .83	37 .00	36 .84	48 .84	64 .27	74 05	72 .17	74 .50	67 .50	52 .46	38 .55	28 .31
1822	28 .69	32 .02	45 .89	53 .70	69 .17	74 .22	75 .36	74 .12	65 .69	51 .96	47 .03	31 .22
1823	32 .50	25 .38	42 .37	....	....	....	....	....	....	....	....	....
....	....	....	....	....	....	....	....	....	....	....	....	....
1826	30 .51	36 .93	48 .53	51 .00	67 .32	72 .38	72 .31	71 .21	66 .52	55 .88	42 .75	33 .06
1827	26 .54	41 .68	46 .29	56 .09	60 .28	65 .24	74 .95	74 .49	66 .90	54 .38	42 .59	41 .58
1828	41 .68	43 .88	48 .69	50 .43	63 .09	73 .69	71 .07	73 .22	62 .32	52 .17	45 .32	39 .03
1829	32 .95	26 .09	37 .44	50 .64	65 .57	71 .25	71 .69	71 .68	62 .81	54 .88	39 .27	43 .72
1830	31 .21	34 .37	47 .00	58 .68	61 .07	68 .35	75 .03	73 .73	64 .30	57 .37	49 .54	35 .45
1831	25 .80	29 .14	45 .28	54 .68	60 .50	70 .47	71 .40	69 .81	62 .67	53 .99	40 .03	20 .49
1832	29 .07	37 .77	43 .45	54 .78	61 .00	68 .63	70 .97	69 .64	63 .36	54 .07	43 .41	35 .72
1833	35 .76	35 .10	39 .73	56 .58	68 .02	66 .33	72 .60	69 80	65 .95	49 .54	40 .56	36 .51
1834	26 .99	43 .03	43 .73	55 .97	60 .82	69 .57	76 .23	72 .49	63 .30	49 .97	43 .34	35 .32
1835	33 .84	24 .37	40 .51	49 .94	63 .54	68 .64	69 .84	68 .35	57 .18	54 .93	44 .55	30 .81
1836	31 .01	26 .87	36 .03	55 .30	65 .69	68 .54	71 .89	68 .94	68 .29	45 53	36 .73	30 .28
1837	27 .79	34 .15	41 .46	46 .56	60 .64	67 .07	71 .56	70 .04	62 .80	53 .46	45 .29	34 .64
1838	34 .65	20 .65	45 .41	48 .59	55 .43	70 .97	77 .10	75 .58	64 .11	48 .20	38 .23	27 .90
1839	35 .10	35 .60	42 .37	57 .58	64 .53	66 .09	72 .25	68 .04	59 .93	58 .21	37 .50	31 .79
1840	24 .32	40 .80	46 .48	56 .58	62 .34	68 .74	71 .41	71 .55	59 .82	52 .81	40 .22	32 .18
1841	32 .04	31 .79	42 .16	49 .66	60 .05	73 .19	71 .90	70 .59	66 .50	48 .53	42 .47	35 .76
1842	36 .15	37 .05	51 .87	56 .21	59 .10	66 .87	70 .40	67 .30	64 .16	50 .34	36 .11	33 .13
1843	36 .53	26 .35	28 .15	51 .14	60 47	67 .49	72 .80	70 .80	68 .77	47 .78	39 .62	34 .64
1844	29 .79	35 .25	42 .79	61 .31	64 .00	68 .34	74 .12	69 .92	63 .27	48 .85	42 .20	34 .29
1845	36 .41	38 .15	43 .15	57 .18	58 .83	68 .89	71 .68	72 .44	63 .88	50 .69	39 ,86	24 .71
1846	33 .05	31 19	43 .40	56 .75	64 .85	67 .05	72 .12	74 .41	70 .01	51 .64	46 ,22	37 .66
1847	31 .29	35 .42	39 .57	53 .90	61 .70	66 .38	70 .92	68 .18	63 .34	50 .99	44 .12	34 .65
1848	35 .77	35 .49	39 .46	52 .36	63 .76	67 .78	70 .51	70 .47	59 .68	51 .81	37 .67	42 .56
1849	30 .33	29 .66	44 .65	50 .64	61 .56	71 .38	71 .31	69 .85	62 .59	51 .93	47 .08	31 .20
1850	35 .37	34 .36	39 .15	48 .17	55 .92	69 .18	76 .32	71 .93	63 .56	51 .56	44 .41	34 .38
1851	34 .14	40 .42	45 .06	51 .30	61 .67	66 .81	72 .66	70 .34	66 .47	52 .27	39 .03	27 .70
1852	24 .84	34 .95	44 .31	48 .78	62 .76	66 .36	73 .24	69 .08	64 .36	57 .96	41 .65	39 .08
1853	32 .55	34 .76	40 .69	53 .05	61 .53	74 .08	72 .39	71 .65	64 .48	49 .36	45 .89	30 .80
1854	30 .72	37 .76	45 .36	50 .94	62 .77	70 .42	76 .39	73 .84	70 .19	56 .06	41 .17	31 .95
1855	34 .96	25 .67	38 .42	55 .44	62 .81	66 .85	75 .35	73 .51	70 .28	50 .33	47 .25	33 .24
1856	18 .61	25 .32	32 .28	54 .35	61 .31	72 .51	76 .67	69 .79	63 .95	53 .89	40 .92	28 .90
1857	18 .75	42 .53	37. 86	42 .56	57 .63	68 .21	72 .70	72 .40	66 .75	52 .03	40 .05	38 .64
1858	40 .11	27 .71	39 .77	53 .62	60 .64	72 .36	75 .09	72 .26	64 .53	56 .53	38 .44	40 .28
1859	32 .86	36 .86	48 .63	50 .85	66 .14	67 .41	74 .01	70 .90	64 .15	49 .15	44 .20	30 .06
Mean	31°.41	34°.00	42 .14	53°.04	62°.25	69°.58	73°.25	71°.54	64°.56	52°.08	42°.16	33°.58

MEAN ANNUAL TEMPERATURE.

Taking the annual means, of the monthly values, given in table A, after substituting the respective monthly means of the whole series, for those months in 1818, and 1823, in which the series is defective, we find the annual mean temperature, for 40 years as follows:

	0	1	2	3	4	5	6	7	8	9
1810	....	....	....	....	....	....	....	....	53°.45	54°.07
1820	53°.07	51°.61	54°.09	51°.86	....	....	54°.07	54°.25	55 .38	52 .88
1830	54 .67	50 .36	52 .66	53 .04	53°.39	50°.54	50 .43	51 .28	50 .57	52 .42
1840	52 .27	52 .05	52 .39	50 .38	52 .84	52 .16	54 .03	51 .62	52 .28	51 .85
1850	52 .07	52 .33	52 .20	52 .61	53 .96	52°.84	49 .71	50 .84	53 .44	52 .93

Mean annual temperatnre from 40 years observation, 52°.46, Fahr. Warmest year, 1828, 55°.38; Coldest year, 1856, 49°.71, difference in the mean temperature for these years, 5°,67; which is comparitively small range of variations.

If we compare the mean of the first 20 years, with the mean for the 40 years, we find it 0°.20 higher. If we compare that of the last 20 years, with the same standard, we find it nearly 0°.10 lower, so that no change in the climate is indicated in the 40 years observations. To ascertain whether the summer and winter temperatures have also remained unchanged, the following comparison is added:

MEAN MONTHLY TEMPERATURE.

	1818 TO 1840	1840 TO 1859		1818 TO 1840	1840 TO 1859
December	33°.38	33°.79	June	70°.14	69°.02
January	31 .38	31 .43	July	73 .40	73 .10
February	33 .91	34 .08	August	72 .03	71 .06
Mean	32° 96	33°.10	Mean	71°.86	71°.06

The differences 0°.14 in winter, and 0°.80 in summer, are too small, and fully covered by their probable uncertainty, to draw any other inference, than that of unchanged temperature of the seasons. The mean deviation of the monthly values for the term of years was found to be as follows:

IRREGULAR FLUCTUATIONS AS EXHIBITED IN THE MONTHLY MEANS.

January	-|-5°.04	July	-/-2°.32
February	6 .02	August	2 .32
March	4 .49	September	2 .76
April	3 .87	October	2 .95
May	2 .87	November	3 .66
June	2 .90	December	4 .48

The irregular fluctuations of the temperatures are therefore greatest in February, and least in July and August. The ratio is nearly 2.6 to 1. Comparing the lowest and highest means, we find them to be as follows:

	Lowest.	*Highest.*		*Lowest.*	*Highest.*
January	18°.61	41°.68	July	69°.84	77°.19
February	20 .65	43 .88	August	67 .30	75 .95
March	28 .15	51 .87	September	57 .18	70 .28
April	42 .56	61 .31	October	45 .53	58 .21
May	55 .43	69 .17	November	36 .11	49 .54
June	65 .23	74 .22	December	20 .49	43 .72

The irregularity in the mean daily temperature, is illustrated by the following table of observed extremes for each month during 31 years. The numbers are corrected for diurnal fluctuations:

	Lowest.	*Highest.*		*Lowest.*	*Highest*
January	— 6°.6	60°.8	July	+55°.5	86°.2
February	— 4 .3	61 .8	August	+53 9	84 0
March	+ 9 .5	74 .0	September	+42 2	80 .9
April	+25 .6	76 .6	October	+28 .8	75 .4
May	+42 .4	82 .3	November	+16 .4	66 .7
June	+45 .9	88 .7	December	+ 3 .4	64 .4

The extreme lowest temperature observed was —23 deg. 0 min. at 7 A. M., January 20, 1852, and the extreme highest temperature was 102 deg. 0 min., at 3 P. M., July 14, 1859. Extreme range observed, 125 deg. of Fahrenheit's scale.

The monthly means at the bottom of the table A, require a small correction to refer them from calendar to average months. Thus corrected they stand:

January	31°.39	July	73°.19
February	34 .16	August	71 .48
March	42 .56	September	64 .44
April	53 .60	October	51 .85
May	62 .50	November	42 .06
June	69 .86	December	33 .48
Mean			52°.55.

The temperature for the Meteorological Seasons is as follows:

Spring	52°.88	Autumn	52°.78
Summer	71 .51	Winter	33 .01

Adding 1°.54, we find the annual mean reduced to the *level of the sea*; 54°.09, Fahr.

MEAN RANGE OF THE DIURNAL FLUCTUATIONS FOR EACH MONTH.

After applying required corrections to the observed ranges, we find the following to be the mean range of Diurnal Fluctuations for each month:

January	12°	July	18°.4
February	14 .3	August	17 .7
March	18 .7	September	18 .7
April	22 .8	October	18 .6
May	22 .5	November	15 .5
June	19 .2	December	11 .2

The diurnal range attains its greatest value in April, and its least value in December; there is also indication of a secondary minimum in August, and a secondary maximum in

September or October. In April, the range is more than double that in December.

DIRECTION OF THE WIND.

Dr. Hildreth's record is tolerably complete over the years from 1829 to 1850, inclusive, and less so for 1852-3-4, and 1858-9. Table B contains 9,467 results of observations, and shows the relative frequency of each of the eight directions of the wind, on record for each year.

TABLE B.

YEAR.	S.	N.	W.	E.	S.W.	N.E.	N.W.	S.E.
1829	51	79	51	20	70.5	16.5	49	26
1830	39	83	52.5	12.5	95	15.5	39	26.5
1831	38.5	58.5	67	6.5	117	12	43	18.5
1832	32	68.5	63.5	12.5	106	14.5	32	36
1833	13	70.5	45	16.5	113	26.5	42	35.5
1834	14	84	62.5	11	87	19.5	30	54
1835	31	54	64.5	8	111	19.5	39.5	34.5
1836	58	84	51	22.5	16	18.5	33	36
1837	62	86.5	57	17.5	74	13	29.5	15.5
1838	49.5	87	41.5	17.5	68	30	35	32.5
1839	71.5	53	61.5	26	54.5	22	35	32.5
1840	45.5	55.5	68	13.5	91	17.5	25.5	41.5
1841	56.5	103.5	45	11.5	79	14	30.5	25
1842	64.5	72	36	20	89.5	7	39	32
1843	81	74.5	46	7.5	79	25.5	25.5	25
1844	83.5	82.5	28	15.5	91	13	27	24.5
1845	50	59.5	45	5	130.5	10	42	22
1846	50	78	36.5	27	99	12	19.5	42
1847	91.5	93	29.5	22	66.5	8.5	11	37
1848	113,5	110.5	30	14.5	45	9.5	10	29
1849	91	97.5	45.5	12.5	42	10	19	46.5
1850	85.5	92	35.5	13.5	58.5	7.5	17.5	32
....	....	....	....	....	....	....	....	....
1852	81	66	38.5	18	57	8	15	35.5
1853	64	91.5	19.5	17	32.5	4	20	26.5
1854	63.5	29.5	42.5	23	17.5	5.5	51	14
....	....	....	....	....	....	....	....	....
1858	64	60.5	69.5	51.5	56.5	6	45	11
1859	94	74	55	48.5	28.5	2.5	23.5	6.5
Sum	1,638.5	2,048	1,287	491	2,019	368	818	797.5
Prop. in 1,000	173	217	135	52	213	39	87	84

These proportional numbers exhibit the relative frequency of the wind throughout the year. The north and southwest winds, are the prevailing ones during the year, and the north-east and east winds are the least frequent. In the following table C, the results of the observations are arranged according to months and seasons, showing the annual variation of the relative frequency:

TABLE C.

MONTH AND SEASON,	S.	N.	W.	E.	S.W.	N.E.	N.W.	S.E.
January	121.5	157.5	137	36.5	181.5	26.5	74	54
February	88	153 5	120	31	171	27.5	107 5	56
March	107	184	121	36	168.5	32	104	58 5
April	110	200	98	43	160.5	37	69	71
May	169	181	85	32	157	28	74	76
June	176	150	95 5	31	205	26	47	49
July	145	187	75 5	48.5	206	27	47	68
August	175	210.5	59 5	39	141	40	33.5	108 5
September	173	178	80.5	52	125	43	46	75
October	155	199	96.5	47	151	30	58	68.5
November	100	114	155.5	41	201	30	72	59 5
December	119	133 5	163	54	151 5	·21	86	53.5
Spring	386	565	304	111	486	97	247	205 5
Summer	496	547.5	230.5	118.5	552	93	127.5	225 5
Autumn	428	491	332 5	140	477	103	176	203
Winter	328.5	444 5	420	121.5	504	75	267.5	163.5
Year	1.638 5	2 048 0	1.287 0	491.0	2,019.0	368.0	818 0	797.5

The results in Table C, show comparatively small changes in the seasons; the W. and N. W. winds blow more frequently in winter, and the S. wind more frequently in summer. The proportional numbers for each season, are as follows:

SEASON.	S.	N.	W.	E	S.W.	N. E.	N. W	S E,
Spring	161	235	127	46	202	40	103	86
Summer	208	230	96	49	231	39	53	94
Autumn	182	209	142	59	204	43	75	86
Winter	141	192	181	52	217	32	115	70

The prevailing winds in each season, are as follows: In Spring, N.; in Summer, N. or S. W.; in Autumn, N. or S. W.; in Winter, S. W. winds. The N. E. wind is least frequent in all seasons.

RELATION OF THE DIRECTION OF THE WIND TO TEMPERATURE.

To find the deviation of the temperature of each wind from the normal temperature, a table of mean temperatures for every day in the year was computed; to these means was applied, with its sign reversed, the correction to the mean of three observations, to the mean of twenty-four observations in a day, in order to make the tabular numbers directly comparable with the observed daily means (uncorrected).

As the deviation from the normal temperature is different in the summer and winter seasons, the year was divided into two equal parts (with regard to temperature), taking the epochs of the mean annual temperature, or April 15th and October 15th, as the limiting epochs. The observations also indicate that unless a certain wind has been *blowing for some time*, it will not indicate its peculiar temperature. An interval of half a day, or a day, however, after a change of wind is sufficient, and the temperature difference (from the tabulated values) of each of the eight winds has been set down whenever the record of the direction shows no change for two days or more. For the directions E. and N. E., single days, on which these winds blew, had to be included in the comparison. The total number of days of comparison of temperature, and direction of wind, is 2,340, with the following results. These show that on the average, during the year, the elevating effect of the south wind is nearly equal to the depressing effect of the northwest wind. The southeast, south, and southwest winds, are the warm winds. *All others are cold.* The temperature effect in winter, is far more marked than in summer, as shown by the extreme range of effect, which is 15°.3 in winter, and 8°.5 in summer.

EFFECT OF THE DIRECTION OF THE WIND ON THE TEMPERATURE.

DIRECTION.	HALF YEAR, INCLUDING		YEAR.
	SUMMER.	WINTER.	
N.	—4°.5	—4°.0	—4°.3
N. E.	—4 .4	—5 .1	—4 .7
E.	—2 .5	-|-2 .3	—0 .2
S. E.	-|-0 .3	-|-3 .3	-|-1 8
S.	-|-2 .7	-|-8 .8	-|-4 .9
S. W.	-|-2 .2	-|-2 .3	-|-2 .2
W.	—1 .9	—3 .5	—3 .0
N. W.	—5 .8	—6 .5	—6 .2

-|- Elevation above the normal.
— Depression below the normal.

RELATIVE DIRECTION OF WIND TO RAIN.

To ascertain the relative amount of rain observed, or to be expected, for each direction of the wind, the latter was tabulated for all the rainy days during 22 years, from 1829 to 1850. Dividing the year into two equal parts, one including summer (April 15th to October 15th), and the other, winter, (October 15th to April 15th), we have in the first 1,018 days, and in the second 803 days on which rain fell, and the corresponding relative frequency, of each direction of the winds, for the two seasons, is given in column 2, of Table D. As each wind does not occur the same number of times, in any given period, the above numbers, to reduce them to a common measure, must be divided by the relative frequency of each wind (made out from the proper table). These numbers are given in column 3, and the ratios, in column 4. The relative frequency of rain and wind, is expressed in percentage.

TABLE D.

DIRECTION OF WIND.	SUMMER.			WINTER.		
	Relative frequency of rain.	Relative frequency of wind.	Ratio.	Relrtive frequency of rain.	Relative frequency of wind.	Ratio.
S	22	20	1.1	14	14	1.0
S.W	31	21	1.5	19	22	0.8
W	13	10	1.3	18	17	1.0
N.W	6	7	0.9	11	11	1.0
N	12	24	0.5	17	20	0.8
N.E	3	4	0.8	3	4	0.7
E	4	5	0.8	7	5	1.4
S.E	9	9	1.0	11	7	1.5

During the summer, therefore, the directions from which most rain comes are S., S. W., and W., the S. W. wind bringing relatively the maximum amount. In winter, these directions are, E., S. E., and S., the S. E. winds bringing relatively the maximum amount. Rain rarely comes from the northward, in summer or winter.

RELATIVE DIRECTION OF THE WIND TO FAIR WEATHER.

The same process of investigation being pursued as above, the result of a tabulation of the winds on fair days, during summer and winter, for the years 1829 to 1833, and 1846 to 1850 (ten years, comprising a total of 1,931 entries), is given in table E., expressed in per centage:

TABLE E.

DIRECTION OF WIND.	Summer, April 15th to October 15th.			Winter, October 15th to April 15th.		
	Relative frequency of fair weather.	Relative frequency of wind.	Ratio.	Relative frequency of fair weather.	Relative frequency of wind.	Ratio.
S.	21	20	1.0	12	14	0.9
S.W.	19	21	0.9	24	22	1.1
W.	9	10	0.9	17	17	1.0
N.W.	5	7	0.7	11	11	1.0
N.	29	24	1.2	24	20	1.2
N.E.	4	4	1.0	3	4	0.8
E.	5	5	1.0	3	5	0.6
S.E.	8	9	0.9	6	7	0.9

Fair weather is accompanied most frequently by N. winds both in summer and winter. In the half year including summer, easterly winds (except S. E.) and in the half year including winter, westerly winds favor fair weather.

ATMOSPHERIC PRECIPITATION.

Table F. Gives the amounts, and frequency of rain (or snow), at Marietta, by Jos. Woods:

TABLE F.

	AMOUNT IN INCHES.							FREQUENCY, NO. OF DAYS.						
	1817	1818	1819	1820	1821	1822	1823	1817	1818	1819	1820	1821	1822	1823
January	......	2.50	3.20	1.46	1.35	1.31	4.42	......	......	7	4	2	2	3
February	......	3.00	3.30	5.79	4·94	1·65	1.28	......	......	8	7	5	1	1
March	......	3.70	5.57	2.95	3.70	2.18	6.21	......	......	7	4	4	2	6
April	......	2.30	1.48	3.93	4.24	5.11	2.86	......	......	4	6	6	5	......
May	......	5.90	4.54	3.50	3.01	2.35	5.08	......	......	9	6	4	5	......
June	......	2.45	2.20	3.80	3.68	4.09	8.07	......	6	5	4	3	7	......
July	......	8.87	3.26	4.73	4.52	4.80	6 91	......	13	10	7	5	7	......
August	......	5.30	6.31	1.58	6.50	2.15	3.20	......	9	5	6	5	4	......
September	......	7.10	1.10	0.20	6.05	4.45	2.03	......	5	5	1	5	6	......
October	......	3.70	2.25	4.73	1.41	4.31	......	......	7	5	8	2	7	......
November	4.45	2.10	0.70	2.66	2 60	8.59	......	......	3	2	4	2	6	......
December	1.00	4 00	2.39	3.83	1.32	2.39	......	......	3	4	4	1	4	......
Yearly Sum	......	50.92	36 30	39.11	43.32	43.38	......	......	......	71	61	44	56	......

The following tables, G. and H., give the amount in inches of rain (or melted snow, and the number of days of rain (or snow), observed at Marietta, by Dr. S. P. Hildreth.

TABLE G.

Amount, in Inches, of Rain (or Melted Snow), Observed at Marietta, by Dr. S. P. Hildreth.

	1827	1828	1829	1830	1831	1832	1833	1834	1835	1836	1837	1838	1839	1840	1841	1842	1843	1844
January	....	4.04	2 75	1.58	4 04	4.50	3.13	5.37	2.42	2.55	0.42	2.12	2.30	2.33	3.87	2.42	1 84	2.42
February	....	6.75	2.33	1.63	2.50	10 25	3.42	2.42	1.50	1.80	1.80	1.79	2.00	3.08	1.31	3.12	2.17	1 08
March	....	2.13	2.04	5.00	2 92	1.33	1.92	1.58	2.00	2.80	3.00	2.25	2.25	3 21	3.42	2.66	3.70	2.83
April	....	6.50	4.00	1.00	2 85	2 00	0.83	1.83	3.87	3.87	1.17	4.45	1 44	4.25	5.80	3.04	4 75	0.70
May	....	6.58	1.08	3.80	4 25	3.17	5.75	1.75	3.13	6 63	4 08	5.71	4.46	5.21	3.37	4.21	2.96	5.75
June	....	4.92	4 00	5.84	7.00	2.85	4.80	5.50	5.50	2.04	7.84	6 92	4.33	4.25	4.30	7.30	4.21	4.12
July	....	5.08	2.12	3.50	12.12	3.08	6.84	5.08	2.58	3 92	5.13	0.96	6.04	2.17	3.50	2.37	1.33	7.75
August	....	3.00	5.54	0 75	7.58	7.92	0.25	1.33	6.54	3.16	4.84	3.50	2 04	5.25	3,17	6 08	1.91	2.17
September	....	3 42	4 00	4 25	3 58	2.08	3 30	0.67	2.75	3.16	4 23	1.33	3.25	2.00	3 37	3.21	9.25	2 87
October	....	2.50	3.16	1 91	3.70	2.75	3.17	3.75	4 80	2 08	4.25	1.9[illegible]	0.25	3,92	1.83	1.58	4 43	3.54
November	....	3.42	4.00	3.67	1.25	3.75	3.88	3.25	5.50	2.50	3.30	3.42	2 50	1.9[illegible]	3 50	3.04	2.63	2.54
December	....	1.16	4.50	4.3[illegible]	1.75	4,66	3.08	2.13	1.87	2.25	3.80	1.08	2.46	1.50	5.38	3.04	2.58	0.87
Sum	41.42	49.50	39.52	37.26	53.54	48.33	40.37	34.66	42.46	36.75	43.86	35.48	33.32	39 69	42.82	42 07	41.76	36.64

Continuation of Table G.

	1845	1846	1847	1848	1849	1850	1851	1852	1853	1854	1855	1856	1857	1858	1859	Mo'thly mean 38 yr's.	Diff'nce Annual mean
January	2.58	3.25	3.66	2.04	4 09	5 25	0 50	2.08	2.20	3.25	2 50	2.75	1 55	1 66	3.10	2.70	--0.84
February	1.50	2.33	2.88	1.33	2.58	3.41	4.88	3 66	4.92	2.33	1.50	1.66	1.50	3.41	7.20	3.00	--0.55
March	2 67	2.37	4.30	3,00	4.37	4.50	1.44	4.30	0 88	4.25	2.67	1.34	1 30	1.[illegible]0	5.08	2.97	--0.58
April	2.50	2.04	2.54	1.38	2.50	3.17	3 04	7.58	5.92	5.42	2.08	2.25	3.08	5.00	6,46	3,85	--0.20
May	1 33	1.37	1.75	5.66	5.92	3.25	6.0[illegible]	4 21	3.21	2.12	5.17	4.16	5.[illegible]6	12.42	1.56	4.20	--0.65
June	6.55	7.04	2.77	3.25	4.42	4.84	2.60	5.70	0.88	3.66	5.68	5.25	4.08	3,09	4,62	4.59	--1.04
July	3.22	6 20	6,80	8.05	1.21	4.41	2.40	3.84	4.12	2.04	6.00	2.50	4.87	5.33	1.08	4.44	--0.90
August	2.00	6.00	2.80	4 86	3.50	6.91	3.60	3.50	2 83	3 66	3.09	2.75	5.21	7.42	4,46	4.02	--0.48
September	4.38	1.68	4.84	1.08	2.63	4.66	2.38	1.08	2.80	2.16	8.00	1.17	1.63	1,37	4,95	3.23	—0.32
October	2.80	4.00	6.42	3.09	3 92	2.54	1·68	2.30	4.29	4.62	1.85	2.42	2.58	7.66	2,79	3.22	--0.32
November	3.04	3.55	2 70	2.86	2.58	2.42	4.00	4 50	2.83	2.29	3 55	4.00	4 84	4.82	2,98	3.30	--0.25
December	1.33	6 44	10.84	6 58	5.17	7.00	2.42	3.75	2.16	3 00	3.66	2 21	4.84	8.66	5.17	3.54	--0.00
Sum	33 90	46 27	52,30	43.18	42 89	52 36	34.94	46.50	37.04	38.80	45.75	32.46	40.64	61.84	48.55	42.56	....

TABLE H.

Number of Days of Rain or Snow.

	1829	1830	1831	1832	1833	1834	1835	1836	1837	1838	1839	1840	1841	1842	1843	1844	1845	1846	1847	1848	1849	1850	1852	1853	1854	1858	1859	M'thly Mean.	Diff. from An. Mean
Jan.....	7	8	9	11	10	8	6	8	4	6	8	3	8	4	5	7	5	8	4	5	6	9	3	......	8	5	6	6.1	—1.0
Feb	5	10	4	11	6	7	3	5	5	4	7	10	4	5	8	5	5	7	5	4	4	8	4	9	5	8	7	5.9	—1.2
March	8	13	8	5	6	5	8	8	8	6	7	8	9	9	5	7	5	6	5	10	6	5	8	4	8	4	10	6.7	—0.4
April..	10	4	6	7	5	6	9	7	5	9	7	10	14	9	10	4	7	9	4	4	6	9	11	11	7	9	12	7.5	+0.4
May ..	6	9	12	11	12	5	8	9	10	14	10	9	7	9	5	11	4	6	7	14	8	7	7	9	5	17	6	8.4	+1.3
June ..	10	11	11	6	13	8	11	8	13	10	10	11	9	11	9	10	10	11	8	10	11	10	7	7	11	10	12	9.2	+2.1
July ..	11	5	18	8	8	9	7	8	10	4	8	6	9	6	5	8	7	9	13	16	7	9	8	8	3	8	4	8.3	+1.2
Aug...	7	3	11	11	2	3	9	8	10	6	7	10	6	11	8	6	5	9	11	8	8	8	9	10	8	9	10	7.6	+0.5
Sept....	12	7	10	6	8	4	4	11	7	2	8	7	8	6	9	5	6	5	7	5	4	6	5	5	6	4	9	6.2	– 0.9
Oct.....	11	8	11	7	5	8	6	8	6	6	3	10	7	3	11	8	5	4	8	8	7	6	5	6	6	12	5	6.8	—0.3
Nov...	15	10	5	11	7	7	10	5	4	8	6	5	8	7	9	6	6	5	7	4	4	5	8	7	6	9	4	6.4	—0.7
Dec.....	10	11	8	10	5	5	6	5	5	2	7	5	9	5	5	2	4	9	10	12	9	...	10	5	......	14	7	6.5	—0.6
Sum	112	99	113	104	87	75	87	90	87	77	88	94	98	85	89	79	69	88	89	100	80	......	85	......	......	109	92	85.6	....

The average amount of rain (and melted snow), from 38 years of observation, is 42.56 inches. The least quantity observed in any one year, is 32.46 inches (in 1856), and greatest quantity, 61.84 (in 1858).

The next to the last column of Table G. gives the monthly means for 38 years (that of October for 37 years), and the differences from the average amount, 3.55 inches, is shown in the last column. The plus sign in the months of May, June, July and August, indicates more than the average amount. The sign minus, with the remaining months, less than the average. Table F. Contains the number of days of precipitation, or the frequency of rain (and snow). The column of monthly means is deduced from 32 years (on the average), and plainly indicates an annual fluctuation, which is better shown in the last column, headed difference from the annual mean (7.1 days). In February, rain or snow, falls on one day *less*, and in June, rain falls on two days *more*, than on the average in any one month.

The average number of rainy days in any one year, is 86, nearly, varying between 44 and 113. If we divide the monthly mean amount, by the average monthly frequency, we obtain the average quantity in any one day.

AVERAGE QUANTITY IN ANY ONE DAY OF RAIN (OR SNOW,)

	Inches		*Inches.*
January	0,44	July	0.53
February	0.51	August	0 53
March	0.44	September	0.52
April	0.44	October	0.48
May	0.50	November	0.52
June	0 51	December	0.55

The copiousness of precipitation is nearly the same throughout the year. In summer, the rains are slightly heavier than in winter. On the average, a fall of rain on any one day, amounts to 0.50 inches. The three heaviest falls of rain recorded on any one day, was October 22d, 1858, 3.1 inches; December 10th, 1847, 3.5 inches; and July 3d, 1844, 4.25 inches. Heavy falls of rain may, therefore, occur in mid-winter as well as in mid-summer.

SNOW.

Snow is recorded to have fallen as late as May 13th (in 1829), and as early as October 4th (in 1836). The heaviest falls of snow occurred February 1st, 1830, when 7 inches fell;

April 18th, 1854, 8 inches; January 14th, 1831, and again December 14th, 1833, 15 inches. Even as late as April 29th (in 1854) as much as four inches fell.

FROST.

Frost is recorded in every month of the warmer half of the year, and quite frequently in the first of June. In 1848 there were 4 mornings of frost between June 1st and 13th. In 1843, June 2d, ice formed ⅛ inch thick. Frost occurred June 22d, and 23d, in 1846; July 1st; 1835; August 1st and 2d, 1842; August 23d, 1835; August 25th, 1832; August 29th, 1859.

STATE OF THE WEATHER.

The number of fair and of cloudy days in each month, were published by Dr. Hildreth, in Silliman's Journal for a number of years. To these were added the fair days recorded by Mr. Wood, making in all, between 1818 and 1859, 37 results for each month, excepting April, May, and December, for which the number of years is but 36.

AVERAGE NUMBER OF FAIR DAYS, DURING THE PERIOD FROM 1818 TO 1859.

Month	Days	Month	Days
January	13.8	July	21.9
February	13.9	August	21.7
March	16.7	September	20.3
April	17.7	October	18.9
May	19.4	November	14.5
June	20.3	December	12.7

The numbers show a regular progression during the year. In December, the number of fair days is least; they increase each month, and reach their maximum in July, after which month, they again gradually diminish.

The greatest number of fair days recorded in any one month is 30 (in July and August), and the least number 3 (in November). The average aggregate number of fair days in any one year is 211¾; and of cloudy days, consequently, 153½, varying between 170 (in 1858,) and 262 (in 1830). It is, therefore, rare that the number of fair and cloudy days in any one year, is equal. Summing up the number of fair days in each year, we have the following results:

TABLE I.

	0	1	2	3	4	5	6	7	8	9
1810	......	......	......	......	......	......	......	......	......	193
1820	181	174	180	......	......	......	......	......	242	208
1830	262	205	216	222	255	221	219	224	248	228
1840	204	205	215	193	209	236	201	198	211	226
1850	233	229	203	221	231	......	228	200	170	190

CHAPTER III.

AGRICULTURAL GEOLOGY.

BY WM. M. FONTAINE.

Under this head, we will give a brief description of the several geological formations found in the State, dealing with them, in their agricultural relations mainly. As, however, topography is so intimately connected with agriculture, we may in this connection, note those special features, not elsewhere, noticed.

But before taking up the Geological Formations, it will conduce to clearness if we first give some account of the character of the different soils, and of the rocks which form them.

THE DIFFERENT SOILS.

The following are the principal soils existing in the State:

Clay Soils.—These contain 75 per cent., and over, of clay. The remaining 25 per cent., is composed of sand, calcareous, ferruginous, vegetable, and other matters. In their physical character, when moist, they are stiff and tenacious. They dry with difficulty, and are rather slowly warmed by the sun's rays. When dry, they become baked to a more or less hard mass, and are also, in freezing and thawing, more apt to injure the roots of plants, than other soils.

With these disadvantages, however, they combine many advantages, and when properly managed, make the best lands for certain crops.

Stiff Clays.—Such as those just described, do not make a large proportion of our soils. They are chiefly to be found in the eastern and southern parts of the State.

Sandy Soils.—Contain 75 per cent., and over, of sand. The remaining components are clay, and the other constituents, except sand, mentioned as occuring in clay soils. In their physical characters, they are the opposite of clay soils, and are much inferior to them. They are loose, thirsty in nature, and do not hold manures well. Hence, a mixture of sand and clay in land is beneficial, the one correcting the defects of the other. Such strictly sandy lands, are comparatively rare, and are mainly found in the N. E. mountain counties, and in the outcrops of the sandstones of the conglomerate series.

Loams.—These are composed of clay and sand, mixed in about equal proportions. They contain also various other substances like those found in the two above-mentioned soils, making 20 to 25 per cent. of the whole. When clay predominates they are called clay loams; when sand, sandy loams; when lime forms a large proportion, calcareous loams, or marls. These make usually the most fertile lands known, since they contain all the elements needed by the plant, combined with the best physical condition, uniting as they do, the good qualities of sandy and clay soils, so far as these arise from the texture and condition of the land. Every farmer knows that the presence of elements of fertility is not all that is needed. Good condition is "half the battle."

Among the good physical qualities of loams, we may mention the following. They are neither excessively stiff nor light, are permeable to water, but do not parch, are quickly warmed by the heat of the sun, permit easy cultivation, and readily respond to the action of manures, while retaining them for some time.

Our State is fortunate in having a large proportion of such lands. Indeed, they may be said to be the characteristic soils of the country, and to form the larger part of our surface. The strata of the coal measures above the conglomerate, which cover so large a portion of our area, are peculiarly fitted to produce the best class of these, since thay consist of shales, argillaceous sandstones, and layers of limestone, or calcareous strata, intimately mixed. These readily break down under the action of the elements, and give a deep, light earth. It will not be necessary to specify localities. Even where the rocks under the coal strata furnish the material, they are usually so compounded of sandstones and shales, as by their disintegration, to produce such soils.

Calcareous Soils.—These are soils in which lime forms a large constituent, mixed with clay, sand, and other matters. Such soils are, from their chemical composition, among the best that are known.

In their physical character, they resemble more nearly the loams, and are especially suited for the production of grass. Of these our State has a large proportion. As localities where they occur, we may mention, Jefferson and a part of Berkeley, which contain the lower silurian limestone of the "Great Valley," with Pocahontas, Greenbrier, Mercer, and Monroe, containing the subcarboniferous limestone, and shales. The northern counties on the Ohio, with the limestone of the upper coal measures belong here also.

Alluviums—The alluviums may be divided into two classes, according as they are produced by deposits from turbid streams, or by slow surface action. We may call the first *stream alluvium*, and the second *upland alluvium.*

Stream alluvium, as is well known, is produced by deposits from streams in seasons of flood. Such soils are generally mixtures of all the kinds of matters found along the water courses which deposit them.

If such deposits are subject to occasional overflow, they receive by this means a renewal of their fertilizing components, and will then last indefinitely. If not overflowed, such soils must, under continued cultivation, eventually be exhausted, provided no return by means of manures, be made to them.

Magnificent soils of this class are found in the State. The "Bottom Lands," along our principal rivers, are widely celebrated for their productiveness, and for the great length of time during which, they have been cultivated. Some of these, have continued without intermission, for more than 100 years, to make heavy yields of that most exhausting of all crops, Indian corn.

Upland Alluvium.—This is produced by the slow action of the surface waters on the hill slopes. Such action tends to accumulate in the valleys, much of the fertilizing constituents of the hills, and to carry down to the lower levels, much of the vegetation which year after year, falls and decays on the higher gronnds.

This has gone on for ages, and has finally produced in the bottoms a soil of from one to to ten feet, and more, in depth, which combines, in the highest degree, all the elements of fertility. Were our hillsides formed of slowly decomposing rocks, this process would soon leave them bare. In fact, however, the rapidity with which they break down, and renew the earth, prevents this denudation, while not checking the accumulation of deep soils in the valleys.

Upland alluvium, is generally more productive than even stream alluvium, since it retains nearly all the fertilizing matters which have been slowly accumulating. On the other hand, stream alluvium, being a deposit from water, has lost most of its soluble enriching matters, from the greater or less length of time, during which, it has been suspended in water. In consequence of this, these have been dissolved, and carried off. This superior fertility of the upland alluvium, explains the great size of the timber which grows on them.

The large amount of vegetable matter, which they contain, is one of the most important enriching agents. The humus of the hill-slopes, gradually works its way down, in the first place, into the bottoms; and then, in the second place, the conditions of moisture, &c., found in such places, specially favoring luxurient vegetation, cause large additions from growth on the spot. This in the dense shade, moulders away with extreme slowness.

From the immense number of hills in our State, the amount of bottom land of this kind is very large, that of the streams and uplands together, being put by some at 30 per cent of the entire area.

THE DIFFERENT ROCKS.

We may now take into consideration the individual rocks, and the part which they play in the production of soil.

Shales.—These rocks are composed essentially of silica combined with alumina. On breaking down into soil they furnish these matters principally in the form of clay. This material by itself is useful to the plant only, in giving body to the soil, and thus acting as a support for the roots, and imparting to the land certain physical properties, which were noted under the head of Clay. Little silica, or alumina, is used by the plant as food, hence a pure shale would form a barren soil.

Shales are however never without other substances, and these, which in one sense, we might call impurities, furnish most of the solid food of the plants. The most common matters mixed with the essential components mentioned above, are as follows. Sand, which when present in large amounts, produces *sandy shales*, Iron, which gives a red color. Carbon, especially in the coal measures, which imparts a dark color. Lime when present in notable amounts, produces *calcareous shales.* Besides these, we have in smaller amounts, Potash, Soda, Phosphoric acid &c. The five last named, are the principal supplies of food to vegeation.

Shales when largely present, excercise an important influence on topography, as was shown under another head. Their presence is always marked by irregular, rounded, or conical hills.

Sandstones.—They furnish essentially sand, or silica combined. Like clay, sand yields almost no food to vegetation, but acts physically, in giving bulk, and in imparting the properties described as possessed by sandy soils. Sandstones also are never pure, but contain the same admixtures as are found in shales, excpt that clay takes the place of sand, among the non-essential ingredients.

Sandstones in their topographical effects, are of even more importance than shales, this was fully shown under the head of topography. It will suffice to say here, that the purer they are, the less prone they are to break down. Sandstones, without impurities, are the most indestructible rocks known. These rocks cause shallow and poor soils of the sandy class.

The sandstones of the coal measure, are always more or less argillaceous, and are broken down with comparative ease, yet it is mainly due to them that our hills maintain their present height. It is remarkabe what preservative influence, a massive plate of sandstone exerts. We of ten find in the tops of our highest hills, a ledge of this rock, covering the summit, which by its presence alone has preserved the crest from being washed away. When situated lower down, it always betrays itself by the formation of a bench.

When the dip of sandstones is gentle, they tend to form flat-backed hills, and table-lands, when they stand at a high angle, mountain ridges and chains, are produced. A mere glance at the country, will often from the topography, give information as to whether shales, or sandstones predominate in a given section. The high mount ins in our north-eastern counties, with their noted scenic effects, are due to the presence, and preservative influence, of sandstones.

Limestones.—Limestone contains, essentially, carbonate of lime, and by its disintegration forms calcareous soils. Lime it itself food for plants. This stone is always mixed here with other rocks, either shales or sandstones, which determine the texture, and other physical properties of the earth, produced by their disintegration.

Limestones themselves are often impure, and contain large amounts of magnesia, when they are called *magnesian limestone*, or *dolomite.* Silica, and almina are often present in considerable amounts, when the rock is fitted for the production of hydraulic cement. Iron and other foreign substances also occur in smaller amounts. Impure limestones are the most common kind in the coal measures, and are better soil producers than pure ones, since they disintegrate far more readily, and furnish a greater variety of materials. The disintegration of all, is much aided by the presence of decaying vegetable matter, which forms carbonic acid, and changes the insoluble carbonate into soluble bicarbonate. In this latter form, it is taken up by plants, or removed by the percolating waters.

Limestones, owing to the evenness with which they wear down, usually give to the country in which they are found, a pleasing undulating surface. These rocks have given to much of Jefferson, Berkeley, Greenbrier, Monroe, &c., the surface features which distinguish them.

It does not follow that all soils, underlaid by limestones, have a large amount of lime in their composition. It often happens that they are mainly produced by the shales which accompany the limestones, owing to their greater proneness to break down. In many cases, as experience has shown, applications of lime, to lands having a substraturn of massive limestone, have proved beneficial.

The above named kinds of rocks are the principal soil producers in West Virginia- It must not be inferred that we will find our lands sharply divided into classes, such as we have made above, for the sake of description. The three kinds of rocks described, occur so intimately blended, and in their decomposition mingle so their products, that no sharp dividing line can be drawn. It is the good fortune of the State, that no one kind of rock, usurps exclusive possession of any great extent of territory.

THE GEOLOGICAL FORMATIONS.

We will take these up in the order in which they occur in passing from east to west, over the State, which is also the order of their age, commencing with the oldest.

We may omit the metamorphic, and primordial strata, as they occur only in the eastern edge of Jefferson, and have no important influence on the soil of the State. The oldest important formation is the *lower silurian limestone,* which with the overlying *Hudson River* shales, make up the greater part of Jefferson and Berkeley. These groups consist of a great thickness of limestone, of every hue and texture, much of which is magnesian, succeeded by soft, easily decomposing shales, and calcareous bands.

From this mass of strata have been produced the splendid calcareous soils of the counties above named, giving some of the finest land in this or any other State.

Farther west, and across the Great Valley, we meet with the first of those long lines of mountains which characterize the Alleghany belt. These continue in parallel folds as we go west, and occupy the northeastern portion of the State as far as Randolph, and Pocahontas. These are composed of silurian and devonian serata. The lower silurian limestone, is not brought up in them, but appears, according to Rogers, in the beautiful valley of Crab Orchard, in Pendleton, and gives to it, its fertility and pleasing topography.

Following the Hudson river shales, we have the *Medina sandstone,* a rock which enters largely into the structure of the mountains of this part of the State, This is a massive sandstone, lying in thick plates, and from its highly siliceous character, it is specially fitted to withstand the destructive action of the elements, and to serve as a protection for the softer strata associated with it. It is essentialiy a mountain-making rock, and is often seen in huge arches, and high cliffs. It is the principal agent in producing the grandest scenic effects of this section. It is extensively exposed in the mountain sides of Pendleton' and along the North Fork of the South Branch of the Potomac.

From its composition it can produce, where it forms the only surface rock, nothing but a thin sandy soil. As it is very unsuited for soil production, or the growth of vegetation, it is fortunate that, within the bounds of our State, it is brought np only along narrow bands, with a steep dip, and is consequently soon buried beneath the softer rocks which overlie it.

From its great permanency, and the elevation to which it has been thrust up, it gives to the county of Pendleton, and the adjacent county, its predominance in altitude. It is conspicuous in Peter's mountain, on the southern border of the State, which, in that quarter, is its most westerly position.

CLINTON AND ONONDAGA GROUPS.

These are mainly soft slates and shaly sandstones, with occasional calcareous bands. All are of reddish hue, and readily decompose, with the production of a fertile soil. These rocks are extensively developed in Hampshire and Hardy counties, and exert an important influence on their soil and topography, from the ease with which they disintegrate. Hence, the mountains which they compose, usually have softly rounded or undulating contours, while the abundant soil which they yield, serves as a covoring for the bare ledges of the Medina Sand Stone.

LOWER HELDERBURG LIMESTONE.

Overlying these, we have the strata of the Lower Helderberg limestone, forming an important element in the agricultural resources of the region. This formation has at the bottom, many alternations of shale, with limestone beds, but it is mainly composed of a rather massive limestone. Toward the top, it assumes a siliceous character, producing a peculiar sandy looking rock on weathering, and causing a decided improvement in the physical character of the soil formed from it.

This limestone is of the more importance, since, as Rogers

says, it is the only one exposed over wide districts of the mountain region, and since it often spreads out along the tops, or on the flanks of the broader ridges. In Hampshire, Hardy, Pendleton, etc., numerous available quarries may be found, furnishing good lime for building or agricultural purposes. This point is of special importance, for, as Rogers has with truth stated, the soils furnished by the Hamilton and Portage groups are spread over an extensive area in this section, and these are of a character to be specially benefiited by applications of lime.

THE ORISKANY SANDSTONE.

This follows next in the order ascending, and is another mountain-making rock. It is an open-grained sandstone of massive texture, occuring usually in massive beds, dipping steeply along the mountain, and quite bare of vegetation. This rock has the same effect as the Medina sandstone, on the topography. A noble specimen of it may be seen in the "Hanging Rocks," near Romney, in Hampshire, where the strata are thrown into three stupendous arches. Nearly all the mountains of Hampshire, Hardy, Pendleton, Pocahontas, etc., exhibit exposures of this formation. As a soil producer, it acts in general like the Medina, but, as it is more prone to disintegrate, forming a white sand, it is not so persistent as that rock.

HAMILTON AND PORTAGE GROUPS,

These are of great importance, for several reasons, as will appear from our description of them. The Hamilton strata are almost entirely composed of shales. and argillaceous rocks, of a slaty nature, while the Portage consist of a mass of alternating thin-bedded shales and sandstones. Both are of great thickness, and are very easily broken down into a loamy soil, which is deficient in calcareous matter, and more or less charged with copperas and other mineral salts.

These rocks overspread a considerable extent of surface, usually forming the hilly broken country, found in the foothills along the main mountain ranges, and the gentler slopes of the mountains themselves. From their likeness to the strata of the coal measures, in their physical character, they produce a topography closely resembling that usually seen in the Hilly Region.

In the vicinity of the White Sulphur Springs, the main Alleghany is entirely composed of them, as well as much of the country between that range and the Greenbrier river. To the softness of these strata, is due the lowness of this range in this section, viz.: 2,320 feet.

Perhaps their greatest importance is due to the fact, that they furnish material to a great number of noted mineral springs, among which, it will suffice to mention, the widely known Greenbrier White Sulphur. They are especially fitted for the production of medicinal springs, from the large amount of iron pyrites, carbonaceous, and other matters which they contain, and from their highly contorted and broken condition.

The pyrites decomposes with great readiness, and the reactions between the products formed, and other components of the shales especially of the Hamilton group, give rise to various sulphates, hydrogen sulphide, &c., which impart to the waters in which they are dissolved, various medicinal properties.

Among the localities in which these strata occur, we may mention the following: They form a large portion of the main Alleghany on the east border of Pocahontas. Along the sides of the anticlinal ridges, of Capon, Sandy, Patterson's Creek, South Branch, Knobbly, and North Fork mountians, they are extensively exposed, as well as in the intervening valleys. The soils which the strata in question furnish, though in physical properties good, yet are apt to be charged with an excess of acid from the abundance of pyrites, and the deficiency of lime. Artificial applications of lime would be especially benefieial to such soils, since they would correct the acidity, and at the same time produce gypsum, which is a valuable fertilizing salt.

CHEMUNG AND CATSKILL.

These groups have never been separated in West Virginia, and indeed we cannot as yet say whether any distinct Catskill group exists at all here. This point, however, for our present purpose, is of little importance, as both groups have the same general character, so far as their relations to agriculture are concerned. They consist of a great thickness of sandstones, generally argillaceous, and shales usually of some shade of red. Some of the shales of these formations are of a very soft and crumbling nature, and readily fall to a stiff red clay soil. The sandstones furnish a loam, and from their predominance, cause the soil formed, to have a much more open texture than it would possess if formed from the shales alone. The products of decomposition have a large amount of peroxide of iron, from the presence of decomposing pyrites. Though not void of lime, applications of this material would be highly beneficial. Thus treated, the soils produced by these strata, would form some of the most productive lands in the State.

These rocks do not occupy so extensive an area, as the preceding Hamilton and Portage. They form a considerable belt, between the Alleghany mountains, in the vicinity of the White Sulphur, and the Greenbrier river, and in the N. E. part of the State, some of the Alleghany ranges themselves are composed of them. They are shown between Huntersville and the Greenbrier river, also in Town Hill, Big and Little Timber Ridges, and in the Shenandoah mountain, forming the most elevated part of the range,

VESPERTINE STRATA.

This is a threefold group, composed at the base, of coarse sandstone and conglomerates; in the middle, of gray, flaggy sandstones, with some little coal; and on the top, of red crumbling shales, like those of the preceding group. The lower, and middle portions, form very little of our surface, but the upper red shales are rather more important, as they overspread some extent of country in Pocahontas, Greenbrier, Monroe and Mercer, lying east of, and immediately adjacent to the limestone soils of the umbral. From the resemblance of these shales to those of the umbral series, overlying the limestone, they have been usually confounded with the latter. The physical character of the soils furnished by these vespertive rocks, is the same with that described above, as belonging to the Chemung and Catskill shale products.

In this case, however, the chemical character is much better, for the vespertine red shales have more or less lime, sometimes enough to render them worthy of the name calcareous, and in all cases they are impregnated with a sufficiency to to produce a fertile soil. These strata are sometimes to be seen within the area occupied by the productive coal measures, appearing as far west as Laurel Hill, in the northern part of the State, also in the western part of Randolph, and in other localities. When thus seen, they usually appear along eroded anticlinal lines of uplift.

THE UMBRAL.

This, the next succeeding series, is, as a soil producer, the most important of all the formations preceding the productive coals, This importance is given it, both by the considerable area which it occupies, and the fertility of much of the land which it produces.

This again is a complex series, being at bottom limestone, followed by a great mass of argillaceous sandstones and shales, most of which are of a deep red color. The limestone is of very various character. The purer kinds are dark bluish in color. and burn to a good lime. The impure varieties, are sandy and shaly, disintegrating readily, and producing a tenacious clayey soil, of a light yellow color, and great fertility. The rocks of this class have given to the counties in which they occur, the productive character for which they are noted. The ease with which most of the sandstones and shales, which overlie the limestone have been broken down and removed, has given to the country that smoothness of surface which we see, and accounts for the fact that the plateau of Greenbrier, as elsewhere noted, is 600 to 800 feet lower than than the conglomerate plateau lying to the west of it. The limestone occupies much of the surface, because the work of denudation has removed the overlying softer, and less resistent shales, and sandstones.

Beginning in the north, the area occupied by this series is less extensive, both because it is thinner there, and the dip which affects it is steeper. Coming south, the group thickens rapidly, and the dip flattens out, so that the rocks in question overspread a wide area, in Greenbrier, Pocahontas, Summers, Mercer and Monroe. The red shales of the umbral, are especially remarkable for their deep and brilliant colors, and the the readiness with which they fall to a tenacious clayey soil. Our strongest clays are found among these lands.

THE CARBONIFEROUS FORMATION.

This overspreads by far the largest area in the State. We have already, under other heads, amply explained the character of the soil, produced by this formation, especially that portion producing coals generally workable, as well as the peculiar topography produced. Of the conglomerate number, we may say in addition, that the highly siliceous character of its upper member, unfits it for the production of either a deep, or fertile soil. It is fortunate then, that generally there is a sufficient remnant left over it, of the softer productive coals, to cover it with a good depth of earth.

Of the productive coals themselves, we may repeat in this connection, that they consist of an intimate interstratification of sandstones, shales, and calcereous bands, all falling readily to earth, and producing a light grey loam, of the best physical character, and with abundant elements of fertility. Calcareous matter is alwas present, whether visible as limestone or not, and this accounts for the great adaptation of these lands for grass. Strangers note the fact with surprise, that the grass grows green and luxuriant throughout the summer, on the hillsides, up to their tops.

This is due to the fact, as suggested by Diss Debar, that these strata are practically horizontal, and the percolating waters, following their upper surfaces, find exit all along up the slope, giving a supply of moisture even in the dryest seasons. On the other hand, when strata are highly inclined, they conduct away the waters into the bowels of the earth.

The uppermost members of the carbonifierous formation, where shown on the Ohio river, in the north of the State, contain important limestones, and these, with their associated calcareous shales, overspread a considerable area in the Panhandle counties, giving in that quarter a soil which, in productiveness, rivals the best Ohio river bottoms.

The stranger, in passing through our State, along the main lines of travel, would be apt to draw conclusions concerning our soil and topography, which would be erroneous when applied to the larger part of our area. The principal railroads, such as the Baltimore and Ohio, and the Chesapeake and Ohio, pass in their search for smaller grades, through the bottoms of gorges, and follow the streams closely in their deeply sunken channels. From what we have said concerning the character of the tops of the hills and plateaus, which adjoin these canon-like stream beds, it will be seen that the inspection of the one can give no idea of the character of the other.

CHAPTER IV.

FARM PRODUCTS.

BY WM. M. FONTAINE.

GENERAL REMARKS.

The present conditions, and the prospects of agriculture in West Virginia, cannot be understood without some explanation. Any present exhibit of her productions from the soil would not give a fair idea of her capabilities. It will be readily seen that the capacity of no new country, can be fairly judged by her productions at any given given time. Census reports, and statistics, may afford us data to determine the resources of old, and well populated regions, where all the branches of industry have adjusted themselves into harmonious working order, and each pursuit is maintained by a sufficient body of laborers. trained for their special calling. This is far from being the case in West Virginia. Almost every condition requisite for the present full development of her abundant resources is wanting. Her population is sparse, much of her land is still in the primeval forests, and her people have not confined their attention to special fields of labor and striven to perfect them. There has also been a great deficiency of labor and capital. Last, but not least, railways and roads, until of late, have been rare within her borders. With respect to this last feature, much has recently been done, and very much more is projected, so that we may soon hope to see generally introduced into our State, that great stimulus to active farming, a ready and cheap transportation to market.

For the general and thorough working of our lands, we greatly need an immigration of industrious settlers. Thousands pass yearly through our State to the far west, not knowing that here they can find an abundance of untouched virgin land, at nominal prices, and with a fertility not surpassed by any which they can hope to gain in the remote west. But suppose that lands were higher, and poorer here, our climate and proximity to the great markets, must ever give us a great advantage over farmers who, when they make a good crop, find it destroyed at one blow, by the ravages of insects, by tornadoes, or floods of rain; and who, if successful in escaping their numerous enemies, find all profits swallowed up in charges for transportation to markets which lie at our doors.

But these are not the only, or chief causes which have lessened the amount of farm products with us. The way in which the State was settled, and the consequent habits of her inhabitants, have been unfavorable to the existence of extensive or skilled farming, and have directed the industry of the people into almost every other channel. The original settlers were to a large extent men without means, who, on entering this country, then cut off from all exit to market, were content to clear small patches of ground, whose generous response to even poor cultivation, yielded returns sufficient to supply their limited wants. His little "clearing," selected in the most convenient spot, was cultivated by the pioneer year after year, in corn, and vegetables, which served to support his family along with a hog or two, and possibly a horse and a cow, with fowls, and the abundant game in the forests around, there was abundance of meat and bread. Even now, in many parts of the State, this is the mode of life.

When the original clearing was exhausted by long tillage, an addition was made by felling more timber. Thus the cleared lands gradually grew around the cabins, until extensive openings were made, but still without causing attempts at establishing communication with the outside world. This independent mode of life impressed upon the people habits of thought and action, which, though calculated to foster industry, frugality, and hardiness, were not most favorable for the promotion of undertakings which require communication with, and dependence upon, other countries.

We see at the present day the influence of this training. Until of late West Virginians have paid but small attention to the raising of agricultural products for exportation. They are usually content with the production of a sufficiency for home consumption. But rarely is an improved system of farming employed, and the cultivation is of the rudest kind. The tendency is to look to other sources than the farm for products of exchange. As an example, this spirit has led our people along all the streams which can float a raft, to denude the forests of the magnificent timber which they afford, often sacrificing it in the most prodigal manner. So, too, they turn their attention, when the finer timber has been removed, to the getting of tan-bark, hoop-poles, &c., &c., which business occupies a very important position among our industries. All of these causes have led to a neglect of agriculture, and stock farming, industries for which, especially the latter, our State is peculiarly fitted. Of course, there are important exceptions, especially along the Ohio, and in the older counties, as in Greenbrier, in the South Branch district, &c. Besides, we are speaking rather of what has been, of late years there has been a marked improvement, and we are being forced into those industrial channels which nature intended that we should follow. The opening of important lines of railroad has brought capital to develop our coals and iron, and the established value of these, bids fair to bring other lines within our limits. The increased amount of cleared land, has given greater impetus to stock rasing, which has been still farther increased by the dictates of a sounder system of agriculture. This has taught us to keep our hillsides, with their easily washed soils, as much in grass as possible, and the ready money returns which our sheep, wool, and the cattle purchased in the fields, bring us, tend strongly in the same direction. Again, our people are no longer satisfied with the miserable roads, which have been no small obstacle in the way of farming. More attention, also, is paid to systematic farming, althought much yet remains to be done in that direction

Our State at present pays more attention to corn, than any other crop. To the production of this, the soil and climate are well adapted. When the lands produce grass, and especially on the calcareous soils, the following rotation has been found advantageous. First corn, one or two years, then oats, then wheat, then grass; clover, timothy, or both mixed. The land, if productive enough, may be grazed during the whole time it is in grass. When the Blue Grass grows spontaneously, as it does over most of the State, it tends to overrun meadows, and hence foreign grasses, such as clover and timothy, cannot be maintained for any great length of time. The farmers on the calcareous soils of the Panhandle, say that their hills grow grass almost as well as the bottom lands, but on neither can they keep timothy longer than five years as the predominant grass. After this period, Blue Grass takes the ground, and this, being indigenous, maintains possession indefinitely, forming excellent pastures. It is claimed that the land improves so long as it is in either grass. The Blue Grass pasture is again broken up and the same routine takes place. The same rotation essentially is followed in other grass lands with beneficial results. Rye and barley may be substituted as small grain crops.

In the uplands of the South Branch district, of the N. E. counties, which is a fine grazing region, and produces fine grain and hay in the bottoms, the rotation of crops is, corn, wheat, clover, and occasionally rye or buckwheat. This rotation may perhaps be taken to represent a good succession for any highland grain district.

The census reports, never absolutely accurate for even old and thickly settled States, are peculiarly liable to error in our State, from the sparseness of the population, the difficulty of procuring data, etc., etc. Thus, among other things, the proportion of woodland, to cleared, and improved land, as given in them, is far too small. Many parts of the State, especially the S. and S. W., are almost in their original condition of forests, and almost the entire acreage should have been given as woodland. In some counties an absurdly small amount of woodland is given. In another important point we are grossly misrepresented. This is in the amount of our forest products. The money value of the forest products of the whole State is put at $363,668. The city of Wheeling alone pays more than that amount. This we mention merely to call attention to the fact that no adequate exhibit of the products of the State, is made in any accessible statistics.

As to the character of the crops, fruits, etc., that may be raised within the State, it will be easily seen that it must be very varied. No State has a greater variety of soil within certain limits, and few have a greater range of elevation, varying as ours does, from 500 feet to 4,000 feet. Between the summits of the mountains in the northeast, and the valley of the Ohio, in the southwest, we have a climatal difference of at least 14°.

INDIAN CORN.

Two circumstances have combined to make Indian corn by far the most important crop in the State. The first is, that the soil and climate are more generally adapted to the production of corn, than of any other grain. The most common soil is a loam, with more or less sand and calcareous matter. As a rule the alluvial bottoms along streams, have more sand than the hills. This soil is usually light, quick, easily penetrated by the heat of the sun, and whether in bottoms, or on fresh uplands, has and abundance of vegetable matter. In such lands, corn produces abundantly, with the very poorest cultivation. The astonishing yields of corn on bottoms formed of such soils, may be best seen by some examples. Some of the Kanawha bottoms have been cultivated in corn eighty consecutive years without diminution of yield. Blenerhasset Island, in the Ohio, in Wood county, has produced, in some parts, for more than fifty-seven years, crops of corn of an average of eighty bushels (sometimes 110), without fertilizers.

Some of the lands in the South Branch district, in Hampshire and Hardy, have been cultivated in corn for one hundred years, with continued high yields (eighty to ninety bushels per acre), though unaided by manures. The Ohio bottoms are not inferior in productiveness.

These examples may serve to illustrate, not only the amazing productiveness of these alluvial loams, but also to show the vicious system of cultivation practiced by too many of our farmers, in continuing the same crop so long.

While the hills do not, of course, usually have a sufficient depth of soil to permit such long continued cultivation, with remunerative returns, yet when freshly cleared and full of vegetable matter, or when properly managed, though not fresh, they are hardly inferior to the lowlands. As an example, many of the hills along the Ohio river, when farmed systematically, not uncommonly produce crops of eighty to one hundred bushels per acre.

We may find the second cause which gives corn the predominance, in the greater usefulness of this grain as a food for both man and beast, and also, to a certain extent, in inherited tendencies. We have seen, in speaking of the pioneer settler, how far this grain alone supplied his wants. With his descendants it plays a no less important part. In the newer counties, settled in the manner above described, corn meal almost excludes flour in the production of bread. Nearly all of the crop is consumed within the State, either as food for the family, or in fattening stock. From the increasing attention paid to stock raising, the amount consumed in the last mentioned way is steadily on the increase. An additional advantage in this mode of disposing of corn, is found in the fact, that from the droppings of the cattle, the material removed is restored to the land.

Whatever corn is not thus consumed, finds ready market in the small towns, or among new settlers. Corn by these means has maintained, especially in the interior, a pretty constant price, almost never falling below 50 cents per bushel.

As might be inferred from what has been said about our soils and climate, it is a sure crop. No total failure has occurred since its first cultivation. Notwithstanding the fact that corn is our principal crop, we may repeat concerning it, what was said above of our productions generally. The present production is by no means a measure of what may be done. Most of the crop raised, is produced on freshly cleared land, in the midst of stumps and roots, with very imperfect tillage.

As illustrating the effect of habit in inducing preference for the cultivation of certain crops, we may take the cultivation of corn in this State.

In those counties which were settled by hunters and trappers, and cleared in small patches, however large a body of cleared land they may now possess, or however thickly they may be settled, we find corn and oats to be by far the most important crop. This is not due entirely to the greater fitness of the land for the cultivation of these grains. On the contrary, the soil of many of these counties, is well adapted for the growth of wheat and tobacco. The exclusive cultivation of corn is due in part to that spirit of imitation, and tendency to travel in well-worn ruts, which, perhaps, are shown more strikingly in the farming profession than in any other calling. On the other hand, we find nearly all the wheat of the State to be produced in the older counties, which were settled by men of some means from the Atlantic slope. Other causes operated to produce this result in the cultivation of wheat. Of these, we we will speak when we come to consider the cultivation of that grain.

Unfortunately, the descendants of the pioneers did not inherit from them only their preference for corn raising, but acquired from that source an almost incurable taste for slovenly agriculture, one of the fruits of which, we see in the disposition, so prevalent, to continue the cultivation of the same grain on a piece of land just as long as it will bring anything.

We have unfortunately no data for the determination of what kinds of corn have been found to succeed best on the different soils, and under the various climatal conditions found in the State. Many varieties, both of white and yellow corn are used. In many parts of the State the yellow varieties are preferred, as it is stated, they give a better flavored and more nutritious meal.

What has been found true of Tennessee will apply to the cultivation of corn in a large portion of our State. The gourd seed, a large cob variety, is preferred in that State for river and creek lands, and the yellow corn for their rolling uplands. Varieties that mature more quickly would be better for the higher plateau and mountain districts.

The total yield of corn in the State, as given in the census of 1770, is 8,198,865 bushels. The average yield may be taken to be 35 bushels per acre.

WHEAT.

We have already adverted to the fact that nearly all the wheat raised in the State, is produced in the older and more thickly settled counties, and intimated that this state of things is not entirely due to the greater fitness of these counties for wheat raising. Here, too, we trace the influence of inherited tendencies. As evidence of this, we may call attention to the fact that in said counties attempts to cultivate wheat are persisted in under the most discouraging circumstances, where other grain crops would pay far better. Another and more important cause which has operated to confine wheat growing mainly to the older counties, is the fact that in such districts, the condition of the land is more favorable for successful cultivation of the grain. Here we find large bodies of open lands which have been long cleared and kept under thorough cultivation. Preparation can be made in time for early seeding, and harvesting, threshing, &c., economically managed. Besides, the inducements are greater. More wheat is consumed at home, and the access to market is often easier.

In some of the more highly cultivated counties, such as Harrison, Marshall, &c., crops of 30 bushels are frequently obtained.

The case is different in the newer sections. Cleared land has been less abundant, the foul condition of the new grounds has permitted no thorough ploughing, and caused great waste in harvesting and threshiug. The greater taste of the people for corn meal, the limited demand for wheat as an article of food for man alone, and the inacccessible position of many of these counties, have all tended to lower the production of this grain in such sections. We may state here that this condition of things is rapidly changing with the increased amounts of cleared land, and the greater attention paid to improved farming.

The above mentioned causes are independent of the conditions of soil and climate. These will ever operate to keep the production of wheat in the State, below that of corn. The kind of soil and climate suited for the successful raising of wheat, is not found in our State so generally as that suited for corn and oats. A well-drained clay, or clay loam with calcareous matter, suits it best. An equable winter climate, dry weather about ripening time, and a freedom from heavy rains when the bloom is on, are all required for the heaviest yields.

Nevertheless, there is no doubt that the amount of wheat raised by us, can, and will be largely increased. Many of the counties do not raise enough for home consumption, but import flour. A sound system of economy will not permit this state of things to continue in those counties where, as is the case in many, all the conditions are favorable for the raising of this grain. Again, much of the present crop in the new counties, as stated above, is raised after corn, on new, imperfectly cleared land. This does not permit the seeding to be done early enough for our climate. The body of cleared land is already large enough in many sections to permit a proper rotation of crops, the good effects of which are shown in no crop, sooner than in wheat. As the roots and stumps decay, cleaner cultivation will be permitted. Thus without an increase of acreage, we may look for increased yields.

Spring wheat is not cultivated to any extent, since it has not proved so successful as winter wheat. Most of the known varieties of winter wheat have been tried with more or less success. The Mediterranean is, perhaps, the most approved in the Ohio counties. In general, the white flinty smooth, and early bearded varieties are the most reliable. The total amount of wheat raised according to the census of 1870, is 2,480,148 bushels, making it the second crop in amount. The average may be taken as 10 bushels per acre. This, when compared with that of corn, seems very low. It must be remembered, however, that corn is cultivated on the best lands in the least exhausted portions of the State, generally bottoms, while wheat is mainly raised on the older and more exhausted lands. Besides, it fails much oftener than corn. These averages, and all others. given for the different crops, are for cultivation without fertilizers· A moderate use of them would largely increase these yields.

OATS.

Oats rank third in the grain production of West Virginia. Their productiveness, adaptiveness to various soils and climates, and the ease with which they are raised, render the crop a favorite one, more especially in the new counties. The crops are limited only by the demand for the grain. In many of the back counties, only enough is raised for feeding at home. When access can be had to market, the largest crops are made. In the mountain and high plateau lands, the conditions of climate cause oats to supercede in large measure other grains. The total amount raised, is for 1870, 2,513,749 bushels. The average may be taken as 30 bushels per acre.

BARLEY.

Owing to the lack of a good market, Barley has received but little attention. It is not consumed as food for man or beast, like wheat, and oats, or corn, among our people, hence as there is no home consumption, there is little inducement to raise it. Some attention was at one time paid to the raising of it, in the counties in the north of the State on the Ohio, for the supplying of the Wheeling breweries. It was found, however, that this grain could be bought elsewhere cheaper than it could be raised in the vicinity. Like oats, this grain flourishes well in almost any soil that is not too heavy and wet. The total amount for 1870 was 50,363 bushels. The amount per acre may be put at 15 bushels.

RYE.

Rye is not much cultivated in the State. It is well adapted, as it would seem, to the higher and colder parts of the country, and it is in such regions that it is mainly raised. The counties of Ritchie, Preston and Hampshire, are the largest producers. It will grow well on almost any of our soils, and is a hardy grain. Since it requires the same season as wheat, and the same cultivation, without being so useful as food, it can never attain any great magnitude as a crop where wheat can be raised. When sown on fertile land in September, it would form a good pasture in winter and spring. This is the chief use of it made in Tennessee, and it mignt be thus employed more largely in our own State. Total yield in 1870, 277,746 bushels. Average yield about 18 bushels per acre.

BUCKWHEAT.

This grain, according to Diss Debar, thrives with little or no care in every part of the State, and is cultivated most extensively in the upper Ohio river and mountain counties. Preston county, according to the same authority, alone produces 95,857 bushels. According to the census of 1870, if correct, there must have been a fearful falling off in this crop, as it gives for the whole State, only 82,916 bushels. But this is only another instance of the glaring incorrectness in the census reports of our productions. Buckwheat seems particularly fitted for the glades, and table lands of the more elevated, and colder portions of the State. On them it is largely raised, and forms an important article of food in such districts. Here, in the form of cakes, in connection with maple syrup, and mountain honey, it is used in considerable amounts. The yield is very variable in different soils, the largest being in good dry loam. In rich alluvial land, it is inclined to go to straw. In the mountains it is sown earlier than elsewhere, in order to escape the fall frosts, which are fatal to it. In the lower counties, the middle of July is early enough for it, and two crops may be obtained from the same field, provided the first be sown early in April. To the new settler, this rapid growth is very useful, as it enables him to get a crop from late cleared land, and extirpates weeds, &c. The census for 1870 gives as the total production, 82,916 bushels. The average yield may be put at 20 bushels per acre.

THE SWEET POTATO.

This root, though forming a palatable and wholesome food, and easily cultivated, is much neglected, being supplanted by the Irish potato. In the predominating clay loams of our State, it grows well and obtains a good size, but is rather lacking in sweetness and keeping qualities. This is especially true of the northern and higher parts of the State. To attain perfection, it requires a sandy, friable soil, of moderate fertility, and a hot sun during the period of growth. In many parts of the State, especially in the southern counties, these conditions are supplied, and there the sweet potato ought to obtain high excellence. Indeed, Tennessee is noted for the size and flavor of her sweet potatoes. Perhaps the greatest trouble in the attempts of our people to raise it, is that they select too rich a soil, which makes too great a growth of vine, and gives the root a sappy, insipid character. In the eastern States, from New Jersey to North Carolina, this crop is raised in the greatest perfection. Poor, sandy loams, are there preferred. They are aided with non-stimulating vegetable matter, such as half rotted straw, &c., where these sandy soils are totally void of vegetable matter. Our soils all have an abundance of this, and would not need such additions. The good prices that the crop brings, $1 to $1,50, per bushel, certainly would seem to make this crop worthy of more attention. The number of bushels report-ed for the State is 46,984, which is no doubt too small an amount. The average yield is about 100 bushels.

THE IRISH POTATO.

This is a favorite crop with our people, and is grown in comparatively large quantities. The Irish potato grows in great perfection all over the State. In size, mealiness, and delicacy of flavor, our Irish potatoes are unsurpassed. Our deep, light loams, charged with vegetable matter, and our cool, moist summers, furnish just the conditions needed to bring this vegetable in perfection. In the high table lands and glades, or upland prairies as they may be called, they excel in all points of excellence. It must be remembered that the original home of the potato, is in the high, cool, and well watered districts of South America, a region not unlike some parts of West Virginia.

The rot has never prevailed in this State. The Colorado bug has been with us three years. Owing to the fierce war waged against him, he has not caused so much damage with us as has been done elsewhere. This insect may now be considered to have done his worst. Irish potatoes in the interior counties, readily command from seventy-five cents to one dollar per bushel. Many varieties are cultivated with success, of which perhaps the Peach Blow is most deserving of mention. Here again we may trace the influence of inherited prejudices, when we compare the amounts of the two vegetables raised. The Irish potato is the mainstay of the laboring class of both Europe and America, while the Sweet potato is confined to comparatively limited districts. It is not to be wondered at then that, in a State settled as ours has been, the Sweet potato should be almost entirely neglected, even where every condition is more favorable for it than for the Irish potato.

The total yield of Irish potatoes in the State is put by the census of 1870 at 1,053,507 bushels. The average crop per acre may be put at 120 bushels.

THE TURNIP.

This is another valuable production, well suited to our soil and climate, which is greatly neglected. It would be especially valuable to the recent settler, since it can be raised with much ease, on imperfectly cleared land. It does finely on virgin soils full of vegetable matter and ashes, and requires a mere scratching of the surface. It furnishes food for both man and beast, being especially fitted for milch cows. The white, sweet turnip, is almost exclusively cultivated, the Rutabaga being almost unknown.

We have no data to determine the total yield in the State. This is small, though increasing. Returns of average yields, indicate 120 bushels per acre, as the general average for all soils.

SORGHUM.

The Chinese sugar cane is cultivated to a considerable extent in the State. Its main production is in the Ohio belt of counties. It is used entirely for the manufacture of molasses, for home consumption. It is not grown so extensively in the inland counties, especially where the lands are wooded, and the maple is abundant. Most persons prefer the syrup prepared from the maple, to the molasses from sorghum. This latter has, too commonly from imperfect ripening, an acid taste. The cane is mainly raised in the counties which have been more or less denuded of their maple trees. The cane succeeds well, and in good soil, when well matured, yields from 200 to 300 gallons per acre. The total production for the State is given as 780,829 gallons, Jackson county leading, with a yield of 57,041 gallons.

MAPLE SUGAR.

This is quite an important production in the better wooded portions of the State, and like most of our forest products, is greatly underestimated in all published statistics. There are two varieties of maple, which, in West Virginia, furnish sugar. These are the Sugar, or Rock Maple, and the Black Maple (*acer nigrum*). The former is the more common tree, and yields more juice than the latter. Both trees grow all over the State, at all elevations, provided the soil be good, and the exposure favorable. Even were the published statistics correct, in the amount of sugar and syrup which they give, in this case also, the present production is no measure of the capabilities of the State. The largest present production, is in some of the old well cleared counties, such as Greenbrier, Monroe, Monongalia, etc., where the trees are fewest. There are millions of acres, according to Diss Debar, where not a tree has been tapped, and thousands of productive trees in the sugar orchards of old and improved farms, are neglected from want of time and labor to save the crop.

The tree in its favorite positions, grows in groups and groves. These are seen in all their perfection in the mountain counties, and here sugar making forms an important and profitable branch of industry. The period of sap running is longer in such regions. The maple sugar production for 1850 is put at

667,178 pounds, while that for 1870 is put at 490,606 pounds. This is far less than the amount reported for 1860, also. Diss Debar was of the opinion that the amount reported for 1860, was much too small. He states, as confirming this opinion, that in Doddrige country, his residence at that time, only 1,623 pounds were given as the entire yield, while to his personal knowledge, the amount sold to the stores, exceeded 2,500 pounds, and no doubt an equal amount was retained for home consumption.

According to the census returns, there must from 1860 to 1870, have been a great falling off in the production (about $\frac{1}{3}$), but as is well known, the production is steadily increasing.

In the more thinly settled counties, such as Randolph, Webster, Nicholas, &c., thousands of acres have nearly half their timber of the sugar maples. Here the price of land is so low that the price of one crop from a tract, would, pay for the whole. The yield per tree varies from 6 to 10 gallons a day, in favorable weather, giving $\frac{3}{4}$ to $1\frac{1}{4}$ pounds of hard sugar, besides a quantity of excellent syrup. This result may be obtained from the same trees upon an average for 25 to 50 days in a season (Diss Debar). Good maple sugar always brings at the country stores, the price of brown New Orleans sugar. This is always a sure crop, giving a large value in small bulk, easy of transportation, and always meeting with a ready market. This source of revenue is as yet practically untouched; it cannot fail to become an important and permanent member of our forest productions.

TOBACCO.

The cultivation of tobacco in the State, for no good reason, as it would seem, is confined to a very limited area. Some of the Ohio belt of counties, and of those on the New and Kanawha rivers, raise nearly the entire crop. The following remarks on the culture of this staple are based on information kindly furnished by the Hon. D. D. Johnson, of Tyler, a large and successful raiser of tobacco. Tobacco has only recently become an important article of production in the State. For a number of years small crops have been raised in the vicinity of the Great Kanawha. Some 25 or 30 years ago, it was also produced in the more northern counties, but in all the section north of the Little Kanawha, the cultivation of tobacco had almost entirely ceased prior to 1860.

During the war, its cultivation was somewhat revived on the borders of the Ohio river. The crop thus raised was sold to packers in Ohio, and by them shipped to the eastern markets, as Ohio tobacco. Hence the absence of quotations of West Virginia tobacco in these markets.

In the county of Tyler, the increase in the production of tobacco, has been more rapid than in any other county in the State. It is estimated for this county, that the production of any one year, for a period of 20 years, prior to 1867, would not exceed 50,000 pounds. Since that time, through the untiring energy of T. J. Staley, Esq., its production has rapidly increased, until in 1873, the crop was estimated at 1,500,000 pounds. The crop of 1874 was a failure, owing to general causes, which affected all the tobacco growing States. In 1875, a larger area was planted in Tyler county than ever before. Owing to the continuous and heavy rains in July, a period of unprecedented rain storms, the crop was lessened materially.

The principal varieties given in Tyler county are the "Maryland Thickset," and the "White Burley." The latter is a recent introduction, and is peculiarly adapted to "old gronnd."

The mode of cultivation is as follows: During the month of February or March, a "brush-heap" is prepared in some favorable locality, generally in newly cleared gronnd, and burned. This is for the purpose of destroying all noxious seeds, that might germinate into weeds injurious to the young tobacco plants. The top soil is then dug up, and thoroughly pulverized, and the tobacco seed sown in the "bed" thus prepared. The young plants appear and grow in this position during the month of May. In June and July, they are pulled up and transplanted in the ground in which they are destined to grow. Of course this must be done when the ground is sufficiently moist to enable the young plant to take root in its new position.

It is almost the universal custom in Tyler county, to select as the growing ground, newly cleared land. From the time of transplanting, until about the middle of August, the growing plant must be kept clear of weeds and worms, and of shoots, or "suckers," which are apt to grow between the leaves and the main stem.

The leaves next to the ground mature first, those in the middle next, and the top leaves last. When all are fully matured, the leaves are stripped from the stalk, and hung up in the tobacco warehouse for "curing." Flues are made by loose stone, and run for about two-thirds the length of the house. In these are placed wood fires, the heat and smoke of which pass up through the tobacco as it hangs in the house.

When sufficiently cured, the tobacco is taken down and put in "bulks," while the house is refilled with green tobacco. When the whole crop is thus partially cured, it is again hung up to be thoroughly cured. It is then taken from the stick, and "rolled," and sold to the packers.

The average yield per acre, is under ordinary circumstances about 1,000 pounds. The price per pound was, in the roll, during 1873, from 3 to 3½ cents; and in 1874, from 4 to 8 cents; in 1875, from 4½ to 5½ cents.

Tobacco grown in the Great Kanawha region, is cured almost entirely by "air drying," and commands a much higher price than cured by "firing," as above described. The smoke in passing through the tobacco very materially injures it. In the northern part of the State, the time between the maturing of the plant, and the early frosts of winter, is too short to permit this method of curing. Air drying also requires a great amount of house-room, which requires too much capital for the limited means of the ordinary tobacco grower.

Col. Johnson suggests that both of these difficulties may be overcome by using air, heated by a stove or furnace, for the purpose of curing the plant, while the smoke is caused to pass to the outside of the house, through a flue or pipe. This would very materially enhance the price of fire-cured tobacco.

The soil and climate of West Virginia, and the large amount of fresh land possessed by her, offer many advantages in the culture of tobacco, and with proper cultivation, and correct modes of curing, the highest prices ought to be obtained.

The production of tobacco for 1873 in that part of the State which lies north of the Little Kanawha, was estimated at

10,800,000 pounds. The number of pounds of West Virginia tobacco inspected in Baltimore, during that year was reported at 7,200,000 pounds. Add to this 2,700,000 pounds, the amount estimated by Col. Johnson, as raised in the Kanawha region, we have an aggregate for the State of 13,000,500 pounds raised in 1873. Col. Johnson estimates the price of the tobacco, raised north of the Little Kanawha, as averaging 3 cents per pound, and that of the Great Kanawha district, as averaging 6 cents per pound, giving a total money value of the crop in the State of $378,000. Two crops of tobacco are usually raised on the same land, which leaves the ground in splendid condition for wheat, since the culture of new ground in tobacco is more effectual than any mode of preparation in getting rid of weeds.

The above account of tobacco cultivation in Tyler county may be taken to represent the entire State. It may be proper to state here, that it is not exactly similar to the method used in Virginia. In that State the tobacco is, immediately after cutting, hung for some days closely together on "scaffolds," in order to give it a bright yellow color, before hanging in the house. The leaves, also, are not stripped from the stalk, but the stalk is split partly down, and hung astride on the sticks. The Virginia farmers attach much importance to the number of leaves left to grow on the stalk. They always break off the lowest leaves, as the plant is growing, since these usually become filled with dirt. If they wish to make heavy shipping tobacco, *i. e.*, tobacco for the European market, they break off the terminal bud low enough down to leave 8 to 10 leaves on the stalk. If thin tobacco, suited for home manufacture, is desired, a greater number is left, and thinner new land selected for planting. They raise their heavy tobacco on old highly manured lands.

Attention may be here called to the great underestimation of the West Virginia tobacco crop in the census report for 1870, where it is put at only 2,046,452 pounds, not much more than the crop of Tyler county in 1873.

MISCELLANEOUS CROPS.

Cotton.—Two bales are reported from Randolph. Cotton, perhaps, might be raised with success for home consumption, in the low valleys of the Southern Ohio counties. It is a very successful and important crop in Tennessee.

Hemp—Succeeds well here, but the demand for it is limited, and where the amount of available labor is small, as it is in our State, attention is turned to more indispensible crops, such as those which furnish some variety of food. The amount returned is 37 tons.

Flax.—Flax is more largely raised, since it supplies in large measure, the material for textile fabrics of home manufacture, taking the place of cotton. It succeeds well in every part of the State, and the production is limited only by the small demand for it. Amount reported, 82,276 pounds, of which Jackson county raises the largest quantity, viz.: 7·286 pounds.

Hops.—These are cultivated only for domestic use. This plant thrives well in all parts of the State. The amount given for 1870 is 1,031 pounds, Preston county producing the largest amount, viz.: 200 pounds.

BUTTER AND CHEESE.

From what has been said about the topography, soil climate, adaptedness for grass of the State, it will be easily understood that with proper inducements arising from ready transportation, and sufficient markets, these products should be a source of large revenue to our people. In a State like West Virginia, where, in consequence of imperfect access to market, the capacity for grain production is far greater than the amount now raised, it is a matter of great importance to discover methods for the conversion of grain. Among the substances into which our grains can be changed with profit, butter, and especially cheese, should rank high.

It requires too much space to properly point out the advantages which West Virginia possesses for dairy farming.

As one pound of cheese is worth 12 to 18 pounds of corn, and one of butter much more, it is plain that large amounts of the corn could be exported in this form with a great saving in the cost of transportion. More attention is being paid to the number of cattle raised, and to the improvement of the breed so far, only for the purpose of beef production. This must react on dairy farming and lead to improvements in milch cows. Indeed, lack of labor and quick transportation, are the only causes preventing a great development of our dairy products: Among the many advantages which we possess for dairy farming we may mention the following:

First, The length of our growing season. It is true our farmers feed from 5 to 6 months in some parts of the State, but this is due in great part to the their having failed to put down a due proportion of their land in grass. In the sheltered valleys in many parts of the State, grass will grow 8 and 9 months in the year. *Second*, The absence of parching droughts, and the luxuriance and succulence of the grass throughout the summer. *Third*, The uniform cool weather of summer, and the abundance of cool springs and excellent water. *Fourth*, The peculiar adaptation of the State for grass. *Fifth*, Our proximity to the large cities. *Sixth*, The cheapness of land for pasture.

West Virginia butter, especially that produced in the mountains, and on the plateaus, commands a higher price in the Baltimore market than that of any other State. We have seen that a considerable portion of the State has these topographical features. During seasons favorable for the shipment of butter, the country stores seldom pay less than 20 or 30 cents per pound. Near the small towns, from September to May, butter commands from 40 to 60 cents. It must be remembered that this is put up in small parcels, and usually poorly prepared.

In 1870 the number of pounds of butter made is put at 5,044,475; the number of pounds of cheese, 32,429, and the number of gallons of milk sold, 144,895. The production of cheese is by no means equal to the home consumption.

HONEY.

Although bees thrive almost without care in this State, honey raising has not formed in any quarter, one of the industrial pursuits. On most farms where bees are kept, they receive little attention. and are provided only with the rudest hives. The principal stock comes from the wild swarms, and the young swarms frequently return to the woods. From the abundance of wild flowers, and the mildness of the climate, it is plain that bee culture can be made a profitable calling in West Virginia. The red maple, with its myriad flowers, in February, affords an early supply of pollen. The Plum, Peach, Spicewood, Dogwood, Sassafras,

Pear, Cherry, Redbud, Raspberry, and Apple, blooming during March and April, afford both food and abundant pollen for cell making. The Willow, in early April, abounding on all the streams, gives splendid pasturage, and is the first source of honey supply. In Tennessee, bees in strong colonies, have been known to store 29 pounds, during the last week in April, per hive. With us the Willow is somewhat later in blooming. Wild Cherry, Dewberry and White Clover bloom in April and May, and being quite abundant, furnish large supplies of food and honey for storage. From this time onward, a constant succession of wild flowers follow. Boneset, the Astors, and Golden Rod give late supplies of abundant and excellent honey. The price of honey in the comb varies from 20 to 25 cents, and the supply everywhere small. The total amount given for the State in 1870, is 376,997 pounds. Harrison county leading with 28,937 pounds.

FRUIT CULTURE,

The nature of the soil and the climate of West Virginia permit the cultivation of any fruit which can be grown in the cooler parts of the temperate zone. A failure of any of these fruits must depend upon special or local causes, or on conditions other than those of climate.

The principal trouble experienced in fruit growing in our State, arises from the early stimulation of the flower buds by warm spells of weather occurring in February, and the first part of March. This trouble is experienced in all the States lying in the same latitude with us. As we are liable to have killing frosts until the middle of April, the fruit crop is, of course, in danger until after this period. This danger can, to a greater or less extent, be avoided, by selecting such exposures as will retard as much as possible the blooming of the trees, or by exposing the roots, &c., &c.

Over the State in general, no great amount of fruit is raised for sale, on account of the lack of cheap and ready transportation. What surplus is disposed of, is mainly in the dried condition. But while the lack of markets prevents exportation, no people raise a greater abundance, or make a freer use of frnit in their household economy than West Virginians.

In all the multitudinous modes of preserving and utilizing fruit, they excel. Every housewife lays up abundant stores of pickles, preserves, jams, fruit butters, besides drying, canning, and storing in bulk. In this respect they stand in strong contrast with the people of the Atlantic slope. A failure of the fruit crop is a misfortune to the West Virginian, but little less grave than that of the grain crop. While the people themselves, owing to the impress of Pennsylvania German tastes, make such large use of fruit, they are alive to the great benefits derived from a liberal feeding of it to stock. As a consequence, an orchard is everywhere an appendage of a well ordered farm.

The Apple.—The apple is by far the most important of the different fruits raised in this State. Owing to the great variety of soil, exposure and elevation, almost every known kind can find conditions well suited to its growth. Speaking for the whole State, the combination of soil and climate is such, that the apple attains with us a perfection of size and flavor, rarely found elsewhere. It is a very sure crop, the bloom not coming out, usually, until the severe frosts are past. Owing to the unprecedentedly cold spell which occurred late in the spring of last year, the apple crop for the year (1875) was almost entirely cut short. We thus are able to compare our native fruit with that grown elsewhere, for our fruit dealers are getting stock from Michigan and elsewhere. None of the kinds thus obtained, equal in flavor those of native growth.

The apple being a pretty sure crop, is cultivated everywhere, and when the farmer confines his attention to one sort of fruit, it is always the apple that he selects. Besides the use made of it for eating in the raw state, drying, preserving and stock feeding, for all of which purposes it forms the chief material, it is largely used for cider and vinegar.

Considerable attention has been paid to securing improved varieties. Along all the lines of public conveyance apples are exported in considerable quantities. Large amounts are shipped from the Ohio belt of counties. In spring the demand always exceeds the supply. Considerable amounts are distilled. Some of the most popular and successful varieties are the following:

Fall and Winter Rambo, Newtown Pippin, Rhode Island Greening, Baldwin, Yellow Bellflower, Grindstone Pippin, Winesap, Yellow Harvest, Red Harvest, June Eating, Summer Sweet, &c., &c.—(Diss Debar).

Peaches—The peach was formerly cultivated more widely over the State than it is now. At present, it is principally produced south of the Little Kanawha. In the northern part of the State, it has been mainly supplanted by the apple, owing to the increasing uncertainty of the crop, due to the danger from early frosts. Many parts of the northern districts used to raise large crops, where now hardly a peach tree can be seen. The counties of Wirt, Calhoun, Gilmer, &c., are very successful, and large amounts are dried and cured for sale. The bloom of this fruit is peculiarly liable to be started forward too soon by the warm spells of February and March.

The varieties most approved are: Morris White, Heath's Cling, Grosse Mignonne, Early Scarlet, Crawford's Late, &c., &c.—(Diss Debar).

Pears.—Pears are not cultivated to any extent, and appear to thrive best in old improvod improved localities. Bartel's, and Sickel appear to give general satisfaction.—(Diss Debar).

Quinces appear to do remarkably well. The fruit is larger and freer from blemishes than that grown on the Atlantic slope in the same latitude. All the varieties of cherries and plums thrive well. The small Damson plum is almost everywhere a profuse bearer, and is used largely in preserving, &c.

The State has not a sufficient number of nurseries to supply the people, and this is a serious drawback to extended cultivation.

The census for 1870 gives the value of the orchard products of the State at $848,773. Harrison stands at the head of the counties, with a production valued at $50,826.

SMALL FRUITS.

Most of the small fruits cultivated in the temperate zone do well in our State. But little attention however is paid to their proper cultivation. Where attention to such cultivation is not promoted by the demand created by the presence of large cities, such fruits are usually cultivated only by persons of means and leisure. Such qualifications are not generally found in our State. Again, the profusion in which the Wild Cherry, Strawberry, Blackberry, Raspberry and Whortleberry grow in all parts of the State, gives a supply of small fruits sufficient to meet the wants of the people. The Strawberry and Raspberry may be cultivated with great success, Currants require almost no attention, and Gooseberries do well generally. Cranberries grow wild in some of the bogs of the mountain glades, but are not cultivated at all, notwithstanding the fact that considerable amounts are used for table purposes, which must be imported. Along the Balt. and O. R. R. access can be had within 18 hours to the Baltimore and Cincinnati markets.

Fowls of all kinds, turkeys, eggs, &c., meet with a ready sale among the people themselves, and are equal to cash. Fat turkeys bring 16 to 17 cents, chickens 10 to 12 cents per pound. Eggs, in summer, 15 to 20 cents, in winter, 25 to 30 cents per dozen.

GARDEN PROCDUCTS.

Market gardening has received but little attention, as the State is thinly settled and has no populous cities. In Wheeling and Parkersburg the markets are often as high as those of New York and Philadelphia, while the supply is irregular and uncertain. The amount of income from this source returned for 1870 is $69,974, a sum considerably below the truth. Of this Marshall raised the largest amount, viz: $15,416.

The following garden vegetables named in alphabetical order attain perfeetion in the open air in every part of the State:

Artichoke, Asparagus, Beans, Beets, Borecole, Broccoli, Brussels Sprouts, Cabbage, Carrots, Cauliflower, Celery, Cress, Cucumber, Egg Plant, Endive, Gourd, Horseradish, Jerusalem Artichoke, Lettuce, Mangel Wurzel, Melons of all kinds, Mustard, Okra, Onion, Parsley, Parsnip, Peas, Pepper (red,) *Pumpkin, Radish, Rhubarb, Salsify or Oyster Plant, Spinach, Squash, Tomato, Turnips of all kinds.*

Of culinary and medicinal garden plants, we have *Aniseed, Caraway, Chamomile, Chervil, Chive, Coriander, Dandelion, Dill, Estragon, Garlic, Hysop, Lavender, Leek, Marjoram, Mint, Rosemary, Rue, Sage, Paragon, Thyme,* and a number of others of less moment.—(Diss Debar.)

GRAPE CULTURE.

In the chapter on climatology it was shown that the whole of West Virginia is within the themometric zone in which the grape matures, and the summer suns are amply sufficient to secure superior strength and quality to the wine:

"On asurface so diversified as that of our State, it would be "difficult to survey off a one hundred acre tract anywhere "without including at least one suitable exposure for a vine-"yard of from five to twenty acres, either in the valleys, or on "slopes of from five to twenty-five degrees. German wine "growers, whoprefer steeper grades, will find the rock neces-"sary for walling upa few feet below tne surface everywhere.

"While every character of West Virginia soil, whether "limestone, clay loam, cacareous, sandy and gravelly loam, "vegetable mould or alluvial, appear to be almost equally "well adapted to the grape, it must be borne in mind that "neither will much avail if resting on a sub-soil of stiff clay, "retentive of water. So soon as this kind of foundation is "reached by the roots of the vine, mould and decay set in, and "fruit and plant are doomed to certain destruction."—(Hand-Book of W. Va. J. H. Diss Debar.)

The number of acres planted in regular vineyards does not exceed 900 in the whole State. Seven hundred of these are claimed for the county of Ohio. Wood county has about 150 acres, and the remainder is divided between the counties of Ritchie, Doddridge, Marshall, Lewis, Berkley, Greenbrier, Mineral, and Randolph. In none of these last eight, excepting Ritchie, is the production sent to markets outside of the county.

For Ohio county the following information was kindly furnished by G. W. Franzheim, a large wine dealer of Wheeling. Tho 700 acres of vineyards of this county are all within six miles of Wheeling. The principal grape grown for wine is the Catawba, while the Concord, Isabella and Delawaro aro raised for both wine and table use. The Ives and Virginia Seedling are cultivated for wine, though not much attention has been paid to the former. Besides these, numerous other kinds have been experimented with, though they give very satisfactory results, yet the tests have not extended over a sufficient number of years to give statistics concerning them.

The wine produced ranks high in market, and is much liked in both the eastern and western cities, going into New York and Boston in the one direction, and as far as Omaha in the other. As regards the yield of wine per acre, it, of course, varies very much with the season, but in seme instances the Isabella has yielded as much as 1,000 gallons. For table use the Concords are the first to come into market—usually about the middle of September. This is followed by the other varieties up to about November. Large quantities are shipped every year to Pittsburgh and other centres, where they sell at an excellent profit. The retail price in Wheeling is from 6 to 10 cents per pound, according to the abundance or scarcity of the fruit.

The grape crop of 1874 was excellent, in both quality and quantity. The average Wheeling wholesale price was 4½ cts. per pound, which gave about $100,000 for the value of the crop in that year. About one-half of this was manufactured into wine, and the rest was consumed as fruit.

As the acreage in vineyards shows, more attention is paid to the grape in this county than in any other. This is a matter of some surprise, as the crop is an exceedingly profitable one, and requires, for the returns yielded, but a small amount of labor, as one man can work 10 acres, except in weeding time in midsummer, when two hands can do all the necessary work in a week.

In Wood county the Messrs. Munchmeyer Brothers, at Washington's Bottom, nine miles below Parkersburg, seem to have taken the most interest in this fruit. Their vineyard extends from the foot of the first bench, or second bottom, almost to the river, on a slope of not over 4 or 5 degrees, inclined to the west. They report but little rot in the Concord, and none in the Seedling, which latter ripens to great perfection. In the same vineyard, in 1870, were rows of Ives' Seedling, Herbemont, Delaware, Iona, and Muscadine, all producing perfect fruit. The latter variety is almost identical, in flavor and appearance, with the Muscat grape of Burgundy, and is decidedly a very superior table grape. It is highly remunerative.

In Ritchie and Doddridge the Ives and Norton's Virginia Seedling appear to be the favorites. From the former county the wine, both Catawba and Seedling, is much superior to that of Wood, owing to a difference in soil and mode of cultivation. It is exported principally to Pittsburgh, where it is much esteemed.

In Doddridge and Lewis the wine is made in a natural and proper way, but in the other counties it is often mixed with sugar and alcohol to make it conform to the taste of the natives, not familiar with the genuine article.

In the other counties, the Concord seems to be the most popular grape, and, upon the whole, that and Seedlings have proved the most hardy and thrifty vines in the State, the Catawba being more or less uncertain every where. The vineyards existing in Kanawha, in 1870, were principally Catawba, but proved so unreliable that the owners have since uprooted them, and are now planting Concord and Seedling, and so little is now done in grapes in that county, that the Charleston market is supplied from the neighboring States of Virginia and Ohio.

In Randolph county, vineyards are beginning to be planted at the head of the Buckhannon river, by a Swiss colony, at Helvetia.

"As to the benefit," says Mr. Debar, "which the State "derives from vine culture, it may be regarded as two-fold: "*First*, In aiding the cause of true temperance, by substitu-"ting a mild and healthful beverage, for adulterated and "intoxicating spirits; and *Second*, by retaining in the State, "the money that would be sent abroad for that obnoxious "article, at least so far as the present rate of production can "do this. When the culture of the grape shall be so extended "as to admit of exporting wine in large quantities to other "States, the benefits of this production of the soil will "become still more apparent. It may be remarked here that "it can be extended considerably without materially "encroaching upon the other productions of the State, "as it requires but little surface, and that of a kind not "very valuable for other crops."

The following tables of the more important agricultural and domestic products for 1870, are here appended. We must again call attention to their inaccuracy, and warn the reader not to consider them as anything more than approximations, which may serve to give the relative amounts by the several counties:

TABLE A.—Statement of the Principal Items of Farm Produce According to the Census, 1870.

COUNTIES.	ACRES OF LAND.			Total value of farm products including betterments and increase of stock.	Wheat.	Rye.	Corn.	Oats.	Buckwheat.
		UNIMPROVED.							
	Improved.	Woodland.	Other Unimproved.						
	No.	No.	No.	Dolls.	Bu.	Bu.	Bu.	Bu.	Bu.
Total	2,580,254	4,364,405	1,583,735	23,379,692	2,480,148	277,746	8,197,865	2,413,749	82,916
Barbour	95,668	120 446	110	664,062	42,008	3.935	173,195	43 367	1,637
Berkeley	111,857	40,004	2,931	1,120,041	296,975	6,265	297,639	187,588	463
Boone	14,762	116,689	....	168,449	2,585	1,398	129,630	13,667	121
Braxton	32,240	133,4[illegible]9	20,824	247,372	20,019	2,883	130,690	29,968	124
Brooke	54,856	366	604	582,583	45,549	1,445	185,576	81,135	35
Cabell	26,866	60,802	24,131	297,673	42 592	2,675	167,600	31.586	35
Calhoun	11,315	67,[illegible]09	......	132,114	5,354	849	52,202	8.357	379
Clay	7,798	627	55,181	121,524	1,955	[illegible]57	39,093	11,497	97
Doddridge	37,752	112,040	116	409,541	15,879	4.196	113 064	18.723	910
Fayette	36.410	5 658	202,375	393,195	13,301	3,003	123 220	41,991	1,566
Gilmer	20,721	93,586	3 567	190,092	9 765	2,402	106,036	17,592	543
Grant	63,145	113.393	59	477,725	31,566	8,255	53,[illegible]0	10.593	1 244
Greenbrier	95 099	170,748	29,740	690,154	50.214	7,734	181,381	92,295	1,511
Hampshire	77,873	163,050	15,221	524,221	76,832	21,885	1[illegible]0,325	46,769	5,599
Hancock	30,947	16,941	2,605	347,055	34,270	11,749	83,180	68,49[illegible]	2,167
Hardy	43,675	127,180	8,521	400,1[illegible]8	33,4[illegible]2	8,939	114,567	13,283	2,020
Harrison	147,488	134,608	1,687	1,302,545	83,462	4,55[illegible]	327,261	56.183	693
Jackson	49 903	100,298	100	510,780	59,8[illegible]5	3,587	272.044	48,524	1,463
Jefferson	92,245	17,898	524	1,139,166	468.836	7,620	336,287	44,[illegible]77	....
Kanawha	59,459	164,598	7,298	774,582	45,587	728	406,826	96,268	144
Lewis	75,878	110,197	118,692	649,527	41,174	3,956	191,556	31,776	652
Lincoln	15,613	84,099	....	136,403	6,260	1,606	104,961	12,054	75
Logan	14,149	666	169,147	143,462	1 784	426	125,273	4,142	22
Marion	37,410	25,480	....	134,811	26,528	1,109	63,643	29 879	272
Marshall	78,852	68 992	601	857,854	131,509	7,363	364,743	211,662	1,944
Mason	67,010	86,426	....	654,570	115,260	598	456,990	43,464	50
McDowell	4,592	358	64,286	51,125	675	460	31,586	3,6[illegible]5	156
Mercer	47,313	7,762	237,890	303,500	25,756	5,597	114,746	43,184	2,444
Mineral	59,119	16,420	92 834	445,144	50,915	13,257	71.895	29,331	2,7[illegible]5
Monongalia	112,045	80,519	143	1,141,914	111 751	5,130	301,328	148 [illegible]72	1,575
Monroe	104,760	164,630	3,429	5[illegible]0,143	52 817	11,320	170,721	59,062	2.054
Morgan	32,729	63,301	1,270	266,436	27,697	9,217	58 142	19,835	1,725
Nicholas	24 455	122,120	36,146	315,854	10.242	1,331	104,300	38,365	402
Ohio	46,059	14,552	300	687,379	41,432	3,975	225,465	97,372	85
Pendleton	54,041	169,895	....	326 656	37,984	10,594	59,228	14,538	3,527
Pleasants	17,098	44,515	1,874	141,247	15,283	1,290	66,580	14,596	15
Pocahontas	43,329	6,9[illegible]4	286,761	224,697	14,901	6,334	46,512	22,343	3,004
Preston	102.062	160,074	15 975	730,462	33 390	20,581	145,004	189,070	27,346
Putnam	36,044	74,695	4,644	323,132	39,980	1,340	[illegible]32,126	49,879	210
Raleigh	20,969	148,413	....	147,916	7 [illegible]09	1,660	73,657	16,278	1,603
Randolph	50 036	188.858	62 991	270 656	8 969	2,493	59,758	33,237	1,504
Ritchie	46,219	112,115	24,881	511,910	25,503	35,63[illegible]	146,235	40,033	1,384
Roane	34 921	130,289	85,441	317,150	24,087	2,479	160.912	28,489	260
Summers	No sta	tistics							
Taylor	53,815	40,557	....	502,070	28,659	2,075	95,439	45,166	483
Tucker	13 078	53,[illegible]17	....	95,403	1,469	1,294	27,813	14,726	1.843
Tyler	45,019	72,86[illegible]	....	382.653	4[illegible],262	2,3[illegible]6	157,302	42,180	682
Upshur	59 812	95,365	62	510,337	[illegible]9,948	6,055	108 49[illegible]	21,4[illegible]	968
Wayne	39,554	115,548	....	453,455	23,192	402	291,863	27,131	39
Webster	6,945	62,708	....	53 079	1,196	8[illegible]6	21,075	4,688	240
Wetzel	34,202	77,118	240	457,563	37,164	4,484	193,111	66,122	2,245
Wirt	20 061	75,77[illegible]	574	237,307	15,532	1 025	128,836	37,988	673
Wood	63,281	94,428	....	715,860	68,190	5,925	327,506	80,839	1,575
Wyoming	9,805	35,876	20	106,615	2,150	973	57,899	11,073	403

TABLE B.

Statements of the Principal Items of Farm Produce According to the Census of 1870.

COUNTIES.	Tobacco.	POTATOES. Irish.	Sweet.	Flax	Maple Sugar.	Maple Molasses.	Sorghum.	Honey.
	Lbs.	Bu.	Bu.	Lbs.	Lbs.	Gals.	Gals.	Lbs.
Total	2,046,452	1,053,507	46,984	82,276	490,6(6	20,209	780,829	376,997
Barbour	4,776	14,526	1,502	2,368	28,575	1,790	27,890	9.883
Berkeley	....	17,738	....	....	40	....	164	5,218
Boone	6,213	12,043	2,676	2,443	3,284	....	6,806	22,547
Braxton	....	9,028	641	2,677	1,360	....	20,281	100
Brooke	....	45,850	355	....	1,060	475	3,795	6,762
Cabell	135,410	17,398	1,189	480	515	....	32,004	2,605
Calhoun	2,181	6,160	632	1,986	2,824	....	10,240	2,172
Clay	3,175	2,411	243	1,868	1,736	....	4,703	5,393
Doddridge	17,568	11,167	907	1.013	3,896	....	28,965	5,457
Fayette	188,165	11,359	3,059	5,056	6,013	....	17,844	12,123
Gilmer	15,931	7,138	579	2,490	6,305	....	21,151	2,825
Grant	519	7,536	....	....	39,445	680	823	5,534
Greenbrier	3,176	13,928	78	185	55,740	6,222	1,562	7,950
Hampshire	285	13,800	60	1,411	44	....	3,583	4,956
Hancock	....	34,578	226	....	500	177	1,605	2.165
Hardy	....	7,069	84	473	13,175	688	180	2,270
Harrison	17,098	26,028	229	743	11,920	73	42,558	28,937
Jackson	96,265	50,397	357	7,286	4,082	....	57,041	3,718
Jefferson	140	24,305	7	....	....	....	....	9,382
Kanawha	412,4[illegible]9	44,300	7,905	533	459	52	45,[illegible]67	14,305
Lewis	51.470	16,071	444	155	9,282	125	30,455	9,337
Lincoln	56,083	....	....	3,177	880	....	11,285	3,499
Logan	3,912	7,957	3,523	110	897	....	5,954	16,447
Marion	....	2,493	45	50	529	20	3,574	701
Marshall	20	54,781	604	50	445	....	24,259	8,542
Mason	58,600	84,534	48	....	200	....	23,722	270
McDowell	3,000	2,310	1,049	1,100	188	....	[illegible],604	6,214
Mercer	117,429	10,867	15	5,313	19,917	467	10,862	8,538
Mineral	....	8,891	....	....	3,722	173	679	9,400
Monongalia	2,73[illegible]	23,772	435	540	24,274	733	36,534	10,710
Monroe	123,321	12,164	443	3,361	42,744	2,829	11,427	14,938
Morgan	1,068	10,915	41	635	50	20	196	2,176
Nicholas	840	6,247	....	....	....	....	12.589	1,000
Ohio	....	46,748	1,454	....	695	209	3,406	6,925
Pendleton	....	8,692	12	3,291	55,391	221	2,107	5,444
Pleasants	11,910	15,925	....	....	300	....	3,319	775
Pocahontas	2,966	8,623	....	1,518	52,448	1,372	515	10,347
Preston	1 673	24,063	[illegible]91	2,222	6,871	626	8,521	13,932
Putnam	47[illegible],765	26.918	1,172	2.481	626	72	19,511	3,771
Raleigh	5,769	6,720	262	2,794	1,745	....	7,163	6,397
Randolph	2,133	10 006	115	81	41,434	154	3.663	10,433
Ritchie	9,907	19,538	850	1,701	4.207	118	29,257	4,344
Roane	16,085	15,[illegible]00	917	6,922	3,511	2,113	28,836	8,512
Summers	....	No	Statistics.		....	....	....	....
Taylor	2,259	10,305	1,256	205	7,983	482	10,368	10,515
Tucker	....	2,083	3	480	7,197	117	1,213	4,408
Tyler	47,969	21,159	228	303	1,815	....	22,768	4,278
Upshur	11,190	11.448	971	4,411	12,639	124	18,164	8,647
Wayne	58,230	21,759	3,281	2.518	368	....	33,776	4,661
Webster	2,508	2,340	26	595	5,286	9	2,591	5,325
Wetzel	47,050	19,209	11	2,208	2,820	60	18,210	7,308
Wirt	8,712	17,809	1,300	1,012	787	....	22,299	2,924
Wood	21,890	138,239	2,982	1,207	....	8	41,720	2,690
Wyoming	889	5.962	2,269	1,834	552	....	3,772	9,287

CHAPTER V.

CATTLE AND GRASSES.

BY WM. M. FONTAINE.

The history of stock raising in our State presents an instance of a people gradually forced by natural causes, out of the channels of industry, in which their prejudices and habits of life impelled them, into others totally different. If we recall for a moment the manner in which much of the State was settled, and the people who first occupied it, we shall easily see that all the conditions then existing, were unfavorable for the promotion of stock raising.

When, however, larger bodies of land had been opened, and experience had taught the farmer the disadvantages of a frequent ploughing of his fields, then, indeed, a change began to take place. The farmer began to seek some means of deriving from his grasses, a more speedy money return than could be obtained from the mere improvement of the soil. He had not far to seek. The successful experience of the thrifty Pennsylvania graziers, was before his eyes. With a similar climate and soil, naturally, similar success was to be expected here.

Many causes operate in West Virginia to induce an extensive cultivation of grasses, and a fostering of stock raising. Some of them may be named here :

When our new grounds have been cultivated for several years, and the small roots which serve to bind the soil together, have been removed, owing to the steepness of our hillsides, and the lightness of the soil which composes them, they suffer much from washing after every ploughing. The most effectual way to prevent such washing is to leave the land in grass.

In most of our lands, even after merely removing the timber, a heavy coating of Blue Grass (*poa sylvestris*) puts up spontaneously, and maintains possession, without any cultivation. This affords a nutritive food for stock, throughout a large part of the year. From the peculiarity of the structure of the hills noted in another connection, grass does not suffer from dry weather on their slopes, but grows green and luxuriant to their summits.

Where there is any lime in the soil, as is the case with most of our lands, decaying vegetable matter, is eminently favorable for the improvement of the land, since, as explained elsewhere, the carbonic acid formed, brings the lime into a condition, in which, it may be used by the plant. Again, grass, while growing, by the action of its roots, breaks down, and brings into an available form, plant food from other rocks besides limestones. Hence the most effectual way to *rest* land of any kind, is to allow it to grow grass.

Many of our shales which show no lime to the eye, contain enough of it to derive a great benefit in the soils which they form, from a course in grass, and it is not necessary to have, in such cases, ledges of limestone among the rocks, in order to have a calcareous soil produced. But whether there be calcareous matter present in the soil or not, a sound system of agriculture teaches the farmer to discontinue at certain intervals, the cultivation of grains on his land, and to allow it to rest in grass. For even if the grass does not produce a positive benefit, it acts beneficially in not taking from the soil, the same materials that grain crops do, and in thus allowing natural processes to accumulate a store of these for further cultivation.

All of these reasons fostering the production of grass, the question arises how to secure the most speedy returns from it.

Our want of transportation, and the bulkiness of the material, forbids its export in the form of hay. The obvious solution is, to turn the grass into flesh, for thus we attain the greatest diminution of bulk, and the greatest concentration of value.

Another strong inducement for the raising of cattle, lies in the fact that they, by their consumption of grain in the latter stages of their fattening, afford a profitable means of consuming, without the cost of transport, a good deal of our surplus corn. Indian corn is our principal grain, and is produced so abundantly, on most of our soils, that the only limit is that imposed by the lack of some profitable way of disposing of it. Here, also, in changing it into flesh, we gain greatly in the cost of carriage, since corn is bulky and difficult of transportation.

These causes have been gradually operating to force upon our farmers a greater attention to cattle raising, until now, in some counties, it forms the leading source of revenue. It must be admitted, however, that nowhere has so great an advance, as is desirable, been made in either improving the breeds of cattle or in adopting a systematic course of grass production.

Over most of the State the cattle are of the so-called *native breeds*, a mixture descended from the original stock of the first settlers. These are hardy, small in size, angular in outline, and do not take on fat well. They are generally left to graze on the native grasses so long as they can pick up enough sustenance in the fields. This is usually until November or December. When feeding begins, shelters are hardly ever made, and when they are used, they are simply a rude covering, affording hardly any protection against the winds. The usual practice is to leave the cattle in pasture, or to put them in enclosures of smaller size, according to the character of the winter, for when this is somewhat open, cattle can get more or less grain all the time.

The feeding is managed in the worst manner, the cornstalks or fodder being thrown into the field, generally in the same place, and in this way there is no distribution of the material, or of the droppings of the cattle, over the field. The failure to provide shelter causes the cattle to consume much more food, to maintain their vital heat, and it is almost impossible for them not to lose flesh.

The time of feeding varies in different parts of the State, being in the north, 5 months, and in the south, 3 to 4 months. This length could be reduced by paying more attention to keeping a portion of the land in sod. It not seldom happens that no feeding is done in the more southern counties. Diss Debar mentions meeting a herd of two-year old steers, browsing in the wilds of Logan, about the middle of January, looking but little the worse in flesh. In many cases, when towards spring, fodder has become scarce, the cattle are driven into the woods, and the beech and linden trees are cut down for them to browse on the young branches and swelling buds.

This is the usual treatment of cattle, except in a few counties, where a better system is maintained. Diss Debar says of cattle raising in West Virginia: "Cows are not, as a rule, "kept for breeding purposes exclusively, and hence the supply of native stock is not sufficient for the wants of the "graziers, who make up deficiencies by purchases in neighboring States, principally Ohio. Stock cattle of all grades "and ages are bought up and grazed in W. Va. until ready "for market. Some dealers, who cut large crops of hay, winter extensive herds of mixed ages, others confine themselves "to grazing more particularly three year-old steers up to market order, and winter but little, beginning to ship in June, "and ending in November. Grain feeding, for later use, is "principally confined to the Ohio river and Potomac counties. In sections where pasture, especially Blue Grass, has "been economized in, the fattening steers are turned out on "grass as early as March, and mature in June or July. This "mode of operation, while requiring the least labor, unquestionably yields the largest profit in proportion to the period "of investment; *i. e.*, 50 per cent on the cost of the animal in "the spring. But to pursue it on a large scale requires an "abundance of first class sod, conveniently portioned off to "afford a change of pasture.

"Within the last fifteen to twenty years, the native stock "has been materially improved, by crossing with shorthorns, "Devons, and grades of these. On lowland farms, with good "winter accommodations, and an abundance of feed all times, "the Durham matures with profit to its owner; but the neat, "compact, and nimble Devon, is the animal for our hills. "Crosses of Devon and common stock are fast being introduced "into every section of the State, and West Virginia beef cattle are successfully competing with the product of other "States in the Baltimore market, where, requiring but a few "hours transportation, they arrive in good condition. The "cost of grazing stock is materially reduced, when the cattle "are summered in the woods, during the second and third "years, with no other trouble and expense, except an occasional "looking-up and salting. When the pea-vine and other succu-"lent herbage abounds, as it does in the greater portion of the "State, the results in growth and flesh, compare favorably "with those of field pasturing, though less tallow may be "formed.

"Many farmers, in the older counties, are in the habit of "sending their stock to be summered in the woods in distant, "and less improved sections, under care of some settler of the "locality. Others use for that purpose, the so-called 'moun-"tain farms,' on the table lands of Randolph, Pocahontas, "Webster, Nicholas, &c., under the supervision of the work-"hands engaged in clearing and fencing them. These moun-"tain farms, which generally produce the finest beef and "mutton in the State, are generally improved at trifling cost. "The land seldom costs more than $1.50 per acre. After con-"structing a worm fence, at the cost of $2.00 per acre, or less, "according to the area inclosed, the largest timber is girdled "or deadened, at the expense of fifty cents, or $1.00 per acre, "making the cost of the improvement, say $4.50, land in-"cluded. The girdled timber dies during the first year, letting "in light and heat sufficient for vegetation. When neither "oak nor hickory grow, no undergrowth is to be found, either "before or after clearing, and the first thing that comes up "after the deadening, is a thick growth of blackberry briers "which will die out in two years, or sooner, if cattle are turned "in to keep them down. By that time, the native spontan-"eous Blue Grass, has taken possession, and the farm is ready "to yield a perennial pasture, worth at least $4.00 per acre. "In the course of a few years, the girdled timber has dried "enough to burn in the log, so soon as cut down, requiring no "piling up in heaps. The cost of the final operation, varies "with the size of the timber, from $2.00 to $2.50 per acre.

"In the remainder of the State, where undergrowth pre-"vails, more or less repeated grubbing is needed, to make a "clear field."

Several other methods are adopted in preparing pasture

lands, which we need not notice here. It will be noted that a vast amount of timber is wasted in these clearings, all of it sooner or later, being consumed. In this rough way, the oldest and most extensive grazing farms were originally cleared, and gradually enriched their owners. Says Diss Debar: "Fortunes of $50,000 to $150,000, were accumulated in the live stock business, by men who started in life as common farm hands, and began their independent career with a brace of calves."

The principal grazing counties in the State are Barbour, Harrison, Hampshire, Greenbrier, Monroe, Hardy, Jefferson, Marion, Monongalia, and Preston, to which may be added Brooke, Hancock, Marshall, Mason, Mercer, Pocahontas, Ohio, and Taylor. The entire product, and that of the several counties, may be seen in table C. It is to be noted that the return for Marion is plainly wrong.

It has been found very difficult to get details of the stock management in different sections of the State. We append some extracts from reports:

Mr. Lot Bowen, a large dealer in cattle in Harrison county, says: "Every breed of cattle of which an introduction has "been attempted, thrives well (in the State), but owing to "the superior natural advantages possessed by the short- "horns and grades, they will maintain the precedence. The "management of our cattle embodies the smallest compara- "tive expenditure of labor. They are wintered without shel- "ter, and are grazed 8 to 9 months in the year. By proper "management, they require attention only 3 months, with "dry feed. Shelter is seldom given, and grain is not fed in "abundance, yet the results are always flattering and prof- "itable. My observation justifies the assertion, that with "parallel advantages, our stock growers may positively look "for results more than equal to those obtained in the neigh- "boring States.

"Not possibly over one-twentieth of our cattle find a home "consumption. Our markets are of speedy access, in Mary- "land, Pennsylvania, and New York, principally in the city "sale yards. Quite a respectable percentage goes to stock the "farms of interior Pennsylvania, and ultimately find their "way to the eastern markets.

"Our cattle in the markets have a flattening average, " returning to our farmers an average of $9 per hundred, net " weight, during 1875. The State ships annually, not less "than $5,000,000 worth of cattle. As a single instance illus- " trative of her capacity, I will state that during the shipping "season of 1875, along the line of the Baltimore and Ohio "Railroad, reaching from Pennsboro to Patterson's Creek, I " shipped over 9,000 cattle, returning to the farmers therefor " more than $700,000.

" From many years experience in the live stock interest, " and varied opportunities for observation, I am led to look " upon our State, as being but in the infancy of a most envi- " able career, as a stock growing country. While her hills " are not adapted to the plough, they are capable, with less " toil, of returning more than parallel results to the grazier.

" The cattle produce of the State is largely on the increase, " and with proper efforts and favorable legislation in mone- " tary interests, soon West Virginia will outrank any of her " area on the continent in this department."

Mr. R. K. Cautley says of the stock in Greenbrier: " It is " nearly all Durham and grades, with an increasing tendency " to pure blood. On the indigenous Blue Grass of the county, " if kept for wintering them, cattle will do well all the win- " ter, and except in the rare case of the land getting ice- " caked, need no feeding."

Orchard Grass, Timothy, and English Blue Grass, and Red Clover, all do well. The usual rotation of crops in this county is Corn, Oats, Wheat, and three years in Grass, of which, two years are mowed, and one grazed. Two careful cow-keepers reported to Mr. Cautley that the best milch cows are the grades, and scrub cows, bred with common Durham bulls. A well fed cow will average four gallons of milk per diem. Two cows made 1,000 pounds of butter in one year, and produced four fine calves. As long as cows are pastured on Blue Grass, at any time of the year, the butter remains yellow. They begin feeding (Pumpkins) September 15th to 30th, and put out on to grass fields May 1st.

The counties along the Ohio river, in the north, pay a good deal of attention to stock raising, and also to the production of grass, for which the hills, as well as the bottoms, are eminently adapted. We have already under the head of rotation of crops, in the general remarks on agriculture, adverted to the method pursued here. It is sufficient to say in this place, that Red Clover and Timothy, are preferred to all others in the production of hay, preference being given to Timothy. Sod and grazing lands are almost entirely formed of Blue Grass (the native), this being indigenous, lasts indefinitely, and takes the land from any other kind of grass. Whether in meadow or pasture, the land improves so long as it is in grass, and they depend upon this treatment, without manure, to enrich their soils.

It must be borne in mind that this land is generally highly calcareous, and of a character to derive the highest benefit from a course of grass.

Mr. St. Geo. Bryan, assistant to the State Board of Centennial Managers, says of the counties of Richie, Wirt, &c.: "Timothy is the grass most usually seeded, on account of its "superior hay making properties. It runs out in about four "to six years. Herds Grass produces finely in this belt. "Orchard Grass is also grown. None of them grow to any "extent during the winter. Red Clover grows finely, but like "Timothy, soon runs out. Blue Grass is everywhere the main "sod producer, for which it is eminently fitted, and through- "out this section, fertilizes the soil, so long as it remains in "it." Mr. Bryan states that it is still within the memory of some of the older inhabitants of West Virginia, when not a blade of Blue Grass was known in the best Blue Grass region of the State. One of its most valuable properties, is that of growing during the winter. It does not grow very well, when exposed to great heat in summer. The soil of the counties in question, though showing no limestone, has a considerable amount of lime diffused through the shales.

From the South Branch district, which is one of the finest cattle regions in the State, if not the very finest, we have few data. The best grass lands here are the splendid valleys, which, long and narrow, run parallel to each other in a N. E. and S. W. direction. Cattle are grazed in summer on the mountains or uplands, and are fed corn in winter. According to Mr. Thos. Maslin, the district probably sends to market every year, 20,-000 head, averaging 1,250 pounds. Of these, the lightest find a market in Baltimore and Philadelphia, and the heaviest in New York. The home price is 5½ cents per pound gross, giving a return of $1,375,000.

With respect to the grasses cultivated in Harrison and other counties, Mr. Bowen says: "Our grasses are principally limited "to the native or Blue Grass, the White and Red Clovers, and "Timothy. The first being indigenious, is all that can be "required for our soil and temperature, while it is unrivalled "as a pasturage, at all seasons, for any kind of stock, and espe-"cially for beef making and dairy purposes. The finest butter "we have ever seen, may be produced with requisite facilities, "from our Blue Grass pastures.

"*White Clover.*—This favorite lawn grass of the Apirian, "may be considered a natural product of our soils. It is exten-"sively grown, and much valued, for summer and fall grazing.

"*Pure Timothy*—Is principally the grass of our best meadows. "Seed sown in August and September is ready to winter safely, "and be mown the following summer. To continue in success-"ful growth, it should not be cut until the seed is fully "ripened. It grows luxuriantly, yet is less capable of with-"standing the extremes of heat and cold, than the foregoing "varieties. A summer pasturage of the three grasses men-"tioned, grown together, cannot be equalled. It is from her "hillsides, thus richly carpeted, that our noble young State "sends to the consumer a beef, which, for *unquestioned health-"fulness*, and rich and delicate flavor, cannot be rivalled on the "continent.

"*Red Clover*—Is somewhat grown, and esteemed for summer "grazing; also, for hay. Its remarkable qualities as a fertili-"zer, if left uncut, or turned under for that purpose, commend "it to all.

"*Orchard Grass*—Is being introduced with the very best "results. It adapts itself to all varieties of temperature and "soil, though it thrives most luxuriantly on a rich loose loam. "It is an excellent grower, producing fine sod, and resisting "close grazing only second to Blue Grass. If cut early, it cures "into an excellent hay."

TABLE C.

Statement of Live Stock, &c., According to the Census of 1870.

	Animals slaughtered or sold for slaughter.	Value of all Live Stock.	Milch Cows.	Work Oxen.	Other Cattle.	Sheep.	Wool.	Butter.	Hay.
	Dolls.	Dolls.	No.	No.	No.	No.	P'unds	P'unds	Tons.
Total	4,914,792	17,175.420	104,434	18,937	178,309	552,327	1,593,541	5,044,475	224,164
Barbour	192,667	658,275	3,622	421	7,647	11,738	31,973	157,317	10,803
Berkeley	154,774	496,532	3,050	24	3.991	9,213	41,147	239.493	8,5.9
Boone	[illegible]8.215	129.213	1,356	446	2,001	3,955	9,699	55,784	191
Braxton	43,890	218,990	2,[illegible]49	375	1,730	9,923	18,507	34,733	1,951
Brooke	92,099	265,944	1,[illegible]60	70	1,439	46,581	185,105	110,307	7,570
Cabell	37,123	146,412	833	685	1,660	4.025	8,676	28,674	680
Calhoun	17,[illegible]74	81,350	666	188	716	3,232	6,555	24,640	985
Clay	15,306	63,096	722	129	552	2,667	5,731	36,595	274
Doddridge	80,264	300,950	1.987	362	2,420	7,183	17,441	113,649	4,649
Fayette	64 594	225,085	2,267	436	2,600	8,709	16,331	72,188	1,649
Gilmer	27,621	162,509	1,295	271	1,426	6,100	12,736	44,929	1,636
Grant	173,719	363,399	1,739	44	4,686	7,551	20,689	67,587	4,787
Greenbrier	187,175	553,856	3,201	496	6,703	13,880	34,051	174,865	7,444
Hampshire	115,575	381.454	2 673	21	3,863	8,317	26,658	114.948	4,587
Hancock	47,996	218,840	869	72	929	26,353	128,642	70,588	4,351
Hardy	179.809	288,204	1,370	146	4,528	4,176	13,566	39,057	2,651
Harrison	403,235	1,267,287	4,906	706	15,149	15,812	45,662	276,955	16,901
Jackson	84,771	370,271	2,289	6[illegible]8	3,036	13,610	29,85[illegible]	87,052	2,934
Jefferson	157,110	581,038	2.489	91	3,222	6,521	28,699	120,374	5,753
Kanawha	124 047	413 450	3,400	1,078	4,011	9,879	20,457	163,142	2,840
Lewis	154,966	564,196	2,962	482	7,654	10,922	26,955	113,259	8,620
Lincoln	32,474	86,626	950	448	1,158	3,874	7,151	48,271	293
Logan	23,429	116,372	1,366	903	1,636	4,505	6,296	29,182	178
*Marion	*1,353	247.090	1,110	173	2,204	4,924	12,780	22,927	3,780
Marshall	128 561	580 730	3,076	515	3,366	37,508	119,579	204,480	5,750
Mason	164,483	544,554	2,332	833	4,350	9,880	22,853	5,002	4,353
McDowell	10,143	39,500	546	86	619	1,300	2,404	15,597	8
Mercer	50,056	297,648	2,722	289	2,906	8,293	18,713	109,355	2,517
Mineral	155,084	277,600	1,534	14	3,624	6,429	23,406	52,078	5,104
Monongalia	304,066	871,260	4,606	761	7,743	17,371	55,856	345,573	12,030
Monroe	158,460	567,053	3,006	281	6,888	11,517	26,694	163,540	5.388
Morgan	36,110	142,792	1 112	27	1.429	2,683	7,564	41,183	1.996
Nicholas	46,567	185,532	1,600	324	3,820	8,171	18,838	164,990	3,029
Ohio	100,407	418 466	1,585	200	1,293	47,201	175,124	120,135	8.389
Pendleton	108,801	328.164	2,270	50	5,105	9,943	26,273	56.876	5,079
Pleasants	12,694	98,257	638	120	1,105	2,918	6,441	110	592
Pocahontas	39,239	358,229	2,440	266	5,476	10.824	24,137	[illegible]65,740	4,797
Preston	118,201	613,369	4 526	187	6,236	22,336	58,388	193.233	11,961
Putnam	70,633	251,049	1,565	813	2,222	6,291	14,992	63,061	1,446
Raleigh	24,880	119,184	1,545	274	1,538	5,462	11,338	41,635	951
Randolph	41,456	369,158	1,970	245	6,258	8,523	17,706	90,840	7,298
Ritchie	106,015	298,199	2,079	383	2,882	11,607	26,828	116,094	4,732
Roane	69,333	241,585	1.858	507	2,970	12,973	24,176	100,379	3,013
Summers	No sta	tistics.							
Taylor	135,141	390,939	1,791	170	4.558	6,009	17,233	97,223	6,710
Tucker	17,719	112.583	637	75	1,009	2,608	6,093	26,769	1,498
Tyler	50,621	330,777	1,566	308	3,307	12,115	26,704	108,080	4,365
Upshur	131,948	383,509	2,354	257	4,304	8,000	21,857	127,158	7,233
Wayne	90,773	259,327	1,827	1,837	2,507	9,723	17 022	68,967	1,039
Webster	8,311	49,607	643	127	642	2,018	4,598	14.563	504
Wetzel	82,314	255,597	1,641	400	1,823	9,545	23,392	119,393	2,947
Wirt	42,450	143,163	954	251	1,008	4,183	9.515	44,000	1,527
Wood	132,055	392,720	2,763	497	2,943	10,419	24,830	215,576	5,578
Wyoming	17,635	80,420	1,042	165	1,417	2,827	5,630	32,328	294

*The value of slaughtered animals put for Marion is plainly wrong.

CHAPTER VI.

SHEEP AND WOOL.

BY C. H. BEALL, OF BROOKE COUNTY.

Prof. M. F. Maury,

DEAR SIR: In compliance with your request of last December, I send you the following facts concerning the wool and sheep interests of West Virginia:

Among the attractions offered to the immigrant by our young and flourishing State, none stand out more prominently, or offer more inducements, than the raising of Merino sheep and the production of Merino wool.

It seems to be impossible to give an intelligent account of our present subject without giving an outline sketch of the origin and history of the present fine wooled sheep of the United States. This we will make as brief as possible.

The original source of the Spanish Merino is unknown. It is generally conceded, however, that at least as early as the commencement of the Christian era there existed in Spain a breed of fine wooled sheep. From this arose several varieties in the different provinces of that country, and importations from these have, from time to time, been made into several countries of Europe, and also into America.

These importations have generally retained the name "Merino," which they bore in Spain, while receiving, as an adjunct, the name of the country into which they were taken.

Thus we have the "Saxon Merino," the "German Merino," the "French Merino," and the "American Merino," sometimes improperly called, also, the "Spanish Merino."

Thus, it will be seen that the three present great branches of the Merino came originally from Spain. These are the French, the German, and the American. Each of these has been repeatedly tried in West Virginia, and the general conclusion is, that the American Merino, improved in its stamina and form, enlarged in its carcass, and having the weight of its fleece almost doubled by a long course of patient and careful breeding, is, for all purposes, the most valuable decendant and representative of the original Spanish Merino which can be obtained.

Having said this much by way of introduction, we will now proceed to deal more specially with the subject of sheep raising in our State.

The raising of sheep, and the production of wool, has, so far, been mainly confined to the "Panhandle," *i.e.* the four counties of Hancock, Brooke, Ohio, and Marshall. What will be said of these, in this connection, may, with some modification, be applied to the entire State.

Soil of the State.—Much of the soil of our State is of that kind called "limestone," or "calcareous." While it has enough calcareous matter usually to ensure fertility, it is of such a nature as to retain no water on its surface. It is generally friable and easily broken up, and is cultivated without difficulty, while it contains no element injurious to the feet and fleece of the sheep. Always covered with a dense coating of fresh, green grass, it is perfectly clean and free from the dust and sand that are so troublesome in some sections.

Such is the freedom of our soil from every thing that can destroy the whiteness, pliableness, and silken character of the fleece, that after washing our sheep in spring, preparatory to shearing, we turn them out in our pasture fields with their coats still saturated with water, without the slightest injury to the wool. When our sheep are shorn, the wool comes from their bodies as soft, white, and pliable, as nature, under tho most favorable circumstances, can make it.

In our water we are peculiarly fortunate. There is, perhaps, no where a section more bountifully supplied with this material. The whole State is broken up into hills and valleys, and watered with never-failing streams and copious springs, so that its entire area might be divided into ten or twenty acre lots, each of which would have either a perennial stream or a never freezing fountain. This water is of the very best character; cold, pure, and invigorating, it meets every requirement of the shepherd.

Another great advantage enjoyed by West Virginia in the breeding of sheep, and growing of wool, is the natural fertility of her soil. This, taken in connection with her genial climate, should make the State permanently the home of the shepherd and his flocks.

Even with our present defective system of cultivation—the natural outgrowh of the fertility of our soil—we can raise a greater variety and quantity of agricultural products than almost all other sections that rank as sheep-breeding and wool-raising districts. This is true, both of our pasture and winter feed. Of the former we have as the principal varieties, Red Clover, Timothy, and Blue Grass. These grow with great luxuriance and are of superior quality. Of the latter, the chief varieties are the grains: Corn and Oats, and as rack-feed Corn-Fodder, Timothy and Clover hay. Such is the excellence and abundance of these products that the cost of wintering sheep, horses, and cattle—the principal farm animals—is much less in our State than in most of the sheep-breeding sections of the country.

As a proof of this, we here present a tabular statement of the comparative cost of wintering these animals in the States named. The table was compiled from statistics that appeared in the Monthly Report of the Department of Agriculture, for the months of February and March, 1875. The States mentioned have been selected, and are the principal sheep-breeding and wool-growing ones of the Union. The costs are as follows:

COST OF WINTERING STOCK.

STATES.	Horses per head.	Milch Cows per head.	Sheep per head.
Maine	$37.00	$29.00	$3.00
New Hampshire	37.00	38.00	2.50
Vermont	38.00	25.00	2.50
New York	37.00	24.00	2.50
New Jersey	48.00	29.00	2.00
Pennsylvania	36.00	23.00	2.00
Delaware	43.00	26.00	2.75
Maryland	34.00	20.00	2.75
Virginia	22.00	11.00	1.50
Ohio	25.00	16.00	1.75
West Virginia	18.00	12.00	1 21

By an examination of the above tables, it will be seen that the cost of wintering a horse in New Jersey, is nearly three times as much as in West Virginia, while there is a gain of $4.00 per head over Virginia, the next lewest State. It will also be seen that, while there is a loss of $1.00 per head, on milch cows, as compared with that State, there is an important gain over all the others. Our State, in the cost of sheep, is 29 cents per head, cheaper than all others.

These gainsare partly due to the fact that our feeding period is shorter than that of some of the States, whose names appear in the list, but chiefly to the superior productiveness of our soil. In proof of this, we may point to the fact that according to the agricultural report above referred to, the feeding period of Virginia is only four months, while in West Virginia, it is four and three-fourth months, with two months partial feeding, and yet it costs 29 cents more to winter a sheep in Virginia than in West Virginia.

But whether these difference depend on soil or climate, or both, they are nevertheless gains, and the foregoing table presents proof not to be overcome, that West Virginia deserves to be placed in the front rank of the sheep-raising and wool-growing States of the Union.

Climate.—Our climate, though much milder than that of the New England and Middle States, is yet sufficiently severe to cause the consumption of food enough to produce an extremely heavy fleece. The fleeces of thoroughbred American Merino ewes, properly summered and wintered, and cared for generally, range from 10 to 18 pounds, while buck-fleeces weigh from 15 to 25 pounds. With the extra amount of feed and attention given in the Eastern States, these weights could, without doubt, be considerably increased.

Our winter weather usually begins in the last week of November, and continues until about the first of April. [For the temperature during this period see Climatology. *Authors.*] The winter temperature is quite variable. In our present winter, 1875, the mercury has not reached the zero point. The coldest weather has been 5° to 6° above zero Fahr. This, however, is by no means common, for the present winter has been exceptionally mild. This comparative mildness of the weather, as might be supposed, renders our feeding period shorter. For the purpose of showing the relative lengths of the feeding periods in the principal wool-growing States, we append the following tabular statement, for which we are indebted to the agricultural report before referred to.

While our climate is thus shown to be comparatively mild, it is very salubrious, and highly favorable for the maintainance of the general health of the flocks.

No such thing as *scab* and the other malarial diseases, so common and destructive in other States, are known to the sheep breeders of West Virginia.

LENGTH OF THE FEEDING PERIOD FOR SHEEP.

STATES.	Number of months of full feeding.	Number of months of partial feeding.
Maine	6	$1\frac{1}{2}$
New Hampshire	6	$1\frac{1}{2}$
Vermont	6	$1\frac{1}{2}$
New York	$5\frac{1}{2}$	2
New Jersey	$5\frac{1}{2}$	2
Pennsylvania	5	2
Delaware	$4\frac{1}{3}$	2
Maryland	$5\frac{5}{6}$	2
Virginia	4	2
Ohio	$4\frac{1}{2}$	2
West Virginia	$4\frac{1}{3}$	2

Surface of the Country.—The character of the general surface of the country, is another advantage, not to be overlooked, in reckoning the facilities of our State for sheep raising. The disposition of the sheep to climb to the top of the highest hills, points plainly to the fact that their nature requires a a high and rolling country. An elevated table-land would render the climate too cold, and the winters too long. This difficulty is obviated by having the surface diversified by hills and valleys, and such we find to be pre-eminently the character of West Virginia. (See topography.—*Authors*). In our deep valleys, watered by cool, pure, never-failing streams, in the smooth slopes of the hills, covered with luxuriant and succulent grass, and in the lofty rounded crests, or table-lands that crown the summits, the shepherd has an assemblage of all the good things that nature can provide for him.

The peculiar topography of our State, furnishes in the the warm months of the year, a high and dry range for the flocks, and enables the shepherd to find in the same pastures, sheltered valleys and nooks which afford an abundance of pure water, while they are protected from the violence of storms and winds. So ample, indeed, is the protection provided by nature, that many do not think it necessary to house their sheep at all. It is no uncommon thing to see sheep fed out in the open field, the entire winter, and though the practice is not to be recommended, yet those who have adopted it, appear in most cases to have realized a fair profit upon their flocks.

The hilly and diversified character of the surface, prevents the occurrence of tornadoes, and such things as "sand storms," elsewhere so injurious to the wool, are unknown.

FACILITIES FOR EXPORTING WOOL.

Having shown that our State is so well adapted to the raising of sheep, and the production of wool, the question naturally arises, what are the markets for these products, and what are our facilities for transportation?

The demand for our sheep is principally from the south, and west. Those who live north and east of us, generally go to the New England States for their stock, and this confines our market for stock sheep, principally to the Southern and Western States, and the Western Territories. We say stock sheep, for the demand for mutton sheep is in the east, chiefly Baltimore, New York, Pittsburgh, and Philadelphia.

For the transportation of stock sheep to the south and west, we have available, the Ohio river and several railroads, which furnish all the facilities necessary, to render such transportation both cheap and convenient.

The demand for West Virginia wool, however, lies in another direction. The great manufacturing section of the United States is in the east, mainly in the New England States. It is to this market, that our wool in the form of raw material must be sent. As we have already stated the market for our mutton is also in the east.

The means of transportation in the northern part of the State, is ample on the two great competing lines of railroad, the Baltimore and Ohio, and the Pennsylvania Central. In the central and southern parts, we have the Baltimore and Ohio with its branches, and the Chesapeake and Ohio. The competition existing between these great routes, bring the the charges down to the lowest figures, while the appliances and facilities of the companies, owning and operating them, afford ample conveniencies to the citizens of every section.

In addition to these, another great thoroughfare is now under course of construction. This is under the management of the "People's Cheap Transportation Company," of New York City. It is to extend from New York to Washington, Pa., and thence to the Ohio river, crossing it at Wellsburg, the county seat of Brooke. From this point it is to extend to St. Louis, Mo., and will there form connection with the roads running westward to the Pacific. This road, when completed, will give us more direct communication, both with the East and West.

FACILITIES FOR MANUFACTURING WOOLEN GOODS.

The discussion of the facilities for transporting our wool to the points where it can be manufactured, naturally suggests the question whether it could not be worked up to advantage at home, and thus enable us to save the cost of the transport of the raw material, and the manufactured woolen goons, which we now import from the East.

The only essentials required for the establishment of manufactories, are a sufficient supply of raw material, water, and coal. The question of a supply of skilled labor does not enter into the problem, for whenever there is a demand for it, there is an ample supply. Manufacturing has been found to pay in New England, and there are many reasons why it should be still more remunerative with us. Our fertile soil produces such an abundance and variety of the necessaries of life, that we can live much more cheaply than the people of the East, and can in consequence of this, pay higher prices to our workmen. Since the laborers could also live more cheaply, the advantage would be twofold. There could then be no doubt about our ability to secure a sufficient number of skilled workmen, to enable us to compete with eastern manufacturers.

The water and fuel which enables us to work our numerous rolling mills, furnaces, and nail factories, would be amply sufficient for the wants of woolen manufactories.

We have quite a number of establishments for the preparation and manufacture of iron scattered along the Ohio river. These have proven themselves both profitable to their owners, and efficient in the work in which they are engaged. Again, the manufacturer here can procure his raw material in the immediate vicinity of the factory, without the payment of a cent for transportion.

This would enable him to pay his workmen higher wages, and at the same time deliver his goods directly, and several per cent cheaper to the consumer than they could be obtained from the factories of eastern States. In addition to this, we would have the same facilities for the transport of our manufactured goods that we now enjoy for the transport of raw material and stock.

Taking all these things into consideration, we may assert with confidence, that in the manufacture of woolen goods we need have no fear of entering into competition with eastern factories.

Cheapness of Labor.—The cultivation of crops, the building and repairing of fences, and the care of sheep, particularly during the winter months, require more labor than the farmer and sheep-raiser can himself perform, and more time than he can bestow. This renders the question of hired labor one of unusual importance to those who contemplate engaging in sheep breeding and wool-raising.

No person, however, need hesitate to engage in such employments in West Virginia through fear of failure to secure all the assistance that he may need. There are here in our State many persons, both married and unmarried, who rely entirely upon farm labor for their employment. This, from the competition afforded, and the original cheapness of labor, enables the farmer to secure assistance at prices that are extremely favorable for his calling.

The services of good farm hands can be secured for prices ranging from $12 to $16 per month.

Farm hands that have families generally expect, in addition to their monthly pay, to be boarded while they are actually employed, and to be furnished with a house, garden, and pasture for a cow, free of charges for rent. Those who have no families expect to be boarded only, and both classes expect pay only for the time they are actually at work. These terms apply only to those hands that are employed for a year or longer. Many can be employed to feed stock during the winter months at much lower rates and upon much more favorable terms. With respect to farm labor also, then, the cost is much less than in many sections where sheep raising and wool production have proved very profitable.

During almost the entire period since the first introduction of Merino sheep into the United States, by Jarvis, Humphrey, Atwood, and others, the citizens of West Virginia have been to a greater or less extent, employed in breeding Merino sheep and raising merino wool. The experience of these breeders extends through a period of more than half a century. The business has employed the talents and energy of some of the first men of their day. The result has been to render this one of the leading sheep-breeding sections of the Union.

The business continues to expand, and is continually taking in new territory and employing new men. As the breeders increase in number, and become more careful in the treatment of their flocks, new evidence is presented of the fact, that as a successful sheep-raising and wool-producing State, West Virginia cannot be surpassed. We may regard the matter as thoroughly tested.

The grade of our flocks, the quantity and quality of their wool, have of late years greatly improved. Our breeders are beginning to realize the fact that if sheep are profitable at all, those are most so that yield the greatest number of pounds of wool of the required degree of fineness. This has induced sheep breeders to exercise more care in the selection of stock rams, and to breed with special reference both to quantity and quality. The more wealthy and enterprising stock owners are, for this purpose, led to get their stock rams directly from Vermont. Here, by a long course of careful and systematic breeding, and by the continued crossing of sheep of the pure Spanish blood, the Merino has been brought to a state of perfection, higher than any where else in the world. Some of our leading breeders have recently, also, imported considerable flocks of pure bred Merino ewes from Vermont.

The result of the increased care in breeding, is that the character of the sheep generally in the State, has been elevated with a decided improvement in the quality, and increase in the quantity, of their wool. Besides, we have to day flocks of pure Merino ewes, which, in their forms and fleeces, rival the finest products of Vermont.

We have thus far spoken only of the American Merino. The French and German varieties, are to be found in our State, but the demand for them is comparatively small, and they appear to be gradually giving way to the American Merino, which is considered to be a hardier and more profitable animal. In addition to the several classes named above, we have several varieties of the English mutton sheep, such as the Southdowns, the Cottswold, the Leicesters, and others. These appear to do well here, but the demand for them, though increasing, is yet small. The long period during which our breeders have been engaged in raising fine sheep and wool, the great care which they have exercised, and the steady improvement that has resulted, have all combined to give us an established reputation in the business.

Not only do the inhabitants of the adjoining States get a considerable per centage of their stock sheep from our flocks, but there is a brisk, and increasing demand, from the Southern and Western States, and the Territories. So important has this demand become, that of late, many of our farmers find it to be a very profitable employment, to breed for the special purpose of supplying it. The demand for West

Virginia wool is not less active. The South and West have always been engaged in agricultural pursuits, and hence cannot be consumers, but are rather producers of wool. Those countries that have a poor soil, but an abundance of water power and fuel, naturally turn their attention to manufacturing; to these the surplus products of producing States must go first, to be worked up. When, however, capacity for production, and all the requisites for manufacturing, are combined in the same State, the manufactories must prove to the producing centers. At present then, we must find the markets for our wools, only in the East, but in the near future, we may, with confidence, expect to find in our own mills and factories, purchasers of our products.

As to the standing of West Virginia wool, we may, with truth, state that, in freedom from dirt, length of staple, fineness, firmness, and strength of fibre, and in its felting properties, our wool is unsurpassed. None meets with readier sale, or commands higher prices than that furnished by our flocks.

Yours truly,

March 1876. C. H. BEALL.

CHAPTER VII.

FOREST TREES, SHRUBS, AND MEDICINAL PLANTS.

BY WM. M. FONTAINE.

Ash (Fraxinus).—The genus Fraxinus, or Ash, is composed of deciduous trees, which are natives of Europe, Northern Africa, a part of Asia, and of North America. They are raised from seeds, or by grafting on the Fraxinus excelsior (European Ash.) These trees have a great tendency to sport, or run into varieties, which closely resemble each other. Hence many, or few species, may be made, according to the value attached to these variations. The most important representative of this genus in America, is the White Ash (F. Americana).

1. *The White Ash* (F. Americana).—This tree is quite common in our forests. In usefulness in the arts, it is surpassed by no tree except the oak. From the rapidity of its growth, the beauty of its foliage, and the valuable qualities of its timber, it is one of the most interesting of American trees. In favorable situations, it sometimes attains the height of eighty feet, with a trunk three feet in diameter, and is often undivided for more than half its length. It grows best in rich or moist ground, near the edge of streams or swamps, where the soil is deep, fertile, and intermingled with fragments of rocks. It is a native of North America, from Labrador to the Carolinas, and is particularly abundant when the climate is cool and moist. It is but little subject to accidents and the attacks of insects. The wood of the White Ash, in young, thrifty trees, is very white from the bark to the center, but in large, old

trees, the heart wood is of a reddish tinge, and the sap wood white. When the annual layers are thick and coarse, it is exceedingly tough and elastic, and may be applied to a great variety of purposes.

It is used by coach and wagon makers for the felloes of wheels, for shafts, and for the frames of carriage bodies, and for those of light wagons. It is used very generally for agricultural implements and domestic wares, especially for the handles of spades, hoes, scythes, &c. In Canada, and the northern part of the United States, it is largely used for hoops and staves. The latter are esteemed best for casks containing salted provisions and flour. For the blocks of pullies, pins for belaying cordage on ships, it is the best material. It is in universal use for oars in all navies. This wood is largely exported to Europe in the form of planks. The inner bark of the tree imparts a very permanent yellow to skins, and may be used in dyeing wool.

The wood is not liable to shrink and swell, when once it has been thoroughly seasoned. It, hence, makes the most beautiful floors of all our timber. Ash lumber always commands a ready sale at high prices.

2. *Ash, Black, Water, or Hoop* (F. Sambucifolia).—This tree, in favorable locations, frequently attains the height of seventy or eighty feet, and a diameter of two, to two and a half feet. The leaves, when bruised, smell like those of the elder. This tree is among the last to put forth its leaves in spring, and the first to lose them in autumn. The leaves are killed by the first hard frost, and in the North of the United States, are frequently all off by the 20th of September. It is generally found in a moist soil, or one exposed to inundations. In the Middle States, this tree associates with the Red Ash, a tree rare west of the Alleghanies, and with the Red Maple. The wood is tougher, and more elastic, than that of the White Ash, but is less durable when exposed to changes from moisture to dryness, and vice versa. Hence, it is less used. Like the European Ash, its timber is more valuable when grown rapidly, and the wood of young trees is more esteemed than that of old ones. The sap wood of this variety is very white, tough, and compact. It is sometimes made into posts, which rank next to the cedar in durability. In Nova Scotia and the Northern

States, it is preferred to the White Ash for hoops. The annual layers, by repeated blows, tends to separate into long strips, and hence the wood is not used for oars, handspikes, &c. This property, however, fits it for the manufacture of baskets, chair bottoms, &c. The ashes of this species, like those of most ash, are very rich in potash.

3. *Ash, Blue*,—(F. quadrangulata).—This variety, in favorable situations, attains often the height of sixty or seventy feet, with a diameter of fifteen or twenty inches. The shoots are quadrangular, and have four membranes placed opposite each other. The Blue Ash is mainly found in Tennessee, Kentucky, and the Southern part of Ohio, where the climate is mild, and the soil fertile in an extreme degree. This fertility seems to serve as a substitute for that degree of moisture, which in the Atlantic States, seems necessary for the growth of the Ash. Hence it may grow well in dry woods, provided they be rich enough. The wood of this tree posesses the characteristic properties of the genus, and in the Western States is extensively employed, and highly valued. Beside the other uses, the wood is selected for the flooring of houses, and for their exterior covering. Where the Tulip tree does not abound, it sometimes serves for shingles. (Browne). It is said that a blue color may be extracted from the bark of this tree, which circumstance may have caused its common name.

4. *Ash, Green*,—(F. viridis).—This tree, sometimes called the Walnut-leaved Ash, in its natural habitat, usually attains a height of 25 to 30 feet, with a trunk 4 or 5 inches in diameter. It is easily recognized by the brilliant green color of its young leaves, which are nearly of the same color on both surfaces.

This variety is native of wet, shady woods, from Canada to the Carolinas, but is more common in the western part of Pennsylvania, Maryland, and in West Virginia, than in any other sections of the United States. It is found in abundance on the banks of the Monongahela and Ohio. Its wood has the same character with the other species of genus, and is applied to the same purposes. As, however, the White Ash is more common where it grows, and is of superior size, the Green Ash is only incidentally employed.

5. *Ash, Mountain*,--(Pyrus Americana).—This tree, though by its common name, placed among the Ash trees, is really found in a quite different genus. It belongs to the same family with the Pear, Apple, &c. It has an erect stem, and sometimes grows to the height of 20 or 30 feet, with a diameter of a foot or more. The varieties are several in number, of which the P. A. Microcarpa, or small fruited Mountain Ash is indigenous, especially in the whole range ot the Alleghanies. It may be propagated from seeds, or by grafting. The Mountain Ash will grow in any soil, and in the most exposed situations, whether on the seashore, or on mountain tops. It attains its largest size in a free soil, with a moist climate, and in an open dry situation. Few trees suffer more than this from extreme heat and dry weather.

The wood of this tree, when dry, weighs 51 pounds to the cubic foot. It is fine grained, hard, homogeneous, and capable of taking a high polish. In Europe it is much used in the small manufactures, such as the handles of knives, &c., and in various articles of turnery. When large enough, it is also used for axle-trees, naves, felloes, &c. In some parts of Europe the berries are also used as a fruit, and even ground into flour. This tree is well adapted as an ornamental tree.

6. *Aspen, or Poplar*,—(Populus tremuloides).—This tree is common in our woods. It attains the height of 20 to 50 feet. As it has no particular value as a timber tree, we need not dwell upon it.

7. *The Beech*,—(Fagus ferrnginea).—This tree is quite common, and attains the diameter of from 2 to 3 feet. It is found commonly along streams, or on the hill sides near streams. It makes a handsome tree with wide-spread, compact foliage, and a trunk which dissolves into very numerous branches.

When seasoned, the wood is extremely hard and solid. It is used for plane stocks, shoe-lasts, and the handles of tools. But little of it is converted into lumber, and it is mainly used for fuel.

8. *Beech, Water*,—(Carpinus Americana).—This tree is not uncommon along streams and in moist places. Though belonging to a different family from the Beech, from its straight veined leaves, and smooth grey bark, it has a considerable

resemblance to that tree and hence the common name. It forms a shrub or tree from 15 to 30 feet high. Its wood is very hard, and from this property the tree in some sections is called "Ironwood," The wood is speckled, or somewhat curled, and would seem fitted for some kinds of furniture.

9. *Birch, Black,*—(Betula lenta).—This is rather a large tree, growing along the Alleghany region. It prefers moist places, and has on the trunk a dark brown, close bark, with a sweet aromatic odor. The timber is rose colored, fine grained, and valuable for cabinet work.

10. *Birch, Red,*—(Betula nigra).—This is rather a large tree, growing on low river banks, rather abundantly in some localities. Its wood is light colored, and is not much appreciated for timber.

11. *Buckeye, Sweet,*—(Aesculus flava).—This tree, which must not be confounded with the Ae glabra, or Fetid Buckeye, unlike the latter, grows in rich woods, and in mountains and knobby districts, where it attains the height of 50 or 60 feet, and is 2 or 3 feet in diameter. The wood is light, soft, and porous, not inclined to split or crack in drying. It is valuable for making troughs, bread-trays, wooden bowls, shuttles, &c.

12. *Buckeye, Fetid,*—(Aesculus glabra).—This is the most common species of Buckeye found in the State. It grows only in the vicinity of streams, and forms a large tree occasionally. It has no particular value.

13. *Cedar,*—(Juniperus Virginiana).— This valuable plant, which in the east grows only to a small size, in West Virginia attain the height of 60 to 90 feet, and a diameter of 2 or 3 feet. It endures in its growth, a considerable variation of soil and situation. It is found both on high hills and along streams. This tree is considered to furnish one of the most valuable of all woods. The wood is compact, fine grained, light, and exceedingly durable. The heart, which furnishes the timber, has a strong red color, and is peculiar for its strong pleasant odor. This is so greatly disliked by moths, that chests made of it are proof against them. It is capable of a high polish, and is more highly esteemed than any other wood in the manufacture of hollow wooden-ware. Great quantities of this timber is manufactured annually into buck-

ets, tubs, &c., &c. For fence posts, &c., it is peculiarly fitted from its great durability, lasting, as does, for generations. The timber meets with a ready sale at remunerative prices.

14. *Cherry, Wild*,—(Prunus Serotina).—This is one of our most valuable timber trees. In the Eastern States it is very common as a shrub, or small tree. With us, it often attains the height of sixty to seventy feet, before dividing into limbs, and often measures three and a half to four feet across the stump. It permits a considerable range of situation, growing both on streams and hills, but delights in a rich, well drained soil.

The wood is light red, compact, and fine grained. and takes a polish as fine as that of mahogany or rosewood. With age and proper treatment, it will compare in polish and beauty, with any wood. The wood is almost entirely used for cabinet work. There are large quantities of this valuable timber in the State. The tree grows everywhere, but the largest number, and the finest for timber, are perhaps to be found near the headwaters of the Elk, Gauley, Greenbrier, and Cheat rivers, in the counties of Randolph, Pocahontas, Braxton, and Webster. It grows usually scattered through the other timber. Many large and fine trees, four feet in diameter, are found on Cherry and Williams rivers, in the above mentioned district. Trees here may be found long enough for three and four, sixteen feet cuts.

15. *Chestnut*,—(Castania Vesca).—This is one of our largest trees, attaining a diameter of seven feet. It grows in dry, elevated ground, in every part of the State, and is more abundant in and near the mountains. It has a rapid growth, and may be renewed from the seed or sprout, in fifteen or twenty years, to a size sufficient to form posts and rails.

The wood resembles the Red Oak in color, being a shade lighter. It is a very valuable timber on account of its durability. In the form of shingles, or rails, it will last until washed away by the rains. Chestnut rails have been known to last over fifty years. When put in the ground, it is not so durable as Cedar or Locust. The wood has a beautifully laminated structure, and when polished or varnished, makes handsome furniture. It furnishes a very valuable edible nut, which is sold in large amounts, and affords a fine mast for hogs. A tree thirty-three feet in circumference has been measured in Kanawha county.

16. *Coffee Tree, Kentucky,*—(Gymnocladus Canadensis).—The Kentucky Coffee Tree grows to a considerable height—sometimes 50 to 60 feet—with a straight trunk, having a diameter of 12 inches to 2 feet, and is often destitute of branches for more than 30 feet.

In its natural habitat, it always grows in the richest soils, and thrives best in sheltered situations. It is generally propagated by seeds, but may be raised from cuttings of the roots.

The wood is of a rose hue, and is very hard, compact, tough, and strong. These properties render it very suitable for cabinet work, and for building. It has but little sap wood, and hence nearly all the trunk can be used. The pods, preserved like those of the Tamarind, are said to be wholesome, and slightly aperient. The seeds were used by the early settlers of Kentucky and Tennessee, as a substitute for coffee, hence the name.

17. *Cotton Wood,*—(Populus Heterophylla).—This tree is not very abundant with us. It attains a large size in Tennessee, and on the Mississippi is used for fire wood. It prefers moist ground and swamps, attaining the height of 40 to 60 feet. The wood is white, soft, and easy to cut and split.

18. *Cucumber Tree,*—(Magnolia Acuminata).—This tree is not uncommon in the State. Its trunk is straight, of uniform size, and often destitute of branches for two-thirds of its length. It attains the height of 60 to 80 feet, with a diameter of three or four feet. It may be propagated from the seeds, or by layers. The situations best adapted for it, are the slopes of mountains, narrow valleys, or the banks of torrents, where the air is always moist, and the soil deep and fertile.

The wood of this species is soft and light, weighing when dry, only 26 pounds to the cubic foot. The timber may be employed in joining, for the interior of houses, and for cabinet making. From its size and lightness, it is well adapted for hollowing out into canoes. The half ripe cores, steeped in whisky, renders it extremely bitter, and it is then, when taken in the morning, considered as a preventative of autumnal fevers.

19. *Dogwood,*—(Cornus Florida).—This tree, or rather shrub, is found everywhere in the State. In its natural habitat, under favorable circnmstances, it forms a tree 30 to 35 feet high, and 9 to 10 inches thick, but is usually only half this size.

The Dogwood thrives best in a gravelly soil, rich in vegetable matter and moisture. It may be propagated by seeds or cuttings.

The wood of this plant is hard, compact, and heavy. Its fine grain renders it capable of a high polish, and hence it may be used for many of the purposes for which Logwood is employed. It is also used for the construction of the handles of light tools, mallets, &c.; as well as for the hames of horse collars, runners of sleds, &c. Being liable to split, it should not be used until perfectly seasoned. The wood as a fuel makes a very hot fire, and gives an abundant pure white ash.

The inner bark of the tree is extremely bitter, and forms an excellent substitute for Peruvian bark. It is even claimed by some physicians that the Dogwood equals Peruvian bark. The bark may also be substituted for galls in the manufacture of ink. From the bark of the more fibrous roots the Indians get a good scarlet dye. A Dogwood 18 inches in diameter is reported from Braxton county.

20. *Elder, Box*,—(Negundo aceroides [Mornch]).—This plant, though bearing the name of Box Elder, has no affinity with the true Elders.

Farther south, the tree attains a larger size than with us. In Tennessee it attains a height of 40 to 50 feet, and a diameter of 15 to 20 inches. It is most abundant in the bottoms which skirt the river, where the soil is deep, fertile, and constantly moist. With us it is not confined to river banks, but grows in the woods with the Locust, Wild Cherry, and Coffee tree. It may be raised from the seeds, and is not a long-lived tree.

The wood has a fine even grain, and is saffron colored, slightly mixed with violet. Except in very old trees, the proportion of sap to heart-wood is very large. In America the wood is used only for fuel, but in Europe it is used in cabinet making, especially for in inlaying. For this, the heart wood of old trees, variagated with bluish and rose-colored veins, affords handsome material.

21. *Elm, Red, or Slippery*,—(Ulmus fulva).—This is a widely diffused, but not very abundant tree. In the Atlantic slope, in our latitude, it is usually a shrub, but with us it attains the dimentions of a large tree. It often attains the height of 50 or 60 feet, and a diameter of 18 to 24 inches. It grows on

the richest lands of an uneven surface, and does well in elevated open situations.

The heart wood is coarse grained, and of a dull red tinge, whence the name. It is less compact, but more durable than that of the White Elm. It is said to be the best of American woods for making the blocks employed in the rigging of vessels. It makes excellent rails, which last long, and the wood is easily split. The bark is very mucilaginous, and contains sugar, gallic acid, and supertartrate of potash. Medically, it is said to be alterative, tonic, and diuretic, and is employed for the cure of herpetic and leprous eruptions. The leaves have been employed as food for the larvæ of the silk moth. The bark, small branches and leaves, macerated in water, give an abundant mucilage, used as a drink in coughs and rheums. This mucilage may be used instead of the roots of the Marsh Mallow in making emollient suppurative cataplasms.

22. *Elm, White, or Rock*,—(Ulmus Americana).—This is our most abundant Elm. Where it grows surrounded by other trees it has a lofty trunk, very clear of branches, attaining the height of 80 to 100 feet, and a diameter of from 4 to 6 feet. It is more often found on river banks, and in more or less open ground. Here it splits up into a great profusion of branches close to the ground.

The tree may be propagated by suckers, by layers and by grafting. It delights in low and humid situations, such as the rich bottoms along streams, where the soil is deep and fertile. It will grow, however, in any soil that is not too dry and barren. The foliage of this tree is the food of several kinds of insects, and its bark is pierced by others.

The wood of the White Elm is of a dark brown color, and liable to decay when exposed to the alternations of dryness and moisture. It may be used for piles, foundations for mills, and canal locks, and other structures which are always under water. When cut transversely, or obliquely to the fibers, it shows many fine undulations. It weighs, when perfectly dry, only 33 lbs. to the cubic foot. The bark, which is easily detached from the tree during 8 months of the year, is used for making bast mats, ropes, and the bottoms of chairs. The wood when burned affords a large amount of ash, which is rich in potash.

23. *Elm, Wahoo, or Witch*,—(Ulmus alata).—This is a small tree, not commonly exceeding 80 feet in height, and 9 or 10 inches in diameter. It is generally found on the banks of rivers.

The wood of this variety is fine grained, heavier, more compact, and stronger, than that of the White Elm. The wood is of a dull chocolate color, and is always in large proportion to the sap wood, In some parts of the country the wood is used for the naves of coach wheels, as it is tougher and heavier than that of either of the other species.

24. *Fir, or Spruce, Black*,—(Abies Nigra).—This tree has a variety of common names, being called in different sections, Black Fir, Black Spruce, and Yew Pine. It is a Fir. The tree is quite common in the higher and colder part of the State, growing on the banks of streams, and on cold mountain sides. It forms a handsome tree, some 60 to 70 feet high, and 2 to 3 feet in diameter. Since it grows mainly in the more inaccessible parts of the State, not much use has, as yet, been made of the timber.

Great numbers of this tree are to be found in suitable locations all through the Alleghanies, the foots of hills near them, and the deep, well shaded hollows of the higher plateau regions. In the region of country around the headwaters of the Gauley, Elk, and Cheat, vast numbers of this tree are to be found. For this reason the district in question is called by the natives the "Yew Pine Region," as they call the tree by this name.

According to Mr. Cecil Clay, President of the St. Lawrence Boom and Manufacturing Company, this tree will often cut 20,000 feet per acre, in this part of the country. Dense masses of it cover the mountains here, the trees growing clear and tall, with trunks several feet in diameter. The country is yet in the original forest, and millions of feet of fine fir timber can be obtained.

25. *Fir, Southern Balsam*,—(Abeis Fraseri).—This tree grows mainly on the highest points of the Alleghanies, and is more abundant to the south of us in Tennessee. From its inaccessible position, it is not used for timber. It is chiefly remarkable for the balsam which gathers in blisters under the bark,

and is used for medicinal purposes. It is found in the high mountains in northern Pocahontas, and in Pendleton and eastern Randolph.

26. *Gum, Black, or Sour*,—(Nyssa Multiflora).—This tree, called variously Black Gum, Yellow Gum, or Sour Gum, seldom rises above 40 or 50 feet, with a trunk 15 or 20 inches in diameter. It permits a somewhat wide range of situation, growing in some parts of the country on dry soil, and in others in wet places. In West Virginia the tree grows in both situations; in Tennessee it grows usually on rich, moist soils.

It may be propagated by seeds and by cutting or layers. The wood holds a middle rank between hard and soft woods. In trees exceeding 15 inches in diameter, frequently more than half the trunk is hollow. The fibres of most trees are closely united, and usually ascend in a perpendicular direction. The Gum is peculiar in this respect, the fibres being united in bundles, and interwoven like a braided cord. This gives it its peculiar toughness. Where it abounds, it is used for the naves of wheels employed for carrying heavy burdens. It is also used for the shaft heads of windmills, and for wooden bowls. As fuel, the wood burns with great slowness.

27. *Gum, Sweet*,—(Liquidambar Styraciflua).—This finds its most congenial home in wet, marshy places.

It forms a handsome and large tree. The leaves, when bruised, have a pleasant aromatic odor.

The wood is fine grained, but decays rather rapidly. It is difficult to split, and resists fire longer than any of our timbers. It is occasionally used for the same purposes as the Black Gum, and sawed into plank, is mainly employed in coarse work. It is compact, and is said to admit of a bright polish. It is sometimes used in cabinet work, and makes a passable article of furniture.

28. *Hemlock, Spruce*,—(Abies Canadensis).—This tree is much more common farther North than with us. It grows on rich mountains and table lands. It forms a large tree, but the timber is comparatively coarse grained and poor. The bark is useful for tanning. Dense strips of large Hemlock grow on the headwaters of the Gauley, &c., rivers.

29. *Hickory*,—(Carya).—Three species of this valuable tree grow abundantly with us. There are: 1st, the Scaly Bark Hickory,

carya alba; 2d, the White Hickory, carya tomentosa; and 3rd, the Red Hickory or Pignut, carya porcina. The common White Hickory (C. tomentosa), grows well on all soils of medium quality. It rarely attains a greater diameter than 18 inches, and grows by preference in dry woods. The wood of this tree is white to the core, hence the name. It is tough, and sometimes stringy, very elastic, hard, and of great weight.

When small, the shrub is used for barrel and hogshead hoops, and for casings, and for wythes for various purposes. It is exceedingly tough, and strong, but easy to split. The bark is useful for tying up grapevines, as it may be easily stripped off in spring, and kept supple under water.

The tree is worked up into axles for wagons, spokes and felloes for carriages, and for axe handles. When seasoned, it makes the best carpenters' mallets, and the most useful handles for chisels. However, when exposed to moisture, it is peculiarly liable to decay, and is also very subject to attacks from worms. Large quanties of the timber are worked up into chairs, &c.

The Scaly Bark Hickory, C. alba, is a much larger tree, and splits more readily. It grows 80 to 100 feet high, and 2½ to 3 feet thick.

The Red Hickory, or Pignut, like the last, prefers a rich soil on hillsides or river bottoms.

The Bitter Nut, C. amara, sometimes called Pignut, also, is a common tree. The wood is less valued than that of the others.

Both the Scaly Bark Hickory, and the Red Hickory, above mentioned, are not rare, and have timber resembling that of the Common White Hickory. They are used for the same purposes. Hickory makes the finest of all fuels. It burns rapidly, and gives out an intense heat. It is preferred for curing tobacco and bacon, not giving so strong a taste of creosote. The ashes of the Hickory are the richest of all in potash.

30. *Holly*,—(Ilex Opaca).—This is a beautiful evergreen tree, growing mainly on mountain streams in gravelly or sandy soil. Its ordinary height in favorable situations, is under 30 feet, with a diameter of 12 to 15 inches, and less. The wood is white, compact, of fine grain, and capable of a brilliant

polish. It is quite heavy, weighing, when dry, about 47 pounds to the cubic foot. Its principal use is for inlaying mahogany furniture, for turning into small boxes for druggists, and for small screws. When perfectly seasoned, it is very hard and unyielding, which makes it fitted for the pulleys used in ships. It takes dye of various colors well, and is used in imitating foreign woods. The bark, medicinally, is emetic and cathartic. Fifteen or twenty berries will induce vomiting, and act as a purgative.

31. *Hackberry*,—(Celtis Occidentalis).—The Hackberry, or Celtis Occidentalis, var. crassifolia, is a common tree west of the Alleghanies. It sometimes attains a height of 80 feet, with a trunk of the very disproportionate diameter of 18 or 20 inches.

It prefers a cool, shady situation, and a deep, fertile soil, or along the borders of rivers and among other trees. Its wood is of little value, from its weakness and liability to decay, when exposed to alternations of wet and dry conditions. It is compact, and fine grained, however, though not heavy. Sawed in a direction parallel, or oblique to its fibres, it shows the fine undulations seen in the Locust and Elm. In some parts of the country, the timber is employed in roofs for the covering which supports shingles. As it is elastic, and may be easily divided, farmers use it sometimes for the bottoms of chairs, and Indians use it for making baskets. Being straight grained, free from knots, and wrought with the greatest ease, it is sometimes used in fencing.

32. *Ironwood*,—(Ostrya Virginica).—This tree is also called Hop Hornbeam, or Lever Wood. It may be distinguished by the hop-like appendages, containing small nuts, which the tree possesses. It forms a small tree, with brownish furrowed bark, and leaves like those of the Birch. It is common in rich woods. The wood is extremely hard and tough, which properties render it unequalled for handspikes, and other purposes requiring these properties in a high degree.

33. *Locust, Common*,—(Robinia Pseudacacia).—The Common Locust, in favorable situations, attains the height of 80 or 90 feet, and sometimes exceed four feet in diameter. Ordinarily the tree does not exceed half these dimensions. It abounds

in West Virginia. The soil in which it grows best is a rather rich sandy loam, and to attain any considerable size, it must have considerable room, and an airy but sheltered position, free from the fury of the winds. It will thrive for a few years, even on poor shallow soils, but soon decays at the heart, and does not attain any size. This is due to the rapid extraction from the soil, of all its nutriment by the large roots, which run near the surface. The only trees that will make timber on such thin soils, are those of the Pine family. The simplest and best mode of propogating it, is by the seeds.

The wood of the Locust is of a greenish yellow color, marked with brown veins. It is very hard, and compact, and is capable of a very high polish. It has great strength, with but little elasticity, its most valuable property being the resistance to decay which it exhibits, this being greater than that of almost any other wood. When newly cut it weighs 63 pounds 3 ounces per cubic foot; half dry, 56½ pounds, or, according to others, only 46. M. Hartig, the German dendrologist, places its value for fuel, when compared with the Beech (Fagus sylvatica), as 12 to 15. For duration, he places it next below the Oak (Quercus robur).

There are at least three popular varieties of the Common Locust, distinguished by the color of the heart wood. These are:

1. *Red Locust.*—With the heart red, and esteemed as by far the most beautiful and valuable timber. Posts of this variety, perfectly seasoned before they are put in the ground, are estimated to last 40 years, or twice as long as those of the White Locust.

2. *Green or Yellow Locust.*—This is the most common variety, being known by its greenish yellow heart, and it is held to be next to the red Locust.

3. *White Locust.*—This has a white heart, and is considered the least valuable.

All the above mentioned variations, are supposed to be caused by differences of soil and situation. In naval architecture, the Locust is much esteemed by American shipwrights. It enters into the upper and lower parts of the frames of vessels. In civil architecture in this country, owing to its scarcity, it is not much used. It is more particularly applied to the support of sills. It has been extensively used in cabinet making, and many small wares. The roots of the Locust are very sweet, and afford an extract which may be substituted for licorice. The flowers have been employed medicinally as an anti-spasmodic.

34. *Locust, Honey*,--(Gleditschia triacanthos).—This in favorable situations, attains a height of 70 or 80 feet, with a trunk 3 or 4 feet in diameter. The tree generally grows in association with the Black Walnut, Red Elm, Common Locust, &c. It is never found except where the soil is good, and its presence is a sign of fertility.

The wood, when dry, weighs 52 pounds to the cubic foot. It is very hard, and splits with great difficulty. Its grain is coarse, and its pores more open, than those of the Common Locust. It is of very little use for timber, and can be only considered as an ornamental tree.

35. *Linden, or Linn*,—(Tilia Americana).—This tree bears various names, being called, the American Lime Tree, Linden, or Basswood. In size it is one of the finest forest trees. It often rises more than 80 feet in height, and is frequently more than 4 feet in diameter, with a straight, uniform body. It prefers a rich, loose, dark soil, on the borders of lakes and rivers, and in moist bottoms, which are little subject to inundation. It may be propogated from seeds, by cuttings, and by grafting.

The wood, when dry, weighs only 35 pounds per cubic foot. When seasoned, it is of a light brown hue. It is soft, easily worked, and is often sawed into boards, which do not warp. In some places it is used for the panels of carriage doors, and the seats of chairs. It is frequently turned into various utensils, and carved into ornamental work. The cellular integument, may be separated from the epidermis, and formed into ropes. The greatest value which it has, is for making firkin staves. It is extremely easy to decay, and hence cannot be used in building. It may be reduced to a pulp, and made into paper. The yonng shoots and twigs are very glutinous, and afford considerable nutriment, and are used in some sections, as food for cattle in winter when forage is scarce.

36. *Maple, Sugar*,—(Acer saccharimum).—The Sugar,or Rock

Maple, as it is sometimes called, is one of our most valuable trees. In our new State the vast numbers of the trees of this species affords large amounts of sugar, which yields a considerable revenue to the inhabitants.

In favorable situations the trees sometimes grow to the height of 70 or 80 feet, and attain the diameter of 2 to 4 feet. The trunk is generally straight, though often studded with wens or excrescences. There is a variety of this tree which in some respects differs from the common Sugar tree. This is called the Black Sugar Maple (or A. S. Var. nigum). The leaves of this tree are of a darker green, thicker texture, and have blunter lobes than the Rock or Sugar Maple. Both trees grow together, and are alike in all other respects.

The natural habitat of the Sugar Maple is the steep and shady banks of rivers which rise in mountanous regions, and in all elevated regions where the soil is cold and humid, free, deep, and fertile, and not too moist.

The wood of the Sugar Maple, when it has been exposed to the light for some time, takes on a rosy tinge. Its grain is fine and close, and when polished its lustre is silky. It is very strong and heavy, but is not durable when exposed to alternations of moisture and dryness. The northern wood weighs, when dry, 46 lbs. per cubic foot, and is heavier than that grown south. It makes, when dry, a fuel equal to the oak. The timber requires two or three years to become perfectly seasoned. It may then be used for axletrees, spokes, mill-cogs, chairs and cabinet work. The wood of this tree exhibits several accidental forms in the arrangement of its fibre, which are utilized in making beautiful articles of cabinet work, and furniture, such as bedsteads, writing desks, inlaying mahogany and black-walnut in bureaus, piano-fortes, and for veneering-slabs, &c. The first of these is *Curled Maple.* The undulations, or medullary rays of this variety, like those of the Red-flowered Maple, are lustrous, and in one light apappear darker, and in another, lighter than the rest of the wood. Sometimes the zig-zag lines are crossed by beautiful veins, but unfortunately the lustre of these shades disappears by long exposure to the light and air.

The second is *Bird's-Eye Maple.* This variety exhibits small, whitish spots, or eyes, not over one-tenth of an inch in diameter, sometimes occurring a little way apart, and sometimes close together. The more numerous these spots the more valuable the wood. They are seen only in old trees, which are still sound; and seem to come from a bending of the fibres across the grain. To get the finest effect, the wood should be sawed as near as possible parallel with the concentric circles.

In addition to the above named varieties, two other kinds occur in the *Wens*. The most valuable variety is called *Variegated Maple Knot*. It presents an assemblage of shades, agreeably disposed, sometimes like Arabic letters, which make the wood well fitted for fancy work, and from its scarcity it commands high prices. The other variety is called *Silver-White Maple Knot*. This shows a silvery lustre by the arrangement of its fibres, and though more common than the other, is highly prized and used for the same purposes.

The ashes of the Sugar Maple are rich in alkalies, and it has been said that they furnish four-fifths of the potash exported from the United States to Europe. In the Torges of Maine, New Hampshire, &c where this tree grows, its charcoal is preferred to that of any other wood. The ripening of the leaves in fall causes them to take on the most beautiful colors. In the mountain counties of the State there are enormous numbers of this tree, and in some districts it forms half the timber.

37. *Maple, Silver*,—(Acer dasycarpum).—The White, or Silver Maple, in good situations, attains the height of 30 to 50 feet, with a trunk 2 to 4 feet in diameter, but sometimes has a diameter as 8 to 9 feet. It is found in a sandy loam on the banks of such rivers as have limpid waters, with a gravelly bed, and is rare in miry, black soils.

The wood of this tree is white and of a fine texture, but is softer and lighter than that of any other Maple in the United States, and from its want of strength and durability, it is but little used. When dry it weighs 38 lbs. to the cubic foot. It is sometimes used in cabinet making, instead of the Holly, for inlaying furniture of mahogany, cherry, &c., but soon changes color on exposure to light. It may be used, for want of a better. in making wooden bowls. Its charcoal affords a more uniform heat, and of longer duration than any other. The inner bark is sometimes used for domestic dying, to produce a black with copperas.

38. *Maple, Red*---(Acer rubrum).---This does not attain the size of the Sugar Maple. The ordinary height does not exceed 50 or 60 feet, but in the "Maple Swamps" of New Jersey, it attains the height of 70 or 80 feet, with a trunk 3 or 4 feet in diameter. This tree flourishes in grounds which are sometimes overflowed. In the East, where it attains its greatest size, it is found only on streams and in miry swamps. Singular to say, west of the Alleghanies, it is seen growing on high ground with the Oaks and Walnuts, but here it does not grow so large as in the eastern swamps.

The wood of this tree, when dry, weighs 44 pounds to the cubic foot, and when green, is soft and full of watery matter. This tree, like others which grow in wet places, has a large proportion of sap wood, and in this case, the heart wood sends rays into the sap wood. The wood has but little strength, is liable to decay when exposed to alternations of moisture and dryness, is apt to ferment, and is exposed to attacks of insects. Yet it is solid and close grained, and for many purposes preferred by workmen to other kinds of wood. It is principally used for the manufacture of chairs, saddle-trees, shoe lasts, broom handles and many other domestic articles. It is easily wrought in the lathe, and acquires, by polishing, a glossy and silky surface. It sometimes happens that in very old trees, the grain of the wood, instead of following a perpendicular direction, is undulated, and this variety bears the name of *Curled Maple*. This singular arrangement is never found in young trees, and it is less conspicuous in the centre of the tree than near the bark. But trees with this feature are rare. The serpentine direction of the fibres produces, when polished, a most beautiful effect of light and shade. These effects are made more striking, if, after smoothing the wood, we rub it with a little sulphuric acid, and afterwards with linseed oil. Bedsteads are made of this wood, which exceed in richness of lustre those of the finest imported woods. One of the most constant uses to which the curled maple is applied is the making of gunstocks. For this it is unsurpassed, since it unites elegance and lightness, with toughness and strength. The cellular matter of the inner bark, boiled with copperas, gives an intense blue black color; with alum, it is used in dyeing black.

39. *Mulberry. Red,*—(Morus rubra).—The Red Mulberry sometimes attains the height of 60 or 70 feet, with a trunk having a diameter of 2 feet, when growing in the forests, but in open situations its statue is low, and the thickness is proportionally increased. This tree has a great tendency to sport. It may be propagated by seeds, by cuttings, grafting, &c. It will grow in a great variety of soils, and situations, but succeeds best in a rich, deep soil, in sheltered valleys.

The wood is of a yellow hue, approaching lemon yellow. It is fine grained, compact and light. It possesses strength and solidity, and when properly seasoned, is almost as durable as the Locust. In the dock-yards of Baltimore, Philadelphia, &c., it is employed in the construction of both the upper and lower frames of vessels, for knees, floor timbers, &c. It is preferred to every other kind of wood except the Locust, for trenails.

Oak,—(Quercus).—The number of species of Oak in the State is very great. All the Oaks growing in the Appalachian belt, are to be found here, and many of them attain here their greatest size and perfection as timber trees. The Oaks grow all over the State, reaching, perhaps, their greatest development in the central and southern parts. They form the bulk of our timber, and certainly the most valuable portion of it. In speaking of them it will not be necessary to dwell on each species, as they all resemble more or less, the most valuable of the genus, viz.: the White Oak.

40. *White Oak,*—(Quercus Alba).—This valuable tree is one of the most abundant and the largest trees in the State. It attains the height of 100 feet, and more than 6 feet in diameter. In the counties on the Little Kanawha river, and to the South of the Great Kanawha, in Boone, Logan, &c., it attains magnificent proportions, and is found in great numbers. In dense woods it grows to $\frac{2}{3}$ and $\frac{3}{4}$ of its height clear of limbs. It grows in a great variety of soil and in very different exposures. It does best in deep, rich alluvial bottoms.

The wood is the most valuable of all the Oaks. The timber is better than that of trees grown farther north. It is strong, compact, hard, durable, elastic, combining most of the valuable properties found in timber.

It is extensively used in making all the parts of wagons, except the axles. For plough handles and beams it is indispensable. It is the only timber east of the Mississippi which will make staves suitable for vessels containing wine and spirituous liquors, not only on account of the tightness of the casks, but because it gives no disagreeable taste to the liquor. —(Resources of Tenn., p. 83).

Owing to this fact, on all the navigable streams and railroads, a heavy business is done in staves for casks, pipes, &c. Large quanties are shipped to the eastern markets, to Europe, the West Indies, and France.

The young trees of the White Oak may be rived into thin splits, which are very tough and elastic, enabling them to be used in basket making, &c. They may also be used for some kinds of hoops, as for tobacco hogsheads. For building purposes and fencing, it makes admirable timber. For floors it is only surpassed by the Ash.

41. *Post Oak*,—(Quercus obtusiloba).—This tree, also called Rough, or Box White Oak, belongs to the White Oak section of the genus. It grows on dry, thin, and gravelly soil, forming a small tree, with timber not so elastic as the White Oak, but more durable. Being solid, tough, close-grained, and hard to split, it is for some purposes more valuable than even the White Oak, especially for railroad ties, &c.

42. *Bur Oak*,—(Quercus macrocarpa).—This forms a handsome middle sized tree, belonging to the White Oak section. It grows in rich soil, and has timber of the same general character with the White Oak.

43. *Chestnut Oak*,—(Quercus Prinus L.).—This tree may be taken as a type of another section of Oaks, which is called the Chestnut Oak section. It is marked by the want of lobing in the leaves, which causes them to resemble more or less those of the Chestnut.

This tree does well on good soil, but delights in thin rocky, or gravelly ridges and benches. It grows from 60 to 80 feet high. The wood is tough and durable, being equal to White Oak for many purposes. Its greatest value, perhaps, is for tanning purposes, yielding a large supply of bark, which is richer in Tannin than any other tree. The leather made by it commands the highest prices, as it is the most solid and durable known.

A variety of this tree growing in rich soil, and quite common, is called Yellow Chestnut Oak. It has leaves more like the Chestnut than any other.

44. *The Swamp White Oak*,—(Quercus bicolor).—This is another of the Oaks belonging to the Chestnut Oak section. It forms a tall tree, common in low grounds.

45. *Willow Oak*,—(Quercus phellos).—This tree is remarkable for its willow-like leaves. It forms a tree from 30 to 80 feet high, growing on low, sandy ground. It is found in small amounts, but furnishes a valuable timber.

46. *Laurel or Shingle Oak*,—(Quercus imbricaria).—This tree grows to the height of 30 to 50 feet, being found on barrens and in open woodlands. It is used mainly for shingles, whence the name. Found only in small amounts.

47. *Black Jack Oak*,—(Quercus nigra).—This tree grows in poor and thin soil by preference, but will flourish in good soil also. It never grows over 30 to 40 feet high. It has a tough, thick bark, and possesses but little durability, decaying in a few years. It furnishes an ash very rich in potash. Otherwise than as a fuel it has no value.

48. *Spanish Oak*,—(Quercus falcata).—This tree is not very abundant. It grows in dry, sandy soil, and attains the height of 60 to 80 feet.

The wood is tough and valuable, making good staves for some purposes. Its chief value is in the bark, which is excellent for tanning.

49. *Scarlet Oak*,—(Quercus coccinea).—This species is common, growing on moist soil. Its timber is about equal in value to the Red Oak, and is used for the same purposes.

50. *Red Oak*,—(Quercus rubra).—The Red Oak does not grow quite so large as the White Oak. It is found both in rich and poor soil, and is quite common.

The timber is rather course and is not so durable or useful as that of the White Oak. Its rigidity and comparative freedom from warping, give it value for sills and house logs. It makes fine slabs for roofing, and is the chief material for the staves of tobacco hogsheads, and flour barrels. The bark is valuable for tanning.

51. *Black Oak*,—(Quercus tinctoria.)—The Black Oak grows from 40 to 80 feet high. It grows both in rich and poor soil. This is thought to be one of the most valuable in the forest for making boards. Its bark also is highly esteemed by the dyers and tanners. It rives easily, and the boards made from it, when nailed on a roof, are not inclined to warp. Great quanties are used for hogshead staves and flour barrels. It is more durable than any of the Oaks, except the White Oak and Post Oak. (Resources of Tenn., page 85.)

52. *Pin Oak*,—(Quercus palustris).—This forms a medium sized tree, growing in low grounds, and is rather common. The wood is hard and heavy, though rather coarse. From the great thickness of its medullary plates, it shows beautiful graining when cut across, or obliquely to the fibres, The wood is considered better than that of the Red Oak.

Besides the above named Oaks, others of smaller size, and of less importance, are to be found, which need not be named here.

53. *Pine, Yellow*,—(Pinus mitis).—The Yellow Pine grows on high ground principally, abounding on poor sandstone soils of the ridges and mountains. It will grow with rapidity on soil too poor to produce other vegetation. It grows to the height of 60 to 90 feet, with a diameter of 2 to 4 feet.

The timber is valuable for many purposes, especially domestic ones. As it is fine grained, durable, and strong, it has few superiors. This tree, so abundant in the Eastern States, and forming so important a source of revenue there, is with us of far less importance, since it does not grow in such abundance as to constitute an important timber tree. It is found in the largest amounts in the sandy and rocky ridges of the plateau districts, considerable quantities growing in Raleigh and the adjoining counties, as well as in Wayne, Logan, and Lincoln. More or less of it is scattered all over the State.

54. *Pine, White*,—(Pinus strobus).—This tree grows in the State on elevated grounds, at 2,000 feet, and over. It attains the height of 120 feet and more, with a diameter of several feet. Some idea of the fine development which this tree attains in the eastern part of the State, may be gained from the statements concerning it made by Mr. Cecil Clay, President of the St. Lawrence Boom and Manufacturing Company

of Roncerverte, Greenbrier county. Mr. Clay is engaged in developing the White Pine district along the Greenbrier river, on its upper waters, which is the only region of the State producing any large quantity of this pine. He says: "The "ordinary run of cuts this winter (1876,) is from four to seven "16 feet cuts per tree, averaging five cuts to the 1,000 feet. "There are several hundred million feet of good White Pine "lumber in this district. The White Pine growing, as it does "here, at the altitude of 2,000 to 2,500 feet, has a climate "about like that of lower Pennsylvania, and has much like-"ness to the Susquehanna pine. Where the White Pine grows, "it takes the ground to itself, and but little of other timber is "found with it. It grows in several localities through the "valley (Greenbrier.) On Deer and Sitlington's creeks are "100,000,000 feet. On Knapp's creek and branches, another "100,000,000; and Spice, Laurel, and Davy's Runs, with An-"thony's creek, and some outlying patches, would yield a "third 100,000,000. This pine timber is perhaps a little "heavier than the Pennsylvania pine, but is soft and smooth "to work. It is generally a sound, red-knot timber, with "remarkably thin sapwood. This often does not average over "half an inch in a lot of 1,000 logs. As much as 40,000 feet "can sometimes be cut on an acre."

This wood, as is well known, possesses great value on account of its great lightness, softness, and freedom from resinous matter. For the manufacture of goods boxes, mantles, shutters, window sash, and for ceiling, it is mnch used.

55. *Pine, Black*,—(Pinus sigida).—This tree, also called Pitch Pine, is found in the same localities in the east with the Yellow Pines. It does not grow so tall or large as the latter, and prefers thin, sandy ridges. It is a tall and slender tree, from 30 to 70 feet high, and from 18 to 2 feet in diamter. The bark is very rough and dark, hence the name. The wood is hard and very rich in turpentine

56. *The Poplar*,—(Liriodendron tulipifera).—This is by far the finest tree in our forests. Nowhere does the Poplar attain greater dimensions than in West Virginia. It often reaches the height of 120 to 140 feet, and the diameter of 7 to 8, and 9 feet, with a distance of 80 feet to the first limb. Several trees are reported as 10 and 11 feet in diameter in this State. It

delights in deep loamy and extremely fertile soils, such as are found in rich bottoms and on rivers or swamps. It will grow, however, on soil of different kinds, but has its timber affected accordingly. A deep sandy loam seems best for it. To attain the greatest size, it must be sheltered from the high winds, and at the same time have light and air enough to ripen its wood. It is generally propagated by the seeds.

The timber, though classed among the light woods, is yet much heavier than the true Poplar, for this tree is properly called Tulip tree, and not Poplar. Its grain is fine, rather compact, polishes well and is easily wrought. When dry, a cubic foot weighs 25 lbs. It affords excellent charcoal, yielding 22 per cent. The heart wood, perfectly seasoned, long resists the action of the weather, and is rarely attacked by insects. When not perfectly seasoned, however, it is apt to warp under alternations of dryness and moisture. The nature of the soil on which it grows has a striking effect on the color and quality of the wood. Mechanics distinguish three kinds, "White," "Blue," and "Yellow." No external marks will distinguish them positively. In general, the White Poplar grows on dry, gravelly, elevated ground, and has a branchy summit, with a small amount of heart wood. The grain is coarser and harder, and the wood decays more rapidly. The Blue has the same general character.

The Yellow Poplar is by far the finest kind, and has all the qualities required for a great variety of uses. It would take too much space merely to enumerate all of these.

It is used extensively in the interior of houses, for shingles and for weather-boarding. Large quantities are used in making trunks covered with cloth or skins; for tables, bedsteads, seats of chairs, &c.; for the supports of veneers, inner work of bureaus, &c.; in winnowing machines, for bowls, broom handles, rails, and planking for fences, for the backing of picture frames, looking glasses, &c., it is employed.

The bark of the tree is considered by some hardly inferior as an antiseptic and tonic to the Cinchona. The aromatic principle resides in a resinous matter in the bark, and when used stimulates the intestinal canal and acts as a gentle cathartic. In many instances the stomach cannot support it unlese accompanied with a few drops of laudanum. The bark mixed with an equal amount of Dogwood, and steeped in whisky, forms a tincture used as a remedy for intermittent fever. The bark reduced to powder and given to horses, is a pretty sure remedy for worms.

The Poplar is one of the most generally diffused and abundant trees in the State.

Great quantities of the finest trees are to be found in the central and southern counties. Perhaps some of the largest timber is to be found on the affluents of the New and Kanawha rivers, and the Big Sandy.

57. *Red Bud*,—(Cercis Canadensis).—This tree, though small, is quite common, and deserves mention for the great beauty of its wood. It does not often surpass the height of 20 feet, or diameter of 12 inches. It grows along the banks of streams, in a deep, free, sandy soil, rather rich than poor.

The wood is very hard and beautifully veined, or rather blotched and waved, with black, green, and yellow spots, on a greyish ground. When seasoned it takes a beautiful polish, and weighs nearly 50 lbs. to the cubic foot. It would serve well to saw into veneers· The bark and young branches are used to dye wool of a nankin color. The flowers are used by the French Canadians in salads and pickles, and might be fried with butter or fritters.

58. *Sassafras*,—(Sassafras officinale).—The Sassafras, west of the Alleghanies, is often a large tree, attaining in West Virginia the height of 70 or 80 feet, and a diameter of more than 3 feet.

The tree will grow in any free soil, rather moist than dry, and is generally propagated from seed. The wood of the large Sassafras tree is of a reddish cast, and has a somewhat compact grain, but is quite weak, breaking easily. Stripped of its bark, it resists decay well, and may be used for the posts and rails of rural fences. It has almost no odor after drying thoroughly. It is not a good fuel, as it snaps too much. The wood imparts to wool a very durable orange color. Medicinally, the wood, roots, and bark of the Sassasfras, are considered to be an excellent stimulant and sudorific. A decoction of Sassafras chips, sold by druggists, is well known as a remedy for scorbutic affections. The bark and pith of the young twigs, abound in a mucilage very pure, and like that of Okra. This mucilage is peculiarly mild and lubricatory, and has been used with much benefit in dysentery and catarrh, and especially as a lotion in the inflammatory stages of ophthalmia. The flowers are considered as stomachic, and purifying to the blood, as is the root, when formed into an infusion, and drunk as tea.

59. *Sour Wood.*—(Oxydendendrum arboreum).—This is a tree, growing from 15 to 40 feet high, and attaining occasionally a diameter of 2 to 2½ feet. It has a large proportion of sap wood, which is white and rather soft. The heart wood is of a pale, pinkish color. It is not abundant enough to make timber of any importance. It grows mainly along the Alleghanies, in rich woods.

60. *Sycamore.*—(Platanus occidentalis).—This is one of the largest forest trees, attaining the height of 120 feet, and occasionally the diameter of 7 or 8 feet, although 3 and 4 feet is the usual size. This tree grows along streams, or in the vicinity of them, since it is a moisture loving tree, and delights in an alluvial soil. It takes a good polish, and sometimes the grain is wavy and strikingly beautiful. It speedily decays when exposed to the weather, and will not split. The old trees are apt to become hollow, and then attain great diameter, even as much as 11 and 12 feet.

61. *Walnut, Black*,—(Juglans nigra).—This fine tree is one of the more important sources of revenue in our forest products. It is generally diffused in rich soils all over the State. It sometimes attains the height of 80 to 90 feet, and the great diameter of 9 feet (this has been actually measured), but is quite commonly 50 to 80 feet high, and 3 to 6 feet in diameter. It grows in the richest soils, perferring deep calcareous loams, full of vegetable matter. It will grow at any elevation, but is especially abundant in the plateau region, where the trees grow 50 and 60 feet without limbs, and 5 to 6 feet in diameter. The exquisite rich, dark brown color of the wood, its hardness, strength, and the high polish which it can take, will always give it value for making the finer kinds of furniture. Among other uses, it is extensively employed in making counters, railings, and finishing work on the interior of houses; also, for gun stocks, picture frames, coffins, &c.

Stumps and knots, when worked up into veneering slabs, have great beauty and value, on account of the ornamental curling of the grain. The bark is used in dying brown.

In the amount and value of her walnut timber, our State is rivalled only by Tennessee among the Appalachian States.

62. *Walnut, White*—(Juglans cinerea).—This tree grows on the margins of streams, and is sometimes found on rich northern slopes. It is not so large a tree as the Black Walnut, and in West Virginia is not nearly so abundant. The wood is much lighter in color, having a reddish tinge. It is durable, but not strong, and is used in some ornamental work. The bark is used in some cases, in dyeing a brown, and a laxative extract is gathered from the inner part of it.

63. *Willow, White,*—(Salix alba).—This is a quite common tree, growing to the height of 60 to 80 feet. No use is made of the wood.

The above are the more important of the timber and other trees, found in the State. The enumeration does not pretend to be a complete list of our forest trees, and might be extended considerably by including in it, those trees and shrubs which, though generally diffused, are of no importance, on account of their small size, or inferior wood.

The following partial list of small trees and shrubs is given to illustrate the character of our smaller growths:

The Alder—Both the *Mountain Alder*, (Alnus viridis,) and the *Smooth Alder*, (A. serrulata), form shrubs, and grow along streams, the former, as its name implies, being confined to the mountains. *The Crab Apple*, (Pyrus coronaria), forms a small tree, sometimes 20 feet high. *The Chinquapin*, (Castanea pumila), sometimes forms a tree 20 feet high. *The Elder*, (Sambucus Canadensis), bears a berry from which a palatable wine is made. It is a small shrub. *The Grape* (vitis), of several species is found. *The Fox Grape*, (V. vulpina), grows close to the banks of streams, and produces, a large, highly odorous, and pleasant tasting berry. *The Summer Grape*, (V. aestivalis), and the *Winter Grape*, (V. cordifolia), are very common.

The Grape merits here a more particular mention, since the size, and mode of growth shown in the wild kinds, is some indication of the degree of success, with which the cultivated kinds may be raised in our soil and climate. So far as the abundance and size of the kinds growing spontaneously with us indicate anything, the conditions for grape culture are very favorable. Vines are not uncommon which attain a diameter of 6 and 7 inches. Some 10 inches in diameter are known.

One well authenticated case is reported of a vine which grew on the banks of Elk river, in Braxton county, and which attained the great diameter of 21 inches.

The Haw, Black, (Viburnum prunifolium), and the *Scarlet Fruited Haw*, (Crataegus coccinea), are quite common.. *The Mountain Laurel*, (Kalmia latifolia), and the *Great Laurel*, or *Rhododendron*, (Rhododendron maximum), are exceedingly abundant in the rocky hills and on the mountain sides. The close-grained, heavy, easily worked wood of the Rhododendron, is largely used in the manufacture of small wares, considerable amounts are shipped north from the counties on the Gauley and New River, and the wood is regularly quoted in the Baltimore market. The *Magnolia*, or *Umbrella Tree*, (Magnolia Umbrella), is not rare, and attains the size of a small tree. *Leatherwood*, (Dirca palustris), also is found. This has a very brittle soft wood, with an exceedingly tough bark, which is used for thongs. It is a small shrub. *Papaw*, (Asimina triloba), is very common on rich alluvial soils. It grows to the height of 10 to 20 feet, and has an edible pleasant fruit. *Persimmon* (*Diospyra Virginiana*), with a hard dark wood, and edible fruit grows to the height of 20 to 60 feet *Service*, or *Shad Bush* (Amelanchier Canadensis), is a very variable shrub or small tree. *Spice Wood*, (*Lindera Benzoin*), is found with highly aromatic wood. *Sumach, Staghorn*, (*Rhus typhina*), sometimes grows to the size of a small tree, with handsome wood. *Sumach, Common*, (R. glabra), is very widely diffused, and valuable in tanning and dyeing. *Willow, Black* (*Salix nigra*), is a small tree with beautiful yellow variegated heart wood. This attains the height of 15 to 25 feet along streams. *Yellow Willow*, (*Salix Viminalis*), useful for basket making, is not rare, also the Common Willow (S. longifolia .

MEDICINAL PLANTS.

The following list of Medicinal Plants growing in West Virginia, was taken from the transactions of the Med. Soc'y. of

W. Va., for 1867 and 1871. These plants were reported on by a committee, of which Dr. A. S. Todd, of Wheeling, was chairman. To him we are indebted for it. The botanical terms used are those employed by Gray, while the common names are those used in West Virginia:

1. Achillea millefolium (*Milfoil*). 2. Acorus Calamus (*Sweet Flag*). 3. Aletris farinosa (*Unicorn*, or *CholicRoot*). 4. Alnus serrulata (*Smooth Alder*). 5. Apocynum androsaemifolium (*Dogsbane*). 6. Archangelica atropurpurea (*Master Root*). 7. Artemisia Absinthium (*Common Wormwood*). 8. Aralia hispida (*Dwarf Elder*). 9. Arisaema triphyllum (*Indian Turnip*). 10. Aristolochia serpentaria (*Virginia Snake Root*). 11. Asarum Canadense (*Wild Ginger*). 12. Asclepias cornuti (*Common Milkweed*). 13. Asclepias incarnata (*Swamp Milkweed*). 14. Asclepias tuberosa (*Pleurisy Root*). 15. Baptisia tinctoria (*Wild Indigo*). 16. Cassia Marylandica (*Wild Senna*). 17. Ceanothus Americanus (*New Jersey Tea*). 18. Chimaphila Umbellata (*Pipsissewa*). 19. Chenopodium Botrys (*Jerusalem Oak*). 20. Comptonia asplenifolium (*Sweet Fern*). 21. Cornus florida (*Dogwood*). 22. Corydalis formosa (*Turkey Corn*). 23. Cypripedium parviflorum (*Small Yellow Ladies' Slipper*). 24. Cypripedium pubescens (*Large Yellow Ladies' Slipper*). 25. Datura Stramonum (*Jamestown Weed*). 26. Daucus Carota (*Wild Carrot*). 27. Epigaea repens (*Trailing Arbutus*). 28. Eupatorium perfoliatum *Boneset*).). 29. Galium aparine (*Goose Grass*). 30. Gaultheria procumbus (*Creeping Winter Green*). 31. Gentiana puberula (*Gentian Blue*). 32. Geranium maculatum (*Spotted Crane's bill*). 33. Hepatica triloba (*Liverwort*). 34. Hydrastis Canadensis (*Yellow Root*). 35. Hamamelis Virginica (*Witch Hazel*). 36. Juniperus Sabina (*Savin*). 37. Inula Helenium (*Elecampane*). 38. Symplocarpus foetidus (*Skunk Cabbage*). 39. Juglaus cinerea (*Butternut*). 40. Lappa Officinalis (*Burdock*). 41. Liatris spicata (*Button Snake Root*). 42. Liriodendron tulipitera (*Tulip Tree*; or *Poplar*). 43. Lobelia inflata (*Indian Tobacco*). 44. Lindera Benzoin (*Spicewood*). 45. Marrubium Vulgare (*Horehound*). 46. Mentha viridis (*Spearmint*). 47. Monarda punctata (*Horsemint*). 48. Nepeta Glechoma (*Ground Ivy*). 49. Nymphaea odorata (*White Water Lily*). 50. Conopholis Americana (*Beech Drops*). 51.

Aralia quinquefolia (*Ginseng*). 52. Pinus strobus (*White Pine*). 53. Phytolaccha decandra (*Poke weed*). 54. Polygala Senega (*Seneca Snake Root*). 55. Podophyllum peltatum (*May Apple*). 56. Prunus Serotina (*Wild Cherry*). 57. Ptelea trifoliata (*Trefoil*). 58. Polygonatum biflorum (*Small Solomon's Seal*). 59. Ranunculus bulboses (*Crowfoot*). 60. Rumex crispus and R. conglomeratûs (*Curled Dock*, and *Narrow Leaved Dock*). 61. Rubus villosus (*Blackberry*). 62. Salix alba (*White Willow*). 63. Sabbatia angularis (*American Centaury*). 64. Sassafras officinale (*Sassafras*). 65. Solanum dulcamera (*Bitter-Sweet*). 66. Sambucus Canadensis (*Elder.*) 67. Sanguinaria Canadensis (*Blood Root*). 68. Taraxicum Dens Leonis (*Dandelion*). 70. Viburnum opulus (*High Cranberry*). 71. Verbascum thapsus (*Mullein*). 72. Veratrum viride (*White Hellebore*). 73. Veronica Virginica (*Culver's Root*). 74. Zanthoxylum Americanum (*Prickly Ash*). 75. Cimicifuga racemosa (*Black Snake Root*). 76. Lycopus Virginicus (*Bugle Weed*).

The large amount of woodland, the great variety of soil and exposures in the State, would lead one to expect to find here a great number of the plants which delight in a virgin soil.—As many of the medicinal plants of the cooler portions of the temperate zone are of this character, perhaps no State of equal size can present a greater variety or larger amounts of these. In many parts of this section, where farming is carried on on a small scale, and there is a great deal of "wild lands," the people suppliment the products of their small patches of tillable land by gathering the medicinal plants for sale. Of course only those plants are thus collected which meet with a sure sale. These are such as employed on a large scale in the manufacture of medicines, or are exported.

A good deal of Blood Root, and of the different varieties of Snake Root, is gathered in the State, especially in the northern part. In the southern counties a great deal of Ginseng (Aralia), is collected. With many of the people of the back counties, the collecting of this plant forms an important business. In Lincoln, Logan, &c., entire families in summer leave their homes and camp out during the whole season. They, with their dogs and guns, make long jounrneys in search of the plant, going even into the mountains of remote eastern counties, such as Pocahontas, &c. Many tons of this material are thus gathered, whose ultimate destination is China. When green, it sells for 50 cents per pound; washed and dried in the sun it commands from $1,00 to $1,25 and $1,50, according to the demands for it.

CHAPTER VIII.

TIMBER—ITS DISTRIBUTION AND DEVELOPMENT.

BY WM. W. FONTAINE.

In West Virginia, as in most thinly and newly settled States, which possess fine forest lands, the first source of income which becomes available, is the timber. Many causes conspire to induce the new settler to turn first to forest products, among the most important of which is the necessity of removing the wood from the soil, in order to prepare for the plough.

He is especially tempted to fell his forests, when, as with us, much of the timber is of good quality, and of the kind most used in the large manufacturing cities of the adjoining States.

Indeed, the only cause which has prevented the almost total demolition of our woodlands, has been the impossibility of getting much of the lumber to market. West Virginia has had much to complain of in her lack of means of transportation, but it is a question, whether in the near future, she will not be more than repaid for any previous lack of revenue from her timbers, by having been compelled to retain them, until from the rapid consumption of the forests in the adjoining States, she will obtain something like an adequate return for them. Indeed, it is not too much to say that ere long, it will pay to build short lines of narrow-gauge railroads to develop the timber alone, of favored districts. That this time is not far off is shown by the greatly decreased exportation of the principal timber producing sections. Of late years, we have seen the lumbermen of Michigan and Maine, investing in the pine forests of Florida and Alabama, and the vast amount of lumber shipped from Pensacola and other Southern ports, points to the speedy exhaustion of this field also. The timber men of Pennsylvania have already secured the greater part of our White Pine forests. But we give this merely by way of illustration, for Pine can never be with us a principal export. It is in our Poplar, hard and ornamental woods, &c., that we look for the greatest development.

Of the 16,640,000 acres of land in the State, between 9,000,000 and 10,000,000 are in the original forest. The older settled counties, such as Jefferson, Berkeley, Harrison, Monongalia, Greenbrier, Monroe, &c., have the smallest proportion of timbered land. In the other part of the State, the main body of the cleared land lies immediately along the principal streams, and their more important tributaries. The first settlements were naturally made where the land was richest and most level, *i. e.*, along the water courses, and later, the streams afford advantages for sending the timber to market, which caused their banks to be more closely cleared.

The rest of the country is covered quite uniformly, with those varieties of trees which permit a pretty wide range of soil and exposure. The trees, of course, vary in size, abundance, and the quality of their wood, according to the adaptation of the locality to supply their special requirements, but are never entirely absent. These are mainly deciduous and hard-wood species.

Other varieties of trees, which require particular conditions for their growth, are found confined to limited areas in particular districts. Such trees are the Evergreens, as the Pines, Firs, &c.

DISTRIBUTION OF TIMBER.

It will be found convenient to retain, in considering this part of our subject, the subdivision of the State, made under the head of Topography. It will be remembered that there, two principal divisions were made, viz.: The Mountain Region and the Hilly Region. It was also stated that the Plateau portion of the Hilly Region, differed in many points from the rest. In speaking then of the distribution of the timber over the State, we will recognize three sections, the Mountain Region, the Plateau Region, and the Hilly Region (proper). This latter, it will be remembered, includes the great body of the central and western portions of the State.

For much valuable information concerning the general distribution of timber over the State, we are indebted to Col.. B. W. Byrne, State Superintendent of Schools, whose extensive acquaintance with the country, makes this particularly reliable.

There is great similarity in the timber over most of the State. It is composed mainly of White, Chestnut, Black and Red Oaks, Chestnut, Hickory, Poplar, Ash, Sugar Maple, Hemlock, Beech, Locust, and Black Walnut. These are almost universally present, and form, in the Hilly Region, almost the entire timber. Some Yellow Pine is found growing in a dispersed manner, almost everywhere in the State, mainly confined to the ridges. This and the Hemlock Spruce (Abies Canadensis), of the Evergreens, seem to permit the widest range of growth. They are both most at home in the Plateau and Mountain Regions. It is said that there was once once a considerable belt of Yellow Pine, growing in the counties near the Ohio river, and some distance back, as in Ritchie county. This has almost disappeared, although scattered trees are to be found even on the ridges along the Ohio itself. There are indications that this tree was once much more abundant, for Pine knots are found in numbers, where the trees do not now grow.

The Hemlock Spruce seems to have crept down from the eastern highlands along the streams, heading up in them, and to have maintained its position along them, for a considerable distance within the deciduous timber of the Hilly Region. Thus we find considerable bodies of this tree far down the Big Sandy and Guyandotte, towards the Ohio, in Wyoming, Logan, &c.

Of the hard woods, the White Oak is by far the most abundant. It forms one-third, and perhaps one-half, of all the timber in the State, and is one of the most generally diffused trees. In the Hilly Region of the northern part of the State, between the head waters of the Cheat and the Ohio, according to Diss Debar, "It grows on heavy rich clay loams, "and in closeness of grain and firmness, is unsurpassed. In "the whole basin drained by Fishing creek, Middle Island "creek, Little Kanawha and branches, Sand creek, Great "Kanawha, and those of its branches emptying into it below "the Falls, and the Guyandotte and Big Sandy rivers, the "Oaks, Poplar or Tulip tree, Walnut, Cherry, Sycamore, Ash, "Chestnut, and Locust, attain a size not surpassed on the "North American continent, east of the Rocky Mountains." To this, we may add that the Oak, Poplar, and Chestnut, seem to increase in size south of the Great Kanawha. Gigantic Poplars are reported reliably from that district, 10 and 11 feet in diameter, and Oaks 6 and 7 feet.

A White Oak from Taylor county, is reported as 8 feet 6 inches in diameter. We mention these merely as instances of extreme size. This belt of country is emphatically the home of the deciduous trees. Only scattered groves of White and Yellow Pine are occasionally found.

The Big Sandy and Guyandotte, with their tributaries, and the country between these rivers and the Great Kanawha, are very heavily timbered, and almost untouched. Along with the hard-woods, and Hemlocks of this district, some Yellow Pine occurs.

In many parts of the State throughout this region, we find Chestnut Oak on the ridges, large Chestnuts on the hillsides, and Beech rather closely confined to the vicinity of the streams. Besides the principal trees above named, we find other varieties distributed all over the Hilly Region. Among them we may name the Black Gum, the Sweet Gum, Buckeye, White Maple, White Walnut, Linden, Cucumber Tree, several species of Maple, Elm, and Ash, the latter quite abundant, &c., &c.

Eastward of this belt of fine deciduous timber, as we ascend the Plateau, the size of the deciduous trees diminishes, and the timber is, in some kinds of trees, poorer, except along the streams and in their vicinity, although still valuable. The Evergreens increase in frequency in this direction, until we pass into certain sections when the timber changes considerably, mainly by the diminution of the Oak, Poplar and Hickory, and the increase of the Walnut, Cherry, Chestnut, Maple, and coniferous trees.

Mr. R. K. Cautley, who has traveled over a good deal of the State, and is an excellent observer, says of this region, in "The Lumberman," that the streams flow in deep gorges, which, however, are not precipitous, and have usually a rich soil. Their benches carry heavy timber, while even the tops of the ridges have good Chestnut Oak. On the great upland plateaus, especially near the heads of the streams, *i. e.*, the New River, there are large tracts of heavy timber, with large lots of Black Walnut, and Figured Maple. He measured on six upland acres, on an average of land, 4 White Oaks to the acre, with a girth 8½ feet, 5 feet from the ground. And again, he says that he finds here a larger proportion of the timber below marketable size, although, as the whole face of the country is timbered, a good deal could be picked out. As an illustration, he mentions that on one tract, some 70 miles up the Gauley river, one-fourth of it was excellently timbered, while a good deal of the remainder was possessed chiefly by enormous Red Oak, Chestnut, and Chestnut Oak, with quantities of Sugar Maple. Each of the numerous water courses, were lined by Hemlock forests, however, such as he had never seen in this section. In two or three other districts, he rode through a great deal of White Oak and Poplar, but the size was too small to justify the title of a finely timbered country, and yet the next valley to such a one would be splendidly clothed with many kinds of valuable trees. He gives the opinion of the head of one of the largest stave houses in New York, on the White Oak of this district. This is: That in size, it is considerably inferior to the Michigan timber, but in every other respect superior to it, and equal, if not superior, to any in the United States, *i. e.*, in strength, grain, absence of streaks, and worm holes. Pennsylvania experts also, place it above their own White Oak. He thinks that the run of the trunks in this section will not give an average diameter in the best trees, of more than 20 inches, at breast high. The larger Oak lies in patches. It will be observed that in this account, Mr. C. is speaking of the timber in demand for exportation, and of the *average* of that. As an illustration of what may be frequently obtained, even in this belt, by selection, we may add the following account by the same person. After speaking of his riding through a good deal of small timber, he says, we entered a big promontory of 800 acres or more, of rich, smooth land, timbered with huge trees, Poplar, Hickory, Ash, Walnut, &c. The Hickory was both shell and close-bark—the largest he ever saw; the Poplar both numerous and large; the Ash very nice, and the White Oak the finest he had yet seen in this country. It grew along the ridges, and dozens of trees were seen, 30 to 40 inches in diameter, at breast height. One was 54 inches, and rose 60 inches, clear of limbs. All the timber was straight, and held its size high towards the limbs.

These examples may suffice to give a fair idea of the two zones of timber to be found in the Hilly Region and on the lower parts of the Plateau district.

We will now turn our attention to the higher Plateau district and the eastern parts of the State:

Here we will find considerable change in the forests. Commencing in the southern part of this belt we find the Plateau terminating on the east in the broad and lofty ranges of the Great Flat-Top and White Oak mountains. The eastern edge of this elevated table-land, after crossing New river into the western part of Greenbrier, no longer presents an unbroken out-crop, but is cut down into irregular, more or less isolated, spurs and knobs, while northward, in the north-western part of Pocahontas, and in Randolph, it passes into the anticlinal and synclinal folds of the Alleghany system; thence the belt of uplands is continued north east to the Potomac, along the west face of the east Front Ridge of the Alleghany. The height of this varies from about 3,000 feet in the south, to 3,200 and 2,500 in the north.

All along this belt, and spreading east and west from it, we have the largest amount of coniferous timber to be found in the State. In the southern portion, on the Flat-Top and White Oak mountain, vast forests, consisting mainly of White Oak are to be found, and this has given the name to the mountains last mentioned. This White Oak timber spreads over the east face of these mountains in Mercer, and covers the Black Oak mountains in that county. Hemlock Spruce grows here also, as elsewhere, in the lower levels, occupying the notches in the mountains and the hollows along streams, along with the Beech, while the Chesnut Oak is found on the ridges, its usual place.

There is considerable body of White Pine on Blue-Stone river, near the borders of Summers and Mercer counties, forming the southern extremity of a somewhat important belt of this timber, which extends towards New river on the east side of Raleigh county, along Glade and Piney creeks. The tree here, from its more southerly position, does not attain the size found further north. The timber, besides, is not so good, the wood being heavier and harder. This, so far as we know, is the most southerly position in which any body of White Pine is found. We find mixed with the White Pine of this belt some Yellow Pine, and Black or Pitch Pine.

Passing northward along the Plateau region, in the vicinity of Big Sewell, and in the western part of Greenbrier, the Sugar Maple is very abundant, and more to the north, on the flat tops of the mountains, the White Birch and White Maple, with scattering Oak and Chestnut, predominate until we reach the "Yew Pine district," as the natives call it. This extends from the north end of Greenbrier along the boundary line between Pocahontas and Webster, and some distance into Randolph along the head waters of the Elk and Gauley.

Mr. Cecil Clay, of the St. Lawrence B. and Mfg. Co., says, of this country:

"As you go west from the valley of the Greenbrier river "towards the mountains, the timber, instead of running out "towards their tops, frequently grows larger and better than "lower down. Sugar Maple, Birch, Ash, and Cherry flourish, "and, in places, fine Tulip trees. On the mountain tops "dense forests of Black Spruce (Abies nigra), are found. This "tree, called by the natives "Yew Pine," would cut often over "20,000 feet to the acre. [The size of the trees has been described under the head of this tree.—*Author.*]

"Along the main Gauley river, Williams river, Cranberry "river, and farther south, Cherry river, is a tract of country "30 miles long and 25 miles wide, which is a perfect wil-"derness. The streams are exceedingly rough, and the "mountains high, and almost no cleared land exists, The "land, however, often produces good grass when cleared of the "timber (as does most of our forest land). The principal "timber is Beach, Sugar, Maple, Cherry, Ash, Poplar, and "farther South, Oak. Sometimes dense strips of large Hem- "locks, grow along the streams, and millions of feet of Black "Spruce are found higher up on the hillsides and mountain "tops.

Col. Byrne, speaking of this region, says the Oak hardly ever appears here, and we may say the same in this higher region of the Poplar and Hickory. On Cherry river, a branch of the Gauley, the Cherry tree abounds as you ascend the Yew mountains. This tree is also found in considerable quantity on Cranberry and Williams rivers, and the headwaters of the Elk. This association of the Cherry with the coniferous trees of the plateau and mountain regions, is also found farther north, in the Canaan district of Tucker and Grant. The greater portion of the Cherry timber of the State, is found in the belt we are now describing.

Southeast and south of the "Yew Pine District," on the Greenbrier and its tributaries in Pocahontas, and Greenbrier counties, we have the largest body of White Pine and the finest timber of this kind in the State. A detailed description of the character of this timber in this section, has been given under the head of the "White Pine," among the trees. Mixed with this White Pine, is some Yellow and Scrub Pine, also some Hemlock, while large Chestnut Oaks cover the sunny mountain sides. About Droop mountain we find Walnut and some Poplar.

Still farther north, the branches of Cheat river, in the Eastern part of Tucker, especially the Black Fork of Cheat, are covered by dense forests of Hemlock Spruce and Black Spruce, the leaves of which have given the Black Fork the dark color, to which it owes its name. The belt of country from Southern Randolph to Grant, adjacent to, and on the west side of the Alleghany Front Ridge, is a vast forest with the Hemlock and Black Spruces predominating, but with large amounts of valuable species of deciduous trees. Diss Debar says of this belt: "The finest specimens of Hem- "lock abound in the Cheat and Greenbrier mountains, and "on the table-lands of Tucker, Randolph, Pendleton, Poca- "hontas, Nicholas and Webster. Here, also, neither Oak, "Poplar nor Hickory are to be found, but in their room thrive

" noble specimens of Sugar Maple, Ash, Beech, Birch, Wild "Cherry, and Black Walnut. Some of the two latter, meas- "uring 4 and 5 feet, and exceptionally even 6 and 7 feet "in diameter. From the Staunton and Parkersburg turn- "pike, near the head of the Greenbrier river, toward the "north, south, and east stretch upwards of 150,000 acres of "the finest forests in the State, scarcely broken by less than "50 scattered mountain farms."

Mr. Guerard, Assistant to the State Board of Centennial Managers, says of the Hemlock of this district, that many of the trees are 130 feet high, and 4 feet in diameter, and of the other woods, that they are not surpassed in the State.

In the higher parts of the lofty country in Pocahontas, and the adjoining counties, the Southern Balsam Fir, (Abies Fraseri), occurs mixed with the Black Spruce. It is stated that a considerable body of it, is found in the high region, between Randolph and Pocahontas, at the source of the East Fork of Greenbrier river.

In Pendleton, some White Pine occurs, and on the South Branch mountain, in Hardy county, a good deal of excellent White Oak and some good White Pine is found.

The parallel mountain ridges, abutting on the Potomac in Mineral, Hampshire and Morgan, are clothed with a mixture of a great variety of trees, among which, besides the usual hard-wood trees, there is a good deal of coniferous wood, composed of Hemlock Spruce, Black Spruce, Yellow Pine, Pitch Pine, and some White Pine, the Evergreens predominating in the higher and colder parts.

On the Greenbrier river, on the eastern side especially, we find hard wood again predominating on account of the comparative lowness of the country (1,800 to 2,000 feet). In the hills and ridges, between the Alleghany mountains, and the river, we find a good deal of Oak, especially Chestnut Oak, which exists in quantities sufficient to furnish a large amount of tan-bark. There is a good deal of good White Oak all along the east side of the river.

It is interesting to note the effect of altitude, and the consequent temperature, on the character of the timber. The deciduous trees attain their maximum developments in numbers, size, and quality, in the lower portions of the State, where they almost exclude the evergreens or conifers. As we ascend the plateau, the former gradually diminish with the the increasing height in numbers, and size, while the latter begin to come in greater force. It must be borne in mind, however, that in our latitude the altitude above tide, is nowhere great enough, entirely to exclude deciduous timber.

In the southern part of the State, in spite of the increased altitude, we find the oaks and other hardwood trees maintaining their supremacy over the lofty slopes of the Great Flat Top, and other mountains, owing to the more southerly latitude. As we advance north, it is only in the lofty ranges along the west side of Pocahontas, where the general level is the highest west of the Alleghany, that we find any great body of conifers.

DEVELOPMENT.

The following are the timbers which have received the most attention: White Oak, Poplar, Walnut, White Pine, Cherry, Ash, Locust, Chestnut Oak, Chestnut, Sycamore. The form in which the timber is sent out depends largely on the kind of transportation available. On the railroads and small streams, the weight and bulk are reduced as much as possible, by partial or complete manufacture, while on the larger streams and those which in floods give water enough, the timber is mainly cut into logs, and made up into rafts, which are floated down on the high waters, either to markets in other States, or to points within our own borders, which are favorably situated for cutting them up into forms suited for more distant transportation, or for manufacture on the spot.

As almost none of the streams have received any improvement, the amount of development in the State at large, is exceedingly small. A vast deal of fine timber, remote from the railroads and streams, and much that is within striking distance of them, is annually wasted by being girdled and left to decay standing, or by being burnt in logheaps. In some sections "worm fences" are made out of the most valuable Walnut and Cherry trees, the sole question being, to get a timber easy to split.

On the eastern boarder of the State, the only development taking place, is in the White Pine along the Greenbrier river, and this is carried on by a single company. The St. Lawrence

Boom and Manufacturing Company, controlled by Pennsylvania capitalists, of which Mr. Cecil Clay is President, has a charter for operating the river, and is engaged in improving its navigation. The spring floods now, give them water enough to run rafts of 100 to 150 feet in length. Logging can be done very cheaply in this country, for the surface is smooth, and supplies for men and forage for teams, are abundant around the camps.

This timber region can readily be reached from the Chesapeake and Ohio Railroad, from Milboro, Covington, or Ronceverte. This latter place has, according to Mr. Clay, fine natural advantages for the concentration of the lumber business of the Greenbrier Valley. Timber can be had in the river suited for the manufacture of cars, wagons, agricultural implements, furniture, woodenware, pump stocks, and for planing purposes.

Lumber can be delivered in Cincinnati so as to compete with the Michigan pine, and in Philadelphia so as to cost less than the Pennsylvania timber. A large market can be had both ways.

The St. Lawrence Boom and Manufacturing Company, has a paid up capital of $60,000, which is increased as needed, and owns and controls 100,000,000 feet of White Pine timber in Greenbrier and Pocahontas counties. It has a boom of several millions of feet capacity, and uses splash dams and tramways in its logging. In times of ordinary prosperity, a good business might be done in square timber, Oak, etc. Mr. Clay thinks that there are several million dollars worth of timber standing, on the Greenbrier river. He says that they are now offered $42.00 per M, Michigan inspection, for timber delivered in Philadelphia.

On the headwaters of the Elk and Gauley nothing has been or is being done to develop that heavily timbered section. Webster county has sent some logs from her western borders down Elk. No timber comes out of the splendid forests on the upper waters of the Cheat. This magnificent timber has never been touched. In the counties along the Potomac, the timber is mainly cut by saw mills within the district. Some Yellow and Pitch Pine is sawed and sent East. The most attention is paid to the hard woods for the smaller manufactures, for cooperage stuff, straps, tanbark, railroad ties, etc., etc. Of the the latter, the Balltimore and Ohio Railroad consumes a great many.

Of the general development of the timber in the central and western parts of the State. Diss Debar speaks in 1870, as follows:

"The lumber trade in West Virginia has been among the "earliest vocations of the pioneers, who settled on navigable "or raftable streams. In the absence of anything like a reli-"able record of the business, some idea of its extent may be "found from the fact that streams like the Little Kanawha, "Guyandotte, or Big Sandy rivers, respectively, bring down, "logs in rafts to the aggregate value of from $40.000 to $50,000 "at a single rise. Up to this date rafting and floating have been "confined to the larger streams and tributaries. Yet the floating "of single logs, and small rafts, is practicable from five to six "miles below the source of almost any stream west of a line "of rapids, extending from the Valley Falls in Taylor county, "to the Kentucky line, and crossing Elk river eight or ten "miles above the mouth of Holly, the Little Kanawha at "Bulltown, and the Great Kanawha, at the Great Falls in the "county of Fayette. East of that line, the rapidity and tor-"tuousness of the streams, and the protruding rocks and "boulders in their beds, interfere more or less with the safety "of rafts, though single logs are floated down without much "trouble, and then caught and rafted in the stiller waters below.

"Not only timber in the log, but staves and sawed lumber, "green and seasoned, are floated down the principal streams "in good sized boats. From counties as far inland as Lewis, "Gilmer, Braxton, Calhoun, Roane, Nicholas, Fayette, "Raleigh, Wyoming, and McDowell, and the counties below "(west of) them, boats with gunwales hewed out from a "single Poplar, over 100 feet in length, are brought down in "ordinary freshets without difficulty. Smaller sized boats "descend Fishing creek, Middle Island, and Sand creek, from "points within 10 miles of their uppermost source.

"As late as 10 years ago, seven-eights of the lumber con-"sumed in the State and exported, were manufactured by "water power but since then, portable and stationary steam "saw mills have rapidly increased. Along both branches of

" the Baltimore and Ohio railroad, from 20 to 30 first-class
" mills are cutting on an average 3,000 feet per day. This pro-
" duct consists of flooring, scantling, furniture stuff, ship and
" railroad timber, for eastern and western markets, the Rail-
" road Company itself being an important customer. Many
" of these mills possess a capacity of 10,000 feet per day,
" which maximum is seldom reached, for want of adequate
" force to supply logs and take care of the lumber. Large
" mills are also in operation on the Ohio and its principal
" West Virginia tributaries.

" A company of enterprising Pennsylvanians, with a capi-
" tal of $300,000, are now engaged in developing 80,000 acres
" of land in Braxton and Webster counties, with saw mills,
" planing mills, and business headquarters at Charleston, on
" the Great Kanawha. One of the first operations of
" this company, was the shipping by river to Park-
" ersburg, and thence by rail to Baltimore, 10,000 feet of
" Black Walnut plank, which, notwithstanding expensive
" freight over a distance of 650 miles, yielded a handsome
" profit. Immense quantities of dressed and seasoned staves
" are shipped along the line of the Baltimore and Ohio Rail-
" road, for coopering in Baltimore, and as far north as Massa-
" chusetts, while several factories along the line of the road
" are turning out from 150 to 200 barrels per day.

" Staves are being made almost at the very source of the
" streams flowing towards the railroad and the Ohio river,
" floated down loosely in times of freshets, and caught by
" booms at convenient points.

" The development of ship timber is receiving much atten-
" tion just now, along the line of the railroad, and late orders
" from abroad have disclosed the fact that not only Oak, but
" other kinds of West Virginia timber were in demand for
" that purpose, as for instance:

" White Oak, for keels, planking, beams, knees, floors and
" ceilings.

" Ash, for blocks, oars, &c.

" Hickory, for capstan bars and handspikes.

" Sugar Maple, for keels, or bottom plank.

" Beech, Red preferred, for frames, planking, &c.

" Poplar, for cabinet work.

" White Oak knees bring higher prices in proportion to " to cost, than any other class of ship timber, and will amply " repay hauling on country roads to the station, over 15 or 20 " miles. Thousands of limbs and tops, admirably shaped for " knees, are thoughtlessly destroyed in our clearings every " year.

" Hoop-poles are among the primitive commodities exported " from West Virginia, and being speedily renewed from the " root or stump, the supply is almost inexhaustible, so long " as the grubbing-hoe is kept out of the woods.

" Wagon and carriage stuff is beginning to be manufac- " tured for exportation, at various points on the railroad.

" The prejudice heretofore prevailing in favor of Connecticut " Hickory, is rapidly waning, to judge from the large orders " now being received for West Virginia spokes, &c. An occa- " sional survey of the Railroad Depot at Parkersburg, when " filled with tons of wagons, carriages, plough-beams, furni- " ture, and twenty other articles of wooden-ware, manufac- " tured from West Virginia timber, outside of the State, and " westward bound, give a faint idea of what is continally lost " through our lack of manufacturing enterprise."

After this general statement, we may give some facts illustrating the present and prospective development of particular points in the central and western parts of the State.

In the northern part of the State, almost the entire development is by means of the Baltimore and Ohio railroad. All along the main stem, and the Parkersburg branch of this road, are numerous mills and manufactories, whose business is almost entirely in cooperage stuff and sawed lumber, and whose aggregate sales cannot be less than $2,500,000 annually.

We will first mention some of the more important points along the line of this road, where lumber is received and shipped.

Cranberry Summit is the center of a consider lumber business, consisting in its collection and preparation for shipment.

At Rowlesburg, where the railroad crosses Cheat river, is another center. As we have stated, Cheat is entirely undeveloped at present. Diss Debar says that main Cheat, for some 20 to 25 miles above the railroad, and the Black Fork of

Cheat, have been to some extent developed, 15 years ago, for ship timber, for the English market, by a company whose mill-works were located at Rowlesburg. It would certainly seem that at no distant day the vast amount of timber, tributary to this stream, would induce capitalists to open it up by tram railroads, booms and splash dams. Cheat would, in tan-bark and coniferous timber, furnish supplies equal to any demand.

At Grafton, we find a lumber center which is just in the first stages of development. All the timber brought by Tygart's Valley river to this point, must of necessity be put in shape at this point, to allow transportation on the railroad.

At this point there is a boom erected, and Mr. Whitescarver says of it. "In last June (1875), there were 12,000,000 feet of " lumber in, consisting of Popular, Oak, Ash, Chestnut, Wal- " Spruce Pine (Hemlock Spruce), and Cherry, but mainly Poplar " and Oak. The boom is supplied from Taylor, Barbour, Pres- " ton, Randolph, and Upshur. In Taylor and Barbour, Poplar, " Oak, Ash, and Walnut; in Randolph and Upshur, Poplar, " Oak, Cherry, Walnut, Ash, and Pine, are the principal tim- " bers. Hickory is plentiful in all the counties. The area of " country that supplies the boom at Grafton, is about 100 " miles in length by 50 in width, all of which is accessible to " streams that empty into the Valley river. The present capac- " ity for manufacturing the timber into lumber in and about " Grafton, is estimated at about 60,000 feet per day.

" The Poplar is principally used in the Eastern markets " for carriages, beds, coffins, pumps, and furniture. Oak is " used for shooks, for railroad, and agricultural implements. " Cherry, Walnut, and Chestnut is employed for furniture and " the inside finish of houses.

"From Philippi up, the Valley river, and all of its tribu- " taries, pass through an almost unbroken forest."

At Valley Falls, in Marion county, a considerable business is done in sawed lumber and cooperage stuff. At Mannington, Belton, and other points on the main stem, a considerable trade is done, and the manufactories in Wheeling consume a large amount.

On the Parkersburg branch, between West Union and Parkersburg, a heavy business is done in timber shipment.

Large amounts of sawed lumber, ship timber, barrel stuff, etc., are shipped from various points along the line of this railroad. Dealers in lumber here, estimate that for from five to ten years back, there have been sent out from Doddridge county, each year, more than 3,000,000 feet of hard, and 2,000,000 feet of soft lumber, to Baltimore and the East, and 1,000,000 feet, westward down the Ohio river. Also, above 5,000,000 Oak staves of medium size, and 5,000,000 hoop poles, to Eastern markets; mainly to England. Harrison county has shipped nearly an equal quantity, while the exports from Ritchie surpass the above amounts.

More attention has been paid here to the development of the country along the railroad by means of short branch roads.

The railroad from Pennsboro to Harrisville opens up a good deal of timber. Mr. Bryan, Assistant to the State Board, says of Ritchie, and the adjoining counties: "The amount of timber, barrel staves, and headings, principally of White "Oak and Poplar, taken out of Ritchie county, is enormous. "The North and South Forks of Hughes river, and the Pennsboro and Harrisville railroad, make the timber very accessible. White Oak of the finest quality abounds. Messrs. Kimball and Shaffer, of Pennsboro, have had in operation a stave "and heading factory, for the supply of their Baltimore barrel "factory. Mr. K. says that in 1875, he shipped from Pennsboro to Baltimore, $800,000 worth of stuff for barrels."

Again, of Calhoun, Mr. Bryan says:

"The timber of this county is splendid. The Little Kanawha, West Fork, Steer creek, and minor streams, have "enabled the people to take out in rafts, a large amount of the "finest logs, but the timber is hardly missed a mile or two "from the streams. The traffic in staves, as in Ritchie and "Wirt, is enormous. Few hoop poles are now gotten out here, "but vast numbers are taken from Ritchie and Wirt. The "Oak timber is gotten for barrel and tierce staves, and headings. As this timber does not float well, Poplar and Walnut "are the principal trees put in logs and rafts. Staves, headings, and all manner of sawed stuff are run out on high "water in flat boats. These same remarks apply to all the "counties between the railroad and the Big Kanawha. Ritchie "has the most White Oak.

"In Wirt county, one Ohio firm got out, in 1875, 10,000,-" 000 staves. Trees are often sold on the stump for $1, or " belted and allowed to die.

" A good deal of Poplar from Braxton, is cut at Elizabeth, " Wirt county, and at Burnsville, in Braxton county, the " Messrs. Burns & Co., have a fifty-horse power engine, and " one of the largest saw mills in the State. They do a large " business, mainly in hard wood, Walnut, &c., and cut " immense amounts of Poplar, &c., and run it out on floods in " flat boats, on the Little Kanawha.

" The branches of the Little Kanawha, afford development " for the timber of Gilmer. Here logs under 2½ feet are rarely " cut or hauled, except for staves."

A good deal of the White Oak, tight-work staves, pipe, hogshead, and claret staves go to Europe from this region, and a great many Red Oak staves are used for the West India trade. Schooners are chartered "to N. side or S. side of Cuba " and return," at so much, and are then loaded with shooks and hoops, and bring back sugar and molasses.—(Clay).

Mr. R. T. Lowndes, of Clarksburg, says of the timber of Doddridge, &c.: "We have a tram road 20 miles long, run-" ning through the S. E. portion of Doddridge county, for " the purpose of bringing the timber to market. It drains " that section of Doddridge, and a part of Harrison, Lewis, " and Gilmer. Our woods consist nearly altogether of Oak " and Poplar, for commercial purposes. We have some Wal-" nut and Locust, and a large amount of Beech, Hickory, Syc-" amore, Sugar, and several varieties of Pine. The Oak is " generally shipped in coopers' stuff, railroad lumber and " ship timber; the roots and crotches for ship-knees and " hames. The Red and Chestnut Oak is used for bark, shook " staves, ties, &c. Our Poplar is generally shipped in lum-" ber, as chair plank, panel boards, &c., sometimes in the log. " Our Yellow Poplar is much sought after by the furniture " manufacturers, and when prime and well seasoned, com-" mands good prices.

" But the White Oak is our princpal timber, and is very " fine. There is a steady demand from Europe for it, but the " cost of handling is so great that prices are not remunera-" tive."

Down the Ohio, from Wetzel county to the Little Kanawha, no large E. and W. flowing river empties into the Ohio, but several considerable creeks, such as Middle Island and Fishing creeks, which bring in a considerable amount of logs from some distance inland. Something is done in squared timber for bridge building, but the main business along the river is in sawed or cooperage stuff, of which a great deal is handled. Some attention is also paid to ship timber, both for river boats and foreign markets.

As an illustration of the excellence of the Ohio river timber for this latter purpose, we may mention the fact, stated by Mr. C. T. Beall, of Mason, that the brig Somers, distinguished in the Mexican war, was built at the mouth of the Kanawha, by the Gilmores, of Mason county lumber.

When this vessel was docked some 8 years ago, her timbers were found to be sound.

While the bottoms along the Ohio are cleared, yet much of the upland, a little back of the river, it still heavily timbered.

In passing down the Ohio, the Little Kanawha is the first stream reaching back a considerable distance towards the Alleghanies. From this river southward, the E. and W. flowing tributaries of the Ohio, are all extensive, and serve to develop considerable tracts of country.

The little Kanawha develops a good deal of the country described above by Mr. Bryan, and brings a vast amount of railroad ties, sawed stuff, cooperage material, square timber, and logs, to Parkersburg and points on the Ohio river.

Mr. L. B. Dellicker, General Superintendent of the Little Kanawha Navigation Company, gives the following as the shipments of timber out of the Little Kanawha, from January 1, 1875, to January 1, 1876:

Four hundred and twenty log rafts, containing about 504,000 cubic feet, 1,816,000 feet of manufactured lumber, mainly inch boards.

Three million five hundred and fifty-two thousand nine hundred and twenty-seven oil barrel staves.

Seventy thousand one hundred and eighty-four railroad cross-ties.

Seventeen thousand hoop-poles.

One hundred and seventy-seven cords of keg wood.

Col. Byrne estimates the product of this stream as follows: The Burns Brothers, at Burnsville, cut and send to the Pittsburgh market, probably $50,000 worth of boards. Other saw mills, between that point and Parkersburg, probably manufacture as much more in boards, and perhaps $10,000 worth of White Oak in ship timber, with $50,000 worth of staves, or perhaps much more. Besides these items, there are $50,000 worth of cross-ties, and $100,000 worth of logs, mainly manufactured at Parkersburg. In all, $310,000 worth of timber, and perhaps much more. The business along the Ohio from Wheeling south to this stream, may be as much, say $350,000.

Omitting for the moment the business on the Great Kanawha and the Chesapeake and Ohio Railroad, we may pass to the region south of the last named stream.

The Big Sandy, the Guyandotte, and Twelve Pole, are the present means of developing the timber of the southern counties, and drain an extensive area of heavily wooded country. We have no details of the business done, but it is known that they all do a heavy business in logs, mainly for Ohio river markets. White Oak is largely manufactured into staves. Large numbers of hoop poles are cut, and a considerable amount of tanbark is sent out. Besides the hard woods, some Hemlock and Yellow Pine is sent West. It would not be an overestimate perhaps to put the trade done in these three streams at $300,000.

On the Kanawha river, the principal development of timber is from the mouth of Elk downwards. Col. Byrne says of the business on the Kanawha and its tributaries: "Elk river " sends out $100,000 worth of logs, cut by mills at and near " Charleston, either for use there or for shipment down the " river. The White and Black Oak, are chiefly manufactured " into salt barrel staves, for use in the vicinity of Charleston. " The mills there have a capacity for producing 1,000 barrels " per day. The Poplar, Ash, Chestnut, Walnut, and other " kinds, are chiefly manufactured into boards, plank, and " scantling at Charleston for the Cincinnati and other mar- " kets on the river, after supplying the home market. Besides " the logs, Elk sends out a large number of coal boats, ($20,000 " worth), for use in shipping coal and salt from the Kanawha " river. The manufactured value of Elk river timber, *i. e.* " boards, staves, hoop poles, etc., is at least $150,000.

"The Great Kanawha, from the falls down, must produce as "much lumber in the shape of logs, staves, hoop poles, boards, "and ship timber, as the Elk, or $150,000."

Pocatalico and Coal rivers contribute largely to this produce of the Lower Kanawha, Pocatalico sending probably $20,000 worth. Coal river sends out some fine Walnut, which goes to Europe. The Lower Kanawha sends out some fine Oak timber for ship building, and a good deal of pine.

At and near the falls of the Great Kanawha, and on Laurel creek, a considerable business is done in cooperage stuff and sawed lumber, perhaps $100,000 worth. Westward to Hinton, hardly anything is done.

At Hinton, a good deal is done. Some staves are, according to Mr. Clay, floated down from up New river, caught at Hinton and shipped by rail. Mr. J. S Thompsen says of the timber trade of Hinton: "Quite a large trade is carried on here "in the lumber business. Large quantities of pipe staves of "Oak, are shipped by rail to the East, and several thousand "Walnut logs have been shipped both to the Eastern markets "and to Europe, from the county within the last 18 months. "There is a large saw mill at this point, owned by New York "men, who ship pine (of a fine quality) lumber; also shingles, "laths, etc. They deal extensively also in Poplar lumber and "and furnish the Chesapeake and Ohio Railroad, with rail-"road ties."

Besides the above localities, the Mononghela river in Monongalia county, and the West Fork from Harrison, carry out some forty to fifty thousand dollars worth of White Oak for ship timber, and other timber in logs.

Taking everything into consideration, we may, without exaggeration, state that the revenue to be derived for many years to come, from the timber of West Virginia must equal that to be obtained from any other of her resources. Putting her acreage in timber at 9,000,000, and estimating 8,000 feet of boards to the acre, at $1.00 per M., a very moderate estimate, we have $72,000,000. It is certain that this State has a larger amount of *surplus* hard wood timber, (and that of the most marketable kinds), than any other State in the Union, and that the excellence of the material is attracting constantly more and more attention.

CHAPTER IX.

THE COAL FIELD.

BY M. F. MAURY.

The most important coal region in America is the Appalachian Coal Field, which is, says Rogers, "almost the largest expanse of continuous coal measures in the world. It possesses "a length of 875 miles, and a maximum breadth, between its "eastern outcrop in southern Pennsylvania and its western "in northern Ohio, of about 180 miles." It extends from northern Pennsylvania to middle Alabama, parallel to the Appalachian chain to the east of it. Its coals are better than those of any other field in America, and, save anthracite, are of every kind necessary to the arts and manufactures. Its area is made up as follows:

West Virginia	16,000	sqr. miles.
Pennsylvania	12,700	" "
Ohio	10,000	" "
Eastern Kentucky	8,900	" "
Alabama	5,000	" "
Tennessee	5,100	" "
Maryland	550	" "
Total	58,550	sqr. miles.

Of these the amounts for Pennsylvania and eastern Kentucky are the results of careful surveys, while the others are estimates taken from the best and latest sources:

By the U. S. census of 1870, these States mined the following tonnage:

Alabama	11,582	tons.
Kentucky	150,000	
Maryland	1,819,824	"
Ohio	2,527,285	"

Pennsylvania	7,798,518 tons.
Tennessee	133,418 "
West Virginia	608,878 "
Total	12,049,505 tons.

These tables, therefore, show that while West Virginia embraces (in round numbers) nearly 28 per cent of the coal area, it produces only 5 per cent of the coal mined therein.

In the absence of an exact and definite location, the eastern boundary of the West Virginia Coal Field may be described as follows: Beginning at the south on the mountain just east Blue Stone river, and proceeding thence to Little Sewell, on the top of which the lowest seam of the lower measures may be seen; thence by, but not a very clearly defined line, with the common boundary of Nicholas and Greenbrier, and Webster and Pocahontas, to Rich mountain in Randolph; following this last named ridge to Laurel mountain, the dividing line between Upshur on the west and Randolph and Barbour on the east: and thence with the Briery mountain into Preston county and on the Pennsylvania line. To the east of this boundary there are small outlying patches of coal, (mentioned at the end of this chapter), as in Greenbrier in Meadow mountain, and possibly in Pocahontas and in some of the synclinal valleys of Tucker, but they are unimportant as compared with the vast area to the west, and in but few instances will yield fuel of any value except for local use. This remark will not, however, apply to the valuable, though small, trough in Mineral and Grant, which is entirely seperated by sub-carboniferous strata from the main West Virginia Coal Field.

In every county west of the general boundary to the Ohio river valuable coal will be found, if not in the hills, then below the surface and accessible by shafting, so that out of 54 counties in the State, only Monroe, Pendleton, Hardy, Hampshire, Morgan, and Jefferson, lack it *in toto*.

Before going into a detailed account of the field it will be well to give a general sketch thereof, which cannot be better done than in the following condensed description of Prof. W. B. Rogers, State Geologist of Virginia from 1836 to 1840, who says, concerning it:

From the eastern margin of the coal field the strata have a general inclination to the northwest, so that as we leave the Alleghany mountains the rocks belonging to the formations below the coal disappear, and the coal measures themselves in their turn become buried as we approach the Ohio river in the region of Point Pleasant, Parkersburg, &c., where we find on the surface the Upper Barren Measures—the highest member of the coal formation—consisting of shales, slates and sandstone, either destitute of coal, or contaning it in variable and unimportant beds as compared to the richer portions of the field. These gently sloping strata, thus gradually depressed, again rise to the surface as we proceed still further west, thus bringing into view over a wide and affluent belt of country in Ohio the counterparts of the lost coal seams and their associated strata, in the reverse order in which they had been seen to disappear in West Virginia some distance east of the Ohio.

As necessary to the general picture of this wide-spread series rocks, it may be added that beyond this belt of productive coal measures in Ohio, as we ascend to the valley of the Scioto, we come into view of a group of underlying, easterly-dipping sandstones, slates and limestones, corresponding to the sub-carboniferous formations ot the Alleghanies, so that, leaving out all the undulations on the eastern side of the tract, we are presented with the imposing scene of a vast *synclinal trough or basin*, spreading from the eastern escarpment of the coal rocks in West Virginia entirely across the largest portion of that State and the eastern half of Ohio, and terminating there in a similar escarpment, in which the rocks are seen inclining to the east, to meet their counterparts dipping in the opposite direction in West Virginia. It is a little west of the center line of this basin that the Ohio river pursues its course for most of the distance, for which it forms the western boundary of our State.

But another feature has yet be introduced to complete the general outline of this interesting region. The eastern and western margins of this basin, though nearly parallel about midway of its length, gradually approach each other as they extend towards the north, and thus bending around, the former in Pennsylvania and the latter in Ohio, at length actually coalesce and form the head or northern termination of the trough. As a result of this configuration, the various coal seams of the whole area may be looked upon as a basin made up of a series of oblong, shallow bowls, whose longer diamters run N. E. and S. W., fitting one within the other and interstratified with shales, sandstones, &c. From the various portions of the margins these would therefore dip towards a common axis, so that along the northern edge of the basin the coals would have an inclination south, and as we follow the rim through West Virginia to Kentucky, first a S. S. W., then S. W., W. S. W, W., W. N. W., N. W., &c., dip would obtain.

Fortunately for the resources of the valuable, though small tract, between Pennsylvania and Ohio, in which are the counties of Hancock, Brooke, Ohio, and Marshall, known as the "Panhandle," this northern termination of the trough takes place at no great distance from where our State begins; so that the Ohio, in its western course along the margin of that tract, intersects the southerly dipping strata in a direction highly favorable for the developement of their rich mineral contents.

Bearing this illustration in mind, it will at once be seen that a river that runs through this basin will first pass over one edge, will then flow through its center, and finally cut the opposite edge, and if, as is the case with the Ohio, it enters near one end and flows nearly along the central axis, it will first cut the edges of the lowest bowls, and then higher and higher ones, till finally all will be exposed by it. Further, if in the course of this passage, it deviates from a straight line, so as to run W. or N. W., it will go into lower strata, or outer bowls, and if it then deflects back to its original position, near the axis, it will come into higher strata, or inner bowls. This cutting of the successive strata is very well shown along the whole river front of the State, for beginning at the northern extremity, near the mouth of Little Beaver, the Ohio flows in the lower part of the Lower Coal Measures, the outcrop of which is further towards the north. Thence, descending the river, the inclination of the rocks being towards the south, these lower coals pass below the bed of the stream, and at the tops of the hills at Steubenville, the lowest coal seam of the Upper Coal Measures, makes its first appearance. The southerly dip still continuing, this seam, as we proceed down the river, comes nearer and nearer the water, till a short distance below Wheeling, it also disappears, and the superior strata come lower and lower in the hills, till Fishing creek, in the southwest corner of Wetzel county, is reached. The river is here a little west of the axis, or center, of the basin, and is therefore in the innermost bowl, or highest strata, all, or nearly all, the coals lying beneath it. Below this point, assuming a direction more toward the west, it flows a little west of, and parallel to, the axis, still exposing only the upper strata, but bending toward the northwest. As it approaches Marietta it displays lower formations, and thence, pursuing a direction nearly parallel to the course from Fishing creek, it passes Parkersburg several miles west of the axis, still continuing to display nearly the same rocks as are met with at Marietta. It now, by various flexures, gradually works back nearer to the axis, and therefore into higher strata, till it reaches the bend below Mill creek, in Jackson county, when, by a sudden turn to the N. W., it penetrates some distance into the western side of the basin, and, the rocks having a dip towards the axis, that is towards the S. E., the strata, which, during its previous course, were buried below its bed, are now seen successively emerging to the surface, and bringing into light, above water level, the seam worked at Pomeroy, and which has not been seen since we left it at a little below Wheeling. Here, resuming its general southwesterly course, and, though having numerous flexures, preserving its general direction as far as Guyandotte, in Cabell county, it continues to expose nearly the same strata appertaining to the western side of the basin throughout the whole distance. Then bending away to the west, it enters the lower coal group (which we have not seen since we left Brooke county, in the northern part of the State), about three miles above the mouth of the Big Sandy, after which, taking a northwesterly course, it emerges from the basin near Porsmouth. This passage of the Ohio through the length of this basin, presents a line of observation of great interest and value to the geologist, for it shows nearly all of the strata of the coal measures.

The coal measures rest upon a well-marked series of rocks, known as the Great Conglomerate, and the following description of them, condensed from Prof. Rogers, is here given, as it may often serve to prevent fruitless exploration for coal in the strata underneath. This formation contrasts strongly in general aspect and composition, with the one immediately below it. It consists of whitish, or light gray sandstones, generally of coarse texture, and comprising heavy beds of conglomerate, usually conspicuous for the white round pebbles of which it is mainly composed. As the rock disintegrates, these latter are set free, and are often profusely strewn over the surface, becoming a useful landmark when the rock itself is hid from view.

At all points, however, this formation does not display the same conspicuous conglomeratic structure, for it passes from a mere mass of large rounded pebbles to a conglomerate of shot like gravel, and thence to a coarse, and in some instances, a fine grained sandstone of even and compact texture, and varies in thickness from 100 feet, and less, to 1,000 feet, and perhaps more.

Nor in all cases does it maintain its character of a purely siliceous rock, for it sometimes contains beds of shale and coal. Yet with all these variations the general characters of the group as above described, are sufficiently definite to enable the practiced observer to recognise it at a glance.

It is the boundary between the Coal Measures, and the Appalachian formations below, and therefore, as a general rule, explorations for coal should be directed to the strata lying geologically above it.

The remarkable expansion and diversified character assumed by this formation for some distance, within the margin of our great coal field west of the Greenbrier river and on New river, has caused it to spread over a wide area, and to include seams of coal of sufficient magnitude to be worthy of exploration. As, for instance, at Quinnimont, on the latter stream.

Having thus hastily sketched the general geology of the coal field, let us now examine the number of coal seams contained therein.

To do this so as to be the more fully understood, the coal strata can be divided into four great geological divisions, viz:

The Lower Coal Measures, resting upon the Great Conglomerate, just described so fully, containing very many important and valuable coal seams, and having a thick bed of sandstone, called the "Mahoning," as its upper limit.

The Lower Barren Measures, composed of reddish and bluish shales and slates, sandstones and limestones—the latter in some parts of the State very important—usually destitute of workable coals, and terminating at the base of a valuable and persistent coal seam known as the "Pittsburgh."

The Upper Coal Measures, containing several important coal seams, of which the "Pittsburgh" is the lowest.

The Upper Barren Measures, composed of sandstones and shales, nearly destitute of coal.

There are also geographical divisions in the field that should be noticed, for, in several cases, ridges, parallel to the eastern margin of the basin, make their appearance, and are composed of sub-carboniferous strata, which separate one coal basin from another, and form well marked boundaries thereto.

These anti-clinals, or upheavals, are more marked in the northern than in the southern portion of the State. In the former, as we proceed west, they become more and more gentle in their slopes, and, as they are traced south, become wider and flatter, until they are more or less lost, and allow the coal measures to coalesce in one grand expanse, or gently undulating plane, that sweeps from Rich and Sewell mountains entirely, across the State, with scarcely a single interruption, save the small and narrow one of the "Oil Break," near the Ohio river.

In fact, in considering this question, the State may be divided by a line running in a northwest direction, from the common eastern corner of Greenbrier and Pocahontas, to the northern end of Pleasants county, on the Ohio. North of this, we find our anti-clinal axes and the rock beds folded, while to the south the upheavals are so gentle, that while they may flatten the strata, we have no positive assurance that they reverse the northwest dip anywhere in the whole territory.

Let us now proceed to show what seams are contained in these several geographical divisions. The first one taken has been alluded to as lying in Mineral and Grant counties, and may be called

THE POTOMAC BASIN.

This is bounded on the east by the Front Ridge of the Alleghany, and on the west, by the Backbone of the Alleghany- In the intervening space are two anti-clinal axes or undula. tions, which divide this area into three sub-fields. As we trace these ridges to the southwest, they more or less coalesce, forming the high land between Tucker and Grant counties, cutting off all continuity of the coal strata between this basin, and the main one of the State.

Continued to the northeast, these two intermediate axes flatten down and die out, so that what in West Virginia, are three basins; in Maryland, is the single one, so well known as the "Cumberland Coal Field."

THE EASTERN TROUGH,

Of the Potomac Basin, is bounded by the Front Ridge of the Alleghany and the anti-clinal ridge, which is the watershed between Abrams creek and Stony river. On the east side the strata dip northwest, and on west they incline southeast. By reason of the proximity to the Appalachian upheaval, the rocks are here inclined at a comparatively steep angle, and by this means the bottom of the trough was rendered sufficiently low to permit the whole of the Lower Coal and Lower Barren Measures, and a little of the Upper Coal Measures, to escape the destructive torrents which have eroded and washed away so much of the coal-bearing formation of this section. The seams found in this basin all furnish a semi-bituminous coal.

The following section was kindly supplied by the Hon. H. G. Davis, and is the result of actual measurements, taken some ten years ago by Wm. Brace, Esq., of Cumberland, at some point near the Baltimore and Hampshire Company's mine, in Mineral county.

	Ft	*In*
1. "Millstone Grit"	...	...
2. *Coal*	3	0
3. Slate	120	0
4. *Coal*	6	0
5. Slate and Sandstone	130	0
6. *Coal*	3	0
7. Slate	1	6
8. *Coal*	3	6

	Ft.	In.
9. Sandstone, Slate, and Shale, etc	150	0
10. *Coal*	4	0
11. Sandstone and Limestone	120	0
12. *Coal*	2	6
13. Shale and Sandstone	90	0
14. Fire Clay	3	0
15. *Coal*—"Big Vein"	14	0
16. Slate	30	0
17. Black Band Ore	....	
18. Shale and Slate	45	0
19. Coal	7	0

By comparing this section with one made on the Maryland side of the river by Prof. Tyson it will be seen that Mr. Brace has mistaken the heavy bed of sandstone under No. 2 of the section for the Great Conglomerate, whereas he should have gone some 39 feet lower. Had he done so, he would have found another coal seam, which is to be seen in the bed of the Potomac, a short distance below the mouth of Savage river, and at Brantzburg, showing itself 2 feet 11 inches thick, 20 feet above the water, where it anyalyzes:

Carbon	72.4
Volatile Matter	19.72
Ash	7.88
	100.00

Beginning now to discuss the section as it stands, Prof. Rogers makes *Coal, No.* 2, only 20 inches at the mouth of Savage, but as measured by Prof. Wm. S. Rowson, of New Jersey, on the head waters of Abrams creek, in Grant county, on the 886 acres of J. Hutton & Co., it shows *Coal*, 4 inches; Slate 2 inches; *Coal*, 1 foot; Slate 4 inches; *Coal*, 2 feet 6 inches. Total 4 feet 4 inches.

Coal No. 4, is well exposed above the mouth of Savage, and from its quality, thickness, accessibillity, and the large area over which it may be wrought, is to be looked on as a very valuable deposit. I have no analysis of it at this place, but samples from up Abram's creek, from the land of Mr. Vandover and Mr. McDonald, show respectively:

Carbon	61.44	74.00
Volatile matter	14.28	18.60
Ash	24.28	7.40
	100.00	100.00

At the head of this creek, on the land of Hutton & Co., Prof. Rowson measured it 6 feet 9 inches, but this shows many partings of slate, the bottom, 2 feet 5 inches, being the thickest bench in the whole height.

Coals, Nos. 6 and 8, show some fine exposures in this, and the next basin on Stony river, to the west, the intervening slate getting thinner, so that at Whistler's opening on Stony, Prof. Rowson found a thickness of 8 feet 3 inches, the slate being represented by a band only 3 inches thick, 5 feet from the floor.

Coal, No. 10, was measured by the same gentleman, on the 100-acre tract of J. W. Shillingburg. Here, including the top shales and coals, it was 5 feet 10 inches, but only the lower 4 feet is solid coal.

Coal, No. 12, in the same locality as the last, shows 3 feet 2 inches, but is worthless, being so much cut by partings that the thickest bench of coal is only 1 foot 3 inches.

Coal, No. 15, some 850 or 900 feet above the river, is the first of the Upper Coal Measures, the same that is so extensively wrought in the Frostburg Region of Maryland. From its great elevation in the hills, it is not only more difficult of access than the lower coals, but is spread over a comparatively limited area, and is, in many cases, likely to be injured by the the insufficient protection of the superincumbent strata. A better idea of its high position may be obtained from the fact that out of 1,933 acres owned by the Hampshire and Baltimore Coal Company, about a mile above Piedmont, a careful survey showed that only 216⅗ acres were underlaid by this seam.*

The mines of this company, and the Virginia Coal Company, are the only ones now in operation in this field, and both are working this great bed, the coal from which is very free from impurities. In the Virginia mine, it is 14 feet thick, with only one parting, 1½ inches thick, 4 feet from the

*Report on the Coal Properties of the Cumberland Coal Basin, by James T. Hodge, Mining Geologist, 1869.

floor. The whole is very tender and soft, the bottom, 4 feet, particularly so, and from this cause, amongst others, only about 60 per cent of the contents of this magnificent bed goes to market. (For analysis see next chapter).

Coal, No. 19, "is called the eight-foot bed, and affords 6 feet "of good workable coal. It is in rectangular blocks, harder "and firmer than the coal of the great bed, and is said to be "more gaseous in character. Its area appears to be full half "of that of the large bed, and is possibly more than this." —(Hodge).

It has been mentioned that the boundaries of this sub-basin coalesce to the southwest, and the coals disappear, so that as we go from the Potomac towards the head of Abram's creek, in Grant county, first the top seams vanish, then the ones below, and so on to the lowest.

Proceeding west, and crossing the dividing ridge between Abram's creek and Stony river, we enter upon the *Second, or Middle Trough*, of the Potomac basin, which has for a western boundary, the anticlinal ridge between Stony river and Difficult creek, and its southwest termination at the head of the former stream. As this upheaval is less sudden and abrupt than the ones to the east, we would expect that the inclination of the strata would be more gentle, and such proves to be the case. Hence, the coal beds were not so well protected from erosion by ancient currents, and as a consequence, we find that all of the Upper Coal Measures have been washed away, and only the Lower Coal Measures are left.

On the lower part of Stony river, in Mineral county, no explorations have been made to show what coals are present, but in Grant county, they were examined in March, 1876, by Mr. A. R. Guerard, of the Royal School of Mines, London, and the following distinct seams were observed:

On Rinker's land, 4 miles below the Falls of the river, is an 8-foot seam, containing a good deal of slate. Lower down the river, and ¼ of a mile from this, is the "Harnes" bed, which is also 8 feet, containing more slate than the last. It is very probable that it is the same as the "Rinker," but this could not be certainly determined, as Mr. Guerard was able to spend but a very short time in the district.

Above the Rinker 8-foot coal, comes in a 3-foot bed, and above this a 4-foot one, near the falls of the river. In connection with these two, it should be said that as the distance between them is some four miles, and there are no intermediate exposures, Mr. Guerard thinks that possibly these may be one and the same stratum, which has undergone an alteration in thickness. Above these, also, at the falls of Stony, is an 8-foot seam—the Whistler seam, with very little slate—and above this Mr. T. W. Evans, a mining engineer, of Pennsylvania, who examined this field in November, 1875, reports a 6-foot seam of good coal.

From Stony river, we now cross over the anti-clinal ridge, between that stream and Difficult creek, and come into the *Western Trough*, which, like the last, has more gently sloping strata than the eastern, and the coals belong to the Lower Measures.

In Grant county, on Difficult creek, up the stream from the crossing of the pike, and about 1½ miles from Lees, are 7 feet of very good coal—the only important parting being 3 inches thick. It is semi-bituminous as, in fact, all in the Potomac Basin seem to be, with some slate in it. Higher in the hills than this, at the bend in the Northwestern Pike, Mr. Evans reports a 4-foot seam, of very fine coal. On Difficult creek, at the crossing of the Northwestern Pike, and apparently below the 7-foot seam, is one that is made up of 3 feet of good coal—1 foot ot slate and 2 feet of bad coal on top. By comparing these thicknesses with those mentioned in the section on page 169, it will be noticed that the last named bed corresponds to *No. 4 Coal, 6 feet*, except that a parting is developed here. The 7-foot seams correspond to *Nos.* 6, 7 and 8, though having suffered a slight diminution in thickness, while the 4-foot seams corresponds to *No. 10 Coal, 4 feet.*

Separating the Potomac Basin from the one next to the west, is a wide region of lofty and broken hills, traversed by the Cheat river, and bounded on the east and west by the Backbone and Briery mountains, respectively, between which the formations which lie below the coal are at, or very near, the surface. This shallow basin expands and deepens in a northwesterly direction, through Maryland, and when traced into Pennsylvania, becomes of great value, as it is the coal field between the axes of the Alleghany and Negro mountains. There are no observations to determine what it does in its prolongations to the south, but as in West Virginia, it is too shallow to contain any valuable coal, we may at once pass on to the consideration of

THE PRESTON COUNTY BASIN,

Which is bounded on the east by the Briery mountains, on the west by Laurel ridge, and is the southerly continuation of the Ligonier Valley, or second basin of the Pennsylvania survey, which, in West Virginia, is divided into two troughs by a gentle anti-clinal axis, lying just west of Kingwood. As this has not been well traced out, both troughs will just now be considered as one.

In it are all the Lower Coal and Lower Barren Measures, and in the southern end, in the tops of the highest hills, the first, or *Pittsburgh*, seam of the Upper Coal Measures.

There is positive information only as to five seams in this field, but it is fair to presume that a careful search will find others which properly belong to this geological horizon, though as they have never yet been discovered, it is just to suppose that they are small and unimportant.

The First Seam, or lowest, is said to be in view, at very low water, in the bed of Cheat river half a mile below Kingwood Ferry, resting, according to Prof. Rogers, upon a limstone. Just below this place the shales, which overlie this seam, contain five bands of rich iron ore within a vertical space of four or five feet, the lowest band occasionally four or five inches thick, and the upper ones generally about two inches.

The Second Seam, varies from 2 to 4 feet, in different parts of the field. Though valuable for fuel, it is often quite sulphurous, and is nowhere worked except for local use.

Between seams Nos. 1 and 2, appears a limestone, often 4 to 5 feet thick, which, from its purity and frequent exposure, is to be esteemed a valuable resource in connection with the agricultural improvement of this region, as well as for other uses to which it may be put. Though often impregnated with iron, it is never so much so as to unfit it for masonry, to which it has been frequently applied with satisfactory results. (For analysis, see table in chapter 13 on Miscellaneous Minerals.)

The Third Seam varies generally from 2 to 4 feet, in some cases swelling to 7 and 8 feet, and contains a very good article of fuel. Three miles south of the mouth of Big Buffalo creek it measures 4 feet, including from 8 to 10 inches of impure slaty coal, and is very compact, breaking with difficulty. Two miles S S. W. of the same point it is 5 feet, with a parting of 6 to 8 inches. At the head of Deep Run hallow it has dwindled to 18 or 20 inches, while opposite Kingwood it is 7 to 8 feet including the partings, and yields about 5 feet of coal, of which 3 feet are in one bed. Corresponding to this increase in thickness, there is also an improvement in the quality, but, unfortunately, the expansion here described is quite local. Two analysis from this place give :

Carbon	67.28	68.32
Volatile Matter	29.68	26.48
Ash	3.04	5.20
	100.00	100.00

As far as the scant data on this region go, it would appear that the 8 or 9-foot seam worked at Austin, on the Balt. & Ohio R. R., and to the S. W. of Kingwood, must be another expansion of this stratum. Just as has been mentioned of it elsewhere, it is here divided by partings, having 4 feet of solid coal at the bottom yielding an excellent article. This is the only part of it worked at present, though if mined on an extensive scale the whole thickness can be utilized.

It is here at Austin a very valuable bed, for, according to a report on it by Prof. J. P. Lesley, "it makes a clear, even, sil-"very coke, sufficiently hard to bear the heaviest burden of the blast furnace."

Above it is sometimes a shale, which, in some localities, as at Fairfax's, south of Kingwood ferry, abounds in nodules of very rich Iron ore of a delicate gray color, while in others the ore is replaced by nodules of impure limestone. At Austin a seam of ore 16 to 20 inches thick. and the same as worked at the Martin Iron Works, is seen 30 feet below it.

In geological nomenclature, this coal is known as the "Upper Freeport." It is near the *top* of the Lower Coal Measures, though, according to Prof. Lesley's report, before alluded to, it would be very close to, if not at, the *bottom* of them, as he locates it 400 feet below the Mahoning sandstone, which is the upper number of the series. There is a coarse sandstone in the Barren Measures at this distance above the Upper Freeport, which, I think, he has mistaken for the Mahoning, for the Lower Coal Series in the Preston basin are not as thick as 400 feet.

Between seams Nos. 2 and 3 is a limestone band, sometimes in nodules and again some 4 or 5 feet thick, often very rich in lime, and associated with a white argillaceous clay and shales of a very peculiar character. It varies very much in its position between the two coal seams, being at some localities 50 or 60 feet above No. 2, while, in others, it is only 4 or 5 feet; on Sypole Run being 8 or 10 feet. This, and the band mentioned as lying between seams Nos. 1 and 2, are so much alike it would be difficult, by aspect or composition, to tell them apart. It is a fine grained, bluish-gray stone, and like many of the limestones of the coal measures, slightly ferruginous—sometimes so much so as to burn with difficulty, slacking slowly, but nevertheless making a valuable lime for agriculture. It has been quarried on Sandy Ridge. Near Kingwood it is a dull, bluish gray, tinged with yellow, compact, fine grained, conchoidal, with specks of iron pyrites and calc spar, *very hydraulic*, sets promptly, and becomes very hard. (For analysis, see table in chapter on Micellaneous Minerals.

The Fourth Seam, 300 feet above No. 3, is in the Lower Barren Measures. It contains 3 feet of an excellent quality of coal.

The Fifth Seam, 150 feet above the last, is the lowest member of the Upper Coal Group, and is the same as that worked in Mineral county, near Piedmont, by the Virginia Coal Co. It occupies the centre of the basin in the tops of the hills at Newburg, where it yields an excellent gas coal, and is 10 to 12 feet thick, though only 9 to 9½ feet are worked, the top being left to support the slate roof.

In Prof. Rogers' report on the Preston field it is not mentioned at all, for the reason, I presume, that his explorations seem to have been in the northern-half of the county, where the hills are too low to catch it. As to whether this will prove to be the case, also, as we go south from Newburg, nothing really deffinite can now be stated, on account of the paucity of data concerning the region, but it may safely be asserted that, if it does exist, it will be in small isolated patches as at the place where it is now worked.

THE LOWER COAL AND BARREN MEASURES IN THE MONONGAHELA BASIN.

The broad elevated tract extending from Pennsylvania into West Virginia, nearly coinciding with the boundary between Preston and Monongalia counties, and which, on the West Virginia map, is called Laurel Hill, contains the last important axis met with in this part of the State. As followed in a southwest direction, the dips of the rocks, on both sides of the ridge, are seen to be rapidly becoming more gentle, and the axis, thus flattened out, soon buries from view the Appalachian rocks previously exposed, while the ridge itself subsides to a less and less elevation, until, at the Falls of the Tygart's Valley river, in the southern part of Marion county, about 30 miles from the Pennsylvania line, it becomes so insignificant that the Mahoning sandstone, the top of the Lower Coal Measures, passes over it unbroken.

Proceeding northwest from that portion of this axis, which is sufficiently marked by an anticlinal to bring to view the sub carboniferous rocks, and so completely separate the Preston from the Monongalia basin, we soon enter upon the Lower Coal Measures. These rapidly dip below the water level, giving place to the Lower Barrens, which, in turn, disappear and are supplanted by the Upper Coal Measures, whose lowest seam, the Pittsburgh, is seen high in the hills, a few miles east of Morgantown, but comes to the water level some 2 miles up Scott's Run, a west branch of the Monongahela river. The northwest dip still continuing, the upper coals sink below the surface as this run is ascended, leaving the surface of the country composed of the shales, &c., of the Upper Barrens.

As these upper coals will form a chapter to themselves, I will at present treat only of the measures below them, for the following, description of which, I am indebted to a paper read before the American Philosophical Society, on 16 Feb., 1872, by Prof. J. J. Stevenson, and to the Geology of Virginia, 1839, by Prof. Wm. B. Rogers. In making the section the line of observation was, in both cases, along Decker's creek to the river, thence down the same to Scott's run, and on up the stream. The following measurements* are those given by the former gentleman, but in the reversed order to that in which they were published. I give them in this way so as to keep up the line of march heretore observed, viz.: from east to west.

SECTION OF THE LOWER COAL MEASURES.

1. Shale	10 feet
2. *Coal*	1 "
3. Sandstone	4 "
4. *Coal*	1¾ "
5. Shale	25 "
6. Sandstone	25 to 30 "
7. Shale	15 to 20 "
8. *Coal*	2 to 3 "
9. Sandstone and Shale	20 to 30 "
10. *Coal*	3½ (?) "
11. Shale	30 "
12. Limestone "Ferriferous"	4 to 5 "
13. Shale	10 "
14. Sandstone	5 "
15. *Coal*	1 "
16. Shale	10 "
17. *Coal*	4 to 5 "
18. Shales	1 to 25 "
19. *Coal*	1¾ "
20. Shale	12 "
21. Sandstone, "Mahoning"	75 "

This would therefore make the Lower Coal Measures in this part of West Virginia from 260 to 300 feet thick.

Shale (No. 1).—Near the bottom of this is an irregular band of a coarse gray or grayish dun carbonate of iron, covered with layers of hydrated protoxide—the result of decomposition. The band has an estimated thickness of one foot, though it sometimes occurs in nodular masses, varying from 2 to 12 inches in diameter. It is generally of inferior quality, though

*In the section, as given by Prof. Rogers, *Coals* Nos. 2 and 4 are not mentioned, while between *Sandstone* No. 14, and *Coal* No. 15, he places 6 to 8 feet of dark blue, argellaceous *shale*, in the lower part of which is a layer of nodules of Carbonate of Iron, coated with Brown Oxide of Iron, and was the material chiefly used at the old furnace on Decker's creek. It was mined on the side of Laurel Hill, in a southeast direction from the furnace. The average thickness of the band is from 6 to 10 inches, through the nodules are sometimes a foot in diameter. (For analysis see Chapter on Iron). This is mentioned to call attention to the matter, so that future exploration may reconcile the slight differences in the sections.

in bygone days it was used in the Decker's creek furnaces, and for this purpose was mined at various points, in isolated patches, along the west base of Laurel Hill.

Coals (Nos. 2 and 4), as exposed on Decker's creek, are of no importance. No. 4 shows a thickness of 21 inches, in which are 3 partings. A very hard refractory sandstone, containing some imperfect specimens of vegetable fossils, mostly of the genus Lepidodendron, lies between these coals. It is a good fire stone, and was so used in the old furnace near by. No. 2 is one foot thick, and of good quality. On Decker's creek these may be seen near the bridge, below Hagadore's mill. On Booth's creek, only one of them was seen. At Nuzum's mill, it is as irregular as the Brier Hill coal of Ohio. Along the railroad cutting for some distance, it shows itself about 3 feet thick, but as it approaches the station, the underlying fire-clay increases in thickness, while the coal diminishes, until at length the latter entirely disappears. At this locality (*i. e.* where 3 feet thick), it has been worked to a slight extent, yielding a coal of excellent quality. The fire-clay seems to be equal to that of Dover, Ohio, which it greatly resembles.

Sandstone (No. 6) varies from moderately coarse comglomerate to fine grained sandstone. Compact and flaggy layers alternate on Decker's creek. On Booth's creek it is mostly compact. At Nuzum's mill it is uneven in texture, and has weathered so as to have huge chambers. The compact layers are very refractory, some of them having been employed for furnace hearths. On Decker's creek, 3 or 4 inches of coal have been found in this rock.

Coal (No. 8) has been opened at several points along Decker's creek and its tributaries, and is in high repute for domestic use. It is friable, free from pyrites, and has been locally termed the "Blacksmith's Vein." Near the furnace, it is of the peacock variety. It was formerly worked near Clinton Furnace, but after the discovery of the larger seam above, the workings were abandoned, and have caved in. So far as known it has not been worked at Nuzum's mill.

Coal (No. 10) was worked many years ago on Decker's creek, a little below the old furnace, but in 1872 it was so closed up by slides that Prof. Stevenson was not able to see it. Old miners said it was 3½ and 4 feet thick, and resembled cannel.

The shales above it are laminated and highly bituminous, burn readily and have been mistaken for cannel.

The Ferriferous Limestone (No. 23) is frequently double with an intervening shale, sometimes several feet thick. For a few inches near its upper surface, it is yellow and so highly ferruginous as in some places to constitute a calcareous iron ore, for which it has been worked in bygone days, in one or two places. It is quite persistent for twenty miles south of the Pennsylvania line, but does not appear in the sections at Nuzum's mill. It was used as a flux at the old furnace on Decker's creek, and at the Clinton Furnace on Booth's creek. It affords a good lime for agricultural and rough work, though but little use has been made of it, notwithstanding that it shows in almost every hill, and lime commands 15 cents per bushel at the kiln.

Shale (No. 13) contains nodular masses of carbonate of iron, which, though of good quality, is in too small quantity to be of value.

Coal (No. 17).—In some places parts of it are rendered quite impure by pyrites, but towards the center it is remarkably free from that mineral. This is the important and most persistent seam of the group. It appears on Cheat river near Ice's Ferry, where it is worked on Tibbs Run, a tributary of Decker's creek, and in some of the various openings near it. In these localities it is 4 feet thick, divided near the bottom by a thin clay parting. The shale above is very bituminous, has a conchoidal fracture, and is a cannel coal of inferior quality, which in some places has been worked with the coal below. The coal in this seam is very friable, breaking into rhombic pieces. Traced southwesterly it crosses Aaron's creek, near the Kingwood road, about four miles from Morgantown, and is worked by Mr. Bell. It also appears at several points along Coburn's creek. On the Evansville road, about seven miles from Morgantown, it is opened by Mr. Howell. Here it lies directly under the Mahoning sandstone, and gives the following section;

	Feet.	Inches
Coal	3	1
Clay Shale		2 to 4
Coal	1	3
Shale		2
Coal		3
	4	11

Evidently the whole bed is not worked here, for on the other side of the hill appears to be a foot or more of coal above, but it does not pay to work more than the lower 4 feet.

Coal, (local).—Ten to fifteen feet below this coal, in a branch of Decker's creek, there is is a seam about one foot thick, which appears to be very local, as it is not found on the main stream, or to the south.

Coal (No. 19).—On Decker's creek, this is about 15 inches thick, was worked some years ago near the Point House, on that stream, and is said to be of excellent quality. This seam does not appear on Booth's creek, nor did Prof. Stevenson see it on White Day. A coal bed occupying the same position has been slightly worked at Nuzum's Mill, and is there 3 feet thick.

Shale (No. 20).—On Decker's creek, this is of dark color, and near the middle contains a band of fossiliferous nodular iron ore. It seems to be present on White Day creek, 12 miles south of Morgantown, but is not persistent in Pennsylvania.

Mahoning Sandstone (No. 21), is for the most part a massive rock, with alternating fine and coarse layers, the latter being sometimes a conglomerate. In some places it is flaggy, while in others it is compact and very suitable for building purposes, as blocks 6 to 8 feet thick can be quarried without difficulty. The lower part descends to the bed of Decker's creek, near the site of the old forge, but, owing to the diminished dip in going west, together with the rapid descent of the creek in the same direction, about 40 feet of it are seen at the mouth. About 2 miles below Morgantown, near Granville, it sinks below the river. To the south, it rises quite rapidly, and at Booth's creek, 4 miles above Morgantown, it is about 40 feet above the river, where it shows in a bluff of about 75 feet, in some portions weathered in large rounded cavities, and in others, showing a strangely honey-combed surface.

THE LOWER BARREN MEASURES.

In this part of the State these are about 400 feet thick. I do not consider it necessary, in a treatise of this kind, to give a detailed section of them, as they contain only one coal seam, out of about five, that is thick enough to be of any importance, and even that appears to be comparatively local. According to Prof. Rogers' section, it is about 180 feet above the Mahoning sandstone. On Decker's creek it has been wrought at several places as high up as the Old Forge, where it runs out on the top of the hills. It sinks below the bed of the Monongahela river, above the mouth of Scott's run, about 2½ miles below Morgantown. Some 30 years ago it was opened in the hill opposite the University, near the village, while 5 or 6 years ago it was worked in a ravine, east of the town, to supply local use, but the mine was abandoned, owing to the thinness of the bed, which made the cost of extraction too great to admit of competition with the openings into the Pittsburgh seam, which is 7 to 8 feet thick in this immediate vicinity. In 1872, it was opened by Mr. Miller and Mr. Fordyce, to supply their own fire-places, and at the opening by the former gentleman, it showed: Bituminous shale, 6 to 8 inches, *Coal*, 3 to 3½ feet. The general structure of the coal is slaty, and contains a considerable a considerable amount of sulphur, which is unfortunate, as otherwise its large proportion of fixed carbon would render it very valuable for manufacturing purposes, for in burning it gives off an intense heat, lasts long on the fire, and makes but little soot. The bed is frequently cut up by "horse-backs" and "mud-seams."

According to the section of Prof. Rogers, the Lower Barrens in this part of West Virginia contain 11 bands of limestone, of an aggregate thickness of 24 feet.

Most of these are ferrugenous, and otherwise impure, but are still generally capable of yielding a lime well suited to agriculture and building, as well as some domestic uses where the color is unimportant.

THE LOWER COAL MEASURES WEST OF TUCKER COUNTY AND RICH MOUNTAIN.

On page 177 *et seq.* it was noted that Laurel Hill formed a distinct boundary between the coals of the Preston and Monongahela

hela basins, but that as it was traced to the southwest it became broader and flatter, until, at Valley Falls, in Marion county, the Mahoning sandstone and its underlying seams passed over it unbroken. Hence, it will be understood that somewhere between this point and Decker's creek, the lower coals will be seen lapping over this anticlinal and joining the the two basins, so that what in the north were two separate troughs coalesce at some place about the northern edge of Taylor county and gradually form one continuous area, which stretches uninterruptedly across the State from Rich mountain in Randolph, which range, as mentioned in the early part of this paper, is practically the eastern boundary of the coal formation in this part of West Virginia. Unfortunately but little reliable information concerning this region is be had, for accurate observations thereon are few and far between, and even these very cursory. It is impossible to give any detailed section of the strata, for none has ever been made, and beyond the fact that the Lower Coal Measures have increased from 250 feet in Monongalia, to a considerably greater thickness in Randolph, but little can be said. Whether the number of the included seams has also increased, as is the case further south, or what changes they have undergone, or what their total combined thickness is, is entirely unknown. Careful examinations may show that other beds, besides those to be presently mentioned, which in the north were small and worthless, are here thick and important; and there is no doubt that valuable seams, now hidden by the soil and loose rock that cover the hills, and of which, at this time, we know nothing, will be found, for it should be borne in mind that western Randolph, the largest part of Barbour, Upshur, and Webster, and parts of Braxton and Lewis, have the Lower Coal Measures and their included seams above water level, while the western portion of Barbour and Upshur, and much of the area of Braxton and Lewis, have also the coals of the Upper Coal Measures.

The following partial section, beginning with the Mahoning sandstone is said to have been obtained in a salt well bored on the Buckhannon river:*

* The detailed measurements given in this and the next few pages were obtained from "Notes on the Geology of West Virginia," by Prof. J. J. Stevenson, a paper read before the Am. Phil. Soc., 5th Feb., 1875.

1. Rock	60	feet.
2. Coal	15	"
3. Shale	32	"
4. Sandstone	40	"
5. Coal	4	"
6. Rock	160	"
7. Coal	4	"
8. Sandstone	40	"
9. Coal	3	"
10. Sandstone	120	"
	478	feet.

There is no evidence in this to show that the boring reached the base of the lower coals.

No. 2. *Coal*, 15 feet, is the Upper Freeport, or the same seam that on Decker's creek, in the Monongalia basin, shows 4 to 5 feet, (page 178), and at Austin, in the Preston basin, 7 to 9 feet, (page 175). As traced south it seems very much to augment in thickness, in some places showing 21½ feet, but its partings so increase that, as a rule, whenever it gets over 12 ft. thick, it is so much cut up that the amount of workable coal in it bears no just ratio to the total size. As an example: In Upshur county, on Sand Run, several miles south of the Beverly road, it measures:

1. Bituminous Shale	5	feet.	0	inches
2. Coal	–	"	7	"
3. Cannel, poor	2	"	6	"
4. Shale, slightly carbonaceous	4	"	0	"
5. Coal, slaty	1	"	10	"
6. Shale, slightly carbonaceous	1	"	3	"
7. Coal partly cannel	2	"	2	"
8. Clay, drab	–	"	8	"
9. Coal, bony	–	"	6	"
10. Clay	–	"	8	"
11. Coal, slaty	1	"	1	"
12. Clay, with streaks of coal	1	"	2	"
Total	21		6	" *

On Grassy Run, another tributary of Buckhannon river, as well as on the river itself, 10 or 11 miles below Buckhannon

* This section is given in detail to especially correct an erroneous impression that seems to be generally prevalent concerning its value, as it is often as important to the interests of a community to know what they have *not* got, as to know what they have, for accurate knowledge and statements concerning the resources of a district will often save both its credit and its money.

town, it is seen in its great thickness, but very much interstratified with slate. In fact, at the former place, out of a thickness of 18 feet $1\frac{1}{4}$ inches there are only two benches that could be worked. The top one is 5 feet 11 inches and the lower 3 feet 8 inches, 3 feet $4\frac{1}{2}$ inches of partings and thin worthless coals being between. On Roaring creek, in Randolph county, however, we find that out of a thickness of 13 feet 10 inches there are 8 feet 11 inches of good coal, (though quite sulphurous when examined under a magnifying glass), with partings so thin on the outcrop that they may all—save one of 4 inches—practically disappear on driving in,* and consequently it is a very valuable seam. On Tygart's Valley river it is seen in many places in Barbour and Taylor, to within a few miles of Grafton, in the latter, but at some of these, though it presents a very handsome appearance to the eye, yet, under a glass, a good deal of sulphur can be distinguished. At Nuzum's Mills, Marion county, it shows: *Cannel*, 1 foot; *Bituminous Coal*, 4 to 5 feet, and is a good, strong fuel. Near Weston, in Lewis county, this coal-bed is said to occur in the bed of the West Fork river.

On Roaring creek and Sand run, Randolph and Upshur counties, we find below this seam, and corresponding to *No.* 5 of section given on page 184, a persistent coal bed, quite regular in thickness, and varying but little from 4 feet. The coal is irised, exceeding rich in bituminous matter, and burns and cokes well.

Still lower than this, and quite near the bottom of the Coal Measures, is the seam from which the town of Beverly draws its supply of fuel. As opened by Mr. S. B. Hart, near the pike, the bed is made up of:

	Feet.	*Inches.*
Coal, sulphurous		
Black Clay		4
Coal		1
Clay	3	6
Coal		1
	1	7
Total	5	7

* Between this point and Beverly, 7 miles from the former, and 9 miles from the latter, on the Staunton & Parkersburg Pike, Mr. J. R. Bestor, one of the assistants to the State Board of Centennial Managers, measured this seam at "Hillary bank," where it is partially worked, and gives, in the ascending order: *Coal* 21 inches; Slate 2; *Coal*, 4 feet; Slate, $2\frac{1}{2}$ inches; *Coal*, 2 feet: total 8 feet $1\frac{1}{2}$ inches. No solid roof had been reached, and coal was found under the floor, which was 8 inches of Slate.

The bottom coal is very inferior, and contains a notable proportion of sulphur.

In February of 1876, Mr. Bestor made an examination of a portion of Barbour county, near the Tygart's Valley river, and reports the following beds. It is to be regretted that the examinations were not sufficiently in detail to identify the various seams, one with the other in the different localities.

On B. Woodford's land, 5½ miles north of Philippi, on the Parkersburg and Webster pike, a 5½-foot seam of bituminous coal is worked. The bed is, in reality, some 8 feet thick, but the top and bottom are so mixed with slate as to be worthless. This is reported to be very generally found in this part of the country, and is used at nearly every farm house in the neighborhood. The abutments of the bridge at Philippi are on a 5-foot coal seam, which is accessible in low water. The total thickness has not yet been discovered. This, or another seam, is found 3 miles below Philippi, in the river bed. Thickness 5 feet, as far as seen, the bottom never having been reached. About 40 feet up the hill, on the east side of the river, at Philippi, is a bed made up of: *Coal*, 2½ feet; Slate, 2 feet 2 inches; *Coal*, 2 feet; total, 6 feet 8 inches. On the west side of the stream it is 5½ feet thick, and is worked at various places along the Philippi and Beverly pike. On Geo. Pitman's land, 4 miles south of Philippi, is 5½ feet bituminous coal, 40 feet above which is 2½ feet of carbonate of iron, and 10 feet higher, a 10-foot coal bank, the upper part being cannel. This latter is seen again on J. H. Strickland's land 4½ miles southwest of Philippi, on the east side of the river, and 40 feet over it is 5 to 5½ feet of bituminous coal. Near C. T. Fisher's mill, 6½ miles south of Philippi, is a 3 foot 10-inch seam, and near Burlington, 11½ miles south of the same radiating point, a 3-foot seam, both the last bituminous.

Before leaving the northern half of the State, mention should be made of

THE LOWER COAL MEASURES OF HANCOCK AND BROOKE COUNTIES.

These appear in Hancock county, at its northern end, and as they dip to the south they disappear below water level before they reach Brooke county, so that they have to be reached by shafting. Two seams have been proven in the northern end of Brooke, being 180 and 210 feet, respectively, below high water mark, and each averaging about 4 feet 2 inches thick. No shafting for these has been done in West Virginia, but at Steubenville, on the Ohio side of the river, there are 9 shafts in operation, raising large quantities of coal considered superior for iron making. One of these collieries has driven their entries under the river to the West Virginia side.

These two seams give a value to the land in this neighborhood of $100 per acre for the "mineral privileges" alone.

THE NEW AND KANAWHA RIVER COAL BASINS.

We now come to that district of the State, which, by reason of the variety of its coals, and number of its seams, is to be considered one of the most valuable portions of the Appalachian coal field, and has helped, in no little degree, to give West Virginia the reputation it enjoys of being one of the richest of any State in the Union in this great element of civilization, wealth and prosperity. For this reason it has a peculiar interest to the capitalist, while from a geological point of view, the great development of the coal measures is very important.

Going back to a pre-carbonaceous period, it would seem that this section was a deep basin, constantly settling down, and being filled up, while the northern portion of the State was nearly stationary. As an indication of this, it may be noted, that the Vespertine formation at Westernport, on the Potomac, is, according to Prof. Rogers, 200 feet thick, while in Greenbrier, it is 800 feet. In this latter measurement, he seems to have taken no notice of some 300 feet of rock, that justly belongs to its upper portion. In the north, at the same place, the Umbral (or Sub-carboniferous) limestone is 80 feet, while in the Greenbrier mountain, in Pocahontas, he gives it as 822 feet. On the Potomac the Umbral shales are 838 feet versus 1,260 feet in the above mentioned locality in Pocahontas, and the indications are that all three of these still increase in thickness as we come south toward New River, so that at Hinton they may be taken as aggregating 3,500 feet versus 1,128 feet in the north. Continuing on up in the geological column, the Conglomerate is 150 feet thick on the Potomac, and on New river, according to Prof. Wm. M. Fontaine, 1,350 feet, including the Passage Rocks, while 400 feet takes in the Lower Coal Measures in the one case, and 1,340 feet about embraces them on the Kanawha. Finally, in the north, the Lower Barrens are 400 feet, against 700 feet in the south.

By an addition of these figures, and dealing in round numbers, we see that while 2,000 feet of strata were forming on the Potomac, or northern West Virginia, some 6,840 feet were being deposited in the New River and Kanawha region; or, in other words, during this period, the latter sank about 4,840 feet more than did the former.

It is to this that we must look for an explanation of the presence of the vàrious anti-clinal axis in the north, and their absence in the south.

As this depression took place, the strain, or tension, of the rock-beds on the eastern border of the basin increased in a direct ratio with the amount of the subsidence; so that the less the latter the less was the former, and it is a self-evident proposition that the less the tension the greater would be the force necessary to break the rocks asunder. Therefore, when the great thrust, or press, on the strata from the east came into effect, it found the strength of the beds on the eastern border of this southern basin so much impaired, that it crushed up the formations adjacent thereto, breaking them into a number of faults of great magnitude, which extend along the southern border of West Virginia, and are nearly coextensive with this depression, and its prolongation, southward, while in the north, the rocks, not being in this very tense state, were not broken, but the Alleghanies and the country to the west were thrown into a series of folds, which became less and less abrupt, as they would naturally do, the further and further we get from the primary force.

The gradation of faults to folds, is well seen in the most westerly of the former, which passes just west of Peter's mountain, in the southern part of the State, and is seen near Caldwell Station, in Greenbrier county, at the Chesapeake and Ohio Railroad trestle, over Monroe branch. In the former place it brings the Silurian rocks agaist the Vespertine, while in the latter it becomes so small that only the highest members of the Devonian abut against the Vespertine.

From this we can see, that, as the strata were elevated along this most western fault, their flank would raise the country to the west as a whole, and give it a gradual slope at right angles to the line of elevation, and as the latter was northeast and southwest, so the former would be northwest. This is really the case, for, from this range on the eastern edge of Greenbrier to the Ohio river the formations have one continual northwest downgrade, save here and there where they become nearly horizontal, and there is no good evidence after we get away from the immediate vicinity of the fault, that a single reversal of dip comes in during the whole distance. In the eastern portion of this vast extent of territory, denudation and erosion have carried off the upper strata, and east of Little Sewell, all of the Lower Coal Measures have disappeared. Going west, the rocks dip faster than the plane of erosion, and thus we get successively into higher and higher strata, so that Gauley mountain is sufficiently high to catch nearly all of the lower coals. Below the Kanawha Falls—the dip still continuing—the conglomerate passes out of view; a short distance west of Charleston, the Lower Measures in their turn sink below water level, and near Pocatalico some 14 miles further on, the highest member of the Lower Barrens is lost to sight, as it goes beneath the bed of the Kanawha.

Between these extremes, of gently inclined formations in the south, and folded strata, in the north, must be an intermediate area where the one passes into the other.

As the depression of the southern basin became less and less as it went northerly, the tension, and therefore the cause for the faults diminished, so that somewhere about opposite Huntersville, in Pocahontas, this system begins to cease, and north of a line drawn from the northeast corner of Greenbrier to the northern part of Pleasants, the strata commence to appear in folds, and as we proceed towards the Pennsylvania line and away from the modifying influence of the faulted country, so these anti-clinals become more and more marked.

NEW RIVER COALS.

In Mercer county, in the valley of the Blue Stone river, are extensive beds of bituminous coal, which would seem to belong to the sub-Conglomerate Measures, and are here developed to a greater thickness than in any other portion of the State. The examinations in this county have not been sufficiently in detail to enable us to state the number of the seams, but it may be mentioned that the thickest one reported is 11 feet, although nothing is said as to the amount of clay partings in it,

In Summers county, in the hills on the opposite side of New river from Hinton, a 6-foot seam of coal has been opened some 800 feet above the stream, and indications would seem to point out that it is the same as the seam presently to be spoken of as worked at Quinnimont.

A carefully observed section of the strata on New river was made by Prof. Wm. M. Fontaine, at Quinnimont, and on Piney river two miles below. The observations were begun at the former place at the base of the hill, for the sake of obtaining as much as possible of the Umbral shales. As the strata dip westerly, Nos. 1 and 2 of these are carried below water level, so that at Piney, the foot of the hill shows only the bottom of No. 3. The measurements marked "not seen" were obtained from observations elsewhere, or were given by Mr. S. F. Morris, the engineer at Quinnimont:

UMBRAL SHALES.

	Feet.
1. Red shales, thinly laminated, visible	50
2. Gray calcareous sandstone	20
3. Variegated shales, with nodules of carbonate of lime near the top	70
Total for umbral	140

TRANSITION STRATA OR PASSAGE ROCKS, FROM THE UMBRAL TO THE CONGLOMERATE SERIES.

	Feet.
1. Thinly laminated grey flags and calcareous shales, with impure *Coal* near the top	50
2. Black fissile slates and sandstones	20
Total for transition	70

CONGLOMERATE SERIES ON PINEY.

	Feet.
1. Lower conglomerate	80
2. Black slate with 1½ foot *Coal* bed (not seen)	11
3. Olive colored marlytes passing into olive and reddish sandstones	100
4. *Coal* and slate, 1 ft 0 in. Sandstone, 8 " 8 " *Coal*, 0 " 8 " Slate, 2 " 6 " *Coal*, 0 " 8 "	13
5. Bright red shales and marlytes	30
6. Variegated marlytes	40
7. Ferruginous limestone	2
8. Sandstones	75
9. *Coal* system with interstratifications of thin *Coal* and slate at base, and on top, sandstones, shales, and flags	80
10 Fine grey flags and sandstones	90
11. *Coal*, not fully seen	2½
12. Firm grey sandstones	50
13. Olive marlytes	40
14. *Coal* system, at bottom interstratifications of slate and coal, one seam 1 foot; on top, flags passing into firm sandstones	80
15 Fire clay, and 1-foot *Coal* seam imperfectly exposed, given as 2 to 4½-feet of impure splint coal	2 to 4½
16. A thick mass of strata not fully exposed at every point, may be divided as follows: (16a) sandstone, 50 feet; (16b) *Coal* seam, not seen, given as 2 feet; (16c) bluish sandy slates, 60 feet; (16d) *Coal*, not seen, given as 20 inches; (16e) olive grey shaly sandstones, 40 feet. Total..	150
17. Quinnimont *Coal* series, which is made up of splint *Coal*, at bottom, 1 foot 2 inches; fire clay 2½ feet; semi-bituminous *Coal*, 4 feet. Total	7⅔
18. Dark blue slate and sandstones	80 to 100
19. Olive grey sandstones and shales	100
20. Black slate, with some thin *Coal*	10
21. Upper, or Great Conglomerate	150 to 200
Total for Conglomerate Series	1,195

The Coal in No. 20, as seen at Quinnimont, is only 6 inches on the outcrop. In Feb., 1875, it was opened, and the first 8 feet down increased to 3 feet, and was still improving when this thickness was measured. It cokes well, and when heated in a pipe in a smith's forge, gave a clear, white, bright light in such quantities as to suggest a good gas coal.

The 4-foot seam of No. 17 is the most important of this section, being the one where the Quinnimont Furnace draws its supply of fuel. It is 1,085 feet above New river. The coal is a semi-bituminous, very soft and friable and makes a most superior coke, not being excelled by even the celebrated Connelsville coke of Pennsylvania. It is, also, a most excellent steam and domestic article, making a very hot, red fire. It will be spoken of more fully in these respects, in the the chap- devoted to the quality of West Virginia coals.

The Great Conglomerate usually forms the tops of the mountains facing New river. As we go back into the country, on each side a second range of hills very soon appears, and in these will be found more coals, which, though usually accredited to the Conglomerate Series, in reality belong to the Lower Measures. In the vicinity of Raleigh court-house, southwest of Quinnimont, on Buckly's Mill tract, is seen one of the lower beds of this latter, which measures 6 feet 2 inches of soft and very pure bituminous coal, with shale overhead. It is seen again on Loup creek, 15 miles from the court-house, on the Fayetteville road, at McCoy's bank, where it measures 4 feet 10 inches in the breast, and 6 feet on the outcrop. In neither place are there any partings, and it is a most valuable seam, for the most part underlying the whole of the Raleigh plateau. Some distance above this, and about 200 feet below the tops of the hills, at the head of one of the hollows of Big White Stick, occurs a 4½-foot seam, with no parting save about 1½ inches of coal dirt and sulphur one or two inches from the roof, which is shale. Continuing in a southwest course from here, the Raleigh plateau gives out, and we descend into the valley of the Marshes of Coal, which, cutting far down into the Conglomerate Series, are marked by an absence of any workable seams till we cross over to the Guyandotte and Cherry Pond mountains, on the borders of Wyoming and Boone, in the upper portions of which the Lower Coal Measures and their included seams again make their appearance; and on Gravel Hollow of Peach Tree creek, near the juncture of the two ranges, four seams belonging to this series have been seen, and measure:

No. 1, 3 feet; No. 2, 2 feet 8 inches; No. 3, 3 feet 3½ inches; No. 4, 4 feet; all free from partings and containing an exceeding pure, though friable, article. The distance between Nos. 1 and 2, and Nos. 3 and 5, are each about 50 feet, that between Nos. 2 and 3, was not ascertained. Several hundred feet above No. 4 and the gaps in the mountains, first a 12-foot, and above that a 4-foot seam have been reported.

The deep valley position of the head-waters of Coal river is not fully appreciated until the observer stands on the mountains last mentioned, where, being some 2,000 feet above the streams below, he has the whole country spread at his feet, and sees that the plateau of Raleigh court-house forms a high eastern rim of the Marsh Fork basin, and is far above its level, while, looking across this, he can note the country rising into White Oak and Flat-Top mountains, over which, so great is the elevation of the observer, can be distinguished the blue out-line of Peter's mountain in Virginia.

Passing from this point in a west-southwest direction into Wyoming and McDowell, the hills become lower than the Guyandotte mountains, though still high enough to contain not only the Conglomerate Series but a portion of those above. This country is accredited with seams as thick as 12 feet, but there are no reliable observations to justify more than a mere mention of this fact.

Returning now to Quinnimont, and proceeding towards the tier of hills back from the river, the same seams observed in the Raleigh plateau ought to be found. However, as they have never been examined, their thickness is a matter of conjecture, but as Big Sewell mountain has a far greater height than the region immediately to the southwest of the river, it will contain a good deal more of the Lower Coal Measures, and hence more seams may be expected. Continuing northeast into the western part of Nicholas, and into Webster, the general elevation of the country is below Sewell, consequently the hills contain only lower strata, and the hill tops west of the Forks of Cherry river are made up of the conglomerate, all the upper coals having been denuded off, and on Hominy, Cherry, Cranberry, Williams, and the heads of Gauley and Elk rivers, are to be found only the conglomerate coals, very thin and very unimportant.*

*The largest seam that we know of in the this region is 3 feet 7 inches. It is seen on Panther run, of Gauley river, near the bridle-path from Kentucky to the Promised Land.

Resuming the northwest line of examination, the New river basin becomes more shallow, and the strata begin to feel the effects of the dying out of the faults, and the beginning of the folds on the eastern border of the State, and we notice that they become more tilted, so that when we reach Rich mountain, in Randolph, they are very much steeper than when seen on New River.

This line of observation from Wyoming to Randolph has been chosen because it is about the eastern edge of the Lower Coal Measures, while that of the conglomerate series may be said to be a line joining Rich mountain and Flat-Top, as explained in the beginning of this chapter.

Returning now to Quinnimont, the course of observation leads us down New River. To better appreciate the dip of the strata, as we go west, I will, whenever possible, refer to the one horizontal line of tide water, so that it will be plainly seen how any individual stratum becomes lower and lower. In some cases these figures will not be *exact*, but very close approximations, not varying more than 15 or 20 feet from reality.

About 16 miles, by railroad, below Quinnimont, in the hill opp site Dimmock station, two seams have been exposed. By aneroid measurement, they are 437 and 703 feet respectively above New river, and both in the conglomerate series. The first, by the side of the path going up the hill, is 4½ feet thick, with no partings, and a very pure and fine bituminous coal, much harder than the average of the New river coals. The second one is a few feet above the level of Rush creek, which mouths at Dimmock, measures 5 feet of clear coal, and was worked by Cary Bibbs.

Twenty miles from Quinnimont, by the railroad, at the mouth of Ephraim's creek, the following seams were opened by J. A. McGuffin, Esq., Superintendent of the Longdale Coal and Iron Company:

Estimated Heights Above Tidewater.	Heights above New River.		Thickness of Seams.
1,020	0	New River Level........	
1,555	535	No. 1 Seam..................	2 feet, 0 inches
1,655	635	" 2 "	4 " 0 "
1,695	675	" 3 "	2 " 6 "
1,707	687	" 4 "	2 " 8 "
1,807	787	" 5 "	2 " 6 "
1,907	887	" 6 "	1 " 0 "
2,135	1,115	About the top of the Great Conglomerate..	
2,185	1,165	No. 7 Seam..................	4 " 10 "
2,375	1,355	" 8 "	4 " 6 "

No. 5 of the table is the seam worked at Quinnimont, but here dwindled to 2½ feet. At that place it is 2,250 feet above tide, while here it is only 1,807 feet—a dip of 443 feet in a straight line of 10 miles, or 44 feet to the mile.

No. 7, the first seam of the Lower Coal Measures, is the only one worked at this place. The mine is about a mile further down the river, and a quarter of a mile above Sewell depot, and shows at that place an average thickness of 3½ feet, yielding a very soft and tender coal that makes a most excellent coke, which is used by the Longdale Coal & Iron Co. in their furnace at Longdale, Alleghany county, Va. The first opening on the seam was at the place noted in the section, but a nipping down of roof caused an abandonment of the work.

Ten miles below Sewell, at Hawk's Nest, on the land of the Gauley Kanawha Coal Co., the following partial section has been made:

Height above Tidewater.	Height above New River.		Thickness of Seams.
751	0	Level of New River.	
928	177	No. 1 Seam, about........................	2 feet, 0 inches
1,351	600	Top of Conglomerate on East side of Mill Creek.	
1,729	978	No. 2 Seam, Bituminous...............	11 " 0 "
1,929	1,178	" 3 " Splint (?).................	3 to 4 feet.
2,079	1,328	" 4 "	4 feet, 8 inches
2,163	1,412	" 5 " Splint and Cannel.....	10 " 0 "
2,220	1,469	" 6 "	3 " 6 "
2,353	1,602	" 7 " Splint........................	9 " 0 "
2,363	1,612	Black Flint Ledge.	

In comparing this with the section at Sewell, the top of the Conglomerate falls from 2,135 feet to 1,351 feet, or, as the straight line, measured on the dip, is between 8 and 9 miles, so the dip will be between 97 and 85 feet per mile. This has brought the Conglomerate so low that Gauley mountain, as it rises above, catches 1,000 feet of the Lower Coal Measures.

Seam No. 1, seen on the railroad, going up Mill creek, is the Quinnimont that has dipped, from an elevation of 2,250 feet, at the place whence it derives its name, to 928 feet at the present point of observation.

Seam No. 2 is the one now operated by the Gauley Kanawha Coal Co., at the head of West Lakes Branch, a fork of Mill creek. It produces a very fine and pure, hard, bituminous coal, and has four partings in it, measuring 10, 3, 3, and 5, inches, respectively. These vary in different parts of the mine, some of them getting thinner as the work is carried to the northwest, till, on the other side of the mountain, the company's engineer reports that the seam shows 9 feet of clear coal in one bench.

Nos. 3, 4, and 6, have not been worked at all.

No. 5 was opened for the sake of its Cannel, which is of a very poor quality. Beginning at the floor this seam shows:

Coal, 2 feet; Slate, 2 inches; *Coal*, 2 feet; Slate, 2 inches; *Coal*, 10 inches; Slate, 2 feet 10 inches; *Coal*, 2 feet.

No. 7. The opening on this shows magnificent splint, having in it 17 inches of bony or bad coal.

The Black Flint Ledge, which is nearly at the mountain top, has usually been taken—by myself and others—as the top of the Lower Coal Measures, which would therefore have a thickness of about 1,000 feet. To do this, however, is wrong, for on the Kanawha, in the vicinity of Paint creek, at least 200 feet of strata that contain valuable workable beds come above it, and above these appears the Mahoning sandstone, which, six miles above Charleston, at Malden,* is 140 feet thick, accord-

* At this place the Mahoning rests on the Flint, showing that as we come west, the intermediate strata give out. Whether the reverse of this is true, as we go east towards the Hawk's Nest, is not known, as there are no data from which we can reason, for the Mahoning is every where above the tops of the hills. In fact the sections in the vicinity of Paint creek are not sufficiently in detail to enable us to say if it is found even there, and future observations may show that the strata between it and the Flint are even thicker than have been given.

ing to Prof. W. B. Rogers, so that to the measurement at Hawk's Nest could be added some 340 feet before the Lower Barrens would be reached, making the Lower Coal Measures of this country 1,340 feet thick.

In the section given for Hawk's Nest, not all of the coals of the Lower Coal Measures are shown, but only those which have been exposed and measured by the company working the property, and these show no less than 6 workable seams, with an aggregate thickness of 30½ feet of solid coal, exclusive of partings.

Continuing our observations down New river and into the Kanawha valley, we see the Conglomerate sinking lower and lower, till at Kanawha Falls it is but a short distance above the stream, leaving all the mountains rising above made up wholly of the Lower Coal Measures, and a short distance below Loup creek it sinks below the water level to rise no more until the north-western margin of the Alleghany basin is reached in the State of Ohio.

THE KANAWHA COALS.

The main body or principal thickness of the Lower Coals may be said to have their practical eastern margin in Gauley mountain, for beyond this the strata rapidly rise above the hills, and are lost in the air, leaving only the lower seams as found in the Raleigh plateau and the adjacent country. A line drawn from the mouth of Elk river, in a northwest direction, passing near the mouth of Big Otter, in Clay county, is the general western boundary, for the Mahoning sandstone comes down to water level on or about this course. Throughout the whole of the distance across this area are to be found various seams of the very finest qualities of splint, cannel, and bituminous coals. The steep hillsides readily expose them; the country is cut, and counter-cut in all directions by numerous streams, up which narrow-gauge railroads can be run with the most favorable grades; there are no faults to seriously interfere with the operations of the coal miner, and the merchant and manufacturer can find every class of fuel, save anthracite that they may need for the use and comfort of mankind. In no other part of the Appalachian coal field are the Lower Coal Measures developed to such an extent, contain a greater number of workable seams, or more varieties of coals, or better or purer fuel.

After leaving Hawk's Nest, the next important disclosure has been made by the Cannelton Coal Company, 9 miles below the Kanawha Falls. A partial section of the hill shows 7 seams above water level. Beginning at the river:

Seam No. 1, bituminous coal, is 4 feet thick, but not worked.

Seam No. 2, some 100 feet above the river, is about 7 feet thick on the average, has two slight partings, and produces a gas coal of so high a grade as to make it rank one of the most valuable seams of the Kanawha Valley. This same bed is worked just across the river by the Coal Valley Coal Company. A half mile below Cannelton it is opened again, but not worked, and shows 6 feet 3½ inches, with 3 inches of shale 2 feet from the floor.

Seams Nos. 3 *and* 4, are seen on the path leading from the old opening on No. 2 to the "Stockton Seam," No. 6. They measure 3½ and 4 feet on the outcrop, and have never been worked.

Seam No. 5, is splint coal, 5 feet thick, and not worked.

Seam No. 6, is 8 or 9 feet above No. 5, 750 feet above the river, and 1,350 feet above tide. On an average it is 7 feet thick in the mine, and is made up of cannel coal at the bottom, which averages about 3 feet 6 inches, and is very variable, and a splinty bituminous coal, known in market as "Cannelton Splint," on top. The whole seam is now worked, though for a long time only the cannel was shipped. This and Peytona cannel quote higher in the eastern markets than any other American cannel.

The Black Flint Ledge is 12 to 14 feet above No. 6, or 767 feet above the river, and 1,367 feet above tide.

Seam No. 7, shows 8 feet thick near the mouth of the opening; with 14 inches of slate 10 inches from the floor, leaving 6 feet of clear coal above. This last is a mixture of hard bituminous and splint, yielding a first class article for steam, domestic wants, and use in the raw state in the blast furnace.

A recapitulation of these seams shows that there is here, above water level,—

No. 1..
" 2.. 4 feet.
" 3.. 7 "
" 4.. 3½ "
" 5.. 4 "
" 6.. 5 "
" 7.. 7 "
.... 8 "

38½ feet.

Including the partings, which are small.

Paint creek empties into the Kanawha from the south side, 5 miles below Cannelton. In the hill at the mouth of the Left-Hand Fork, about 4 miles from the river, the following section was made in 1873. The height above tide is obtained by allowing Paint creek a fall of 20 feet per mile, and adding the result for 4 miles to the elevation of the mouth of the creek, which is 570 feet above tide.

Height above Tidewater.	Height above the Creek.		Thickness of Seams.
650	0	Level of Paint Creek at the mouth of the Left Hand Fork.	
690	40	Seam, No. 1..................	2 feet, 6 inch
702	52	" " 2..................	3 " 0 "
713	63	" " 3..................	2 " 0 "
742	92	" " 4..................	3 " 6 "
763	113	" " 5..................	2 " 0 "
778	128	" " 6..................	2 " 0 "
857	207	" " 7..................	Out Crop
892	242	" " 8..................	" "
950	300	" " 9..................	" "
959	309	" " 10..................	" "
997	347	" " 11..................	" "
1,020	370	" " 12..................	2 feet, 6 inch
1,037	377	" " 13..................	Out Crop
1,080	420	" " 14..................	6 feet, 0 inch
1,113	453	" " 15..................	3 " 6 "
1,166	506	" " 16..................	11 " 4 "
1,208	548	" " 17..................	4 " 0 "
1,274	611	" " 18..................	4 " 0 "
1,285	625	Black Flint Ridge.	
1,295	635	Seam, No. 19..................	3 " 6 "
1,317	657	" " 20..................	2 " 0 "
1,341	691	" " 21..................	Out Crop
1,624	974	Top of Hill.	
		Total thickness, including partings..............	51 feet, 10 inch

There are, in this, 8 seams 3 feet thick and over, measuring 38 feet 10 inches, including the partings that may be present.

The next section is made 5 miles below the mouth of Paint creek, on the land of Col. Wm. Dickinson, opposite Coalburg. It is complete, showing every seam in the hill.

Height above Tidewater.	Height above the River.		Thickness of Seams.
563	0	Level of Kanawha River.	
589	26	Seam, No. 1	4 feet, 6 inches
608½	45½	" " 2	3 " 0 "
626½	63½	" " 3	3 " 0 "
655	92	" " 4	1 " 0 "
685½	122½	" " 5	0 " 6 "
733½	170½	" " 6	3 " 7 "
819	256	" " 7	1 " 0 "
884	321	" " 8	2 " 0 "
955	392	" " 9	5 " 0 "
1,036½	473½	" " 10	2 " 0 "
1,046½	483½	" " 11	4 " 6 "
1,085	522	" " 12	5 " 6 "
1,131	568	" " 13	2 " 6 "
1,145½	582½	Black Flint Ledge.	
1,218½	655½	Seam, No. 14	3 " 2 "
1,321½	758½	" " 15	15 " 0 "
1,393½	830½	Top of Hill.	
		Total thickness of seams	54 feet, 3 inches

The top seam, No. 15, shows 4½ feet of coal at the bottom, then 2 feet of slate, 4½ feet of coal, 2 feet of slate, and 2 feet of coal. In mining, the upper 2 feet of slate would most probably be left as the roof, so that this would leave 9 feet of workable coal out of the 15 feet. This, together with the other eight seams, 3 feet thick and over, and including what partings may be present therein, gives an aggregate thickness of 41 feet 3 inches.

At Cannelton, seam No. 2, (7 feet thick) is about 667 feet below the Black Flint ledge, and below No. 2 is a 4-foot seam (No. 1). Assuming that this well marked stratum of flint has this same relative position to the seams below it in the last two sections (the Dickinson and Paint creek) in the Paint creek measurement, the 7-foot seam should be 42 feet below, and in the Dickinson section, 85 feet below water level. The 4-foot seam is of course still lower, but whether these thicknesess continue from Cannelton to the other points, only an actual sinking to them can determine.

SYNOPSIS OF THE SECTIONS OF THE LOWER COAL MEASURES ON THE KANAWHA AND NEW RIVERS.

Locality.	Nature of the Sections.	Number of Seams over three feet thick that have been opened.	Aggregate Thickness of Seams, including partings.
Hawk's Nest...	Partial........................	6	41 ft. 2 in., to 42 ft. 2 in.
Cannelton......	Partial above Water Level.............	7	38 " 6 "
Paint Creek....	Complete above Water Level............	8	38 " 10 "
Oppoisite Coalburg.....	Complete above Water Level...........	9	41 " 3 "

Other sections could be given, but these are deemed sufficient to show, better than could any words, the great richness of the Lower Coal Measures in this region, and I would call especial attention to the uniformity that exists in the aggregate thickness of workable seams.* In this connection it is well to state that as we recede from the Kanawha river towards the heads of the many creeks which flow into it from each side, the seams become thicker. I have personally noticed this up Paint and Campbell's creek, and on Gauley river, 8 or 9 miles from its mouth. But more openings and extended observations will have to be made to enable me to say positively whether this, as a general thing, is so, or whether the increase may not be confined to individual localities. To elucidate such important points as this, is one great argument in favor of the necessity of a careful State geological survey.

---

*Taking the specific gravity of coal at 1.3, 40 feet would give 48,000 tons per acre, from which, if even *one-third* is deducted for partings and waste in mining, there would still be left 32,000 tons per acre, which, at 12½ cents royalty, the common one in the district, would give an income of $4,000 to the owner.

From Hawk's Nest to Cannelton, (20 miles by river and 10 miles on the dip), the Black Flint Ledge falls 1,000 feet,. r about 100 feet per mile. Continuing down the Kanawha it becomes very much flatter, and in some cases horizontal, until Burning Springs, 21 miles further down the river, is reached, and from that point to where it disappears below the water, (8 miles by road and some 6 miles on the dip), it once more resumes its slope of 100 feet per mile to the mouth of Elk river, at Charleston. Between these extremes of Gauley mountain on the east, and Charleston on the west, these Lower Coals have an average width of about thirty miles, and a point a little below the mouth of Paint creek is about the centre of the belt. Drawing a line North 60 degs. East and South 60 degs. West, receding from each side of the Kanawha into Nicholas, Clay, Braxton, and Webster, on the one hand, and Boone, Lincoln, Logan, and Wayne, on the other, these vast amounts of coals still continue to be found, and in every direction abundant evidence of them is discovered; sometimes they form the bed of a stream, or crop out to view in the cliffs and steep mountain sides; in other places they are exposed by slides on the hills, and are everywhere indicated by the presence of lumps of coal lying, smooth and water worn, in the beds of the creeks. Going North 30 degs. West, or South 30 degs. East, from this axis, the Measures rise in the latter case till they pass into the air above the hills, while in the former, they gradually dip below the water level, and are lost to sight, though shafting will still reach them in many counties where at present they lie untouched.

The Lower Barren Measures on the Kanawha.—Of these very little can be said beyond the fact that they have been estimated at 700 feet thick, and probably contain one workable seam of 5 or 6 feet, as seen at the head of Two Mile creek, of the Kanawha, some 3½ miles from the river. On Elk river, above Clay court house, in Clay and Braxton, they become of great importance, from the fact they bear several beds of valuable Iron Ore, which are now worked by the Elk River Iron and Coal Company. Mention will be made of these in the chapter on Iron.

THE UPPER COAL STRATA OF WEST VIRGINIA.

Having now—perhaps at the risk of prolixity—described

those portions of West Virginia which have to look to the Lower Coal Measures for their fuels, we would draw attention to those sections where the Upper Coal Measures form the important series.

On reaching the upper limit of the Lower Barrens, the circumstances which gave rise to the enormous development of the Lower and Conglomerate Measures seem to have ceased, and in the south the formation of new strata was slow, but in the north very fast, so that, while in the former case there were only about 400 feet of Upper Coals and Upper Barrens forming; in the north, as in Monongalia county, about 600 feet of the former, and some 1,200 feet of the latter were deposited. There is also another marked difference between the two sections, viz.: on the Kanawha the Upper Measures contain principally.shales, no limestone of any great consequence, and only one workable coal seam*—the Pittsburgh—which, at Raymond City, measures 6½ feet; while in the north—as in Monongalia—they contain heavy ledges of sandstone, some 8 or 9 strata of limestone, aggregating 50 or 60 feet, and often yielding most excellent limes, both hydraulic and agricultural; and five workable coal seams, having an aggregate thickness of 28 to 33 feet, and containing, as a rule, fewer partings than exist in the larger seams of the Lower Coals on the Kanawha. In the Upper Barrens there is no evidence that any coal seams exist in the south, but in the north there are several, though none are workable.

As might be expected from what has been said, all the mines, save only the Austin in Preston county, in the northern portion of the State, are on the seams of the Upper Measures; while in the south, with the exception of the Raymond Coal Company, and the Oak Ridge Coal Company, in Putnam county, and the Hartford City, &c., mines, in Mason county, all working the "Pittsburgh," the present mines look to the Lower Coal and Conglomerate Measures for their supply.

In preparing the following account of the Upper Coal Measures, we are largely indebted, especially in the general description of the beds, to Prof. J. J. Stevenson, Professor of Geology in the University of New York, and of the Geologi-

*There may be one or two more, but on this nothing definite can be said till the country is more thoroughly explored.

cal Survey of Pennsylvania, who has paid more attention to them, as developed in this State, than any one else.

The Upper Coal Region embraces all that portion of West Virginia, in which the exposed rocks overlie the Pittsburgh coal bed. The eastern and southern limits are marked by the outcrop line of that coal, which passes through Monongalia, Marion, Taylor, Barbour, Upshur, Braxton, Clay, Kanawha, Putnam, and Cabell counties, and crosses the Ohio river in the vicinity of Guyandotte. Westward this area extends into Ohio, and northward into Pennsylvania. Its northern line crosses the Ohio river near Steubenville.

No close survey of this region has ever been made. Its eastern limit was studied out, and several reconnoissance lines were run across it by the State Surveyors during the survey under Prof. W. B. Rogers, but only scanty references to the work were made in the annual reports. Almost the only material respecting this region now accessible, is to be found in the brief memoirs published by Prof. Stevenson, in 1872-3-5, and these refer exclusively to the northern portion.

Within this region, a small area, embracing the greater part of Ritchie, Wirt, Wood, and Pleasants counties, has been deprived of the coals by the oil break. The effects of this disturbance extended westward to the Ohio river, from a line passing almost N. and S. through Ellenboro, on the Parkersburg Branch of the Baltimore and Ohio railroad. How far this line extends north and south from that place has not been determined. Aside from this limited space, the whole region is underlaid by the coals of the upper group; but as the thickness of the rocks in this series is not far from 1,800 feet, where fully exposed, the more important beds are so deeply buried in some counties that many years must pass before they can be made available. All the coals attain their greatest thickness between the Pennsylvania border, near the Monongahela river and the Baltimore and Ohio railroad, and diminish somewhat rapidly southward, so that before reaching the Parkersburg and Staunton pike, in Lewis and Gilmer, they, with the exception of the Pittsburgh, have become comparatively worthless.

The principal coals of the upper series are known as the *Pittsburgh*, *Redstone*, *Sewickley*, *Waynesburg* and *Washington*, having received these names from localities in Pennsylvania. Besides these, several other beds occur, but as they barely cross the line from Pennsylvania into West Virginia, and never become of any value in that State or this, it is unnecessary to make farther reference to them here.

Of all these, the *Pittsburgh* alone maintains its importance throughout, as far as the examinations go. The available area of this bed, therefore, is of economical interest, and we give its limits in detail, as observed by Prof. Stevenson in 1874:

The eastern limit of the *Pittsburgh* bed, and therefore of the Upper Coal Measures, aside from small outlying areas, is marked by a line beginning on Cheat river, near the Pennsylvania border, in Monongalia county, and extending west of south to Fairmont, in Marion county, crossing the Tygart's Valley river a little distance above that town; thence irregularly to Pruntytown, in Taylor county, where it turns east by south to Flemington. From this point it follows a south of southeast course almost to Tygart's Valley river, thence southward, crossing the Buckhannon river near the Upshur county line. There it again turns east by south, and so continues almost to the Middle Fork of that river, where it is changed to southwest, which is maintained to the line between Upshur and Lewis counties. From this point to where it crosses Pocotalico river, near the Great Kanawha, in Putnam county, it has not been followed. The extreme eastern exposure occurs in Upshur county, on the Staunton pike, about five miles east from Buckhannon.

The western limit, or the line along which the coal passes below the surface, cannot be given accurately without entering into great detail, as it is farther east or west, as the case may be, according to the depth to which the streams have eroded their channel-ways. The extreme limit may be regarded as marked by a line which begins at the Pennsylvania line, about four miles west from the Monongahela river, and crosses that river about a mile below Fairmont. It lies a little west from the West Fork River, and crosses Harrison county from Shinnston to Wolfe's Summit, on the railroad; thence it passes southwestward through Lewis county, reaching Gilmer, near Troy, on the Staunton pike, and the Little Kanawha, just below Glenville.

Owing to the abruptness of the Laurel Hill anticlinal, the area is very narrow at the north, hardly more than six or seven miles wide, but southward this fold becomes gentler and the area rapidly widens, until, along the Staunton pike, the coal is available for a distance of nearly 40 miles. The coal has its greatest thickness, ten feet, at the Pennsylvania line, and diminishes south and southeast, becoming only five feet at Glenville, and barely four feet at Buckhannon.

In the Ohio Pan-Handle the same coal is available. There it is known as the Wheeling coal. Openings in it are numerous from Moundsville to a little way above Steubenville.

MONONGALIA COUNTY.

The Pittsburgh Bed is worked on both sides of the Monongahela river, and varies in thickness from eight to somewhat more than ten feet. In this estimate is included only the workable portion, for above that, and separated from it by clay, is a roof-division, which is from zero to four feet thick. The coal in this county is quite variable in quality, but for the most part is an excellent fuel. It is hardly equal to that obtained from the same bed at Connellsville, in Pennsylvania.

The Redstone Coal is exceedingly variable. In this county it is exposed on both sides of the Monongahela river, near the Pennsylvania line, where it is from three to four feet thick. In some localities it is a little better than a richly bituminous shale, while in others, not far distant, it is one of the handsomest coals in the whole trough west of the Alleghanies. No sulphur is usually apparent to physical examination, but chemical analysis shows that it is present to the extent of from 1.75 to 2.8 per cent. The coke is hard and bright, but sometimes shows as much as 2.85 per cent. of sulphur, which, however, seems to be present in combination with lime and magnesia, and not as sulphide of iron, and consequently will not be so injurious for iron making.

The Sewickley Coal is from 70 to 100 feet above the Pittsburgh, and is quite as variable as the Redstone. It is very thin where exposed east from the Monongahela river, but west from that stream, it is a very valuable bed. On Robinson's, Dent's and Scott's runs, it is found varying from 4 to 6 feet. A parting of cannel occurs at irregular distances from the base. The coal is comparatively free burning, would bear shipping well, and contains from 1.5 to 3 per cent. of sulphur, which exists mostly as sulphate of lime and magnesia, and not as iron pyrites, and is not, therefore, as deleterious as the percentage would seem to indicate. It is a very handsome coal, and in many places, says Prof. Stevenson, is well fitted for gas making.

The Waynesburg Coal is a very persistent seam, but is marked by a constant diminution southward, so that like the last two beds, it becomes of no economical value whatever. It is found from 190 to nearly 400 feet above the Pittsburgh, the interval being greatest near the Pennsylvania line.

It attains its greatest thickness in West Virginia, in this county, where it is a double bed, occasionally triple. The total thickness, including the clay partings, varies from 6 feet 8 inches to nearly 10 feet. The clay sometimes thins out so as to be barely perceptible, while at others, it thickens up and forms a "horseback," which is grievously annoying to the miners.

MARION COUNTY.

The Pittsburgh Coal has been mined very extensively, and shipped for use in the manufacture of gas, for which purpose it ranks very high. The bed in this county varies from 7 to 10 feet thick, and averages 8 feet, and shows no roof division. The percentage of sulphur is much larger than in the Youghiogheny coal, but compensation for this drawback is found in the fact that it yields a much greater amount of gas per ton. Experiments have been made to ascertain the value of this as a coking coal, but they have not proved altogether satisfactory. The coke is very compact and handsome, in these respects excelling the Connellsville, but the percentage of sulphur is so great as to render it utterly unfit for use in smelting iron, even when mixed with Connellsville in the proportion of two to one. It is a very excellent steam coal, but the distance from the eastern cities prevents it going on those markets as such.

The Redstone Coal, about 80 feet above the last, is from 3 to 6 feet thick, and, as far as one may judge from the outcrop, it is a good article.

The Sewickley Coal is from 100 to 150 feet above the last, and verages 3 feet thick.

The Waynesburg Coal, as seen in the eastern portion of the county, is high up in the hills, and only 3 to 4 feet thick.

Further northwest along the railroad, it is mined for local use. It is extremely variable in character, showing from 2 to 4 benches of coal, of which the bottom one varies from 3 to 4 feet.

TAYLOR COUNTY.

The Pittsburgh Coal.—In the southwestern portion of this county, this underlies some 10,000 acres, of which 5,000 acres are now owned by foreign capital, and the rest by the farmers whose land it underlies. It is found high up in the rolling or hill lands, and is about 9 feet thick, yielding an article of high reputation for gas, and producing an excellent coke. It is now worked by the Tyrconnel and the Flemington Mines.

This seam appears, from the reports on it, to be so high, that the hills do not catch the other seams that lie above the Pittsburgh, though below it we find three coal beds, measuring 5, 4 and 3½ feet, respectively. At the mouth of Lost run, on the Tygart's Valley river, there is also reported a 7-foot seam of cannel and bituminous, the former being 2 feet thick (and of very inferior quality), 18 inches from the roof. The information concerning all these is not sufficient to enable them to be identified.

HARRISON COUNTY.

The Pittsurgh Coal in this county is mined extensively at Clarksburg, Wilsonburg, and Coketon for shipment. Here it shows the same defects and excellencies as at Fairmont. The percentage of sulphur is considerable, but the amount of volatile combustible matter is very great. At Clarksburg the bed is 8 feet 10 inches; at Wilsonburg, from 7 feet 6 inches to 8 feet 4 inches, and at Coketou, from 5 feet to 7 feet. This is a solid mass, broken about midway by a thin parting of clay. Above this the coal is hard, but below, it is soft. The base for about one foot, is usually poor and not marketable. This feature, however, is characteristic of the bed throughout its whole extent. We have been unable to learn that any careful attempts have been made to test the value of this as a coking coal. Pyrites is largely present, but it occurs mostly as lumps, which are easily separated. The larger portions can easily be removed as the coal is taken out, and washing would take out the rest. The coke is so handsome that the experiment is well worth trying. The Pittsburgh disappears at Wolf's Summit, on the railroad, where it is six feet thick. From this point to within one eighth of a mile of Ellenboro, it is at no place more than 400 feet below the surface, and from Long Run to West Union, it can be reached at less than 200 feet.

The Redstone Coal may be seen at several localities along the railroad, but varies so in thickness as to be utterly useless. At Wilsonburg it is one foot thick and twenty-five feet above the Pittsburgh; while at Coketon it is four feet thick and twenty feet above that coal; and at Wolfe's Summit it is only three inches thick. On the Staunton pike it could not be found.

Sewickly Coal.—The "blossom" of this has not been observed north of the railroad. At Clarksburg it is found 70 feet above the Pittsburgh, and 2½ feet thick, but no attempt has been made to ascertain its character. At Wolfe's Summit, 8 miles west of Clarksburg, it is only 2 inches thick, and one the Staunton pike it has not been found.

Waynesburg Coal.—Of this we have no information.

MARSHALL, OHIO, AND BROOKE COUNTIES.

In Marshall the *Pittsburgh Coal* is worked as far south as Moundsville, though at that place it is a little below water level. As we go south it could easily be reached by shafting. As we come north it rises above the level of the Ohio river, and is extensively mined in the vicinity of Wheeling for steam and puddling uses. The working portion of it here averages about 5 feet. Above this comes in a slate parting from ½ to 26 inches thick, and then the roof coals, which are from 24 to 26 inches, divided in the middle by a thin slate parting, which often swells to 6 or 8 inches. It is available as far north as Steubenville, being within easy reach in many localities in Brooke county. The *Redstone* and *Sewickly seams* in this district are usually almost worthless. The latter is separated into two beds, of which the upper is occasionally 2 or 3 feet thick. This is mined near Triadelphia, in Ohio county, but is of only local importance. The *Waynesburg* is very thin in this portion of the State, seldom more than 2 feet thick and always of poor quality.

The following section of Chapline hill, at Wheeling, made by Messrs. Hubbard and Gilchrist, may be interesting as showing the seams of coal that have been discovered in this locality:

Height above the Pittsburgh Seam in Feet.	Character of Seam.	Thickness.
0	*No.* 1. Pittsburgh Seam, the lower 5 feet workable, and the rest of slates and roof coals not worked...	7 to 9 ft.
34	*No.* 2. Divided near the middle by a slate parting, the portion below being but little better than a bituminous shale. At Jim's Run, 5 miles south, this seam is 4 feet 9 inches, making a fair fuel for domestic use..........	3 ft.
67	*No.* 3. In two layers, separated by a 4 inch parting. The lower layer is 14 inches. The seam is not worked in this vicinity..........	2 ft. 4 in.
88	*No.* 4. Coal..........	1 ft.
96	*No.* 5. Coal..........	8 in.
202	*No.* 6. One foot of the lower part is an impure cannel, while the upper portion is a block coal, and is good for domestic uses..........	3½ ft.
249	*No.* 7. Slate parting in the middle..........	1½ ft.
	No. 8. Has a 5-inch parting near the middle. Locally used for domestic purposes, but is not a desirable coal..........	5 ft.
	No. 9. Coal..........	9 in.

LEWIS COUNTY.

The Pittsburgh Coal is accessible along the Staunton Pike all across the county. It varies from 4½ feet to nearly 8 feet, the thickness increasing northward, though at one opening on the Pike it approaches the maximum. It is worked only to supply local demands.

Of the *Redstone*, *Sewickley*, and *Waynesburg Coals* in this county, we have no information, though they no doubt exist.

GILMER COUNTY.

The Pittsburgh Coal in this county is from 5 to 5½ feet. The quality is good, but it seems to have rather more sulphur in it than at Clarksburg, though no analysis has been made to definitely settle this point. As is the case in Lewis county, it is worked only to supply the local demands. Of the *Redstone* and *Sewickly*, we have no information beyond the fact that they exist, but of the thickness nothing is said.

The Waynesburg Coal is rarely more than 2 feet thick in this county.

UPSHUR COUNTY.

In this county the openings on the *Pittsburgh* are quite numerous in the vicinity of Buckhannon, where the thickness varies from 3 feet 9 inches to 4 feet. Farther north, near the Barbour county line, it is 5 feet 6 inches. The quality is superior, and no doubt the coal would prove well worth working for market, notwithstanding its thinness.

Of the other seams of the Upper Coal Measures we can state nothing, except the fact that they exist, but of the thickness and quality there are no reports.

DODDRIDGE COUNTY.

Here the *Pittsburgh*, *Redstone*, and *Sewickly Coals* seem to be below water level, and would have to be reached by shafting.

The Waynesburg Coal.—An opening is seen near the Balt. & Ohio R. R., just west from Wolfe's Summit, where the coal is 4 feet thick and divided mid-way by a parting of clay. At a little beyond this it goes under, but is seen again near the mouth of Long Run, and is available thence to West Union, there being numerous openings along the railroad. It is mined at West Union, where it is in three benches, and has a total thickness, including the clays, of 4 feet. The middle bench is 31 inches thick.

BRAXTON, CLAY, CALHOUN, ROANE, AND KANAWHA COUNTIES.

In portions of Braxton, Clay, and Kanawha, that lie northwest of Elk river, and in southern Calhoun and Roane, the seams of the Upper Coal Measures exist above water level, but it is impossible to speak of their quality or thickness, as no explorations have ever been made in these districts.

PUTNAM COUNTY.

The Pittsburgh Coal, is worked at Raymond City and Oak Ridge, containing in the former case an average of 6 feet 2 inches of workable coal in the lower bench, and in the latter about 4 feet.

Of the other coals but little is known.

CABELL AND MASON COUNTIES.

Here the *Pittsburgh* is seen cropping out along the Ohio. At the Hartford Coal Company Mines it is from 5 to 6 feet thick, but in the main portions of the counties it, as well as the others, are below water level, and would be reached by shafting. At West Columbia, in Mason, it is 100 feet above the river, and has a seam about 2 feet thick, 70 feet above and 30 feet below it.

THE OTHER COUNTIES ALONG THE OHIO.

In these and Wirt, and the main portions of Roane, Calhoun, and Ritchie, all the coals would have to be reached by shafting. In Wetzel, on Fishing Creek, we find a seam reported 10 feet thick, and in Tyler, some of the Upper Coals may be above water level, and in Cabell the *Pittsburgh* outcrops, but beyond these facts, we know, at this time, nothing definite concerning their values.

Above the four seams that have been described as occurring in the Upper Coal Measures, is found a fifth one, called

The Washington Coal, which seems to be confined to the northern half of the State. It is often 3 feet thick, and is found at from 300 feet to nearly 600 feet above the Pittsburgh. the smallest interval being along the Parkersburgh Branch of the Baltimore and Ohio railroad. It is referred to here simply because it is of local importance as a source of supply, where all the other coals, already described, are so deeply buried as to be unavailable, except at great expense. It occurs in Monongalia, Marion, Wetzel, Doddridge and eastern Ritchie, as well, no doubt, as in Tyler. No examination of the latter county has been made, so that a definite statement respecting the availability of the coal in it is impossible. The coal from this bed is poor, very slaty, and contains much sulphur. At the same time, as it is frequently quite thick, it is a source of fuel not to be despised, especially when the Pittsburgh is several hundred feet under the surface.

In this Upper Coal Series we find in the northern tier of counties a great mass of limestone, which grows thinner and poorer southward. It is represented by a few thin and earthy beds on the Parkersburg Branch of the Baltimore and Ohio railroad, but has almost completely disappeared in the southern portion of the Upper Coal Region. This limestone is finely exposed along the Ohio river in the vicinity of Wheeling, where it has been quarried for use as a flux in iron smelting. Some of the layers are well adapted to this purpose, and others, which are injurious as flux, yield a very fair hydraulic cement if carefully prepared.

COAL IN THE EASTERN PART OF THE STATE.

On page 163, the general eastern boundary of the coal field was given, but it was mentioned that small, though unimportant, patches of coal are found still more easterly. We see these in Greenbrier and Pocahontas counties, in the valley of the Greenbrier river, but the coals occur in the geological formation next below the true Coal Measures, and are called the "Vespertine Coals," because they are found in the geological horizon of that name. There are several seams, but all thin and worthless, though one them has a local expansion of 3 feet on the land of D. C. B. Caldwell, near Ronceverte Depot, in Greenbrier county. A short distance from this place, at the railroad bridge over the river, it has split up into a number of strings, and is of not the slightest value. Near the White Sulphur Springs are several exposures of these seams, but they are of no account because of their thinness.

In Pocahontas, west of the Cranberry, Black and Elk mountains, the seams that may be present belong to the true Coal Measures, though it is extremely problematical, whether they are here of any value, for to the west, on Williams' river and the east side of Gauley, they are thin and unimportant.

In Randolph county, between the Alleghanies and Cheat Mountain, and in Tucker county, between its eastern boundary and the Backbone mountain, there are vague reports of an abundance of coal which, in all probability, will prove to be those of the Vespertine formation, and especially may this be said of the latter county, for in the geological reports of Virginia, made in 1839, a series of observations was made on Cheat river and the Black Fork thereof, and in not a single instance was a workable bed reported.

In Berkeley county these same coals are seen again, though here converted into anthracite of a very pure quality, and in sufficient quantity to answer some slight local demands, and have given rise to many bright visions concerning their importance in the mineral resources of this county. In March 1876, they were visited by Mr. A. R. Guerard, of the Royal School of Mines, London, for the State Board of Centennial Managers, and that gentleman reports, that "between "Sleepy Creek and Third Hill mountains, at an opening on "the Meadow Branch, by Embry & Cushwa, a shaft 45 feet

" deep has passed through three seams from 1 to 3 feet thick, " and a tunnel from the hillside strikes a 4-foot seam below. " The coal appears to be of fair average quality, but some- " what broken up and intermixed with slate. There was " nothing in this opening to lead me to the conclusion that " the problem which has been on hand for the last 40 or 50 " years, as to the coal being here in paying quantities, was at " last satisfactorily solved."

CHAPTER X.

THE QUALITY AND VARIETY OF COAL, AND THE MINING ADVANTAGES.

BY M. F. MAURY.

The coal mining advantages of West Virginia arise from the great number of seams found accessible above water level, and from the fact that they contain coals of various compositions adapted to all the requirements of trade and manufacture. The fat coking, gassy bituminous, the hard and valuable splint, and the rich and oily cannel in this highly favored region, are found in great purity, and made easily accessible to the miner, through the agency of running water, which has exposed the seams in thousands upon thousands of places, and in consequence of this, and their size, coal, as a general rule, can be mined cheaper, and with more economy, under the same rates of labor, than in any other part of the Alleghany coal field.

In fact, when the northern portion of the State was wrinkled into folds, and the southern tilted gently from its original horizontal position, water, with its vast planing and eroding power, washed off the superincumbent strata, and cut and counter-cut the country by deep and narrow valleys, thus preparing this field with numerous objective points for safe and economical working, for it left vast areas of the coal measures above water, accessible at many points by simply removing from the outcrops of the seams the alluvium that has formed there by the decaying work of ages.

This will more clearly appear by a comparison of the position of the coals here and in Great Britain in this respect.

There the coal is deep below water level, and to reach it requires years of labor and vast sums of money. In its great northern coal field, the shafts are rarely less than 150 feet deep, and many have the great depth of 1,800 feet, sunk at an expense, in some cases, of $240,000,* while the Dukinfield colliery was taken down 2,600 feet, at a cost of $500,000, mainly to reach the "Black Mine Coal," a seam 4 feet 8½ inches thick.

Here mighty natural forces have sunk pits which need neither repair or renewal. The inclination of the strata, coupled with the laws of gravity, have provided the most costless, perfect and permanent pumping machinery, and the perfect ventilation of the mines is but a matter of the most simple and ordinary care, as, except in one or two instances in the northern portion of the State, there are none of those noxious gases to be dealt with which oftentimes render coal mining so dangerous.

There are, however, many districts where the seams are below the surface, though easily reached by shafting, but when we consider the number that are over 3 feet thick, and that such an one is workable and yields about 4,800 tons per acre, it will be seen that we need not treat of the deeper ones, for we have no need to sink shafts at all, as it will be a long time before the cost of winning coals from day levels will be so far raised as to necessitate other styles of working, and West Virginia can justly be proud of the numerous advantages it holds in this respect.

The coals may be divided into three great classes, viz.: Bituminous. Splint, and Cannel.

BITUMINOUS COAL

Is the most abundant, occurs in all portions of the field, and some of it is found in nearly every seam of the other two classes. It is the only class worked in the northern half of the State, and with but few exceptions, is the only one of value of that region, so far as present explorations show.

The Redstone, Sewickly, Waynesburg, and Washington seams were shown in the last chapter to be of great importance in the north, but dwindle down and are little value,

---

*Sweet's Special Report on Coal to the New York Legislature, 1865. Page 11.

or are not even found, as the case may be, in the southern part of the State. Owing to the general prevalence of the more important and valuable Pittsburgh seam, none of them are worked except to supply local demands, though the coal produced is often a most excellent and superior article, though varying in this respect in different counties and localities, as we would naturally expect it should.

The following are analyses of the first three from Monongalia county, near Morgantown; and of the Redstone, as seen 5 miles north of Fairmont, in Marion county, on the land of R. S. Radcliff, where it is 6 feet 4 inches thick.*

SEAM.	Fixed Carbon.	Volatile Cumbustible Matter.	Moisture.	Ash.	Per cent. of Sulphur in Coal.	Per cent. of Sulphur in Coke.
Redstone, Monongalia............	54.36	37.88	0.37	7.39	2.87	2.85
Redstone, Marion	50.33	40.97	1.01	7.69	4.27	2.86
Sewickley, Monongalia.............	54.31	35.78	0.44	9,47	3.10	2.78
Waynesburg, Monongalia.......	56.36	35.36	0.74	7.55	0.70	0.55

On these analyses Mr. Dwight makes the following remark: "The color of the ash from the Redstone is dark gray, and the sulphur in the coal seems to be in combination with lime or magnesia, and not as sulphide of iron; consequently it will not be injurious for iron making. The coke is hard and bright. The ash from the Sewickley is gray, and the sulphur seems to be in the same form as in the last. The coke is medium hard. From the Waynesburg the ash is light buff, and the coke moderately hard."

The Pittsburgh seam is the present source of the shipping coals of the northern half of the State. Except from the Potomac basin, its fuel goes on the market as "West Virginia Gas Coal, and for that purpose ranks among the highest of the United States, being extensively used in the large cities of the Atlantic seaboard. But where mined on the Potomac, in Mineral county, it has lost this quality, though it is very valuable and highly prized for steam, foundrys, rolling-mills, smiths work, &c.

*These, and all other analyses given in this chapter, are by C. E. Dwight, of Wheeling, unless some other chemist is mentioned.

28

Where wrought by the Newburg Orrel Coal Co., in Preston county, this seam is from 10 to 11 feet thick, but only 9 to 9½ are worked, the rest being left to support the roof. The coal is shipped to the eastern markets for gas purposes, yielding, by the tests of the Manhattan Gas Light Co., of New York, over 10,000 cubic feet per ton of 15½ candle power. In Monongalia county it produces a most excellent fuel, which is extensively used in Morgantown and various other portions of the county. It often contains as much as 2 per cent of sulphur, which unfits it for the manufacture of iron and coke, and renders its value for gas somewhat doubtful, though at the same time it should be said that analyses of coal extensively used for this purpose in New York, show that the Monongalia coal is not much inferior. But apart from any value it may have for this, its other excellent qualities will command a ready market for it when the completion of the locks and dams on the Monongahela river give it a ready and cheap exit to consuming centres.

The Flemington and Tyrconnel mines, in Taylor county, do their mining on the same bed, the product of which, as tested from the latter, shows itself, according to the report to the company, by C. M. Cresson, of Philadelphia, to be much superior for gas making purposes to the celebrated Penn coal of Pennsylvania. From the mines at Fairmont, in Marion county, it goes on the eastern and western markets, but, particularly on the former, with an exceedingly high reputation for gas, and it is also a good steam generator, but at present prices the mines are too far from the seaboard to enable it to bear the expense of transportation, for it would have to come into competition with the cheaper and less distant fuel of the Cumberland Coal Field of Maryland.

To show its rank in this respect, with other coals from other States, the following table is given. The Fairmont coal spoken of in it, was from the West Fairmont mines :

OFFICIAL TESTS OF COAL,

At Chicago Water Works.

Number.	Month.	1870 Date.	Name of Coal.	State.	Hours Run.	Quantity.		Revolutions.	Total Gallons Water Pumped	Gallons of Water per lb. Coal.	Comparative val. per cent.
					Hs M	Ts	Lbs.				
1	May..	3 to 5	Triplet..............	....	71-45	51	360	55,563	37.110,743	362-5	100-0
2	Apr..	25 to 28	Willow Bank...	....	71-10	75	....	83,975	56,241,232	374-9	103-4
3	"	22 to 23	Briar Hill.........	Ohio ...	50-40	52	272	60,876	40,592,071	389-2	107-3
4	....	....	Glenco............	Ohio ...	35-05	47	420	49,376	38,896.790	412-0	113-6
5	May..	5 to 7	Peal.................	....	52-55	51	1,250	63,748	42,581,673	412-4	113-7
6	Apr..	23 to 25	Fort Pitt..........	....	54-30	51	1,860	63,952	42,957,960	413-6	114-0
7	"	18 to 21	Pittsburgh........	Penna	54-50	51	140	63,907	42,559.962	416-6	114-9
8	"	28 to 30	Walnut Hill....	Ohio ...	56-50	53	1,510	67,353	45,107,868	419-5	115-7
9	Oct...	18 to 19	Lackawana......	Penna	48-00	49	1,150	49,416	42,208,364	425-6	117-4
10	Sept.	9 to 20	Hocking Valley	Ohio ...	288-00	352	260	347.667	300,416 866	426-5	117-6
11	May..	1 to 3	Cherry Mines...	......	60-25	54	1,590	69,706	46 800,855	427-0	117-7
12	Sept.	1 to 9	Hocking Valley	Ohio ...	192-00	235	1,900	240,083	206.293,815	437-1	120-5
13	"	21 to 22	Fairmont.........	W. Va...	42-30	44	1,470	56,658	47,251,650	528-1	155-7

In Harrison county, at the Despard and Murphy's Run collieries it (the Pittsburgh seam) is again extensively mined and sent on eastern markets for the same use as mentioned above and is also excellent for steam, but the same reasons that operatea gainst the Fairmont coals do not allow these to be burnt under the boilers of the eastern cities. Compared with the Penn and Westmoreland coals, of Westmoreland county, Pa., (which have no superior in that State), the gas from the Harrison county coal is superior in illuminating power, but not quite equal to them in purity, requiring more lime in purification, but this slight additional cost, say 10 cents per ton, is more than compensated for by the higher illuminating power, coupled with the larger yield.

At and near Wheeling, in Ohio county, this coal is extensively used in the puddling furnaces, but contains too much sulphur for gas. As worked on the Kanawha river, at the Raymond Mines, in Putnam, it produces a domestic fuel of the highest grade, and as such goes on the western markets. It is also excellent for steam but does not seem to be in demand for gas, as there is an abundant supply of other more noted coals for that purpose.

In Mason county, and on the opposite side of the river in the State of Ohio, it is largely worked, both for consumption at the salt furnaces, and for exportation down the Ohio river.

In 1875, in Mason, there were 9 nine mines in operation, producing 301,000 tons, of which 101,000 were used at the salt furnaces and the rest was shipped to market.

Its quality, however, seems to have deteriorated very much, for in the Cincinnati market we find it, as shipped from Pomery, quoting about 2 cents per bushel lower than the coal from Raymond City.

The following table shows the analyses of the coal of this seam from the different localities just mentioned:

County.	Mine.	Thickness of Seam in Feet.	Coke.	Volatile Matter.	Water.	Ash.	Sulphur in the Coal	Sulphur in the Coke.	Cubic Ft. of Gas per 2,240 pounds.	Candle Power.	Chemist.
Mineral.......	Virginia Mine, Top Coal..................	10	79.82	20.18	0.82	3.95	0.71	0.81	....	....	C. E. Dwight.
Mineral.......	Virginia Mine, Bottom Coal...........	4	81.99	18.01	0.50	2.98	1.13	1.12	....	....	" "
Monongalia.....	Near Morgantown.....	9 to 10	60.98	39.02	0.38	6.20	2.54	2.19	....	....	" "
Marion..........	Gaston..................	9	67.50	32.50	....	2.10	0.95	1.01	11,043	16.00	S. C. Ford.
"	American...............	9	65.00	35.00	....	5.00	....	....	10,471	15.17	Manhattan Gas Light Company.
Taylor..........	Flemington.............	9	61.27	38.73	0.74	7.68	0.88	0.69	....	....	C. E. Dwight.
"	Tyrconnel	9	....	....	....	....	....	....	9,856	16.63	C. M. Cresson.
Harrison........	Despard	9	60.00	10.00	....	6.70	....	....	9,500	20.41	Manhattan Gas Light Company.
"	Murphy's Run.........	9	....	....	....	....	2.84	....	11,401	17.20	Harlem Gas Light Company.
Ohio...........	Wheeling Top Coal..................	5	55.28	44.72	1.75	4.30	2.88	3.06	....	....	C. E. Dwight.
Ohio...........	Wheeling Bottom Coal..................	to 7	60.03	39.97	1.52	12.26	3.82	4.88	....	....	" "
Putnam	Raymond.................	6 to 7	66.00	33.00	....	6.00	....	....	....	....	C. Vinton.
Mason	Hartford City...........	5 to 6	52.19	47.81	3.43	5.31	1.57	1.93	....	....	C. E. Dwight.

In connection with these results, it should be mentioned that the analysis of the American Mine is from the practical workings on two cargoes; that of the Despard from the practical workings of six months, and of the Murphy's Run coal, for three days. The others are laboratory tests.

As showing the results of locomotive use of the fuel from this seam, the following letter is very useful:

BALTIMORE AND OHIO RAILROAD,
OFFICE OF CHIEF ENGINEER,
MARTINSBURG, W. VA., 6 April, 1876.

M. F. Maury, Esq.:

DEAR SIR:—I give you results of observations on the consumption of fuel in Locomotives on this road:

First Division—Baltimore to Martinsburg, 100 miles:

Weight of Engine	72,900	pounds.
" " train	834,000	"
Maximum grade (per mile)	80	feet.
Minimum radius of curvature	600	"
Ascent westward	1,282	"
" eastward	913	"
Consumption of coal per mile run	60	pounds.

Coal was from large vein near Piedmont (in Mineral county).

Third Division, trip from Keyser to Grafton and return, 157½ miles:

Weight of engine	95,300	pounds.
" " train	831,000	"
Maximum grade (per mile)	117	feet.
Minimum radius of curvature	600	"
Ascent westward	2,518	"
" eastward	2,334	"
Consumption of fuel per mile run	134	pounds.

Coal was from large vein near Piedmont (in Mineral county).

Fourth Division, Grafton to Benwood, 95¼ miles:

Weight of engine	73,400	pounds.
" " train	795,000	"
Maximum grade (per mile)	80	feet.
Minimum radius of curvature	600	"
Ascent westward	825	"
" eastward	1,167	"
Consumption of fuel per mile run	90	pounds.

Coal was from the mines at Fairmont, (in Marion county).

Parkersburg Branch, Parkersburg to Grafton, 104 miles:

Weight of engine	73,400 pounds.
" " train	600,000 "
Maximum grade (per mile)	52.8 feet.
Minimum radius of curvature	600 "
Ascent westward	1,644 "
" eastward	2,086 "
Consumption of fuel per mile run	85 pounds

Coal was from the mines at Clarksburg, (in Harrison county). Respectfully, JAMES L. RANDOLPH,*

Chief Engineer.

Returning now to the general discussion of the quality of the bituminous coal in West Virginia, the only seam of it in the Lower Coal Measures, in the northern half of the State, that is largely worked, is the Upper Freeport, at Austin, in Preston county. It is here 8 or 9 feet thick, though only the lower bench, say, 4 feet, affords in all places a first-rate quality of coal, though if mined on an extensive scale the whole bed can be utilized. It makes a clear, even, silvery coke, sufficiently hard to bear the heaviest burden of the blast furnace. (J. P. Lesley). An analysis is shown in the next table.

In Upshur, Randolph, Barbour, Taylor, Monongalia, and Marion counties, this seam has been examined at various places† by Prof. Stevenson, and while it is often of great thickness, and yields a good strong fuel for domestic use, it is usually much contaminated with sulphur, which, in many cases is not discovered without the aid of a magnifying glass or chemical tests. In many places in these counties it has an inferior cannel associated with it.

On the land of the Kingwood Gas Coal and Iron Company, near Tunnelton, in Preston county, several seams of very excellent bituminous coal are found. An analysis of one of 4½ feet is shown in the first two items in the following table:

---

*These results given by Mr. Randolph are. I believe, for freight trains.

†For measurements, see description of these counties in the last chapter.

	Fixed Carbon	Volatile Matter.	Ash.	Water.	Sulphur in Coal.	Sulphur in Coke.	Remarks.
Top of Seam	65.66	31.47	2.53	0.34	0.58	0.58	Ash buff. Coke hard and bright.
Bottom of Seam	66.13	31.19	2.17	0.51	0.61	0.53	
Austin Mine	66.29	31.12	2.48	0.12	0 64	0.64	Coke: medium hard. Is being used at the Belmont Furnace in Wheeling, and gives general satisfaction.
" " (Coke)	87.55	....	11.25	0.54	....	0.65	

In the Southern portion of the State the bituminous coal is very pure and hard, and often approaches splint so closely that it is almost impossible to draw a dividing line between the two, or to know to which class a certain seam may be considered to belong. As found here, its seams furnish admirable coals for gas, domestic use, and steam, and, where interstratified with splint, for use in the blast furnace, in the raw or uncoked state.

In 1874, the Richmond (Va.) Gas Company tested various coals from the Kanawha valley with the following results:

LOCALITY.	Bushels Tested.	Cubic Feet of Gas per 2,240 pounds.	Candle Power.
Coalburg	951	8,534	14.5
Houston Mining and Manufacturing Comp'y	876	10,281	17
J. B. Lewis & Co.	993	9,766	15
Cannelton Coal Company	1,049	8,892	14
Hampton City Coal Company	609	9,184	15.5
Gordon and Seal	648	8,064	13.9
H. C. Replier (Coalmont)	1,003	9,699	17.1
Coal Valley Coal Company	....	10,080	17

"The coal from the Houston, Coal Valley, and Coalmont "mines, is superior to any tested so far, is more free from "slate and sulphur, produces greater heat, yields more gas, "and makes the best coke." (Report of Richmond Gas Works, 1875.)

In order to better appreciate these figures, it should be mentioned that the Penn Gas Coal, which is generally adopted as a standard in the United States, gives 9,856 cubic feet of gas, of 14-candle power, per ton, of 2,240 pounds.

The coals given in the table are from various localities in the valley, the distance between the extreme eastern and western ones being 15 miles.

The test of Coalburg was on the rich bituminous coal at the bottom of the seam. The main portion of the bed, which is usually called splint (though in reality a mixture of that and bituminous), gave, when tested by the Chelsea Gas Company, the remarkable result, for this class of fuel, of 10,640 cubic feet, of 17½-candle power.

The coal from the Cannelton Coal Company was from the splinty bituminous division of their cannel seam.

The coal from the lower 5 feet 8 inches of the seam of the Coal Valley Coal Company shows:

Fixed carbon	61.602
Volatile combustible matter	35.203
Ash	18.73
Moisture	1.322
	100.000
Sulphur in coal	0.658
" " coke	0.865

Dr. C. M. Cresson, analysed the coal from the same seam, from just across the river from the land of the Cannelton Coal Company, and in his report speaks of it as "a bituminous coal of first-rate quality, and as especially adapted for gas making. It exceeds in value for such purposes, the best bituminous coal in use in this or the New York market by about 7 per cent, and is remarkably free from sulphur."

The 4½ to 5-feet 2-inch seam, at the old Winnifrede mines on Fields creek, in Kanawha county, is bituminous with 1½ feet of splint at the bottom. An analysis by Prof. Locke, of Cincinnati shows:

Carbon	68.53
Volatile matter	27.01
Ash	3.22
Water	1.24

An analysis from the labratory of the Royal School of Mines, in London, of the coal from the 11-foot seam, worked by the Gauley Kanawha Coal Company, on Gauley Mountain, in Fayette county, gives:

Coke	65.99	Ash	2.15 per cent.
Volatile matter	32.61	Sulphur	0.74 "
Water	1.40		
	100.00		

Volatile gas per ton, of 2,240 pounds, 10,100 cubic feet, of 17.9-candle power.

Proceeding east from the Gauley Kanawha Coal Company, the hard bituminous coals disappear, and the semi-bituminous come in. They are almost altogether shipped to the eastern market, and in Richmond quote 50 cents per ton, of 2,240 pounds, higher than the coals from the Richmond field. They make a most excellent fuel, but their great value is in the admirable coke they produce. As mined at Sewell Station, by the Longdale Coal and Iron Company, it is mostly made into coke for use in the Company's furnace, at Longdale, in Alleghany county, Virginia, where they succeeded in reducing their fuel bill to a little over 2,200 pounds of coke per ton of pig metal produced.

At the Nuttallburg Mines, it is extensively shipped both raw and coked, the latter being done in open kilns. At Quinnimont, it is largely worked by the New River Car Company, for use in their furnace, on the spot, as well as for shipment. The first of the following tables gives analysis of the coals from these three localities, and the second of the cokes. In the latter is added, for the sake of comparison, an analysis of a sample, composed of 49 different pieces of the celebrated Connellsville coke, of Pennsylvania:

COALS.

MINE.	Carbon.	Volatile Matter.	Ash.	Sulphur.	Water.	Chemist.
Nuttallburg	69.00	29.59	1.07	0.78	0.34	C. E. Dwight.
Sewell	72.32	21.38	5.27	0.27	1.03	
Quinnimont	75.89	18.19	4.98	....	0.94	J. B. Britton.

COKES.

MINE.	Carbon.	Volatile Matter.	Ash.	Sulphur.	Water.	Chemist.
Nuttallburg	91.[illegible]		7.53	0.92		C. E. Dwight.
Sewell	93.00	....	6.73	0.27	....	
Quinnimont, No. 1	93.85	....	6.15	0.30	....	J. B. Britton.
" " " 2	91.72	....	5.57	0.48	....	" "
Connellsville	87.46	....	11.33	0.69	....	" "

No. 1, Quinnimont, is of the coke made from the coal, as usually mined. No. 2 is of the coked slack, or mine screenings and refuse. The ash in the Nuttallburg coal and coke shows that the former was either a picked sample, or else that the latter was a poor specimen.

Connellsville coke has obtained so high a reputation, and justly, that there are many persons prone to believe that it can have no superior, and for such it would be well to state that the analyses from Sewell and Quinnimont were made for the private use of the companies using the coal, and that of Nuttallburg was made by the State Board of Centennial Managers.

At various points in the surrounding counties, beds of this variety of fuel are found up to 6 feet 2 inches thick, as, for instance, near Raleigh court-house. Everywhere that I have examined them they contain the same tender, friable, rich, bituminous coal. As far as a physical examination goes—for no analysis has ever been made from this region, beyond those given—they are exceedingly pure and would make excellent coke, and the seams have the advantage of being very free from partings.

Returning to the hard bituminous coals of the Kanawha valley, I have measured very many exposures, varying from 2 to 9 feet, on Gauley, Elk and Coal rivers, and their tributaries. In Logan, Lincoln, Wayne, &c., are, also, many valuable seams as shown in the following analyses, which are from Wayne county, and as far as I can learn, all that have been made for the district. In the table there is no attempt to separate Splint from Bituminous, the list being given merely to show the general purity of the coals:

LOCALITY.	Fixed Carbon.	Volatile Matter.	Ash.	Water.	Sulphur in Coal.	Sulphur in Coke.	Cubic ft. of Gas per 2,240 pounds.	Chemist.
Mouth Camp Cr'k of 12 Pole........	56.35	37.60	6.05	1.60	0.57	0.14	....	Wormley.
Stephen's Br. of Laurel of 12 Pole	60.10	36.40	3.50	1.70	0.72	0.18	....	"
Tug Fork	61.18	38.74	1.88	....	....	0.02	....	Taylor.
" "	60.54	36.66	2.80	....	....	0.03	....	"
Cassville	44.89	43.22	10.33	1.56	0.824	....	....	Dwight.

As showing the thickness of the seams in this portion of the State, the following measurements of outcrops were obtained from a report on the coals of Twelve Pole river, by Prof. E. B. Andrews, of the Ohio Geological Survey :

LOCALITY.	Character of Coal.	Thickness of Seam.		No. of Partings.	Am't of Clear Coal.		Remarks.
		Ft.	In.		Ft.	In.	
Mouth Camp Creek..	Bituminous.........	6	4	2	5	5	Dry burning and very pure.
Sulphur Spring Creek	Splint.....................	6	0	1	5	8	Excellent quality.
Stephen's Br. of Laurel.......	"	4	9	3	4	5	
Wm. Wileys Cove Creek.....	Spl't and Cannel	6	6	...	6	6	Contains 4 ft. 6 in. Cannel.
Hezekiahs Cr'k	" "	8	2	2	7	3	Contains 5 ft. 6 in. Cannel.
Brush Creek.....	" "	4	1	1	3	10	Contains 2 ft. 0 in. Cannel.

The coals from all of these are spoken of in the highest terms by Prof. Andrews. On numberless other creeks and ravines in Wayne and the counties of Lincoln, Logan, Wyoming, and Boone, exposures of equal thickness and purity can be found.

SPLINT COAL.

Except in a local expansion on one of the seams above the Pittsburgh, near Wheeling, there is no well authenticated instance of this class of coal being found in the Upper Coal Measures, or in the northern-half of the State. Possibly this may arise from the fact, that the attention of the miner is there mainly directed to gas coal. Hard, open burning, bituminous fuels exist, but they lack the highly laminated, sonorous characteristics of splint.

Without saying that it occurs nowhere outside of the following limits, the area where it is known positively to exist in workable beds is in the Lower Coal Measures in Braxton, Webster, Clay, Nicholas, Fayette, Kanawha, Boone, Logan, Lincoln, and Wayne counties, and its boundaries may be roughly outlined as follows: Beginning at the juncture of Louisa and Tug Forks of Big Sandy river, on the Kentucky line, and thence in a straight northwesterly line to the Forks of Coal, in Lincoln and Kanawha; thence to Charleston, on the Kanawha; thence to the point where Elk river crosses the Clay and Braxton line; thence bending to the east and runningto where the Elk crosses the Braxton and Webster line; thence southeasterly to the vicinity of Addison; and thence southwesterly, passing though Summersville, in Nicholas, Gauley mountain, near the Hawk's Nest, in Fayette, the extreme southern corner of Kanawha, and thence on to the common corner of Wayne and Logan, on Tug Fork of Big Sandy. It should be clearly understood that these boundaries are only general, and that instead of being straight, as laid down, they will run in and out in curves, so as, in some cases, to add to this area, and in others to subtract from it.

In this region it is abundant, and in admixture with more or less bituminous coal is found in seams as thick as 10 and 11 feet. For the combined purposes of steam, domestic use, and the manufacture of iron, it may be looked upon as the most useful and valuable coal of the State, and even now it ranks so high that in the New York retail market it quotes higher than any other West Virginia coal, except cannel. Its value is due to its firmness and solidity, which enables it to be handled, shifted and stored with very little loss; it burns well; leaving but little ash; has both high calorific power and intensity; is usually remarkably free from sulphur (iron pyrites) and other impurities; has little or no tendency to clinker; is free from the danger of firing by spontaneous combustion—a great desideratum in storage and ocean transportion: is first-rate as a steam and household fire, and it has a particular adaptability in the raw state to the manufacture of iron in the blast furnace, for which purpose it is eagerly sought in districts accessible to market, as it makes a quality of iron which can only be surpassed by the use of charcoal. In this latter connection, it is well to point out how this fuel is esteemed in other States:

The Block Coal of Ohio, in its position in the coal measures, its structure, composition and its appearance, is exactly the same as the "Splint" of Kanawha, and is well adapted, in the raw state, to the smelting of iron ores. It is, indeed, a typical furnace coal, and forms the fuel by which fully half of the iron in the State is manufactured. It is the only fuel used in the furnaces of the extensive iron district of Cleveland, and is, in fact, the basis of the great iron industry of Northern Ohio. (Geology of Ohio, 1870, page 26 and 27.)

The "Block Coal" of Indiana, also, is the same as Kanawha Splint. "As a blast furnace fuel to smelt iron ores it has been amply tested in the five furnaces that are now using it in Clay county, and leaves nothing to be desired. The pig iron made at the Clay county blast furnaces from Iron mountain and Lake Superior iron ores, by use of block coal as fuel, commands from $2 to $3 more per ton, at the furnace than the same grade of pig iron made in Kenucky and Ohio will command in Indianapolis."—(Geology of Indiana, 1869, page 70).

"The reputation of the 'block coal' for smelting iron ores continues to be fully sustained by its excellent behavior in the blast furnaces that are using it. * * Mr. Hicks, the founder, assures me that the furnace (the Brazil) now runs with the utmost regularity, and he finds no difficulty in making a uniform grade of gray pig." (Geology of Indiana, 1872, page 9.) In the same book (page 37) Prof. Cox, the State Geologist, notes a case in Clay county where only 4,250 pounds of raw block coal are required to make a ton of iron.

After four years examination and trial of these splint coals in Indiana, Prof. Cox says: "I have every reason to believe that, when used under the most favorable conditions, we will obtain as large yields of iron with Indiana block coal fuel as can be obtained from the same ores with coke."—(Geology of Indiana, 1873, page 115.)

Let us now look at Pennsylvania. "There is no bituminous coal in Pennsylvania that can be used in the raw state for smelting iron except the splint or 'block coal,' as it is commonly called, of this region close to the Ohio line, in Mercer county, on the Pittsburgh and Erie R. R. and the Beaver and Erie Canal. * * * There was nearly 500,000 tons of block coal produced in Mercer county in 1871, and twenty-three blast furnaces in the district above mentioned were running on this coal in that year."—(Coal Regions of America, page 209).

As regards practical tests of this coal from West Virginia, the following is about all that has been done.

Mr. Mendenhall, of C. C. Mendenhall & Co., tried it, and speaks of it under date of October 10, 1867, thus: "We have thoronghly tested its quality for this purpose (a blast furnace fuel) in our own furnace, near Wheeling, with the most satisfactory results; regarding it as better adapted to smelting iron than any known coal of the Alleghany coal field. We used Campbell's creek and Coalburg coals with about equal results. The estimate in which our furnace manager holds these coals is evidenced from the fact that I am authorized to contract for a supply to be carried up the Ohio river to Wheeling, for use in our furnaces there."

Coalburg splint has also been used in the furnaces at Ironton on the Ohio; but they, as well as Wheeling, stopped their orders several years ago, because, on account of the uncertainty of the navigation of the Ohio and Kanawha rivers, they could not get a regular supply, and had to keep large stocks on hand. This stoppage I should mention, was before the Chesapeake and Ohio railroad was completed.

The Kenton furnace, of Newport, Ky., up to 1873, had used some 10,000 tons of Campbell's creek splint, mixing it with an equal amount of Connellsville coke. Of this mixture it took $1\frac{3}{4}$ tons to make one ton of iron.

In the summer of 1873 I visited the Elizabeth Furnace, Augusta county, Virginia. They were then using two-thirds charcoal, and one-third Coalburg splint, with very satisfactory results. Since then the Lewiston splint has been a good deal used and very much liked, but I am not aware that Kanawha coal alone has ever been tested here.

The same summer I also visited the Buffalo Gap Furnace in the same county. At that time Coalburg splint, mixed with a little charcoal was the fuel, and the iron went on the market as charcoal iron. On one occasion, before my visit, the supply of charcoal gave out, and they ran on raw coal alone for three days, and Mr. McClure, the Superintendent, estimated that one ton of pig would take 1¾ tons of coal, which he thought would produce a better iron than coke.

In the spring of 1875, the Powhatan Iron Company, near Richmond, Virginia, made a test of Kanawha splint, with a view of substituting it for anthracite, which they were then using, but abandoned it, returning a verdict that the coal was not suited for iron making. This can be amply accounted for by the fact that they attempted to use it without making the proper and necessary changes in their furnace. Exactly the same difficulty was met with in the early days of the use of splint (or block coal, as there termed), in Indiana. The furnaces originally put up had a tendency to chill, and what grade of iron would be tapped, was always uncertain. After many experiments with changes in the interior form of the furnace, they learned exactly what was required, and in 1872, the Brazil "was running with the utmost regularity, and the founder experienced no difficulty in making a uniform grade of gray pig."

The following table shows the analyses of various West Virginia splint coals. For the purpose of comparison, there is also added the block coal of Indiana, and the Mahoning Valley, Ohio, the Pittsburgh coal, and two of the best iron making coals of Great Britain :

LOCALITY.	Volatile Matter.	Fixed Carbon.	Ash.	Water.	Chemist.
Campbell's Cr'k, Kanawha	35 64	61.07	1 21	1.88	Riverside Iron Company.
Coalburg, 4-foot Seam, Kanawha	33.26	62.61	1.81	2.14	Riverside Iron Company.
Coalburg Main Seam, Kanawha	40.50	56.50	1.50	2.00	Levette, Indiana.
Paint Creek Mines, Kanawha	30.13	63.74	6.13	....	Doremus, N. Y.
Kelley's Cr'k, Kanawha..	37.08	60.92	2.00	....	Rogers, Virginia.
Stephen's Branch, Wayne	36.40	60.10	3.50	1.70	Wormley, Ohio.
Tug Fork, Wayne	38.74	61.18	1.88	....	Taylor, Ohio.
" " "	36.66	60.54	2.80	....	" "
Coal Valley Coal Co., Upper 16 in. of Seam Fayette	38.32	57.20	4.30	0.18	Dwight, W. Va.
Briar Hill, Ohio	32.58	62.66	1.16	3.60	Wormley, Ohio.
Star Mine, Indiana	32.50	61.50	2.50	3.50	Levette, Indiana.
Pittsburg Coal	41.10	56.90	1.00	1.00	" "
Clyde Splint	36.80	59 00	4.20	....	Mushet.
Worsborrough, Yorkshire	48.18	60.32	1.50	....	"

In conjunction with this table, I would submit an extract as to what analysis gives as a good furnace coal :

"It would appear that a furnace coal, to have sufficient reducing power, should have from 58 to 62 per cent. of fixed carbon, with little hygrometric moisture and few impurities. There should be also such physical structure as to prevent the bitumen from running together in the process of combustion and cementing the mass, and at the same time sufficient firmness to bear up under the burden of the furnace charge. 'The effects produced by such a coal,' says Mushet, 'in a blast furnace, either as to quality or quantity of cast-iron, far exceed anything in the history of the manufacture of that metal with charcoal.' With these coals, a greater quantity of iron, in proportion to the fixed carbon, is produced than with anthracite; the quality of iron is better, and the wear upon the furnace is less destructive."*

Now note the reputation of some of the coals given in the table: The Briar Hill coal has been spoken of page 230. The praise bestowed upon it is very high, indeed, but in the same letter, from which an extract was quoted on page 231, Mr. Mendenhall says: "The coal in the Mahoning valley† which is now used in the works of Governor Todd and others there, has hitherto been regarded as of the finest quality known by the works which use it, but our founder, who has managed furnaces for many years in the valley, places the Kanawha coal unquestionably before it."

The coal from the Star Mine is that used for making iron at the Planet furnace, Clay county, Indiana, and for manufacturing iron it is not surpassed by any in the country."‡

The Pittsburgh specimen is a coking coal. The analysis was made of a picked sample obtained from one of the Indianapolis coal dealers, by Prof. Levette, chemist on the State Geological Survey of Indiana. In his report on the Wayne county coals, as shown on Twelve Pole, Prof. Andrews, of the Geological Survey of Ohio, says, in speaking of the 4-foot 9½-inch seam, on Stephens' branch: "I have seldom "found a coal I can commend so strongly and positively as "this."

Thus we have the testimony of analyses that the West Virginia splint ranks with the most celebrated iron coals of the United States, and with two of the best British ones, whilst the verdict of practical tests places it in the front rank of valuable furnace fuels, one of the large iron making firms of the West giving it as their opinion, that "it is better adapted to smelting iron than any known coal of the Alleghany coal field."

*Report on the iron smelting coals of Southern Indiana, 1871. Page 14. Prof. J. W. Foster, LL. D.

†Briar Hill, in this valley.

‡Geology of Indiana, 1869. Page 49. Prof. E. T. Cox, State Geologist.

Another glance at the table will show a very small proportion of ash. This fact has a two-fold importance:

1. The smaller the quantity of ash the less limestone is required in the furnace to flux it; less slag is formed from that particular source, and consequently less heat and less coal are needed in forming that chemical compound in the blast furnace.

2. It is well known that phosphorus makes iron "cold short," *i. e.*, brittle under a blow; imparts fluidity to cast iron, but spoiling it for the manufacture of steel.

Prof. Wormley, Chemist on the Geological Survey of Ohio, in his analysis of the ashes of coal, finds phosphorus present in every case, though, of course, in variable quantities.* The same was found to be the case in the analysis made of ten noted coals for Prof. S. Newberry, State Geologist of Ohio.

Phosphorus no doubt, therefore, occurs in those from Kanawha; but as in all cases it forms but a small percentage of the ash, and as in the Kanawha splints the ash forms such a small percentage of the coal itself, *therefore* the phosphorus will form but a small percentage of the coal itself.

It is due to this fact, amongst others, that splint coal, wherever found, owes its superiority in the blast furnace; and also, I have no doubt, that it is said, that iron smelted by it is especially adapted to the manufacture of steel by the Bessemer process, which process is superseding all others.

Its firmness and capability of bearing handling and transportation has been remarked on: but this will be better appreciated when it is stated, that where it has been thrown out on the mountain side many years ago, from old openings, it may be found in many cases covered with moss, while on the shoals of the creeks and rivers are scattered lumps, varying from the size of a pebble up to 20 and 30 pounds weight, smooth and water-worn. How long they have been there no man can tell, and yet break them in either case and they are as black, rich, pure, sound and solid as when first severed from the mother seam.

This hardness has an admirable illustration in a cargo of lump coal that was shipped to New York by the Kanawha Semi-Cannel Coal Co. It was closely examined during the

* Geological Survey of Ohio, 1870, page 428.

loading of the vessel in Richmond, and while discharging in New York, out of the whole cargo only about two tons had been broken up into sizes of "egg" and "nut."

As regards its advantages for steam and reheating furnaces, it has been largely tried both in the east and west, and is rapidly gaining popularity wherever introduced, but, unfortunately, the mines are usually careless in getting the results of such practical tests, so that but very few detailed ones are accessible, and all that I have been able to obtain for this work are as follows: On the completion of the Chesapeake and Ohio R. R. in 1873, a trial of this coal was made by the Tredegar Iron Works of Richmond. This test brought forth the report, "that we have made a limited trial of the Kanawha "splint coal. That, however, was sufficient to satisfy us of "its admirable qualities for the heating furnace. The only "question as to its use on a large scale here, is the price at "which it can be delivered."

In the winter of 1875–6, the steamers of the New York and Harlem Steamboat Co. were using Kanawha coal, and the engineers report a preference for it, as they could raise steam on short notice and could bank their fires over night with the certainty of quick combustion and ready steam in the morning, which they could not count on without re-lighting when other coals, to which they were accustomed, were in use. The Bridgewater Iron Co., of Massachusetts, made a very limited trial of the coal from the Kanawha Semi-Cannel Coal Co., which induced them to give an order for some 307 tons, which they used under their boilers and in the rolling mills. They reported it as being superior to any bituminous coal formerly used, and entered into contracts for further supplies. This same Coal Co. is also supplying the Mantanzas and Havana R. R. Co., in Cuba, with its fuel.

For steam purposes the most satisfactory tests (because the most in detail), have been obtained from the Kentucky Central, Chesapeake and Ohio, and the Atlantic, Mississippi and Ohio railroads. The former made a months careful tests of Youghiogheny, Pa., and Ashland, Ky., coal, with a result of 39 pounds in the former case, and 43 pounds in the latter, consumed per mile run, for freight and passenger traffic. The road then bought its fuel from the Coalburg mines, in Kanawha, and a months trial gave 25 pounds per mile run. At the end of 12 months the fuel books showed that the average for the year (including what had been used of all three kinds named above) was 32.1 pounds per mile run for all kinds of service. The difference between the 25 pounds and 32.1 pounds can be accounted for by the care exercised while testing, with a view to contract for a year's supply, the difference in the seasons, and condition of the track (the first trial being made in the summer), and the one month's use of the lower grade Youghiogheny and Ashland, which, of course, tended to bring down the average. For the following information concerning the trials on the Chesapeake and Ohio, and Atlantic, Mississippi and Ohio, railroads I am indebted to the kindness of Gen. J. M. St. John, the Consulting Engineer of the former:

"Our best monthly average for C. & O. engine performance is 29.62 pounds coal, per mile run, for passenger service, with *loaded* engine and tenders, weighing 88,000 to 90,000 pounds, and five cars weighing 220,700 pounds. Sum of ascents, Richmond to Huntington,* west, 6,271 feet; descents, west, 5,639 feet. This monthly average includes all wastage and deterioration of fuel on hand, and for train detention, a per centage of loss that should always be considered in comparing statements of engine performance, and which is often large enough to explain the difference cited in your letter of 11th of February, between the 25 pound trial trip on the Kentucky Central and their 32.1-pound average.

In this connection, I have just received from the Atlantic, Mississippi and Ohio railroad, a report of Lewiston (Kanawha) coal, which may interest you:

Weight of engine and tender, loaded	110,300	pounds.
" " train, west, 6 cars, exclusive of engine	273,250	"
" " " east, 5 " " " "	214,000	"
Sum of ascents, west, (Lynchburg to Bristol)	4,815	feet.
" " descents, " " " "	3,755	"

Maximum grade, 70 feet per mile; curve, 7 degrees; coal consumed per round trip, of 408 miles, 29.02 pounds per mile run.

Allowing for the difference of grades between the Atlantic, Mississippi and Ohio, and the Kentucky Central the results

---

*Distance, 427 miles; maximum grade, going west, 72 feet per mile; lowest radius of curve, 1,000 feet.

of the two trial trips do not vary essentially, while the Chesapeake and Ohio monthly average is probably a more reliable guide than either for estimating the value of Kanawha coals."

The fuels used during this monthly average, by the C. & O. R. R., were from Lewiston, Coalburg, and Coal valley, the two last being respectively about 4 and 13 miles east of the first, thus showing the distribution, in the Kanawha valley, of a first-rate article for steam.

CANNEL COAL

May be termed a "fancy" article, as it sells at high prices, and the seams are erratic, varying from zero to 5½ feet. It is universally associated with some other kind of coal, usually bituminous, a very fortunate circumstance, as in mining the "bearing in" can be done in this latter, leaving the whole of the cannel available, and as it separates very easily from the others, a 10 or 12-inch stratum in a large seam can be gotten out profitably and shipped by itself. Were it otherwise it would have to be mined with the rest and sold at the smaller prices of lower grades.

Unfortunately, from the peculiarity of its geological deposition, it cannot be stated over what area any given seam of it will be found, or how long it will last of any given thickness, so that it cannot be reasoned that, because a 5-foot seam is found on the northern edge of, say 5,000 acres, it will be found on the southern edge. The *seam* will be found, but the cannel may have been completely displaced by another kind of coal. This will be made more clear by a few examples:

The celebrated Bog-head cannel, of Scotland, varied from 1 inch to 2 feet 6 inches. The cannel in the seam at Cannelton, on the Kanawha, has extremes, in the present mine, of 10 inches and 5 feet, the average being 39 to 42 inches. About half a mile to the west the seam has increased to 10 feet 4 inches of splint and bituminous, but without out a semblance of cannel, while to the east, and across the river, the latter is so thin as not to be workable. At Peytona, on Coal river, the thinest place yet found in the seam now worked is 2 feet 6 inches, and the thickest 3 feet 8 inches. The entry is about half a mile from the river, on the other side of which the cannel has disappeared.

Another example: Some four miles up Paint creek, before

the war, two companies made oil from this mineral. On the east side of the creek a seam was opened and worked till the cannel stratum became too thin to get out easily. An opening was then made on the west side, about 800 yards from the first, and the cannel was found 40 inches. A mile to the west the same bed is opened to its usual thickness, but the cannel has dwindled down to 14 inches.

From its frequency in the southern portion of the State, there is no telling where it may not be found, but only an actual opening on it can prove its existence, and in searching for it, and in determining the extent of a deposit, the annular diamond drill can be most advantageously used.

Its principal development in West Virginia appears to be in the area assigned to Splint Coal, though with more contracted boundary lines, and in this the thickest exposures yet observed, are as follows:

County.	Locality.	Thickness.	
		Ft.	In.
Wayne.....	Laurel Branch of Hezekiah (outcrop)..................	5	6
"	Brush Creek (outcrop)..	2	0
"	Cove Creek "	4	6
Logan.......	Nine mile of Guyandotte (outcrop)......................	3	1
Boone......	Workman's Branch "	4	6
"	Peytona Coal Co. Lower Seam (average)..............	3	4
Kanawha..	Paint Creek Coal Co. (thickest place).................	3	4
"	Mill Creek Coal Co. (reported)...........................	4 to 5 ft.	
Fayette....	Cannelton Coal Co. (average)............................	3	6
Nicholas...	Little Elk of Gauley (outcrop)............................	4	0

In the northern half of the State this coal seems to accompany only one bed, viz: the Upper Freeport, and but little is known of it, for it has never been worked—except in one case noted hereafter—and there are no analyses except of the exposure at Lost run, in Taylor county.

In Monongalia county, on Tibb's run, a branch of Decker's creek, the Upper Freeport was examined by Prof. Stevenson, who reports that "the shale above it for several feet, is very "bituminous, with a conchoidal fracture, and is undoubtedly "a cannel coal of inferior quality." In an exposure of this seam on Sand run, Randolph county, is a poor cannel of 2 feet 6 inches, which a mile distant shows 1 foot 1 inch; at Nuzum's

Mill, Marion county, it shows 1 foot. On Prickett's creek, in the same county, we have the general statement that the cannel is thicker, but no measurement of it. On Lost run, in Taylor county, is a seam composed of

Bituminous Coal,	1 ft. 6 in.
Cannel "	2 " 0 "
Bituminous "	3 " 6 "
Total,	7 ft. 0 in.

In this the cannel, though very handsome in appearance, is of very poor quality, as will be seen by its analysis in the next table.

On White Day creek, in the northern part of Taylor county, is a seam composed of 2 feet of bituminous and 3½ feet of cannel. In 1859 the White Day Cannel Coal & Oil Company, purchased 1250 acres here, and erected extensive buildings and machinery for the purpose of distilling oil from the cannel. After five or six weeks profitable running, a careless management allowed fire to reach the gas in the condensing pipes, which exploded the works. It was decided to rebuild them, but the discovery of petroleum caused an abandonment of the idea, and the property was sold. Mr. Hiram Winchester, who was formerly connected with these works, and who kindly furnished the above account, writes that the coal yielded about 37 gallons of crude oil per ton. This is very low, and would seem to indicate that the coal would be poor in gas, which is the element that gives cannel its great value. The Peytona cannel of Boone county, gives

Crude Illuminating Oil,	20 gals.
Crude Lubricating Oil,	52 "
Oily Parafin,	7.2 "
	79.2 " *

Cannelton cannel, Fayette county, yielded by the treatment of the Union Oil Company, 2 gallons per bushel, or 56 gallons per ton. This is really not the full yield, for when the retorts were taken up, the present company found there had been considerable waste and leakage. Two companies on Paint creek, and one on Mill creek, Kanawha county, formerly distilled oil from this mineral. They were stopped chiefly on

*The New York *Times*, 1856. This is the latest information on this point I can find. The coal was never distilled on a large scale, that I am aware of.

account of the war, and have not resumed operations since, partly from lack of capital, but mainly from the discoveries of the cheaper Petroleum. There are now no oil works of this class, in operation in the State.

The chief value of this coal is as a gas producer. For this purpose, that from West Virginia has no superior in America. The only two mines in operation within our borders at this date, are the Cannelton Coal Company, on the Kanawha, and the Peytona Coal Company, on Coal river. The quotations for their article are higher, without an exception, in all markets that they reach, than any other fuel mined in the United States.

To better appreciate the high results of the analyses, from Peytona and Cannelton, in the following table, the reader should compare them with the bituminous coal some pages back:

COUNTY.	Locality.	Fixed Carbon.	Volatile Matter.	Ash.	Cubic ft. of Gas per 2,240 pounds.	Candle Power.	Chemist.
Boone......	Peytona*	41.0	46.0	13.0	13,200	32.36	Manhattan Gas Light Co., N. Y.
Fayette.....	Cannelton....	23.5	58.0	18.5	12,025	45.6	Manhattan Gas Light Co., N. Y.
Kanawha.	....	....	....	.....	....	....	....
Taylor.....	Lost Run.....	42.32	23.08	34.01	....	....	C. E. Dwight.
Wayne.....	Twelve Pole.	42.59	49.40	7.41	....	....	" "

Before leaving this coal, attention should be called to the bituminous or cannel shale that is very often mistaken for it There are many outcroppings of it varying from a few inches to 5 or more feet. In appearance it is like cannel, but from which it can usually be distinguished by its greater specific gravity and slaty structure, this latter being particularly observable where the blocks have been exposed for some time to the weathering action of the atmosphere. It burns well, evolving great heat, and igniting readily, but leaves so large

*At 10.000 cubic feet per ton, the illuminating power was 41.16 candles.

an amount of ash as to be unfit for fuel. It seems to be almost, if not quite, as rich in oils as the cannel itself, and, if Petroleum was still undiscovered, would be a very valuable source of illuminating oils, whereas, at present, it is of no value.

The similitude to cannel is so marked that in some cases the most practiced observer has to be very careful not to be deceived, and it has been the cause of erroneous rumors and many false hopes started. As an example we can cite the case of a company, in West Virginia, improving a property, building an incline, and opening a mine, to find out, after their money was gone, that they were shipping an unmarketable article, and of another, so deceived were they by appearance, that built the incline and opened the mine, to discover that their "cannel" contained 52 per cent of ash. *Experientia docet.*

MARKETS.

First, there is the Eastern one of the Atlantic seaboard states which are reached by the Baltimore and Ohio railroad, in the north, and the Chesapeake and Ohio railroad, in the south, and next is the Western one, of the great Mississippi valley, with its 16,674 miles of waters navigable for steamboats, and its system of 20,000 miles of railroads now in successful operation, and its hundreds of thousands of coal burning engines, locomotives, factories, furnaces, machine shops, &c.

These rivers and railroads traverse the country of 16 magnificent, populous, and growing States, of an aggregate of one million square miles, and minister to the wants of abont one-third of the population of the United States.

To form a better idea of the wealth and demands of this western country, it may be stated that the tonnage of the Upper Ohio, in steamers, barges and boats, exceeds that of New York, and that the trade of the Ohio river, as estimated by Government Engineers, exceeds the entire foreign commerce of the United States.

Before the war, the consumption of mineral fuel was increasing year by year, at a rapid rate throughout the West, and as the growth of that region in population and wealth has been even more rapid since that time, so the demand for coal has increased, and must do so, to enormous bounds.

Again, not only does the market become greater by increase of population, but it makes larger demands, year by year, from additions and improvements to the arts and manufactures; for every new invention of a labor saving machine usually implies a new source for the use of coal, either directly, in the production of steam to run it, or indirectly, in producing heat or steam for its manufacture, and often for both.

Surely with so excellent fuels as West Virginia possesses, it may with all reason, look forward to the time when it may contribute no small per centage of this growing increase.

The cannel and the gas coals will, from their superiority, grow yearly in favor, and become more in demand, and the State can expect larger and larger exportations. But for splint and pure coking coals that are suitable to iron making, the greatest demand will not be from abroad, but in home markets. By this is meant the consumption that will be found within or near our own borders in the blast furnace and its attendant industries.

Besides the iron ores found in the Coal Measures of West Virginia, its eastern side forms part of the great iron belt of the United States, which runs from northern Pennsylvania to middle Alabama, and is so richly developed in our State and Virginia, between the Alleghanies and the Blue Ridge.

In this belt the ores, for the most part, are the brown oxides, yielding in Virginia from 40 to 50 per cent. of iron. They are usually worked in open quarries, and though fine in the northern portion of the State, increase, both in quality and quantity, as we follow the belt in its southwesterly course, till in the last counties to the south they are very rich.

In treating of the geology of this portion of Virginia and West Virginia, Professor Rogers says: "Of the twelve rocks, each marked by certain distinctive characteristics, composing the mountains and valleys of this region, it has been determined that at least eight are accompanied by beds of iron ore."*

General Haupt,† in speaking of the minerals along the line of his road, which runs in this iron belt across the State of Virginia, says: "The iron deposits are very numerous, and of superior quality. Pennsylvania, rich as she is, is poor in iron ores as compared with Virginia."

*Geology of Virginia. 1836. W. B. Rogers, State Geologist.
†Chief Engineer of the Shenandoah Valley Railroad.

On the eastern edge of this iron country, on both sides of the Blue Ridge, are the magnetic and red haematite ores. On the James river, in the counties of Bedford, Amherst, Nelson, Buckingham, &c., the magnetics are exceedingly fine, and in Patrick, Henry. Grayson, Floyd and Carrol counties, they, as well as the brown oxides, also abound.

Scattered throughout this belt are many charcoal furnaces, some of them producing metal of such quality that in 1871 it was bringing $55 to $56 per ton in Philadelphia, while the Pennsylvania iron on the Lehigh, was selling for $35.

A furnace of 6 to 7 tons daily capacity, requires about 200 acres of ordinary Virginia forest to supply it with fuel for a year, and hence it will be seen that timber is too soon stripped from the vicinity of a furnace to depend on it as a smelting agent in very large and extensive works; while in rolling mills, &c., coal is a necessity. These ores will, therefore, look to other sources for their reduction, and they *must* turn to West Virginia coal, for besides being most excellent for this purpose, they are the nearest.

In the history of the iron trade, the ore usually has come to the coal, and not the coal to the ore; but in this case, owing to the nearness of the one to the other, a reciprocity of freights will be established, and each will be taken into the other's district, and when brought into communication along the length of the State, we can look forward to the day when West Virginia and the bordering iron counties of Virginia will be teeming hives of industry and wealth, and one of the most important centres of the iron manufacture of the United States, while the ever consuming fires of the blast furnace will furnish one of the largest markets for our fuels.

The following tables show the quotations of the chief West Virginia coals in the principal eastern and western markets to which they are carried. For the sake of comparison, their greatest rivals from other States, are also added. The prices are taken from the quotations given in the *Engineering and Mining Journal*, on the first Saturday of each of the six months ending 1st April, 1876.

NEW YORK.

Wholesale Per Ton of 2,240 Pounds Alongside.

COAL.	State.	Nov.	Dec.	Jan.	Feb.	March	April.
Westmoreland and Penn	Penna...	$6.50	$6.50	$6.50	Not quoted.	$6.00	$6.00
Youghiogheny, Waverly County..	" ...	6.50	6.50	6.50		5.75	5.75
Despard	W. Va...	6.50	6.50	6.50		6.00	6.00
Murphy's Run	"	6.50	6.50	6.50		6.00	6.00
Fairmont..................	"	6.50	6.50	6.50		6.00	6.00
Newburg Orrel...........	"	6.50	6.50	6.50		6.00	6.00
Red Bank Cannel	Penna...	8.50	8.50	8.50		8.50	8.50
Straitsville "	Ohio......	10.00	10.00	10.00		....	....
Cannelton "	W. Va...	11.00	11.00	11.00		10.50	10.50
Paytona "	"	11.50	11.50	11.00		10.50	10.50
Cannelton Splint........	"	6.50	6.50	6.50		6.00	6.00

RICHMOND, VA.

Wholesale Per Ton of 2,240 Pounds on Ship Board.

COAL.	State.	Nov.	Dec.	Jan.	Feb.	March	April.
Kanawha Cannel.......	W. Va.	$12.00	$12.00	$12.00	$9.00	$9.00	$9.00
Coalburg Splint.........	"	4.90	4.75	4.75	4.75	4.75	4.75
Lewiston "	"	4.90	4.75	4.75	4.75	4.75	4.75
Kanawha Gas...........	"	4.50	4.50	4.50	4.50	4.50	4.50
New River bituminous	"	4.50	4.50	4.50	4.50	4.50	4.50
Clover Hill	Va.	4.25	4.25	4.25	4.00	4.00	4.00
James River Bituminous.........	"	3.30	3.30	3.30	3.30	3.30	3.30

CINCINNATI, OHIO.

Wholesale Per Bushel Afloat.

COAL	State	Nov.	Dec.	Jan.	Feb.	March	April.
Youghiogheny..........	Penna...	10c	10c	9c	7½c	7½c	7½c
Pittsburgh	Penna ..	10c	10c	9c	7½c	7½c	7½c
Pomeroy..................	Ohio	8c	8c	6c	5c	5c	5½c
Kanawha.................	W. Va ..	10c	10c	10c	7½c	7½c	7½c

LOUISVILLE, KY.

Retail Per Bushel.

COAL.	State.	Nov.	Dec.	Jan.	Feb.	March.	April.
Pittsburgh	Penna...	14c	14c	14c	14c	14c	12c
Raymond City	W. Va...	13c	13c	13c	13c	13c	11c
Pine Hill..	Ky.......	13c	13c	13c	13c	13c	13c
Peytona Cannel ..	W. Va...	20 to 22c	20 to 22c	20 to 22c	20 to 22c	20 to 22c	20 to 22c

A final summing up of the advantages possessed by the West Virginia coal field, are:

1st. A very large area of coal strata of unusual regularity, great thickness and excellent quality.

2d. In this coal field are numerous seams of splint, cannel, and bituminous coal, which rank with, and sometimes excel the best coals of the United States.

3d. It has railroad connection with the western markets, as well as communication with 40,000 miles of western river navigation and railroads, along which are many large and manufacturing towns.

4th. Within its boundaries, and skirting its eastern borders, are deposits of iron ore of good quality, in great profusion, and of all the varieties necessary for the manufacture of first rate iron.

5th. The vast deposits of ore in the adjoining State of Virginia, have to look to the West Virginia coal field for the fuesl for their reduction.

These facts should commend our State in the most confident terms to the careful notice of those who desire an advantageous location for mining coal, and for the erection of blast furnaces and their allied industries.

CHAPTER XI.

IRON.

BY M. F. MAURY.

The iron to be found in West Virginia may be divided into two classes:

1. Those ores which belong to, and are found in the Appalachian Coal Measures, consisting of Brown Oxides, Carbonates, and Black Bands, and in some places, nodular red hæmatite.

2. Those which belong to the region lying between the eastern escarpment of the coal formation and the eastern border of the State, forming a part of the great iron belt of the Atlantic States, and consisting of the brown and red hæmatites, which are much more rich and abundant than those of the first class.

IRON ORES OF THE COAL MEASURES.

Little attention has been paid to the iron of this geological horizon, except in the northern counties, where a few small blast furnaces have worked the native ores. With these exceptions, as there was generally no cheap and convenient outlet, and consequently no great value for this mineral or its product, it has not possessed much attraction for the people at large, and but little attention has been paid to it.

A careful geological survey may, and no doubt will, show that we possess more workable beds of it than are now known, and in fact, within the last two years most valuable seams of Black Band ores have been uncovered, the presence of which was not thought of before.

Laboring under these disadvantages, and with a great lack

of data, only a very imperfect sketch of this mineral element of wealth can at present be given.

In the chapter on Coal, it will be remembered that the Coal Measures were divided into four great divisions, viz.:

The Lower Coal Measures.

The Lower Barren Measures.

The Upper Coal Measures.

The Upper Barren Measures.

With but one exception (in Jackson county), so far as examinations go, it is only the first two that in West Virginia contain workable beds of ore, which may be divided into Carbonates and Black Bands.

Black Band Iron Ore.—This is nothing more than a Carbonate of Iron, of a more or less black color, by reason of an admixture of bituminous matter. So far as yet known, it is confined entirely to the southern part of the State, where it has been discovered only within the last few years. From the fact of its very often resembling black slate in its structure, it may often have been passed over unnoticed, and careful search will no doubt show it in many places, where it is not now suspected.

It is a class of material that makes an excellent iron, and from which much of the celebrated Scotch pig is smelted. It possesses an especial value, from the fact that, in many cases, a low grade ore can be roasted into a higher grade. For instance, take that from Davis creek, in Kanawha county. Where mined, it contains 33 per cent of metallic iron, and 26 per cent. of carbonaceous matter. By piling it in heaps, and setting fire thereto, the carbonaceous matter is burnt out, and in the process of combustion, generates enough heat to convert the carbonate of iron in the ore into a richer oxide, so that the mass, after being thus roasted, analyses 65 per cent. of metallic iron.

Unfortunately, we can never reckon or depend upon any seam of it continuing of a uniform value, for in one place it will contain an ore well worth working, while half a mile off it may become so mixed with slate or earthy impurities as to be utterly valueless. As an example: On Bell creek, Fayette county, an excellent bed about 4 feet thick was found by Mr. L. Bemelmans, of Charleston. Some 2 or 3 miles from this place, up a ravine a short distance below the mouth of Bell, the same seam showed only 12 to 14 inches of the good material, while on Little Elk run, of Gauley river, some three miles to the north, the results of two analyses from the same seam gave only 5 and 7 per cent. respectively, of metallic iron. If we search for it in another direction, it may open to a very valuable deposit. From this irregularity, and from the fact that it has been well proven in this field, it will be readily understood that careful search may find it in many places where it has never yet been noticed, and wherever it is found in workable quantity its presence adds great value to the land.

So new is this ore to our people that it has been discovered in workable strata in only two counties.

The first is in Wayne, near the Big Sandy river. There has been no analysis of it from this place, but one made by E. S. Wayne, of Cincinnati, from the 2½-feet seam in Kentucky, a short distance from the West Virginia line, shows:

Prot. Oxide Iron	34.07
Per Oxide Iron	2.31
Alumina	.43
Lime	7.31
Magnesia	6.30
Carbonic Acid	37.40
Phosphoric Acid	.17
Sulphur	.34
Organic Matter	6.45
Insoluble Matter	3.34
Water	2.30
	100.00
Metallic Iron	28.12 per cent.

The second is on Davis and Briar creeks, in Kanawha county, where many openings have been made, and its extent over a large area well proven. The seam is 6 to 7 feet thick, and in this are from 4 to 5 feet of good workable ore.

An analysis by Otto Wuth, of Pittsburgh, Pa., gives:

Silicic Acid	4.64
Carbonate of Iron	68.35
Phosphoric Acid	0.58
Sulphur	0.42
Carbonaceous Matter, some Lime and Alumina	26.02
	100.00
Metallic Iron	33 per cent.

"Thoroughly roasted, it would then contain about 65 per cent of metallic iron, while there is more than enough carbonaceous matter to roast it. I consider it a Black Band ore of the first quality."—(Otto Wuth).

On Bell creek, in Fayette, Little Elk run, in Nicholas, and Little Sycamore creek, of Elk river, in Clay, outcrops of it have been observed.

Carbonate of Iron.—Under this head may also be classed the Brown Hæmatites of the Coal Measures, as they are merely the results of the decomposition of the Carbonates, and in fact, when a seam of the former is discovered, we may expect it to turn into the latter as soon as we go far enough under ground to get beyond atmospheric influences.

We see the result of this decomposition in the pieces of Brown Oxide that are found on the hills in every portion of the State. These have lead to many erroneous ideas as to the richness of certain localities in this mineral, which came originally from the carbonates of iron existing in the beds that were once superimposed upon the present strata, and have long since been worn away by erosion. As this took place, the lighter materials were washed off by the currents, while the heavier ore settled down and was left resting on our hill sides. Sometimes a great deal was deposited in one place, and the soil is full of it, while in others but a single lump was left, and hence it is that on many of our mountains we find the "blossom" of good ore, and yet have no bed of it near by.

Like the Black Band, the seams of Carbonate of Iron are quite variable, so that in one locality they will be workable, while in another they may have thinned down or degenerated so much from an admixture of earthy impurities, as to be worthless. They usually contain more or less Carbonate of Lime, which is of much importance in the blast furnace, in helping to flux out any earthy impurities that may be present.

By roasting, the carbonic acid of this ore is driven off, and the mass is converted into the red oxide. As the former, when pure, contains 48.3 per cent of iron, and the latter 70 per cent., it will at once be perceived that a thorough burning will raise the per centage so that an ore of low grade can often be roasted to a higher one—a very fortunate circumstance, as otherwise many of our seams would be too poor to be of value.

With the present lack of information, we are not able to trace the various seams from point to point, showing how they thin out or thicken up, and can only mention the individual localities where they have been opened. This will show the frequent occurrence of this mineral, and gives reason to believe that very many more localities with workable deposits, can be found.

Mineral and Grant Counties.—In that portion of these counties that is underlaid by the Coal Measures, the ores that have been discovered, though very good, are not usually workable, on account of the thinness of the beds. The following are the analyses that have been made from this region by Prof. Rogers:

	No 1.	No. 2.	No. 3.	No. 4.	No. 5.
Carb. Iron	79.56	71.00	77.20	61 64	68.68
Carb. Lime	3.36	5.76	3 24	3.48	1.80
Carb Magnesia	2.56	4.00	2.80	2.24	3.12
Silica	10.16	12.20	11.40	24.88	20.72
Alumina	1.84	3.60	2 44	4.60	2.76
Water	1.40	1.80	1.32	2.04	1.56
Carb. Manganese	trace	trace	trace	trace	trace
	98 88	98.36	98.40	98.80	98.64
Metallic Iron	38.42	34.29	38.28	29.77	33.17

No. 1, is from Grant county, on Stony river, 4 miles from the crossing of the Northwestern pike. It occurs in nodules of from 8 to 10 inches in diameter, in a band of calcareous shales, which latter also contain, irregularly distributed, another and coarser kind of ore, quite siliceous, and sometimes having the appearance, when freshly fractured, of a poor article, but upon exposure assuming a deep ferruginous hue. An analysis of this latter is shown in

No. 2, from the Falls of Stony river, 7 miles above the Northwestern pike. Here the shales are 15 to 20 feet thick. The ore is found in a 5 foot bed, which would yield about 3½ feet of solid ore.

No. 3. In the same band, 6 miles below the mouth of Abrams creek, in Mineral county, on the Potomac, the ore occurs again, being in some places 18 inches thick, though very variable.

No. 4, Is still from the same band, from Wilson's Mill, 2 miles below the mouth of Abrams creek, in Mineral county. The ore occurs in nodules 1 to 12 inches in diameter. It would be well to state that these shales in many places, especially on Stony river, contain bands of very pure limestone.

No. 5. From a seam 6 inches thick, from the shales above the second seam of coal, at Brantzburg, on the Potomac, in Mineral county.

These analyses are given mainly to show the quality of the ore in this basin, with the hopes that they may encourage further investigation as to the quantity of this valuable mineral.

Preston County:—The following are the analyses that were made of the ores of this county by Prof. Wm. B. Rogers.

	No. 1.	No. 2.	No. 3.
Carbonate of Iron	68 64	92.00	82.56
Carbonate of Lime	5.84	1 20	2.24
Carbonate of Magnesia	12.04		3.76
Silica	10.48	4.80	8.44
Alumina	1.80	1.20	2.12
Water	2.12	1.12	1.04
Carbonate of Manganese	trace	trace	trace
	100.92	100.32	100.16
Metallic Iron	33.15	44.43	39.87

No. 1. One mile below Kingwood Ferry the shales which overlie the lowest coal seam of the basin, contain 5 bands of rich iron ore within a space of 4 to 5 feet; the lowest band is occasionally 4 to 5 inches thick, and the upper ones generally about 2 inches.

No. 2. In the vicinity of German Settlement, on the summit of a high hill on the north side of the Rhine, is the outcrop of a body of iron ore of a superior quality. It occurs on the surface over a wide area in large fragments, and is also found a short distance beneath. These fragments are evidently in place, and are portions of a bed which occurs near the surface. (W. B. Rogers.)

No. 3. Two and a half miles up Muddy creek from its mouth, at Deep run hollow, the ore varies from 3 to 12 inches. Beneath this is a cacareous shale containing nodules of impure iron ore 8 to 10 inches in diameter.

A very rich ore occurs at Mr. Mich. Hartman's old place in Crab Orchard. The fragments are strewn on the surface over a wide area and seem to indicate a contiuous vein.—(W. B. Rogers.) It is a deep red, inclining to brown, compact, fine grain. It shows 24.96 per cent of silica, and 46.67 per cent of metallic iron.

The Austin Coal Co., on the Balt. and Ohio R. R., have a seam of iron ore 16 to 20 inches thick, 30 feet below their coal mine. The material is shipped to the Lancaster Furnace, Irontown, in Taylor county, and the seam is the same as that worked at the Franklin or Martin Iron Works, on Three Forks creek.

From the northeast portion of Preston, in Grant township, we have reports of two veins of ore, each 4 feet thick, but no details concerning them are given.

In the western portion of the county, from the vicinity of Reedsville, two seams are reported: one 22 inches of honey comb ore, and the other 6 to 36 inches of red lump, which were formerly worked at the Rock Forge, in the adjoining county of Monongalia.

On Three Forks river the ores are said to be of superior quality and to occur under peculiarly favorable conditions for working.

On the estate of the Kingwood Gas Coal and Iron Co., at Tunnelton, is a seam of carbonate of iron that is reported as averaging 2 feet thick. It crops out in many places on the company's land, and also for several miles over the adjacent country.

An analysis of an average of various samples, by Otto Wuth, of Pittsburgh, shows:

Silicic Acid	2.64		
Alumina	0.31		
Carbonate of Iron	67.36	Metallic Iron	32.52
" " Lime	18.89		
" " Magnesia	6.41		
Manganese	0.51		
Sulphate of Lime	0.56	Sulphur	0.13
Phosphate of Lime	3.32	Phosphorus	0.66

"When roasted the ore will yield about 50 per cent in the "furnace. It being a limestone ore, remarkably free from sili- "ca, other more siliceous ores can be worked with it without "using an additional flux."

Four iron furnaces have been worked in this county, though none are now in operation. Hardman and Lancaster Furnace (the Franklin or Martins), on Three Forks, near the Balt. and Ohio R. R., went out of blast in the spring of 1875. The other three are Muddy Creek Furnace (Landon's), on Muddy creek; the Gladeville Furnace, and Carlisle's Furnace, in the northeastern portion of the county, near the Pennsylania line. This last is said to have been one of the original furnaces in the country.

Monongalia County.—The workable beds of iron ore seem to be found in the eastern portion ot this county. Samples from nine distinct seams were gotten and sent to the Centennial office in Wheeling in February, 1876, to be forwarded to the International Exhibition to be held in Philadelphia. Beginning at the lowest and ascending in regular order, they were described in the invoice that accompanied them, as follows:

No. 1. "Martin Vein," about 18 inches thick at the outcrop.

No. 2. "England Ore." Thickness 18 inches. Formerly used at the Decker's Creek Furnace.

No. 3. "Stratford Ore." Thickness 18 inches. Formerly used at the Decker's Creek Furnace.

No. 4. "Spring Hill Ore." Thickness 30 inches. This is the same seam as that worked at Duncan's Furnace, Pennsylvania.

No. 5. "Swisher Ore." Formerly extensively used at the Decker's Creek Furnace.

No. 6. "Haine's Ore." Thickness 2 feet. Formerly used at the Decker's Creek and Cheat River Furnaces.

No. 7. "Scott Ore." Thickness 18 inches Formerly used at the Decker's Creek Furnace.

No. 8. "Hastings Ore." Thickness 18 inches. Formerly used at the Cheat River Furnaces.

No. 9. "Clippart Vein." About 2 feet thick. The analyses* of samples from each of these give:

---

*These and all other analyses given in this chapter, were made (unless another Chemist is mentioned,) by C. E. Dwight, of Wheeling.

CONTENTS.	Martin Seam, 18 in.	England Ore, 18 in.	Stratford Ore, 18 in.	Spring Hill Ore, 30 in.	Swisher Ore.	Haines Ore, 2 ft.	Scott Ore, 18 in.	Hastings Ore, 18 in.	Clippart Vein, 2 ft.
Carbonate of Iron.......	61.01	69.31	31.19	......	50.60	......	49 81	51.67	62.00
Sesquioxide of Iron......	3.44	1.79	11.89	70.49	18 76	57.71	23 80	7.55	2.54
Protoxide of Iron........	......	......	......	0.71	......	1 22	......	......	......
Oxide of Manganese–...	0.01	trace	tr'ce	1.07	1.41	3.34	2.43	0.23	0.02
Carbonate of Lime......	11,95	4.91	26.05	2.28	5 22	5.60	13.25	19.26	8.37
Carbonate of Magnesia.	2 10	0.21	2.45	1.01	0 31	2.10	3 11	1.35	0.31
Silica.....	15.14	29 75	15.55	14.41	13.04	18 19	4.06	15,98	21.62
Alumina....................	4.48	1.23	2.12	2.10	0.31	2 10	1.48	1.25	3 21
Phosphoric Acid.........	0.53	0.71	0.80	0.44	0.37	1.39	0.63	0 69	0 41
Sulphuric Acid...........	0.37	0.30	0.42	0.32	0.49	0.74	0 54	0 82	0.22
Moisture	0.64	0.48	1 02	6.93	0 38	6.80	0.68	0.76	0 48
	99.69	100.00	99 59	99.69	99 97	99.80	99 80	99.56	99 78
Metallic Iron...............	31.86	34.69	27.24	49 69	41.94	41.35	40.71	30 24	32.00
Phosphorus.................	0.23	0.31	0.39	0.19	0.16	0.87	0 27	0.30	0.18
Sulphur........	0.15	0.12	0.17	0 13	0 20	0 30	0.22	0.33	0 09

These thicknesses appear to be somewhat exceptional and, local, as neither Profs. Wm. B. Rogers or J. J. Stevenson, who have both examined this county on the line of Decker's creek and Scott's run, make any mention of so many seams of these sizes.

According to this latter gentleman, the most extensive ore deposit (the Clippart vein,) of this county, is in the Lower Barren Measures, in the shale immediately underlying the Pittsburgh coal seam. It is a proto-carbonate of iron, rich and pure, in some places locally known as the "Olyphant blue lump." Near Uniontown, in Pennsylvania, it is well developed, and Mr. Olyphant has worked it successfully there for many years in the Fair Chance Furnace. On Scott's Run, near Haigh's Mill, the quantity is considerable. It is said to be found south of Fairmont, in Marion county, on the Monongahela river.

The following are the analyses that have been obtained of the ores of this county, by Prof. Wm. B. Rogers, who gives the following account of these.

	No. 1.	No. 2.	No. 3	No. 4	No 5.	No. 6.	No. 7.
Carb. Iron	93.08	64.32	60.60	71.16	89.12	76.72	78.20
Carb. Lime	trace	trace	trace	} 1.40	} 0.80	3.72	4.40
Carb. Magnesia	trace	trace	trace			2.80	3.00
Silica	4.48	27.20	31.20	22.48	7.78	12.72	11.20
Alumina	0.80	4.16	3.76	2.96	1.40	2.04	1.40
Water	1.24	1.20	2.00	1.64	0.88	1.76	2.00
Carb. Manganese	trace	trace	trace	trace	trace	trace	trace
	99.60	96.88	97.56	99.64	99.98	99.76	100.20
Metallic Iron	44.95	31.06	29.27	34.37	43.04	37.05	37.77

Nos. 1, 2, 3, 4, and 5, are from three bands from a black shale from 20 to 30 feet thick, that immediately underlies the Great Conglomerate. It is the ore from these bands that supplied the Henry Clay and Grenville Furnaces.

Nos. 1 and 5 come from the *Upper, or Castile* band, which is the most uniform in thickness of the three. It varies from 8 to 15 inches, and, having but a slight covering of shale, has been less protected from weathering than the others, and is therefore, found in a decomposed state, the whole bed sometimes presenting the appearance of a friable, shaly oxide much valued on account of the ease with which it works. Occasionally it occurs in nodules merely incrusted with oxide, the nucleus being in the original state of carbonate of iron.

Nos. 2 and 3 are from the *Rock Vein* at the Grenville Furnace. It is some 8 or 10 feet below the "Upper Vein." The ore is generally 8 or 10 inches thick, though varying from 3 feet to 3 inches.

No. 4 is from the *Lower Vein* at the Grenville Furnace, and is 8 or 10 feet below the "Rock Vein." It varies from 2 to 6 inches—averaging 4 inches—and is usually coarse and siliceous, and chiefly valuable at the outcrop, where it has been decomposed.

No. 6 *and* 7 are both from the lower part of a 6 to 8 feet bed of dark blue argillaceous shale on Decker's creek. The ore consists of a layer of nodules, and was the material chiefly used at the old furnace (the Valley), on that stream prior to 1837. It was mined on the side of Laurel hill, in a southeast direction from the furnace. The average thickness of the band is from 6 to 10 inches, though the nodules are sometimes 1-foot in diameter.

There are no furnaces now in operation in the county. The Valley (?) (Mr. Clair's), on Decker's creek, and the Henry Clay, and Grenville, near the State line on Cheat river, were started at a very early day in the iron history of the region. The others that have been worked are the Pridevale, on Cheat River, and the Clinton on Booth's creek.

Taylor County.—The Centennial Local Board of this county report as follows: "There is a large amount of iron ore and it is in various parts of the county. By the side of the Balt. and Ohio R. R., on the Valley river, at the mouth of Lost Run, there is a seam of excellent ore, and more than 50 years ago an iron furnace was erected there. In the northeastern part of the county, next to Preston, on Three Fork creek and the railroad, a company from Lancaster county, Pennsylvania, erected a furnace named the "Lancaster," and made iron from the ore obtained. The property was afterwards purchased and is now owned by the "Lancaster Furnace and Mining Co.," who built entirely new, large and costly buildings, furnaces and machinery, and shipped to market a large amount of metal made from the ore obtained from that neighborhood."

Two miles from the mouth of Lost Run, on the steep hill in front of John Riley's house, are three strata, each 8 inches thick, of an excellent carbonate of iron, imbedded in 8 feet of rotten slate and clay. Below these are nodular pieces of 3 to 15 pounds weight in blue clay.

On Plummer's run a very fine article of the same class of ore has been discovered, but never worked, and its thickness is not known, though it is said that it is in workable quantities.

The following are the analyses made of ores from this county:

	Lancaster Furnace.	Mouth of Lost Run	Lost Run, near J. Riley's.
Carb. Iron	31.34	24.576	33.141
Peroxide Iron	33.98	34.443	33.100
Binoxide Manganese	....	trace	0.256
Carb Lime	16.52	13.913	12.495
Carb. Magnesia	5.28	3.478	3.214
Phosphoric Acid	0 68	0.477	0.536
Sulphuric Acid	0 13	1.201	1.050
Silica	9.36	16.260	7.536
Alumina	1.31	2.982	4.978
Water and Loss	1.40	2.673	3.697
	100.00	100.000	100.000
Metallic Iron	38.91	35.983	39.100
Phosphorus	0.296	0.207	0.284
Sulphur	0.052	0.480	0.420

Barbour County.—About 2¼ miles south of Philippi, on the east side of Tygart's Valley river, and some 30 feet above the water, is a reported2 feet seam, and still above this is another of the same thickness. Both of these are carbonate of iron of very excellent quality by the samples that were forwarded to the Centennial office in Wheeling.

Braxton and Clay Counties.--In 1874 the Elk River Iron and Coal Co. built a furnace at the mouth of Strange creek, in Braxton, close to the Clay line, and since that date have gone into operation, making a No. 1 cold blast charcoal iron. Their developments have shown some most excellent beds of ore, on which the following notes were made in 1874, when I last visited them.

In Clay county, at the mouth of Standing Rock Run, 246 feet (barometric measurement,) above Elk river, is a fine deposit of nodular brown oxide of iron, the result of decomposition from the carbonate. The nodules are very thickly embedded in a soft, gray clay, and will yield from 35 to 40 per cent. of metallic iron, and being soft and cellular, work well in the furnace. The bed averaged 4 feet thick, but when examined, there was no roof exposed, and the ore was still under foot. Mr. J. Savage, the President of the company, who made this opening, said that at one place he went to the bottom of the bed, and found the total thickness 6 to 7 feet. He also traced the seam for 3½ miles by walking along the out crop, and striking his pick in at every 80 or 100 yards, till he rolled out nodules of the ore, and, having noted it in the same way at many other places, feels confident that it runs for many miles up and down Elk river. About 15 feet lower down the hill was a very encouraging out crop, which, however, was not sufficiently opened to speak of its thickness.

About a mile higher up the river, and below the last, is another seam of the same class of ore, though not quite so rich. It was opened enough to prove the existence of a workable bed, but the exact thickness could not be measured. Just across the river it is partially opened again. Here the ore is of better quality, and in very valuable and easily workable quantities. Above this, on the east side of the river, Mr. Savage opened a 2½ foot bank.

These 3 seams are found again from 2 to 4 miles below the company's furnace in Braxton county. Concerning the mineral at these points, Mr. Savage, under date of 22nd March, 1876, writes: "Our heaviest seam of ore, which is of a grayish color before it is burnt, lies 50 feet above Elk river, and is a regular bed. We also have two more regular beds which are 100 and 150 feet respectively, above the stream. There is another seam in which the ore lies in pockets or bunches, sometimes 3 or 4 feet thick, and again running out completely. Near the top of the hill is what we call the 'top hill ore,' which is scattered promiscuously over the country, and appears to be more plentiful in Clay than in Braxton county."

Besides the places mentioned, Mr. Savage has noticed one or more of these seams at various points on either side of the river for many miles down, but as to the continued thickness nothing can be said, as few or no openings, beyond the discovery of out crops, have been made, though the indications are very encouraging.

The furnace of this company is 42 feet high and 11 feet across the boshes. Concerning its working, the same gentleman mentioned before, has kindly furnished the following points: "We are making only about 8 tons per day at this time,* using 18 tons 580 pounds of roasted ore, 4 tons 600 pounds of limestone, and 1500 bushels of charcoal. These cost us—

Charcoal,..5 cts. per bushel, delivered.
Limestone, ...$2.00 per ton.
Ore,.. 2.25 " "

"Expenses of manufacturing about $21 per day. These items give a cost for the pig iron of about $17 per ton. In good weather on dry stock we can make an average of 10 to 11 tons a day, which will make the pig cheaper. The reason that we are not making more now is because last season was a very bad year to make charcoal, and it was out in the weather and is in bad condition, as we had not gotten up our coal house. The in wall bosh and hearth rock were obtained from this neighborhood and is superior to fire brick." It may be proper to remark that all of the ore beds of this region just described occur in the lower barren group of the coal measures.

Kanawha County.—As far as examinations have gone, only the northwestern half of this county can lay claim to iron ore. Those exposures that have been observed are: a 2-foot bed in the hills across Elk river, opposite Charleston, from which the Kanawha Iron Company, whose furnace is now building, expects to draw a portion of its supplies; a bed, 2 feet 2 inches thick, one and a quarter miles up Campbell's creek, of a brown oxide, lying just above the Black Flint Ledge. It has, however, a good deal of sand in it, and would have to be mixed with other and richer ores for furnace use.

A seam, on the Davis creek side of the dividing ridge between that stream and Rush creek, was opened some 15 or 20 years ago, with the intention of starting a small furnace, but the idea was abandoned. It is 2½ feet thick, according to the recollection of General L. Ruffner, and is on the Black Flint. It is, therefore, the same bed as the last. The ore that is still lying about is a siliceous brown oxide, containing some 30 or 35 per cent. of iron. It would mix well with the richer ores of Virginia.

Lower down Davis creek several workable seams of carbonate of iron, or the results of its decomposition, are reported, an

*22nd March, 1876.

analysis, by O. N. Stoddard, of Woocester University, Ohio, of one 80 feet above the Mahoning Sandstone, giving—

Iron	34.927
Carbonate Lime	9.400
Carbonate Magnesia	2.450
Siliceous Matter	15.400
Alumina	4.210
Manganese	2.900
Sulphur	0.243
Loss of Water by Drying	0.400
Loss of Combined Matter by Ignition	27.800
Loss	2.270
	100.000

This shows that after the ore is roasted, and the 28.2 per cent. of water and combined matter are driven off, the remaining mass will contain 48.6 per cent. of matallic iron.

Wayne County.—Perhaps the best idea of the iron ore of this county can be obtained from a section made at Cassville, on the Big Sandy river, by Mr. Dwight:

LEVEL OF SANDY RIVER.

INTERVAL, 155 FEET.

1. Clay and Fossiliferous Iron in kidneys ..... 5 feet.

INTERVAL, 8 to 10 FEET.

2. Shale containing lumps of Blue Carbonate of Iron, containing 34 per cent. of metal ..... 5 feet.

INTERVAL, 104 FEET.

3. Carbonate of Iron ..... 2 feet.

INTERVAL 12 FEET.

4. Black Manganiferous Iron Ore, containing 25 per cent. of Binoxide of Manganese, and 27 per cent. of Iron ..... 2½ feet.

INTERVAL, 52 FEET.

5. Mixed stratum of Limestone and Iron Ore, the latter containing 42 per cent of Iron ..... 2½ feet.
6. Clay with kidneys of Red Hæmatite, containing 55 per cent. of Iron .....

INTERVAL, 37 FEET.

7. Carbonate of Iron and Limestone ..... 2 feet.
8. Clay and kidneys of Iron Ore ..... 3 feet.

INTERVAL, 14 FEET.

9. Limestone Ore ..... 1 foot.

INTERVAL, 138 FEET.

10. Clay with kidneys of Red Hæmatite, containing 58 per cent. of Iron .... 3 feet.

INTERVAL 60 FEET.

Top of Hill ....

Nos. 5 and 6 are locally known as the "Wilson Seam," and an analysis of the mixture of the ores therefrom shows:

Peroxide of Iron	16.20
Protoxide of Iron	25.70
Protoxide of Manganese	20.85
Caustic Lime	30.22
Silica	3.56
Alumina	3.11
Phosphoric Acid	0.64
Sulphur	Trace.
	100.00

In December, 1875, 58 tons of this ore was tried at the Belmont Furnace, Wheeling, and so much liked that an order for 1,000 tons was at once given:

Mr. Dwight's analysis of the Black Manganiferous Ore, from No. 4, shows:

Sesquioxide of Iron	27.400	
Binoxide of Manganese	26.802	
Carbonate of Lime	37.214	
Carbonate of Magnesia	1.908	
Silica	1.866	
Alumina	1.000	
Phosphoric Acid	1,557	
Sulphuric Acid	0.354	
Moisture	1.770	
Loss	1.029	
	100.000	
Metallic Iron in raw ore	19.18	per cent.
" " " roasted ore	27.87	"
Phosphorus	0.679	"
Sulphur	0.142	"

It will be noticed that, in the extensive belt from the Pennsylvania line, in Monongalia and Preston counties, to the Kentucky line, at Cassville, the workable beds of ore that have been discovered, are confined to four localities; viz: 1st. Monongalia, Preston, Barbour, and Taylor counties. 2d. Braxton and Clay counties, near the furnace at Strange creek; 3d, Kanawha county, near Elk river, and 4th, Wayne county, on the Big Sandy. Of the gaps between these, we know nothing, but it is fair to presume that, in these blank spaces, a careful and systematic search will develop beds fully as good as those of which we now know.

Jackson County.—A bed of Oxide of Iron, 6 miles from the mouth of Mill creek, has lately been purchased by the Bellaire Iron Company, in the State of Ohio, just below Wheeling, but we have no data showing its thickness.

Raleigh County.—A bed of Brown Hæmatite, 3 feet thick, has recently been discovered 3 miles north of the Court House, on the land of Wm. McCreery. It is very soft, porous and earthy, as taken from the outcrop. By an analysis, it gives:

Peroxide of Iron	79.350	
Silica	3.599	
Alumina	1.593	
Phosphoric Acid	1,880	
Sulphuric Acid	0.895	
Lime	0 821	
Magnesia	0.034	
Water	11.232	
Organic Matter (rootlets) and Loss	0.589	
	100.000	
Metallic Iron	55.545	per cent.
Phosphorus	0.819	"
Sulphur	0.358	"

Red Hæmatite.—In several places mention has already been made of this, which occurs in nodules in a series of bands of red and reddish-yellow shales, which are found in the Lower Barren Measures along the general line that has been indicated for the carbonates of iron. These nodules often contain from 50 to 60 per cent of metal, but in no place as yet, with, perhaps, the exception of Wayne county, have these been found in sufficient quantity in the shale to constitute a workable deposit. If they should be, the probability is that the continuation of such would be uncertain, and would not justify the erection of any works looking to them as the main source of supplies.

IRON ORES EAST OF THE COAL MEASURES.

We now come to the consideration of what may be called, *par excellence*, the Iron Region of West Virginia, as the ores are far richer and in greater abundance than those of the coal measures. It is to be regretted that the present knowledge concerning them is so scant that we are not able to trace the beds from point to point along the whole border of the State, showing where any individual one has its greatest development, and we shall, therefore, have to be satisfied with pointing out those localities in the various counties where beds or deposits have been observed and their value examined into.

The same remarks that were made about the ores in the coal measures can be reiterated for this district, viz: that in many localities a proper exploration will develope valuable deposits of which we have now no information, and this can be said with all the more positiveness because the beds are more strong and continuous, and less likely to die out in this geological horizon than they were in that.

Mercer County.—"The northern slope of the East River mountain shows considerable deposits of iron ore, ledges of variegated marble, very pure barytes and fine mill-stone-grit extending along Peter's mountain into Monroe county. Iron ore does not exist in such masses as in Giles county,* but Bluestone river, above the mouth of Brushy creek, presents fine bodies of ore, * * chiefly lying upon the spurs of the Black Oak mountains, as well as in ridges and spurs of the Flat Top mountain, upon the opposite side of the Bluestone river."

(Report of C. R. Boyd on the Minerals of New River. Exec. Doc. Nov. 25. 3rd Ses. 42d Congress).

Monroe County.—" Little Mountain, lying next to Peter's mountain, on the south boundary, possesses a very fine deposit of iron, from which metal of good quality has been manufactured." (Boyd's Report).

On Peter's mountain, on the road from Union to the Salt Pond, a very fine outcrop of brown haematite has been observed, and along the eastern border of the county it is probable that other deposits will be found.

* Giles is the adjoining county in Virginia.

Greenbrier County.—On Howard's creek, within 4 or 5 miles of the White Sulphur Springs, iron ore of fair quality and apparently in large quantities has lately been discovered; and on Anthony's creek the fossiliferous and block ores make their appearance. At the point of observation the fossil ore was 9 inches thick, but the block ore has been opened at two places, each showing 7 feet. It inclines at a good angle for mining. A bluff ore, also, shows itself at numerous points in large masses. (Report of T. S Ridgeway on the Minerals along the C. & O. R. R). Analyses of several of these ores by J. B. Britton, show:

Fossil Ore	52.23	per	cent	Iron.
Pipe "	61.75	"	"	"
Hæmatite Ore	57.17	"	"	"
Bluff Ore	36.69	"	"	"

Pocahontas County.—Beyond the fact, that large bodies of iron ore are usually accredited to this county, nothing positive can here be stated, there being no data to show the quality of the mineral or the thickness of the deposits. We may, however, look with confidence for the same classes as are found in Greebrier, for the strata of the two counties are, in many places, identical.

Pendleton County.—A. R. Guerard, Associate of the Royal School of Mines, England, and one of the assistants of the State Board of Centennial Managers, made a reconnoisance of this and the counties presently to be mentioned, in February 1876.

He writes: "So far, there have been no detailed Geological examinations of the great iron belt between the Blue Ridge and Alleghany mountains, passing through this State; and the only authentic information on the subject at all, is the now scarce report of W. B. Rogers, made in 1838, as State Geologist of Virginia· Nor is it now to be expected, in the very short time allotted to me, in so extensive a region, that I should have been able to arrive at anything like adequate details, or indeed to make more than a confirmation of the existence of workable deposits of iron ore in this section of the State. I submit my report to the Board, therefore, with this reservation, prompted by the hope that if it cannot satisfy all demands, it may at least call attention to the valuable mineral resources of this region, and awaken a desire for further investigation and development.

"The principal deposits of this county (Pendleton,) are in the eastern portion, along the South Fork mountain, a few indications only of no special importance being observed on the ranges of the North Fork. The ores comprise the red, brown and red fossiliferous haematites peculiar to, and always associated with, this Geological formation, and traceable over a large extent of surface in West Virginia, including the counties of Hampshire, Hardy, Grant and Pendleton.

"The red fossiliferous haematite, the most uniform and important of this group, displays itself at many points along the sides and summit of the South Fork range. This ore, from its occurrence in layers arranged parallel with each other, interstratified with friable red shales, and from its being usually filled with impressions of hollow castings of shells, admits of being readily identified and is traceable in a series of seams, though seldom very thick, in considerable numbers, and for a great distance; it presents everywhere the same natural advantages, indicating the abundance in which it might be procured, as well as the facility with which it might be mined. Of its extraordinary value to any region, the experience in Pennsylvania furnishes the most conclusive evidence, where, since the discovery of its admirable adaption for the furnace, it has been keenly sought after, and seams, which from their thinness, would, if composed of any other material, have remained unnoticed, have not only been diligently but profitably worked. This formation, which further north and south is not so well developed, expands in passing through this State, and here attains a thickness not found elsewhere.

"Associated with these strata, at the junction of this with the overlying formation, are found valuable deposits of red and brown haematites, derived probably from the former. These appear in out crops and scattered boulders along the entire length of this mountain."

The following analyses were made of the samples of the ores of this county, exhibited at the International Exhibition of 1876:

	No. 1.	No. 2.	No. 3.	No. 4.	No. 5.	No. 6.
Sesquioxide of Iron.........	63.470	80.336	80.838	50.010	70.201	55.706
Binoxide of Manganese......	3.150	....	trace	....	trace	....
Silica..............................	18.000	5.722	17.544	37.151	17,361	18.110
Alumina...........................	5.707	7.291	1.266	8.390	3,503	13.463
Lime................................	.146	1.517	trace	.756	.456	1.321
Magnesia.........................	.713	.482	trace	.432	1.489	.120
Phosphoric Acid...............	.300	1.331	.026	.080	2.400	.090
Sulphuric Acid.................	1.575	1.070	.423	.925	1.345	2.147
Combined Water...............	6.197	....	....	} 1.877 (Combined and Hygroscopic Water)	} 2,754 (Combined and Hygroscopic Water)	7.799
Hygroscopic Water............	.432	} 1.864 (Hygroscopic Water and Loss)	} 1.02 (Hygroscopic Water and Loss)			.732
Loss................................	3.10			.379	....	.512
	100.000	100,000	100.199	100.000	100.000	100.000
Iron................................	44.42	56.232	56.586	35.010	49.137	38.994
Phosphorus......................	.131	.580	.012	.035	1,046	.039
Sulphur...........................	.730	.428	.169	.370	.538	.858

No. 1, is a Brown Hæmatite, from the neighborhood of Franklin.

No. 2, is a Red Fossiliferous Hæmatite, from Dickenson's land, on South Fork mountain.

No. 3, is a Red Hæmatite, from the vicinity of Upper Tract.

No. 4, is a Red and Brown Hæmatite (mined), from George Miller's, South Fork mountain.

No. 5, is a Red Hæmatite (part of No. 4).

No. 6, is a Brown Hæmatite, from Col. Johnson's place near Franklin.

Hardy County.—Mr. Guerard in his report on these counties goes on to say: "Large and important bodies of iron ore, identical with those already mentioned, are conspicuously developed in this county on the ranges of the Middle and North mountains.

"On the west side of Elk Horn Knob, 13 miles south from Moorefield, three separate seams of the Red Fossiliferous Hæmatite crop out with the usual favorable characteristics of this valuable formation. They measure respectively:

(1) 0 feet, 8 inches	} Ketterman's Farm.
(2) 1 " 6 "	
(3) 3 " 3 "	

"The upper ores of this group are remarkably well shown on the same range:

(1) Red Haematite, 25 feet (16 feet solid ore)—Pine mountain, $1\frac{1}{2}$ miles from Ketterman's.

(2) Brown Haematite, 30 feet (from outcrop)—Salt Spring Run Knob, 5 miles from Ketterman's.

(3) Brown Haematite (very pure), 14 feet—Cunningham's Tract, 3 miles from this and 9 from Moorefield.

"The Brown Haematites occur largely again on the spurs and ridges of the North or Capon mountain. These have long been mined and smelted by various iron works in this portion of the county. The only furnace now in existence, is that known as the Capon Iron works, six miles from Wardensville, on the east side of the mountain.

"The ore bank shows in an open drift of a 100 yards, a remarkable deposit of ore. Having sunk 70 feet on the vein, which is inclined at an angle of 40°, it still appeared to be continuous. The deposit lies between sandstone and limestone, of which there is a large supply, and the outcrop can be traced some distance along the mountain. Three smaller veins of the same ore crop out above this larger one, and some hundred yards below, a vein of Brown Fossiliferous Haematite, the counterpart of which has been worked at Bloomery, in Hampshire, has lately been discovered. It is 2 feet thick near the outcrop, but has never yet been worked.

"The following data show the general charge and working of the Capon furnace:

Cold blast at $\frac{5}{8}$ of an inch pressure........	800 to 1,000 pounds, limestone	To 1 ton pig.
	140 to 160 bushels, Charcoal	
	2 to 3 tons, charred ore	
	25 to 30 tons pig a week.	
	$15 cost per ton at the works.	
	Shipping point Winchester, distant 20 miles.	

"The ores worked are said to produce an excellent quality of iron, especially adapted to the manufacture of car wheels and boiler plate.

"Of the furnaces formerly worked, but now abandoned, there were three in this county: One on Orr's mountain, west of Moorefield, and two on the east side of the mountain. In the neighborhood of Wardensville, Messrs. Saliard and Bryan carried on a furnace many years ago, and 8 miles from Capon Iron Works, on the same range, was the Crack Whip Furnace, owned by Charles Carter Lee. A large deposit of ore was developed in this locality, as shown by the old workings still exposing several feet of solid ore.

The following are analyses made of the ores from this county:

	No. 1.	No. 2.	No. 3	No. 4.
Sesquioxide of Iron	84 80	72 990	83.47	64.287
Protoxide of Iron	....	....	4.64	....
Binoxide of Manganese	....	....	trace	7,680
Silica	5.90	23.500	9.40	11.771
Alumina	....	....	1.81	3.184
Lime	....	....	....	2.657
Magnesia	....	....	....	1.141
Phosphoric Acid	1.60	.122	.373	1.110
Sulphuric Acid	.10	.870	.120	1.180
Water } Loss }	4.60	2.518	.187	6.695
				.295
	100.000	100.00	100.000	100.000
Iron	59.36	51.09	62.01	45.00
Phosphorus	.698	.053	.163	.483
Sulphur	.040	.035	.048	.472

No. 1, is a Red Fossiliferous Hæmatite, from the 3-feet 3-inch seam on Ketterman's farm.

No, 2 is a Red Hæmatite, from the 25-feet vein on Pine mountain.

No. 3, is a Brown Hæmatite, from the 14-feet vein on Cunningham's tract.

No. 4, is a Brown Hæmatite, from Capon Iron Works.

Grant County—Mr. Guerard reports from this county: "The associated Haematites are exhibited in a still more remarkable manner in Grant than in Hardy and Pendleton. The beautiful symmetry of arrangement, too, of the mountain strata here particularly well-defined, as well as the striking development of iron ore in close proximity to the coal basin of the Alleghany, render this county more than usually interesting, both in a geological and economical point of view.

In the vicinity of Greenland Gap, the Red fossiliferous Haematite shows itself in 5 parallel layers, on the east side of Walker's bridge, dipping N. W., and on the west side of Little or Knobly mountain, dipping S. E., indicating the wreck of a denuded anticlinal arch over the New Creek mountain. These seams, workable in Pennsylvania when only a few inches thick, here assume the following large dimensions:

(a)......	8 feet	Walker's Ridge (measured from outcrops).
(b)..........................	18 "	
(c)........................	13 "	
(d)........................	11 "	
(e)	7 "	Little Mountain (measured from section).
Total	57 feet.	

On either side, and overlying these strata, massive beds of limestone (partly hydraulic) and sandstone are exposed. Above the latter, the Brown Haematites crop out along the summits of Walker's ridge and Knobly mountain. From these ores, the Fanny furnace, 4 miles from the village of Greenland, on Hasard's creek, was formerly worked, being long famous for its iron.

These ores are only 6 miles from the coal of the Alleghany, and 20 miles from Keyser, on the Baltimore and Ohio railroad.

The following table shows analyses of the ores of this county:

	No. 1.	No. 2.
Sesquioxide of Iron	75.033	68.750
Binoxide of Manganese	.025	....
Silica	14.354	15.555
Alumina	7.445	13.733
Magnesia	.230	......
Lime	.521	....
Phosphoric Acid	2.020	1.842
Sulphuric Acid	.240	0.120
Loss, &c	.132	....
	100.000	100.000
Iron	52.52	48.13
Phosphorus	.880	.803
Sulphur	096	.048

No. 1, is a Fossiliferous Red Haematite, from the 7-feet seam near Greenland Gap, Little Mountain.

No. 2, is a similar variety, from the 13-feet seam on Walker's ridge, in the same neighborhood. The 13.733 per cent, ascribed to alumina, includes, according to Mr. Dwight's report, also the moisture and loss.

Hampshire County:—Mr. Guerard goes on to report—"The Iron ores of this county are more scattered and not so conspicuously developed as those of the counties previously mentioned; but my observations led me to estimate the deposits of this county, (though small when compared with those of Grant, Hardy, &c) as still of economical importance.

At various points along the slopes and ridges of the Patterson's Creek, Short and Capon mountains boulders may be observed lying thick over the surface, and here and there occasional outcrops of true beds of ore.

The only deposits at present worked are those occurring at Bloomery, on the east side of Capon mountain, in the north eastern portion of the county. Here a fossiliferous variety of brown haematite occurs in a vein, varying from 18 inches to 4 feet. This and a vein of the ordinary Brown Iron ore (thickness not known) has been mined and smelted here for many years. The furnace has been out of blast for the last few months, but will probably soon be in operation again. Limestone, charcoal and fine water power are easily obtained anywhere along this valley, The following are the general proportions of the charge and the production of the furnace, as given me by Mr. Withers. the present Manager and part owner.

Cold blast................	800 lbs. limestone, 120 bushels, charcoal. $2\frac{1}{2}$ to $2\frac{3}{4}$ tons of raw ore	To 1 ton Pig...... ....

Cost $20 00 per ton, Pig delivered at Paw-paw station, distant 14 miles.

The following table gives the analyses of the ores from this county·

	No. 1.	No. 2.
Sesquioxide of Iron	73.531	75.250
Binoxide of Manganese	4.380	trace
Silica	13.329	12.035
Alumina	3.025	2.199
Lime	.024	1.254
Magnesia	.251	.631
Phosphoric Acid	,241	,089
Sulphuric Acid	1.204	2,058
Combined Water	3.082	.750
Hygroscopic Water	.632	.631
Loss	.301	,524
	100.000	100.000
Iron	51.471	52.675
Phosphorus	.105	.038
Sulphur	.481	.823

No. 1, is a Brown Haematite from Short mountain, 15 miles from Romney.

No. 2, is a Brown Hæmatite, from the same locality.

Morgan County.—Mr. Guerard continuing his reconnoissance into the Valley of Virginia, reports on this county:

"There are no iron ores of any importance in this county. On the slopes of Sandy ridge, near Sir John's Run Station, are two veins of ore of a siliceous character, one measuring 6 and the other 2 feet, but not workable, except under peculiar circumstances.

"At various points along the summit of Sleepy Creek mountain boulders of ore may be observed, but indicating no workable deposits.

"It may be mentioned, more as a mineralogical curiosity than as of economical importance, that specimens of micaceous red haematite may be picked up frequently in both this and Berkeley county, at the base of the mountain."

Berkeley County:—Mr. Guerard reports, "two deposits of iron ore have been developed in this county, one owned by Charles J. Faulkner, about a mile south of the town of Martinsburg, and the other by Adam Small, five miles in the opposite direction. These form a part of a series of irregular deposits imbedded in arenaceous limestone extending through this valley along the western base of the Blue Ridge. The ores consist of the cellular, honey-combed and pipe, or stalactitic varieties of brown haematite, in many cases proving valuable, and said to produce a very good iron. Both of the deposits abovementioned have been worked and the ore shipped to Pennsylvania."

Jefferson County.—Mr. Guerard's report on this county contains the following: "The ores of this county are analogous to those occurring in Berkeley, and belong to the same formation. Deposits have been worked on the Virginia side of the Potomac river, below the mouth of Antietam creek, to supply the Antietam Iron Works, opposite, and also near Bolivar Heights at Harper's Ferry, furnishing the old Keeptryst furnace with its stock when it was in blast, many years ago. But the most recent working is on the west side of the Shenandoah river, 6 miles from Charlestown, at what is known as Maltby's ore bank. Here is a large body of fine ore, giving every indication of a continued heavy yield. This bank has lately been abandoned in consequence of the furnace, which it furnished with ore in Maryland, having stopped.

CHAPTER XII.

SALT AND PETROLEUM.

SALT.

BY DR. J. P. HALE, OF CHARLESTON.

CHARLESTON, W. VA., APRIL 5TH, 1876.

Prof. M. F. Maury:

DEAR SIR: In compliance with your request, I send you, herewith, some facts in regard to the early history, subsequent developments, and present condition of the salt manufacture and salt interest of Kanawha and Mason counties, and of West Va., generally.

Hoping that the paper may, in some degree, furnish the information you desire, I am

Very Respectfully,

Yours Truly,

J. P. HALE.

Rich as is West Virginia in coal, iron, timber, &c., she is scarcely less rich in that indispensable necessity to human health and comfort, and to animal life—common salt. Fossil or rock salt has not been found in the State; but salt brines of greater or less strength, and in greater or less abundance are found by Artesian borings, at greater or less depth throughout the Appalachian coal field, which underlies the greater portion of our state.

The strength of these brines varies in different localities, and in different wells in the same locality; the range may be stated at say 6° to 12° by the salometer, Baume scale (distilled water being 0 °, saturation 25°), but the average strength of the brines from which salt is now made is about 8° to 10°. The value of these brines depends, of course, upon their location, as regards accessibility, and cheap transportation of the products to market, as well as the convenient proximity of cheap coal for fuel, and timber for barrels. Only locations on the navigable rivers, or lines of railways at present fulfill these indications; but, as population increases, aud new routes of travel and traffic are opened up, it is probable that new salt manufacturing localities will be developed.

The principal points at which salt has been manufactured in the state, are Charleston on the Great Kanawha river; from West Columbia to Hartford City on the Ohio river; at Bull-town on the little Kanawha; at Louisa on the Big-Sandy; in Mercer county on New river; near Birch of Elk river; (at the mouth of Otter creek on Elk. Authors.) and at a few other less important points, on a very small scale for local use. At present, owing to the greater facility of reaching the markets of the great west by cheap water transportation, and the advantages of cheap fuel, salt is only manufactured, on a commercial scale near Charleston on the Great Kanawha, and in Mason county on the Ohio. It is of these localities that I propose to give some account; and of the latter first, reserving for the Kanawha works, the oldest in the State. a fuller account and description, much of which will apply to the Mason county and other works as well.

The Mason county Salt works, now the most extensive in present productive capacity in the State are of conparatively recent development.

In 1849 Messrs. Williams & Stevens, aided by Capt. Tom Friend—all Kanawha Salt makers—bored for salt water at West Columbia, in Mason county on the Ohio river; they succeeded at about 700 feet in getting a fine well of water of good strength, and at once proceeded to erect the first Salt furnace on the Ohio river; they also bored several other wells in the vicinity, none of which, however, proved so good as the first They, shortly after, sold the property to New York parties who remodeled and rebuilt the furnace on a much larger scale, giving it a productive capacity of some 1200 bushels, or more per day. The success of this enterprise gave a great impetus to to salt boring, and coal mining throughout the available coal frontage of this region. This developed coal frontage along the river extends from West Columbia to Hartford City, about 7 miles. Up the river the coal dips, until it passes under water level at, or just above Hartford City.

The second salt furnace was erected at this upper limit of the coal frontage in 1854 by a Hartford City, (Conn.), company, then under the management of W. O. Healy, Esq; since, and now under the management of G. W. Moredock, Esq.—who has three large furnaces, with abundance of good brine, and cheap and convenient coal. These two operations, one at the extreme lower, and the other at the extreme upper limit of the coal frontage, demonstrated pretty clearly the existence of good brines throughout that extent, and at once gave a value to furnace sites and coal lands which the owners had not hitherto suspected them to possess.

In 1855 Mr. R. C. M. Lovell, another Kanawha salt manufacturer, bored wells and erected a large furnace about half way between the two points above named, and laid out a town which he called "Mason City."

This valuable salt and coal property was afterwards purchased by L. H. Sargent of Cincinnati, O., and more recently has passed into the hands of Messrs. Roots & Kilbreth of the same city.

Following these three furnaces, and within the next few years, were built the New Castle, Burnup, Clifton, Bedford, Hope, German, Jackson, Valley City, Starr, and New Haven City, in all 13 in number.

These 13 furnaces have a present productive capacity of over 3,000,000 bushels per year.

The usual depth to which the wells in this neigborhood are bored, is about 1,100 to 1,200 feet: the strength of brines 8° to 10°: the quantity, 15 to 50 gals. per minute per well. The wells are tubed with iron tubing, usually about 4 inches internal diameter, and bagged at 600 to 800 feet depth, at which depth the pumps were worked, run by steam power.

The coal used here in the manufacture of salt, and also shipped to a considerable extent to the lower markets, is, geologically, the same as the well known Pittsburgh seam, so extensively mined and shipped near the city of that name. It is here a fine seam of coal, 4½ to 5 feet thick, easily mined, accessible and cheap.

From the natural advantages of this locality, salt is produced here very cheaply, and cheaply freighted to the markets of the west, where it is in ready demand and its reputation deservedly excellent.

From the bitterns or waste liquors from the salt furnaces here, a considerable quantity of bromine is manufactured, the uses and demand for which are steadily increasing.

Chloride of calcium is also manufactured to some extent from these waste, bitter waters.

The following table, kindly furnished by G. W. Moredock, Esq., of Hartford City, the largest manufacturer in Mason county, gives a very clear understanding of the present status of the salt manufacture in that county.

SALT WORKS, MASON COUNTY, W. VA.

NAME OF FURNACE.	Capacity.	Depth of Wells	OWNERS' NAMES.
	Bush.	Feet.	
New Haven	300,000	1,200	Hartford City Coal and Salt Co., 1,100 acres of coal land,
Hartford City	300,000	1,150–60	
Star	325,000	"	
Valley City	350,000	1,125–35	Valley City Coal and Salt Co
Jackson	200,000	1,120–30	V. B. Horton, jr.
German	250,000	"	German Salt Co
Hope	350,000	"	Hope Salt Co.
Mason City	325,000	"	Mason City Salt Co.
Bedford	300,000	1,150	Bedford Salt Co.
Clifton	300,000	"	Not running.
Burnup or Quaker City	150,000	"	" "
New Castle	250,000	1,155	" "
West Columbia	300,000	1,125–40	" "
Actual capacity	3,700,000		
Actually made in 1875	2,500,000		

"It takes one bushel of coal to make a bushel of salt, Strength of brine from wells at Hartford City, 9° to 10°. measured by Baume's salometer; saturated brine 25°, making the brine stand 40 per cent salt." (G. W. Moredock).

The Kanawha salt works are situated in Kanawha county, on the Kanawha river, commencing about three miles above Charleston and extending up the river for several miles, on both sides.

These "Licks," as they are called, have not only been known and extensively worked, from the first settlement of the valley by the whites, but have been known and used, from time immemorial, by the Indian tribes, and frequented by swarms of buffalo, elk, deer, and other wild animals, before the advent of the white man.

In 1753, when all this region was an unbroken wilderness, which had never been penetrated by the most adventurous white man, a party of Shawnees who dwelt upon the Scioto, in what is now Ohio, made a raid upon the frontier settlements of Virginia, in what is now Montgomery county. Having taken the settlers unawares, and after killing, burning, and capturing prisoners, as was their custom, they retreated, with their captives, down New river, Kanawha, and Ohio, to their homes. One of these captives, Mrs. Mary Ingles,* who afterwards made her escape, and was returned to her friends, related that the party stopped several days at a salt spring on the Kanawha river, rested from their weary march, killed plenty of game and feasted themselves on the fat of the land; in the meantime, boiling salt water and making a supply of salt, which was carefully packed and taken with them to their western homes. This is not only the first account we have of salt-making on Kanawha, but anywhere else west of the Alleghanies. In fact, if there is any earlier record of salt-making from brine springs, anywhere in the United States, I am not aware of it.

The earliest settlement made by whites, in the Kanawha Valley, was by Walter Kelley and family, at the mouth of the creek, which bears his name, in the spring of 1774, several months before the battle of Point Pleasant, where the combined Indian tribes, under the celebrated Sachem, Cornstalk, were defeated and driven back by the Virginians, under Gen. Lewis.

Kelly and his family paid the forfeit of their lives to their temerity; they were all killed by the Indians, but after the battle of the Point, when there was greater security for life,

*The great grand-mother of the writer.

the valley was rapidly settled, mostly by Virginians, and in great part by the hardy soldiers who had followed Lewis to Point Pleasant.

The early pioneer settlers, in a wilderness, without communication with other settlements, except by foot or bridle paths, depended upon the Kanawha Licks for their scanty supply of salt. In those days of simple economy and provident thrift, when everything useful was made the most of, the women's wash-kettles were put under requisition for a fourfold duty; they boiled the daily hog and hominy, and other wholesome, frugal fare; once a week they boiled the clothes, on wash day; semi-occasionally they boiled the salt water for a little of the precious salt, and every spring they went to the sugar camp, to boil the annual supply of maple sugar and molasses.

It is related that at one time, when there was an apprehended attack from the Indians, the few early settlers were posted at the mouth of Coal river, for protection. Being out of salt and suffering for the want of it, they sent some of their hardy and daring young men in canoes up to the salt spring, where they dipped the canoes full of salt water; and, getting safely back, the water was boiled, and the precious salt made under cover of the fort.

Among the earliest land locations made in the valley, was one of 502 acres, made in 1785, by John Dickinson, from the Valley of Virginia, to include the mouth of Campbell's creek, the bottom above, and the salt spring. Dickinson did not improve or work the property himself, but meeting with Joseph Ruffner, an enterprising farmer from the Shenandoah Valley, Virginia, in 1794, and describing this salt spring to him, Ruffner became so impressed with its value, that he then and there purchased the 502 acres upon Dickinson's own report, without himself seeing it, agreeing to pay for it 500 pounds sterling without condition, and other sums conditioned upon the quantity of salt to be made which might increase the price to 10,000 pounds sterling. Having gone thus far, he sold out his Shenandoah estates, and in 1795 removed himself and family to Kanawha to look after his salt property. Upon arriving here, however, his penchant for rich farming lands overcame him, and he purchased, from George and William Clendenen, the large river bottom of 900 acres extending from the mouth of Elk river up Kanawha; and, upon 40 acres of which the village of Charleston had been laid out and started the previous year. This last purchase, and the subsequent attention to clearing and improving the farm diverted Ruffner's attention for a time, from the salt project; the delay was fatal so far as he was concerned; he did not live to execute his pet scheme or realize his cherished hopes. Dying in 1803, he willed the property to his sons, David and Joseph, enjoining it upon them to carry out, as speedily as practicable, his plans of building up extensive salt manufactories to supply not only the increasing local demand, but a larger and still more rapidly growing demand which was now coming from the many thrifty settlements throughout the Ohio Valley. During the elder Ruffner's life, however, he had leased to one Elisha Brooks, the use of salt water and the right to manufacture salt; and in 1797 this Elisha Brooks erected the first salt furnace in Kanawha, or in the western country. It consisted of two dozen small kettles, set in a double row, with a flue beneath, a chimney at one end, and a fire bed at the other.

To obtain a supply of salt water he sank two or three "gums," some 8 or 10 feet each in length, into the mire and quicksand of the salt lick, and dipped the brine with a bucket and swape, as it oozed and seeped in through the sands below.

In this crude, rough-and-ready way, Brooks managed to make about 150 pounds of salt per day, which he sold at the kettles, at 8 to 10 cents per pound. No means were used to settle or purify the brines or salt, as the salt water came from the gum, so it was boiled down to salt in the kettles, with whatever impurities or coloring matter it contained. As it issues from the earth it holds some carbonate of iron in solution; when it is boiled, this iron becomes oxidized, and gives a reddish tinge to the brine and salt.

This Kanawha salt soon acquired a reputation for its strong, pungent taste, and its superior qualities for curing meat, butter, etc. A great many who used it and recognized these qualities in connection with its striking reddish color came to associate the two in their minds in the relation of cause and effect, and orders used to come from far and near for some of "that strong red salt from the Kanawha Licks."

Almost the only mode of transporting salt beyond the neigh

borhood, in those early days, was by pack-horses, on the primitive, backwoods pack-saddle. So much of this was done, and so familiar did the public mind become with the term, as used in that sense, that even to this day, among a large class of people, the verb "to pack" is always used instead of other synonymous or similar terms, such as carry, transport, fetch, bring, take, etc., and the "tote" of Old Virginia.

It was not until 1806, that the brothers, David and Joseph Ruffner, set to work to ascertain the source of the salt water, to procure, if possible, a larger supply and of better quality, and to prepare to manufacture salt on a scale commensurate with the growing wants of the country.

The Salt Lick, or "The Great Buffalo Lick," as it was called, was just at the river's edge, 12 or 14 rods in extent, on the north side, a few hundred yards above the mouth of Campbell's creek, and just in front of what is now known as the "Thoroughfare Gap," through which, from the north, as well as up and down the river, the Buffalo, Elk, and other ruminating animals made their way in vast numbers to the lick. I may mention *en passant* that so great was the fame of this lick, and the herds of game that frequented it, that the great hunter, explorer, and conqueror of the "bloody ground" of Kentucky, Daniel Boone, was tempted up here, made a log cabin settlement, and lived just on the opposite side of the river, on what is now known as the Donnally farm or splint coal bottom. I have had, from old Mr. Paddy Huddlestone, who died a few years ago, at nearly one hundred years of age, many interesting anecdotes of their joint adventures in hunting and trapping. Boone still lived here in 1789–90, when Kanawha county was formed, and in 1791 served as one of the delegates for the county, in the Legislature at Richmond.

But to return to the Lick, and the operations of the Ruffner brothers. In order to reach, if possible, the bottom of the mire and oozy quicksand through which the salt water flowed, they provided a straight, well-formed, hollow sycamore tree, with 4 feet internal diameter, sawed off square at each end. This is technically called a "gum." This gum was set upright on the spot selected for sinking, the large end down, and held in its perpendicular position by props or braces, on the four sides. A platform, upon which two men could stand, was fixed about the top; then a swape erected, having its fulcrum in a forked post set in the ground close by. A large bucket, made from half of a whisky barrel, was attached to the end of the swape, by a rope, and a rope attached to the end of the pole to pull down on, to raise the bucket. With one man inside the gum, armed with pick, shovel, and crowbar, two men on the platform on top to empty and return the bucket, and three or four to work the swape, the crew and outfit were complete.

After many unexpected difficulties and delays, the gum, at last, reached what seemed to be rock bottom at 13 feet; upon cutting it with picks and crowbars, however, it proved to be but a shale or crust, about 6 inches thick, of conglomerated sand, gravel and iron. Upon breaking through this crust the water flowed up into the gum more freely than ever, but less salt.

Discouraged at this result, the Ruffner brothers determined to abandon this gum, and sink a well out in the bottom, about 100 yards from the river. This was done, encountering, as before, many difficulties and delays; when they had gotten through 45 feet of alluvial deposit, they came to the same bed of sand and gravel upon which they had started, at the river.

To penetrate this, they made a 3½ inch tube of a 20 foot oak log, by boring through it with a long shanked augur. This tube, sharpened, and shod with iron at the bottom, was driven down, pile-driver fashion, through the sand to the solid rock. Through this tube they then let down a glass vial with a string to catch the salt water for testing.

They were again doomed to disappointment; the water, though slightly brackish, was less salt than that at the river. They now decided to return to the gum at the river, and, if possible, put it down to the bed rock. This they finally succeeded in doing, finding the rock at 16 to 17 feet from the surface.

As the bottom of the gum was square, and the surface of the rock uneven, the rush of outside water into the gum was very troublesome. By dint of cutting and trimming from one side and the other, however, they were, at last, gotten nearly to a joint, after which they resorted to thin wedges, which were driven here and there as they would "do the most good."

By this means the gum was gotten sufficiently tight to be so bailed out as to determine whether the salt water came up through the rock. This turned out to be the case. The quantity welling up through the rock was extremely small, but the strength was greater than any yet gotten, and this was encouraging. They were anxious to follow it down, but how? They could not blast a hole down there, under water; but this idea occurred to them; they knew that rock blasters drilled their powder holes two or three feet deep, and they concluded they could, with a longer and larger drill, bore a correspondingly deeper and larger hole.

They fixed a long iron drill, with a 2½ inch chisel bit of steel, and attached the upper end to a spring pole, with a rope.

In this way the boring went on slowly and tediously till on the 1st of November, 1807, at 17 feet in the rock, a cavity or fissure was struck, which gave an increased flow of stronger brine. This gave new encouragement to bore still further; and so, by welding increasing length of shaft to the drill, from time to time, the hole was carried down to 28 feet, where a still larger and stronger supply of salt water was gotten.

Having now sufficient salt water to justify it, they decided, and commenced, to build a salt furnace; but while building, continued the boring, and on the 15th January, 1808, at 40 feet in the rock, and 58 feet from the top ot the gum, were rewarded by an ample flow of strong brine for their furnace and ceased boring.

Now was presented another difficulty: how to get the stronger brine from the bottom of the well, undiluted by the weaker brines and fresh water from above; there was no precedent here; they had to invent, contrive, and construct anew. A metal tube would naturally suggest itself to them; but there were neither metal tubes, nor sheet metal, nor metal workers—save a home-made blacksmith—in all this region, and to bore a wooden tube 40 feet long, and small enough in external diameter to go in the 2½ inch hole, was impracticable; what they did do, was to whittle out of two long strips of wood, two long half tubes of the proper size, and, fitting the edges carefully together, wrap the whole from end to end with small twine; this, with a bag of wrapping near the lower end, to fit, as nearly as practicable, water tight, in the 2½ inch hole, was cautiously pressed down to its place, and found to answer the purpose perfectly; the brine flowed up freely through the tube into the gum, which was now provided with a water tight floor or bottom, to hold it; and from which it was raised by the simple swape and bucket.

Thus was bored and tubed, rigged and worked, the first rock-bored salt well west of the Alleghanies, if not in the United States. The wonder is not that it required eighteen months or more to prepare, bore and complete this well for use, but, rather, that it was accomplished at all under the circumstances. In these times, when such a work can be accomplished in as many days as it then required months, it is difficult to appreciate the difficulties, doubts, delays, and general troubles that beset them then. Without preliminary study, previous experience or training, without precedents in what they undertook, in a newly settled country, without steam power, machine shops, skilled mechanics, suitable tools or materials, failure, rather than success, might reasonably have been predicted.

The new furnace, which for some time had been under construction, was now complete. It was simply a reproduction of the Elisha Brooks kettle furnace, or a larger scale. There were more kettles, of larger size, and better arranged.

On the 8th of February, 1808, the Ruffner Bros. made their first lifting of salt from this furnace, and simultaneously reduced the price to the, then, unprecedentedly low figure of 4 cents per pound.*

From this time forward, salt making, as one of the leading industries of Kanawha, was an established fact, and Kanawha salt one of the leading commercial articles of the west; and wherever it has gone, from the Alleghanies to the Rocky mountains, from the Lakes to the Gulf, its superior qualities have been recognized and appreciated.

The neighboring property owners, who had watched the progress and result of the Ruffner well with such deep interest, now instituted borings on their own lands, above and below, and on both sides of the river. Among these earlier, enter-

* For interesting facts in this history of the boring of the first well, I am indebted to a MS by the late Dr. Henry Ruffner—and for personal recollections and traditions I am indebted to Gen. Lewis Ruffner, Isaac Ruffner, W. D. Shrewsberry, Col. B. H. Smith, Col. L. I. Woodyard, W. C. Brooks, and others, and my own experiences for the last 30 years.

terprising experimenters, were William Whitaker, Tobias Ruffner, Andrew Donally, and others. All were more or less successful in getting a supply of brine, at depths varying from 50 to 100 feet, and by 1817 there were some 30 furnaces and 15 or 20 wells in operation, making in the aggregate 600,000 to 700,000 bushels of salt.

In this year an important revolution in the manufacture of salt was effected by the discovery of coal. Although, in one of the finest coal fields of the world, coal had not, hitherto, been found here in workable seams, nor been used at all, except for blacksmith purposes. Wood had been the only fuel used in salt making, and for other purposes, and all the bottoms and convenient hill slopes for several miles up and down the river had been stripped of their timber to supply this demand.

David Ruffner, true to the spirit of enterprise and pluck which bored the first well, was the first here to use coal as a fuel. This would appear to be a very simple matter now; but was not so then. It was only after many months of discouraging efforts, and failing experiments, that he finally succeeded in getting it to work to his satisfaction. Its value established, however, its use was, at once, adopted by the other furnaces, and wood ceased to be used as a fuel for salt making in Kanawha.

Other important improvements were gradually going on in the manner of boring, tubing and pumping wells, &c. The first progress made in tubing, after Ruffner's compound wood-and-wrapping-twine tube, was made by a tinner who had located in Charleston to make tin cups and coffee pots for the multitude. He made tin tubes in convenient lengths, and soldered them together as they were put down the well. The refinement of screw joints had not yet come, but followed shortly after, in connection with copper pipes, which soon took the place of tin, and these are recently giving place to iron.

In the manner of bagging the wells, that is, in forming a water-tight joint around the tube to shut off the weaker waters above from the stronger below, a simple arrangement, called a "seed-bag," was fallen upon, which proved very effective, which has survived to this day, and has been adopted wherever deep boring is done, as one of the standard appliances for the purpose for which it is used. This seed-bag is made of buckskin, or soft calf-skin sewed up like the sleeve of a coat or leg of a stocking; made 12 to 15 inches long, about the size of the well hole and open at both ends; this is slipped over the tube and one end securely wrapped over knots placed on the tube to prevent slipping. Some six or eight inches of the bag is then filled with flaxseed, either alone or mixed with powdered gum tragacanth; the other end of the bag is then wrapped, like the first, and the tube is ready for the well. When to their place—and they are put down any depth, to hundreds of feet—the seed and gum soon swell from the water they absorb, till a close fit and water-tight joint are made.

The hydraulic contrivance for raising salt water from the gums, consisting of a bucket, a swape and a man, was simple, slow and sure; but the spirit of progress was abroad and it soon gave place to a more complicated arrangement, consisting of a pump, lever, crank, shaft, and blind horse or mule, that revolved in its orbit around the shaft. This was considered a wonderful achievement in mechanical contrivance, especially by the men who had worked the swapes.

For several years this "horse-mill," as it was called, was the only mode of pumping salt water on Kanawha, but in the fulness of time it also went to the rear in 1828 and the steam engine came to the front, not only for pumping, but also for boring wells and various other uses.

In 1831 William Morris, or "Billy" Morris, as he was familiarly called, a very ingenious and successful practical well borer, invented a simple tool, which has done more to render deep boring practicable, simple and cheap, than anything else since the introduction of steam.

This tool has always been called here "Slips," but in the oil regions they have given it the name of "Jars." It is a long double-link, with jaws that fit closely, but slide loosely up and down. They are made of the best steel, are about 30 inches long, and fitted, top and bottom, with pin and socket joint, respectively. For use they are interposed between the heavy iron sinker, with its cutting chisel-bit below, and the line of augur poles above. Its object is to let the heavy sinker and bit have a clear, quick, cutting fall, unobstructed and unencumbered by the slower motion of the long line of augur poles above. In the case of fast augur or other tools in the well, they are also used to give heavy jars upward or downward, or both, to loosen them. From this use the oil well people have given them the name of "Jars."

Billy Morris never patented his invention, and never asked for nor made a dollar out of it, but as a public benefactor, he deserves to rank with the inventors of the sewing machine, reaping machine, planing machine, printing cylinders, cotton gin, &c.

This tool has been adopted into general use wherever deep boring is done, but, outside of Kanawha, few have heard of Billy Morris, or know where the slips or jars came from.

The invention of this tool, the adoption of the heavy sinker and some other minor improvements in well boring, gave a great impetus to deep boring in Kanawha. Wells were put down 500, 1,000, 1,500, and 1,800 feet, and one, the deepest in Kanawha, by Charles Reynolds, to about 2,000 feet. These borings would doubtless have been carried to a much greater depth, but that the fact soon got to be understood, that the salt-bearing strata had been passed, and that no brines were obtained at a greater depth than 800 to 1,000 feet. The limit of the salt-bearing rocks is readily told by the character of the borings. Within this limit are sandstones, shale, coal, &c., of the Coal Measures lying nearly horizontal, though dipping slightly to the northwest; below is the Carboniferous Limestone which underlies the Coal Measures, and crops out 100 miles to the eastward. This limestone, when penetrated, is known to the well-borers as the "long-running rock," from the fact that a boring-bit will run a long time in it without being dulled.

No regular suites of samples of borings from the Kanawha wells have ever been kept. This is not important, however, as the strata are well known, and can be examined along the New river canon as they crop out to the eastward.

The Kanawha borings have educated and sent forth a set of skilful well-borers, all over the country, who have bored for water for irrigation on the western plains, for artesian wells for city, factory, or private use, for salt water at various places, for oil all over the country, for geological or minerological explorations, &c., &c.

Nearly all the Kanawha salt wells have contained more or less petroleum oil, and some of the deepest wells a considerble flow. Many persons now think, trusting to their recollections, that some of the wells afforded as much as 25 to 50 barrels per day. This was allowed to flow over from the top of the salt cisterns, on to the river, where, from its specific gravity, it spread over a large surface, and by its beautiful iridescent hues, and not very savory odour, could be traced for many miles down the stream. It was from this that the river received the familiar nickname of "Old Greasy," by which it was for a long time familiarly known by Kanawha boatmen and others.

At that time this oil not only had no value, but was considered a great nuisance, and every effort was made to tube it out and get rid of it. It is now the opinion of some competent geologists, as well as of practical oil men, that very deep borings, say 2,500 feet, would penetrate rich oil-bearing strata, and possibly inexhaustible snpplies of gas.

In 1775, Gen. Washington visited the Kanawha valley in person, and located some very valuable lands for his military services. About three miles above the Salt Lick, he set apart and deeded to the public, forever, a square acre of land near the river, on which was a great natural wonder, then little understood, called a "burning spring."* For many, many years after, it was visited by every one who came to or passed through Kanawha, as one of the great curiosities of the region. It was simply a hole in the ground, which filled with water when it rained, and up through which issued a jet of gas, giving the water the appearance of boiling, and when lighted burned with a bright flame till blown out by high wind.

In 1841, William Tompkins, in boring a salt well a short distance above the burning spring, struck a large flow of gas, which he turned to account by "boiling his furnace" and making salt with it, effecting a great saving in fuel and economy in the cost of salt.

In 1843, Messrs. Dickinson & Shrewsberry, boring a few

*The following is an extract from George Washington's will: "The tract of which the 123 acres is a moiety, was taken up by Gen. Andrew Lewis and myself, for, and on account of, a bituminous spring, which it contains, of so inflammable a nature as to burn as freely as spirits, and is as nearly difficult to extinguish."

rods below, tapped at about 1,000 feet in depth, nature's great gas reservoir of this region. So great was the pressure of this gas, and the force with which it was vented through this bore-hole, that the augur, consisting of a heavy iron sinker, weighing some 500 pounds, and several hundred feet more of augur poles, weighing in all, perhaps 1,000 pounds, was shot up out of the well like an arrow out of a cross-bow. With it came a column of salt water, which stood probably 150 feet high. The roaring of this gas and water, as they issued, could be heard under favorable conditions for several miles.

It would have been difficult to estimate with any approach to accuracy, the quantity of gas vented by this well, and no attempt was made to measure it. I heard it roughly estimated as being enough to light London and Paris, with, perhaps, enough left to supply a few such villages as New York and Philadelphia. But as this is a *salt* well, as well as *gas* well, I suggest that the gas estimates be taken, "*cum grano salis.*"

While this well was blowing it was the custom of the stage drivers, as they passed down by it, to stop and let their passengers take a look at the novel and wonderful display. On one occasion a professor from Harvard College was one of the stage passengers, and being a man of investigating and experimenting turn of mind, he went as near the well as he could get for the gas and spray of the falling water, and lighted a match to see if the gas would burn. Instantly the whole atmosphere was ablaze, the Professor's hair and eyebrows singed, and his clothes afire. The well-frame and engine-house also took fire, and were much damaged. The Professor, who had jumped into the river to save himself from the fire, crawled out, and back to the stage, as best he could, and went on to Charleston, where he took to bed, and sent for a doctor to dress his burns.

Col. Dickinson, one of the owners of the well, hearing of the burning of his engine house and well frame, sent for his man of affairs, Col. Woodyard, and ordered him to follow the unknown stage passenger to town, get a warrant, have him arrested and punished, for wilfully and wantonly burning his property,—unless concluded Col. Dickinson, as Woodyard was about starting, unless you find that the fellow is natural d—d fool, and didnt know any better· Arriving at Charleston, Woodyard went to the room of the burnt Professor at the hotel, finding him in bed, his face and hands blistered, and in a sorry plight generally. He proceeded to state in very plain terms, the object of his visit, at which the Prof. seemed greatly worried, and alarmed, not knowing the extent of this additional impending trouble, which his folly had brought upon him. Before he had expressed himself in words, however, Woodyard proceeded to deliver, verbatim, and with great emphasis the codicil to Dickinson's instructions. The Prof. notwithstanding his physical pain and mental alarm, seemed to take in the ludicrousness of the whole case, and with an effort to smile through his blisters, replied that it seemed a pretty hard alternative; but, under the circumstances, he felt it his duty to confess under the last clause, and escape. Well, said Woodyard, if this is your decision, my duty is ended, and I bid you good morning.

The salt water and gas from this well were partially collected, and conveyed through wooden pipes, to the nearest furnace, where they were used in making salt.

For many years this natural flow of gas lifted the salt water 1,000 feet from the bottom of the well, forced it a mile or more through pipes, to a salt furnace, raised it into a reservoir, boiled it in the furnace, and lighted the premises all around at night. About the only objection to the arrangement was, that it did not lift the salt and pack it in barrels.

The success of this well induced other salt makers to bore deep wells for gas, and several were successful· Messrs. Worth & English, Tompkins, Welch & Co., Wm. D. Shrewsberry, J. H. Fry, and J. S. O. Brooks, got gas wells and used the gas either alone, or in connection with coal, for fuel in salt making. Gas was also struck in a few other wells, but did not last long, and was not utilized.

The first flow of gas ever struck in Kanawha, was as far back as 1815, in a well bored by Capt. James Wilson, within the present city limits of Charleston, near the residence of C. C. Lewis, Esq.

The Capt. had not gotten as good salt water as he expected; but instead of being discouraged, he declared in language emphatic, that he would have better brine or bore the well into —— lower regions, with higher temperature.

Shortly after this the augur struck a cavity which gave vent to an immense flow of gas and salt water. The gas caught fire from a grate near at hand, and blazed up with great force and brilliancy, much to the consternation of the well borers and others. Capt. Wilson thought it would be a reckless tempting of Providence to go any deeper, and ordered the boring stopped.

This well is now owned by the Charleston Gas Light Company, who at some future time contemplate re-opening it to test the gas for lighting the city.

Of the many wells in the neighborhood, that have furnished gas, some have stopped suddenly, and some by a slow and gradual process. Whether these stoppages have been from exhaustion of the gas, or sudden, or gradual stoppage of the vent-ways, has not been definitely determined. It is known, however, that in the Dickinson and Shrewsberry well, which blew longer than any other, that the copper pipes in the well, and the wooden pipes leading to the furnace, were lined with a mineral deposit, in some places nearly closing them. This deposit has not been analyzed, but may possibly be silicate of lime. A system of torpedoing might break up these incrustations from the walls of the well and rock cavities, and start the gas again.

From the results of such wells in Pennsylvania, and New York, we have large encouragement to hope for similar results here.

A few wells intelligently manipulated, might give gas enough to boil all the salt manufactured here, and run all the machinery, in the neighborhood.

After the introduction of steam power, and the use of coal for fuel, no striking change was effected in the process of salt manufacture for a number of years. What improvements were made, were simply in degree. Wells were bored deeper, the holes were bored larger, the tubing was better, the pumps and rigging simpler. The furnaces were larger, better constructed, and more effectively operated, the quality of the salt improved and the quantity increased, but still they were kettle furnaces of the original type.

The mammoth of the kettle era was that of Joseph Friend & Son, at the mouth of Campbell's creek, on which they made 100,000 bushels of salt per annum. The usual capacity of other furnaces was 25,000 to 50,000 bushels per annum.

This was about the condition of the salt manufacture here in 1835, when there were, all told, about 40 furnaces, producing annually about 2,000,000 bushels of salt.

During this year Geo. H. Patrick, Esq. of Onondaiga, New York, came here, to introduce a patent steam furnace.

The furnace proper, after it was developed and improved, consisted of cast iron pans, or bottoms, 8 to 10 feet by 3 feet. Eight or ten of these pieces were bolted together by iron screws, forming one section 24 to 30 feet long, by 8 or 10 feet wide. There were two, three, or four of these sections according to the size of the furnace. Over each of the sections was constructed a wooden steam chest, bolted to the flanges on the sides of the pans. and otherwise held together by wooden clamps and keys, and iron bolts and rods, all made steam and water tight by calking. These several sections are set longitudinally on the furnace walls to form one continuous furnace.

After the furnace comes a series of wooden vats or cisterns, a usual size for which, is about 10 feet wide and 100 feet long. The number of these cisterns varies according to the size of the furnace, They are constructed of poplar plank, 4 to 5 inches thick, dressed to joints, and fitted in a frame of oak by sills and clamps. They are tightened by driving wooden keys, and then calked to make them water tight. This system of clamping and keying cisterns, was introduced here from a model brought by Col. B. H. Smith, from the navy yard at Norfolk,. It was very simple and effective, and has been retained to this day, without improvement or change.

There are two sets of these cisterns, the first in which the brines after boiling in the furnace proper, are settled, and at the same time strengthened up to saturation. The latter in which the salt is graduated from the clear saturated brines. These settling and graining cisterns are very much alike, except that the grainers, are but 15 to 18 inches deep, while the settlers may be double that or more. Through each and all of these cisterns from end to end are three rows of copper pipes, usually 5 inches in diameter.

After the salt water is boiled in the furnace proper, it runs into these settling cisterns, and after being thoroughly settled and saturated, is drawn into the grainers, where the salt is deposited, and once in 24 honrs is lifted out by long handled shovels, on to a salt board, suspended above the grainer, and from which, after proper draining it is wheeled in wheel barrows to a salt house, where it is packed in barrels ready for shipment.

The steam generated by the boiling in the furnace proper, is carried from the steam chest, by wooden pipes, to the copper pipes and through the settlers and grainers. This steam giving up its heat in passing through these cisterns, keeps up the temperature of the brines, and causes rapid evaporation. The temperature of these cisterns varies from 120° to 190°, an average would probably be 165°.

This in short, is a description of the steam furnace, after it was improved, and the first mistakes and crudities eliminated. In the first experiments only very slight heat was imparted by the steam to the brines, and only very coarse or alum salt made. It was very simple, accomplished all that was expected, and so soon as it was fairly tested, improved up to its working condition, and its advantages demonstrated, the days of kettle furnaces were numbered.

Andrew Donnally and Isaac Noyes were the first to try and adopt the plan. Then followed John D. Lewis, Lewis Ruffner, Frederick Brooks, and others, till all had made the change; and when the Ohio river furnaces were built, the system was fully adopted there.

It is now about 40 years since George Patrick introduced the steam furnace, but it still holds its position securely, and without a rival.

Minor improvements have been made, and the furnaces much enlarged, but the general plan has not been changed. From the 2,000 or 3,000 or 4,000 bushels per month of the earlier furnaces, the production has been increased to 20,000, 30,000 or 40,000 bushels per month. The writer's furnace, Snow Hill, has made in one year, independent of all stoppages, delays, etc., 420,000 bushels, the largest single month's run being 41,-000 bushels. This furnace has 20,000 square feet of evaporating cistern surface, and over 1,300 square feet of metal-pan furnace-surface. About 1.200 bushels of coal per day are consumed in the furnace proper, and about 300 more for engines, houses, and other purposes.

How far this will be exceeded in the future remains to be seen. The same progress has occurred in freighting salt, as in the manufacture. In the days of Elisha Brooks, the neighbors took the salt from the kettles in their pocket handkerchiefs, tin buckets, or pillow cases. Later, it was taken in mealbags, on pack-horses, and pack-saddles.

The first shipment west, by river, was in 1808, in tubs, boxes, and hogsheads, floated on a raft of logs. Next came small flat-boats, 50 to 75 feet long, and 10 to 18 feet wide, "run" by hand, and in which salt was shipped in barrels. These boats increased in size up to 160 feet or more long, and 24 to 25 feet wide, and carried 1,800 to 2,200 barrels of salt.

These boats were all run by hand, at great risk, and although the Kanawha boatmen were the best in the world, the boats and cargoes were not unfrequently sunk, entailing heavy loss upon the owners of the salt. The late Col. Andrew Donnally used to ask, when he heard of one of his boats sinking, whether any of the boatmen were drowned; if not, he contended it was not a *fair sink*. But all this is now done away with. Salt is now shipped eastward by rail, and to the nearer westward markets by daily and weekly steamboat packets, and to the more distant markets by towboats and barges. A towboat will now take 8,000 to 15,000 barrels at one trip, landing them at Louisville, Evansville, Nashville, Memphis, St. Louis, or elsewhere.

In the matter of packages, no change has occurred here since the first use of barrels, the principal change being a gradual improvement in the quality of the cooperage. Our neighbors in Mason county, ship some salt in bulk, and some in bags, but the larger portion in barrels.

Kanawha uses barrels exclusively. We use two sizes—280 pounds and 350 pounds net salt, respectively. The pork packing trade takes the larger size, and the retail trade, the smaller chiefly.

These barrels are made of white oak staves and hickory hoops, and it is believed that nothing cheaper or better can be devised for salt packages. They are cheaper than bags, more convenient to handle, more convenient to store, stand rougher usages, and more exposure to the weather. Markets having choice of salt in bags or barrels, generally prefer the barrels.

In the earlier times of salt making here, various substances were experimented with for the purpose of settling or separating the impurities from the brine. Blood, glue, jelly, lime, alum, etc., were used. Something of the sort was necessary when the brine was boiled down in kettles with all its impurities, but they are all useless, and worse than useless in the present process, and have long been abandoned. Plenty of settle-room and plenty of time, are all that are needed to have the brines as clear as spring water. The bitterns, after the salt is granulated, are thrown away, or used for other purposes.

It has long been known that a small portion of some greasy or oily substance, on the surface of the brine helped "to cut the grain," and hasten the granulation. Butter, tallow, lard, rosin, oils, etc., have been tried. Of these, butter is far the best, and next to butter, tallow; lard and some of the others are positively detrimental.

What the action of butter is, whether chemical or mechanical or both, I think has never been determined, but certain it is, that a very small quantity of butter on the surface of brine, while it is granulating very much improves the salt, making the grain finer and more uniform.

Heat, too, is an important condition in making fine salt. The higher the temperature, other things being equal, the finer the salt. In making the finer grades of table and dairy salt, it is necessary to have the brine up to, or near, the boiling point.

On the other hand, the coarser grades of salt, preferred for meat packing and other purposes, are made at temperatures of from 100 to 150 F.

A still coarser grained, or larger crystalled salt, known as alum salt or solar salt, and made in the open air by solar evaporation, is not made here, but there is no reason why it should not be to great advantage, as we have longer summers and warmer suns, than at Onondaiga, New York, where it is very largely made, and with more profit than other grades of salt.

Some of the waste products from salt making, are recently being utilized. Mr. Lerner, an enterprising German, is manufacturing bromine, both here and at the Mason county furnaces, from bitterns, and Mr. Bemmelmans, a Belgian chemist, is erecting works to manufacture hydrochloric acid from bitterns, and pigments from the impalpable oxide of iron which is deposited from salt brines.

The cost of manufacturing salt on Kanawha varies, of course, from time to time, with the varying price of living, labor and supplies. It also varies with each particular furnace according to size, and the greater or less advantages which it possesses. The larger the furnace, other things being equal, the cheaper it will make salt. The general superintendence and management of a large furnace, costs very little, if any more, than for a small one; and a given quantity of coal will make more salt on a large furnace than a small one.

The best furnace will make 100 bushels of salt with 80 to 90 bushels of coal. A good average result is, a bushel of salt for a bushel of coal, and the least economical consume about 125 bushels of coal per 100 bushels of salt.

Some of the furnaces mine their own coal, and some buy fine or nut coal from mines that are shipping coal. Even the best furnaces do not use coal at all economically or to the best advantage. There is, in this respect, great room for improvement.

The cost of coal delivered at the furnaces, ranges from 2¾ to 4 cents per bushel. The present cost of barrels is 25 to 28 cents for the smaller size and 28 to 32 cents for the larger. The cost of common day labor is $1,00 to $1,25 per day. Coal miners get 2 cents per bushel.

The cost of producing salt at these figures may be stated at 8 to 11 cents per bushel in bulk, or 13 to 16 cents in barrels, ready for shipment.

The present cost of boring a salt well here, say 1,000 feet, after engine, well frame, &c., are ready, is $1,200 to $1,500. The time necessary to bore and ream it complete, is 60 to 90 days. The cost of a salt furnace, complete, depends upon size, &c., and varies within wide limits. It may be stated roughly at $40,000 to 100,000.

The people of the United States consume more salt than those of any other country, the estimated average consumption being one bushel of 50 pounds, per capita, for the entire population. The great western markets, where our product goes, consume even more largely than the general average, as this is the largest pork-packing region on the globe. This portion of the country is rapidly increasing in population, and as rapidly in its meat crop and salt cousumption.

It is well known to chemists that salt is a valuable fertilizer on most soils for wheat, cotton, grass, potatoes, turnips, and other crops; and as an ingredient in compound manures it has a wide range of value. It is often recommended by the highest authorities, but, as yet, very little is so used in this country. When agriculture gets to be better understood and practiced, and agricultural people nnderstand their interests better, a large demand and consumption will doubtless be developed in that direction.

The most important and prospectively promising development in the manufacture of salt here, is its probable use on a large scale in the manufacture of alkalies and other chemicals having salt as a basis or important constituent.

With a population of 40,000,000, and covering the greater part of a continent, it is an astonishing fact that our last census does not report a single Soda Ash works in operation in the United States, while the official returns show the importation of these chemicals into the country to be enormously large.

In 1872 the importation of soda ash, caustic soda, &c., was over 100,000 tons; in 1873, 118,000 tons; in 1874, 140,000 tons; in 1875, ——— tons.

These figures, together with the following article, cut from the New York *Tribune* a few years ago, are strikingly suggestive and instructive, and present, in a very forcible manner, the great and rapidly growing importance of this manufacture to this country.

"GIVE US THE SODA ASH MANUFACTURE."

"Soda ash, within ten days, has gone up ½ a cent a pound. Well, what of that? Just this: For the bread we Americans eat, for the window glass that lights our houses, and in fact shelters us from the weather, for every pound of hard soap that we use, for every sheet of our letter, cap, and printing paper, for the bleaching of our cotton cloths, and very many other blessings, we are absolutely dependent upon Great Britain. Her manufactories of soda ash have the monopoly of furnishing the United States with that article, indispensably necessary in itself, and in its correlative products, to the supply of the commonest wants of our social and domestic life. There is not a soda ash manufactory in the United States.

There are the skeletons of many, killed dead under a competition under Free Trade Tariffs, or Free Trade clauses in Protective Tariffs, which represents the difference of wages paid to common laborers in the United States and Great Britain, 50 cents a day there, and $1.50 a day here. But there is not a single living, kicking soda ash factory in our whole country. Let us re-state this, our nation's dependence. If a war should break out between Great Britain and the United States we would be instantly cut off from the supply of the materials to make bread, soap, glass, and paper. The manufacturing interests dependent upon soda ash and its correlations, would torthwith be brought to the greatest distress, or to absolute ruin. So soon as the imported stock on hand was exhausted, we should have to depend on blockade running to obtain the chemical element necessary to enable the nation to wash its clothes and raise its bread and cakes. In the event of such a war, soda ash would go up to $2.00 per pound, indeed it could not be gotten at any price. Our people would expiate with widespread distress their folly in not having encouraged and established this article of prime and indispensible necessity, at least to the point of independence from foreign supply.

But soda ash has gone up ½ a cent a pound. It is a new fluctuation, which we simply wish to employ in urging the solemn duty to make this nation independent of Great Britain, for the comfort of its social and domestic life. The fluctuation in the price of soda ash in 1865 was between 3½ cents the pound and 12½ cents. During that time, the profit the British manufacturers and importers made out of us, ranged between 200 and 400 per cent. Money enough was sent out of this country, to pay inordinate profits to foreigners, to have paid for the successful establishment here of the soda ash manufacture in at least eight different States, and to have secured a permanently low and steady price of the article in all the American markets. This rise of ½ a cent a pound, a British tax on every glass, soap, paper, and cotton manufacturer in this country, will not excite a protest. How wise it would be for these manufacturers, quitting forever their chronic protests against a tariff on soda ash, to unite in demanding one that should immediately establish the manufacture here, and save them forever from those inevitable fluctuations in the price of the foreign article, and the extravagant profits from which only home competition between established producers, saves the consumer."

All, or nearly all, of our supply of these chemicals comes from Great Britain. Official reports of 1870, giving the operations of 1869, will give an idea of the extent and importance of the manufacture in that country.

In that year the manufactories there consumed 10,184,000 bushels of salt; 26,908,000 bushels, or 961,000 tons of coal; 281,000 tons of limestone and chalk; 264,000 tons of pyrites; 8,300 tons of nitrate of soda, and 33,000 tons of timber for casks.

The manufacture, I am told, has largely increased since 1869, but I have not seen official reports of a later date.

Is there any sufficient reason why this manufacture should be so neglected and ignored in this country? On the contrary, the advantages are so great and so palpable that it is difficult to understand why capital and enterprise have not been enlisted in it. To illustrate, compare the conditions of manufacture at New Castle, on the Tyne, the seat of the largest manufacture in England, with what they would be on the Kanawha.

The New Castle manufacturer buys his salt in Cheshire and transports it several hundred miles by rail. He buys his coal from neighboring collieries, paying railway transportation on that to his works. His pyrites and manganese come from Spain, and his timber for casks from Canada or Norway.

When the chemicals are made, he sends them to Liverpool or Glasgow by rail for American shipment, thence by steamers to New York, paying ocean freight, insurance, and government duty. At New York he pays commission, cartage, &c., and thence railroad freight to the western markets, say to Pittsburgh, St. Louis, &c.

Per contra, the Kanawha manufacturer would have salt and coal at his doors, at a small margin over producer's cost, if he did not produce them himself at actual cost. On the line of the Ches. & Ohio R. R., accessible, cheap and convenient, are inexhaustible mines and beds of superior pyrites, manganese and limestone, and timber of the finest qualities abounds throughout the region, and is extremely cheap.

The product, when ready, could be rolled from one door of the factory into boats or barges, and in a short time, by cheap water transportation, be landed at these same large western consuming markets from Pittsburgh to St. Louis, inclusive; or from the opposite door of the factory, on the cars of the Ches. & Ohio R. R. for early delivery into any of the eastern cities.

It will be readily seen, I think, that the advantages are greatly in favor of the American manufacture, and especially at Kanawha, where there are, probably, more advantages combined than at any other point in the country.

With cheap salt, cheap coal, cheap sulphurets, cheap manganese, cheap limestone, cheap timber, cheap labor, and cheap transportation, there is nothing lacking but *capital* to make the Kanawha the Tyne of America.

West Virginia should at least supply soda ash, caustic soda, and bleaching powder, to the great chemical consuming markets of the west, so near and cheaply accessible to us, if not, indeed, to the whole continent, thus saving to the consumers millions of dollars of extra cost for the foreign article, and saving the country from the risk of the unpleasant contingencies described in the foregoing *Tribune* article.

The inauguration of this industry here on a large scale, it is believed, would promote other enterprises depending largely upon these products as well as upon cheap coal and cheap timber.

Glass works, soap factories, paper mills, &c., might, with advantage, be located here convenient to salt and chemical supplies. The products of these establishments would, of course, have the same advantages of cheaply reaching the great consuming and rapidly growing markets of the west.

The Great Kanawha Coal Field, within which lies the Kanawha salt basin, is one of the finest known coal fields in the world. We have coal of the finest qualities, splint, bituminous and cannel, hard block coal, suitable for iron making; soft, rich coal for gas; good coking coal; steam coal and grate coal. Our cannel coals for parlor use or gas making are unexcelled. Iron ores, carbonates of the coal formation, are found throughout the region, red and brown haematites and specular ores are cheaply accessible by rail, and black band of superior quality is found here in large abundance. As a timber region, especially for the hard woods, this can hardly be excelled on the continent.

It is not my purpose, however, in this paper, to describe the coal, iron or timber; they will doubtless be written up by others; but I wished, simply in a few words, to call attention to the conjunction, or convenient proximity of these great leading staple, raw materials, herein described or mentioned, and all on a great line of railroad and a navigable river, connecting with all the 16,000 miles of water-ways draining the interior of the continent into the "Great Father of Waters," the Mississippi, and reaching the teeming millions of population who dwell upon his fertile shores to their farthest limits.

It is upon such valuable, staple raw materials, as I have named, and so favorably located as here, that communities and nations, found their industries, and build their wealth.

I will not undertake to give any detailed description of the geology of this salt basin, to do so, would be to give the geology of the Appalachian coal field. The strata here, are simply the usual strata of the coal measures, lying nearly horizontal, and saturated in an unusual degree, with valuable brines.

Pure salt, or chloride of sodium, is the same under all circumstances, but no commercial salt is entirely pure. Sea water, brine springs, rock salt, and all sources of commercial supply contain, associated with common salt, other saline ingredients.

These are chiefly sulphates and chlorides, in greater or less quantity, and varying proportions.

Probably the most common, as well as the most deliterious of these compounds is sulphate of lime. Our salt has the advantage of being absolutely free from lime and other sulphates, our process of manufacture, perhaps better, than any other, enables us to separate the hurtful compounds and purify the brines.

The salt when carefully made analyzes 98.00 to 99.00 per cent of pure chloride of sodium. the remaining fraction being made up of chlorides of magnesium, and calcium. These absorb a little moisture from the atmosphere, relieve the salt from a chappy dryness, and impart to it that valuable property of penetrating and curing meat in any climate or weather, for which it has so long enjoyed a high reputation. In fact the distinctive characteristics of Kanawha salt may be stated as follows:

1st. It has a more lively, pungent and pleasant taste as a table salt than any other known.

2nd. It is the only commercial salt that is absolutely free from sulphate of lime.

3rd. It does not, under any conditions of climate and weather, cake or crust on the surface of the meat, but penetrates it and cures it thoroughly to the bone, so that in large pork packing establishments in Cincinnati and elsewhere, it is found to save meat in very unfavorable weather, where with any other salt known or used the meat would have been injured.

4th. On account of its pungency and penetrating qualities a less quantity of it will suffice for any of the purposes for which it is used—whether table, dairy, grazing or packing.

Certificates from numerous western firms show that the Mason county salt quotes with this; though at the same price consumers prefer that from the Kanawha wells.

There are in this salt district, about 120 salt wells, all told. Some of these being inferior, have been abandoned, and will probably never be used again. Others are good wells, the furnaces connected with which, have been dismantled by "dead rents," or other causes. These furnaces may be rebuilt, and restarted. The good wells, if all run, would supply brine for about 5,000,000 bushels of salt per year. Each furnace requires three to five wells.

There are at present ten furnaces here, of which the following is a list, with name of furnace, name of owner, and capacity. The aggregate capacity is about 2,500,000 bushels per year, if all were run full time. Two of the furnaces, however, are not in repair, and some others that had been idle, have only recently been repaired, so that the product of 1875 was very small.

LIST OF KANAWHA SALT FURNACES.

Name of Furnace.	Name of Owner.	Productive Capacity.	Remarks.
		Bushels.	
Daniel Boone	W. B. Brooks	300,000	
Crittenden	W. D. Shrewsberry	280,000	Not in repair.
Snow Hill	J. P. Hale	420,000	
Washington	J. D Lewis	230,000	Not in repalr.
Pioneer	Gen. L. Ruffner	180,000	
Quincy	J. Q. Dickinson	210,000	
Burning Spring	Mrs. R. Tompkins	160,000	
Alden	Mrs. S. Dickinson	240,000	
Lorena	Splint Coal Company	240,000	
Kenton	Splint Coal Company	240,000	
10		2,500,000	

Statement Showing the Production of Salt in Kanawha.

Date.	Bushels.	Date.	Bushels.
1797	150 pounds per day.	1850	3,142,100 bushels per year.
1808	25 bushels per day.	1851	2,862,676 " " "
1814	600,000 bushels per year.	1852	2'741,570 " " "
1827	787,000 " " "	1853	2,729,910 " " "
1828	863,542 " " "	1854	2,233,863 " " "
1829	989,758 " " "	1855	1,493,548 " " "
1830	906,132 " " "	1856	1,264,049 " " "
1831	956,814 " " "	1857	1,266,749 " " "
1832	1,029,207 " " "	1858	No records.
1833	1,288,873 " " "	1859	
1834	1,702,956 " " "	1860	
1835	1,960,583 " " "	1861	
1836	1,762,410 " " "	1862	
1837	1,880,415 " " "	1863	
1838	1,811.076 " " "	1864	1,300,991 bushels per year.
1839	1,593,217 " " "	1865	861,973 " " "
1840	1,419,205 " " "	1866	1,275,017 " " "
1841	1,443,645 " " "	1867	1,321,066 " " "
1842	1,919,389 " " "	1868	1,528,282 " " "
1843	2,197,887 " " "	1869	1,822,430 " " "
1844	1,874,919 " " "	1870	1,721,963 " " "
1845	2,578,499 " " "	1871	No records.
1846	3,224,786 " " "	1872	
1847	2,690,087 " " "	1873	
1848	2,876,010 " " "	1874	
1849	2,951,492 " " "	1875	967,465 bushels per year.

CHRONOLOGICAL LIST OF EVENTS AND INCIDENTS CONNECTED WITH THE KANAWHA SALT INTEREST.

1753. Indians made salt at the Kanawha salt springs. Reported by Mrs. Mary Ingles, then a captive.

1774. Walter Kelley and family, first white settlers in Kanawha Valley.

1775. General Washington reserved from his lands, and gave to the public, the Kanawha Burning Spring.

1785. John Dickinson "located" the Kanawha Salt Spring.

1790. (Before and after) Daniel Boone lived here opposite the Salt Spring.

1794. Joseph Ruffner purchased the Salt Spring, and in 1795, moved to Kanawha.

1797. Elisha Brooks put up a little kettle furnace, made 150 pounds of salt per day, and sold it at 8 to 10 cents per pound.

1806. David and Joseph Ruffner, commenced to bore the first salt well.

1808. Same parties started their kettle furnace, made 25 bushels per day, and sold it for 4 cents per pound.

1808. Wm. Whittaker Tobias Ruffner, Andrew Donnally, and others followed, boring wells and building furnaces.

1808. First salt shipped west by river, in tubs and boxes on a log raft, and in canoes.

1810–12. The late Tom Ewing, of Ohio, boiled salt and studied law and Latin here.

1815. First gas well struck by Captain James Wilson.

1816. First steamboat ever in Kanawha, called the Eliza.

1817. Coal first used in salt making.

1817. The first Kanawha salt company, "Steele, Donnally & Steele."

1822. Highest water ever known in Kanawha to that time.

1822. Second salt company, "William and Robert M. Steele."

1827. Lewis Ruffner and Frederick Brooks introduced the first steam engine to pump salt water.

1827. Third salt company, "Armstrong, Grant & Co."

1830. F. Brooks laid the first wooden tramway to haul coal.

1831. Billy Morris invented the "Slips."

1833. Fourth salt company, "Donnally, Bream & Co."

1834. Col. B. H. Smith brought from the Norfolk navy yard, model for keyed clamped cistern.

1835. Geo. Patrick introduced steam evaporation in salt making.

1835. Lewis Ruffner built the first keyed cistern (20 by 7 feet), and put a cast iron pipe through it.

1836. Fifth salt company, "Hewitt, Ruffner & Co."

1841. John D. Lewis first used steam under copper pans for making salt.

1841. Frederick Brooks first used copper pipes and steam through cisterns.

1843. Big Burning Spring gas well struck.

1849. Williams & Stevens bored and built first furnace on the Ohio.
1851. Sixth salt company, "Ruffner, Donnally & Co."
1856. Seventh salt company, "Ruffner, Hale & Co."
1856. Lowest water ever known on the Kanawha and Ohio rivers.
1856–7. Coldest winter and longest freeze-up ever known here.
1861. Disastrous flood in river, the highest water ever known here.
1861–5. War.
1864. Eighth salt company, "Kanawha Salt Co."
1872. The Chesapeake and Ohio Railroad opened.
1875. The ninth and present salt company, "The Kanawha Salt Co.," organized.
1875. United States Government commenced to improve the Kanawha river by locks and dams.

PETROLEUM.

BY HON. WM. E. STEVENSON, OF PARKERSBURG.

Prof. M. F. Maury:

DEAR SIR: In accordance with your request, I give you some account of the oil interests of West Virginia, and am sorry that sickness and a press of business prevented my writing a fuller statement of this very important item in our natural resources.

A source of considerable wealth to the State since 1864, is found in the production of Petroleum. This production at present, is confined principally to what is known as the "Oil Break," a geological upheaval of the earth's surface, giving it a roof shape or bulge, especially the rocky portion. This break, passing from Ohio into this State, crosses the Horse-Neck Fork of Bull creek, Cow creek, and French creek, all of which flow into the Ohio river, a few miles above Marietta; then passes in a direction to the southeast, across Goose creek, Hughes' river, and the valley of the Little Kanawha, in the direction of Charleston.

Petroleum in small quantities was found within, and even outside the territory of this break, at a very early day. As far back as 1771, Thomas Jefferson gave an interesting description of a burning spring, and the oil connected with it, found in the Great Kanawha valley.

But it was not until modern discovery and invention had transmuted the oily treasure into a source of money making, that its abundance and multifarious uses became rapidly known.

The main development of the oil districts of West Virginia commenced soon after the close of the war in 1865. There had been partial developments in different sections of the State prior to that period, but it was in a very primitive way.

At Burning Springs, in Wirt county, and at different points along "The Break," wells had been bored and oil obtained in paying quantities, but the difficulties found in getting it to market, deterred operators from making "developments" in any satisfactory manner.

Petroleum has been obtained near Morgantown, in Monongalia county, and at points on a line from Morgantown to Charleston, Kanawha county. This fact has given rise to the theory that the "Great Pennsylvania Oil Belt" extends into West Virginia, and crosses the State from north to south, Acting upon this theory, parties are now actively "prospecting" for new oil territory. A beginning will be made during this summer, on territory at the head waters of the Little Kanawha river.

It is thought by practical oil men, that this line is to be the future oil field of the State. Everything in this direction, however, is in the future. A few months will, it its believed, confirm, or disappoint the now pronounced belief of some of the most successful operators of Pennsylvania, in the success of the attempt. Many of them propose to make large investments in this direction.

But looking to the past, we must consider what has already been done, in the way of actual accomplished facts:

Up to 1865, the oil busines in West Virginia had been almost entirely speculative. Large amounts of money had been expended, and but little return had been made on the investments. In 1865–6, however, the business assumed a legitimate form. Oil men came to an appreciation of the fact that this, like any other legitimate calling, had to be followed with an eye to economy, and to a proper regard for order and system, in the management of oil and oil wells. As a consequence of this, oil development assumed a more scientific and business-like shape. Operations commenced almost simultaneously at Burning Springs, Oil Rock, California House, Volcano, Sand Hill, and Horseneck. Large quantities were produced at all of these points. Light oil was obtained at each of these places except at Volcano and Sand Hill. At these points were produced the "Heavy Oils," which have obtained a world wide reputation as "Lubricators."

The amount of *heavy* oil produced in the West Virginia oil regions, is about 300 barrels per day. Its gravity runs from 26° to 32° Beaume. It is used, in its crude state, almost exclusively for the purpose of lubrication. It will stand a lower degree of cold test than any other oil lubricator; this, added to its extreme cheapness, gives it the preference to all other lubricators, for general purposes. By different processes of reducing and admixture with oils of a lighter gravity, most excellent lubricators, at still lower rates than the crude article, are produced. These, as well as the crude heavy oil, are used in all parts of the country, and even form a large item in our export trade. The wells producing heavy oil are durable in their character, yielding not a large but steady flow of their oily treasure. It is the opinion of the most experienced operators, that there is still undeveloped, heavy oil territory of large extent within the State.

Whilst the light oil regions ran a rapid course, giving a large yield during their productive career, the heavy oil district continues to remunerate the producer.

Some idea may be gained of the extent of the oil development in the districts just named, by the inspection of a few figures. As far as can be estimated, there have been produced not less than 3,000,000 barrels of oil. The specific gravities of these range from 27 to 45 degs., Beaume, the greater portion varying from 27 to 33 degs.

The estimated value of this product is about $20,000,000. The number of producing wells at present, is 292, averaging about 3 barrels per day each. If the price and the times justified it, this number would probably be doubled in twelve months. One noticeable feature in the development of oil in West Virginia, is the cheapness of putting down wells. In Pennsylvania, it costs from $5,000 to $10,000 to bore a well, while in the oil district of West Virginia, it costs not exceeding $1200. Men of small means can operate in this State, but in Pennsylvania, the operator must have a fortune to make success certain. In this respect, West Virginia affords advantages not shown by any other section.

Notwithstanding the fact that oil had been developed in Pennsylvania long prior to 1865, and that large sums had been expended in the production of the crude product, in Venango county, in that state, to West Virginia belongs the honor of first furnishing the means of transporting it to market in the modes now recgnized to be cheap, safe, and expeditious. By means of tubing lines, and iron tank cars, oil is shipped to the seaboard and to all parts of the country in bulk, thus cheapening transportation, and bringing the article to the door of the consumer.

By means of steam pumps, adapted to the purpose, oil is propelled for miles through iron tubing to such termini as are accessible. It is cheaply pumped to the Ohio river, or to the Baltimore & Ohio R. R., and to the Laurel Fork, and Sand Hill R· R., and from thence transported in tank cars, to its destination, the product being handled with safety, and great expedition.

By these means the producer is enabled to send his oil to market from the most inaccessible points.

Parkersburg is the great oil centre of the state. Here is the market for the crude article, both for West Virginia and Ohio. Here are large refineries, which not only consume our own production, but import largely from Pennsylvania. The refining capacity of Parkersburg is about 2000 barrels per day,

In connection with most of the refineries, "are reducing" and and "treating" houses, for putting the heavy crude oil into shape for lubrication.

Being at the junction of the Little Kanawha, and the Ohio river, and the center of railroad connections which give it the advantage of river and rail transportation, it has become a recognized point in the sale and delivery of crude oil and its products. The trade gives employment to several hundred operatives, besides furnishing facilities by which great prosperity has been brought to this active and well-to-do city.

A few words about the uses of Petroleum may be of interest to the general reader. The "heavy oils" are extensively employed for lubricating purposes, taking the place almost wholly of the various articles heretofore in use for this purpose. For illuminating purposes, the light oils, when refined are extensively, almost universally used.

This is not to be wondered at, when it is known that the intensity of the light of refined Petroleum, is eighteen times as great as that of burning fluid; six times as great as that of sperm oil, and more than twice that of camphene, while the oil itself is furnished more cheaply than any of the above named articles.

Printing inks of all colors are made from Petroleum, the black especially, being an excellent article. Many varieties of soap are made from it, and are held in high repute. The medicinal qualities of Petroleum, especially the crude article, have long been known; its use as a liniment, more especially for cutaneous diseases, is quite extensive. As a specific for Consumption. by the inhalation of its vapors, it has acknowledged virtues.

Recently, it has been applied with very satisfactory results as a motive power in running the machinery of steam boats, iron mills &c. It is also used successfully in smelting iron ores, and as a coating for iron and wood to preserve them from decay, indeed for almost numberless other purposes which cannot be even named in a brief article like this.

Yours very truly,

WM. E. STEVENSON.

Parkersburg, W. Va., April 1876.

CHAPTER XIII.

MISCELLANEOUS MINERALS.

BY M. F. MAURY.

Having, in the three preceding chapters, spoken of the Coal, Iron. Salt, and Oil, of the State, its most abundant and valuable minerals, it is proposed, in this, to speak of the others that may be of interest and importance, giving such information as may be deemed of practical utility.

LIMESTONE—COMMON.

In great abundance and of great purity, this stone is found in the region between the coal measures and the eastern border of the State. In the counties in the coal formation in the northern-half of the State it is also very abundant, the Lower Barrens and the superincumbent strata containing, in some districts, an aggregate of 75 to 80 feet.

In the southern counties of the coal field there is a striking scarcity of this mineral, the seams being thin and usually of very poor quality.

The limestones of West Virginia are suited to all the purposes of the farmer, builder and blast furnace use. Where there is so much land that would be most materially benefitted by the use of lime, this material should attract the attention of the agriculturist far more than it does. Indeed it is rather a matter of surprise that the agriculture of this State has hitherto been suffered to reap so little benefit from this source of improvement so easily within reach. As yet, its application as a manure has been restricted to particular neighborhoods, though there is no portion of the uplands, especially of the limestone regions themselves, where it could not be used advantageously. The impression that the soils of a limestone country are already impregnated with calcareous matter. in consequence of the proximity of the limestone, which in many places rises to the surface in the fields, seems more than any other circumstance to have lead to the erroneous idea that lime could be of no benefit to the soil. It may, therefore, alter the opinions of many to state, that in a great many cases the soils even when in contact with this class of rock of the best quality, contain little or no available calcareous matter, for to have it, the material must be in the form of a soluble salt, and the ledges which crop out on the surface are carbonate of lime, which may be said to be insoluble for all practical purposes. When, however, it is burnt and applied to the land as *quick-lime*, it imparts fertility partly by being dissolved in the surface waters, and so passing into the soil in such a shape that the roots of plants can seize hold of it, but mainly by tending to decompose vegetable matter and so form a fertilizing humus. In the chapter on Agricultural Geology we have treated of the soils that would be particularly benefitted by an application of this class of manure.

The following are analyses from various portions of the State, and will tend to show the great purity in which this mineral may be found:

COUNTY.	LOCALITY.	Carbonate of Lime.	Carbonate of Magnesia.	Alumina and Oxide of Iron.	Insoluble Siliceous Matter.	Water and Loss.	CHEMIST.
Grant	Knobly Mountain..	90.08	4.00	0,72	4.56	0.64	W. B. Rogers
"	Near Petersburg.....	88.52	3.24	1.52	6.00	0.72	"
Greenbrier...	Fort Spring..........	90.11	2.49	2 02	5.04	0 34	J. B. Britton.
" ...	On C. & O. R. R.....	93.76	0.29	1.12	3.92	0.91	C.E Dwight.
" ...	Blue Sulphur Sp'gs	98.20	0 00	0 48	0.40	0.92	W.B.Rogers.
" ...	Muddy Creek Mt ...	88.64	9.60	0.12	1.20	0.44	"
Harrison......	Near Clarksburg....	95.52	1.88	0.96	0 92	0.72	"
Jefferson......	Harpers Ferry.......	81 16	10.80	0 52	6.68	0 84	"
"	2 miles s.w. H. F....	53.88	43.40	0.48	1.68	0.56	"
"	4 " w. "	95.86	1.46	tr'ce	1.83	0.85	"
Mineral	Patterson's Creek...	92.44	1 40	0 76	4.96	0.68	"
Monongalia..	Grenville Furnace..	88.32	0.00	2 52	7.24	1.92	"
Monroe	Red Sulphur Spg's..	90.92	tr'ce	1.20	6 20	1.68	"
"	Union	95.92	"	0.56	1.88	1.62	"
"	Dunlap's Creek......	86 52	9 52	0.52	2.96	0.48	"
"	Little North Mt.....	78.48	9.20	1.00	10 80	0 52	"
Ohio	Willow Grove........	85.95	1.38	4.10	7.61	0 96	C.E.Dwight.
Preston	Jenkins' Lime-kiln	88.16	2.32	1.16	5,80	2,56	W.B.Rogers.
"	Richard Foreman's	91.80	5.72	0.40	1.36	0.72	"
"	Below Coal No. 2...	79 52	2.80	3 12	13.80	0.76	"

LIMESTONE—TUFA.

This is another valuable class of lime within our State, in the counties on the eastern border, that has been much neglected, though occurring in some places in enormous beds. It is formed by the precipitation of calcareous matter from limestone water, and may therefore be looked for in those neighborhoods where the springs, thus impregnated, are of general occurence. In Jefferson, Hardy, Hampshire, Grant,* etc., this chalky deposit forms beds of great thickness, mingled with but little extraneous matter, and yields a lime of very superior quality. Its utility in agriculture, added to the facility with which the

*A deposit on Patterson's creek, in Grant county, has a surface from 6 to 8 acres, and a depth of 25 to 30 feet, the mass being very friable and extremely easy to work.

deposit may often be obtained (no quarrying being necessary to separate it from the mass), renders it a very advantageous substitute for the limestones of the same neighborhood. Moreover it should be remembered that in its more friable and powdery state, it may, as in Europe, be very beneficially applied as a marl without being burnt. Although it is of the same composition as limestone, yet when it is spread on the ground in a pulverized state, it presents so large a surface to the action of the carbonic acid that exists in the atmosphere, and is generated by the decay and decomposition of vegetable matter, that a portion of it is converted into a soluble bicarbonate of lime, which can then be taken up by the soil. But, as this chemical change is slow, a larger quantity has to be applied to the land, than if it was first burnt. If the ordinary pure limestone was ground to powder, it would have the same effect, but the expense forbids it being done, and besides, the burning the hard stone is cheaper, as well as produces a more active fertilizer.

The immense improvement that tide-water Virginia has derived from calcareous marl must render any illustration of its beneficial effects quite superfluous, when it is understood that its composition cannot be distinguished from the better classes of pulverulent marls, independent of which, its value has been unequivocally tested in other countries, where it has been found to have the most decided ameliorating effects upon land to which it is properly applied.

LIMESTONE--HYDRAULIC.

Associated with the common limestone strata of all portions of the State, are many bands of most excellent Hydraulic Limestone, which can be converted into a cement to suit all the requirements of trade. In Jefferson county, near Shepherdstown, quarries on a stratum from 10 to 15 feet thick are now in operation, and have been, since 1825, the product being used in the various public buildings in Washington for many years. At Wheeling, a band some 9 feet thick, is being worked by Mr. A. J. Long, and it produces a very valuable article. These are the only two places in the State where this mineral is at present wrought. In our southern counties some three seams of it have been observed, but never tested to any practical extent.

The following are analyses from some of the principal localities where it has been observed, and received high indorsement, according to laboratory tests.

COUNTY.	LOCALITY.	Carbonate of Lime.	Carbonate of Magnesia.	Alumina and Oxide of Iron.	Insoluble Siliceous Matter.	Water and Loss.	CHEMIST.
Hampshire..	Near Bloomery Furnace	46.64	30.68	6.32	15.60	0.76	W. B. Rogers.
Jefferson	"Gray Cement," Reynolds' Quarry, Shepherdstown ...	23.90	24.36	42.90	2.10	6.74	"
"	Near Charlestown..	38.66	9.50	42.50	3.50	5.84	"
Monongalia..	Near Morgantown..	52.04	17.12	8.60	19.36	1.40	"
Ohio...........	Riley's Hill, Wheeling.....................	43.44	26.44	4.40	24.64	1.08	"
Preston ...	Cheat river, mouth of Laurel...........	41.60	25.92	9.68	20.00	2.80	"
"	Near Kingwood, below Coal No. 3	57.16	23.80	9.12	8.52	1.40	"

LIMESTONE—MARBLE.

There are no true marbles in West Virginia, though in the counties on our eastern borders are many varieties of dark variegated, and nearly white limestones, susceptible of a high and beautiful polish, which bear that name. This is especially the case in Jefferson, where they appear to be very abundant, for here we see pink and gray, red and yellow, white, dove colored, etc., stones. A light gray stone shows a thickness of 25 feet at Shepherdstown, and crops out along with strata of colored marbles, on the river cliff, where a quarry might be advantageously located. A very beautiful black variety has also been found, and if it should prove to be free from flaws and fissures when gotten out in large slabs, will be a valuable element of wealth to this county. Five miles from Charlestown, a marble of this color has been worked by a Pennsylvania company for tiles, but is now abandoned. Not far from here is a small outcrop of a beautifully crystalline variety of a pure white stone, and it is possible that it may belong to a very valuable deposit. In Berkeley, also, are some gray and black limestones approximating to a compact marble. In Greenbrier a bed of this black ornamental stone has been found on the land of the Hon. James Withrow, near Lewisburg, but the quarry has not been opened so as to show the size. In this county some of the lighter shaded varieties of the limestone can be polished into very handsome facings and trimmings. The same remarks would seem to be applicable to other portions of the limestone belt of our eastern borders.

BUILDING STONES.

From various limestone and sandstone strata over the State most excellent building material of innumerable shades and colors can be had.

Many of the limestone bands of our eastern borders yield a most beautiful and durable material for any class of work, but except for foundations, chimneys, and dams, they have been put to very little practical use.

Among the beds of the conglomerate coal measures, sandstones of almost any size and texture can be quarried. Near Morgantown, in Monongalia county, a portion of the Mahoning sandstone can be quarried without difficulty, into blocks 6 or 8 feet long. Some distance higher in the hills than this is a stratum 15 feet thick, that furnishes a most beautiful and superior sandstone for all kinds of building. It is a light buff and dove color, dresses well, and when the improvement of the Monongahela river is completed and the material can be cheaply shipped, will form a most valuable source of revenue to the county, as it has but few equals and no superiors in the building market; in fact, it is of so excellent a quality that Col. Merrill, who has charge of the river improvement, expresses the opinion that it could well bear the expense of transportation to New York. It is now being used in the construction of the locks and dams in the Monongahela by the United States Government, and it forms the facings and dressings to the two main buildings of the West Virginia University.

In Taylor county, the Grafton sandstone as it is called, is of a most superior order. The texture is close, the grit sharp and clean, and the color gray. It has been used by the Baltimore & Ohio Railroad for their most superior masonry in this State. In Ritchie county, the Baltimore & Ohio Railroad have for many years worked a large quarry of a very handsome and durable gray sandstone, which has been used in the construction of their bridges, etc. An extremely valuable quarry of gray sandstone was opened at Weston, in Lewis county, and from it was constructed the Insane Asylum, located at that place. In architectural beauty this stone is said to have but few, if any, superiors in the United States. In Greenbrier county, near Ronceverte, large deposits of an extremely hard, durable and handsome sandstone occur. One is of a gray color, and was largely quarried and boated 6 miles down the Greenbrier river to build the piers, etc., of the railroad bridge over that stream, the contractors preferring to do this to using the stone nearer at hand. The other is of a chocolate color, and has a local use for building purposes.

On the upper portion of the Kanawha river, the sandstones of the Lower Coal Measures furnish the materials for the locks and dams now being built by the United States Government, and from the various hills along its line, the Chesapeake and Ohio Railroad obtained the stone for the construction of its bridges, culverts, etc., while the Mahoning sandstone at Charleston furnishes a beautiful gray and easily wrought trimming for many of the houses of that city.

Many other instances could be cited, but it may suffice at present to merely mention the fact that in nearly all portions of the State can good and first-class building stone be obtained

FIRE CLAY.

Fire clay is frequently found in the Coal Measures, often underlying a seam of coal. It results from the decomposition of siliceo—argillaceous shale, and its plasticity and impervious nature, when collected in a bed, prevents it from being carried away by infiltration.

A very valuable seam, 4½ feet thick, is mined by the Glade Fire Brick Company, at Nuzum's Mill, Marion County. The bricks are used in all parts of furnaces where great heat is required. The capacity of the works is 4,000 bricks per day. Of this Mr. Dwight, who made the analysis given in the next table, says: "The clay is superior to Mt. Savage clay, which has obtained such a reputation here (Wheeling,) as to exclude all other clay for blast furnace use. The analysis of Mt. Savage clay shows 1.5 per cent. of Protoxide of Iron, while this clay has no trace of this greatest enemy to the refractory nature of fire clays."

This seam shows across the Monongahela river, in Taylor county, one mile up Lost Run, where, to all physical examination it is of exactly the same quality.

On the property of the Kingwood Gas Coal and Iron Company, at Tunnelton, in Preston county, is the out crop of a very good article, which varies from 20 inches to 3 feet, being 2 feet thick on the average.

In Monongalia county, a very promising bed 4 feet thick occurs near Morgantown, and this class of mineral was also worked by the Pridevale Furnace Company, though nothing has been done in this line at that place for many years.

The following table shows the analyses of the clay from these places:

CONTENTS.	Glade Fire Brick Co.	Kingwood Gas, Coal and Iron Co.	Near Morgantown, Monongalia Co.
Silica	45.86	68.16	54.27
Alumina	44.23	24.11	33.83
Oxide of Iron	0.00	0.01	0.01
Lime	0.24	trace	trace
Magnesia	0.36	trace	0.02
Potash and Soda	trace	trace	trace
Moisture, hygroscopic	.70	0.85	1.00
" combined } Organic matter. }	8.35	6.66 trace	10.86 0.15
	99.74	99.79	100.14

In Hancock county some 20 firms, employing from 200 to 300 hands, are employed in working a fire clay which makes a good refractory brick.

On Two Mile creek of Elk river, in Kanawha county, a few miles from Charleston, very excellent fire clays have been worked and shipped to western markets. In Wayne county, near Cassville, a bed apparently of the best quality, is found. Also, one and a half miles from Savageville, on J. W. Johnson's farm, Braxton county, is a stratum about 3 feet thick, and frequently of excellent quality.

Taking into consideration the process by which this mineral is formed, we may expect to find it in very many places in the Coal Measures of the State.

POTTER'S CLAY.

This clay results from the decomposition of granites and shales. That in West Virginia comes from the latter source entirely, of which there is a great abundance and variety, so that we may look for very many deposits of the material. When it is yellow or red, it denotes the presence of oxide of iron, which tinges the manufactured articles red. When the clay is white, there is no iron present. Potter's clay has a peculiarly unctous feel, and has the valuable property of resisting heat without cracking. Within our State are several establishments that carry on a very successful business in this material Notable amongst these, is that of Mr. James Smith, at Point Pleasant, Mason county, who manufactures all sizes of tiles, the demand for which is double the capacity of his present works.

In Berkeley this clay is worked and made into crocks at Martinsburg; in Barbour county it is worked by Messrs. Burley & Holler; in Greenbrier county, near Alvon, on Anthony's creek, a blue variety of excellent quality is found; in Harrison county it is worked at Shinnston by Wilkinson & Flemming into crocks, jugs, jars, vases, drain pipes, &c. This clay, which is white, burns blue and very compact, forming a strong ware, and is found two miles from Shinnston, on the Clarksburg road. In Hampshire county potter's clay is wrought on North river, and again in Hardy county on the outskirts of Moorefield and in Capon mountain ridge; also, in Jefferson county at the Shepherdstown pottery, as well as in Lewis county by S. A. Colvin, where it is white. It burns blue, forming a strong ware and all forms of pottery used in the country is manufactured. Also, on Kincheloe creek, in this county, on the farm of A. Davis, a clay is abundant which will make table ware, where very hard burning is not demanded. At Palatine, in Marion county, Knotts, Swindler & Co. work an excellent article, found two miles from the town down the river road. It is 6 feet thick, and on R. M. Hill's property. This firm manufactures excellent wares—jugs, jars, crocks, vases, &c. There is, also, at Mr. Hill's, a clay which presents all the physical properties of an excellent slip. In Mercer county, on East river, potter's clay is manufactured into crockery and pipes by Messrs. Brown & McKenzie.

At Morgantown, in Monongalia county, there are crockery works, and at Parkersburg, in Wood county, is a large establishment making jars, jugs, vases, tiles, drain pipes, &c. In Wirt county, on the farm of Mr. Bibbee, 1½ miles from Newport, is found a 4-foot seam of white potter's clay, which has been tried with great success.

On the land of I. S. Boggs, on Steer creek, near Kennedy's mills, in Gilmer county, is a deposit of clay, 4 feet thick, so white, and sand so fine and clear, as to lead to the belief that excellent ironstone china and terra cotta ware could be made therefrom. This stratum, from surface indications, is extensive.

A very fine article is found, extensively, near Cassville, in Wayne county.

GLASS SAND.

In Hampshire county, in Blue's Gap of Short mountain, occurs a very remarkable deposit of pure, white, siliceous sand, that would be most admirably adapted to glass making, as it seems to contain no trace of any deliterious coloring matter. The cliffs, for a height of several hundred feet are composed of it, forming a hard rock where in mass, but quickly disintegrating when exposed to the air. From its great quantity and purity it will form a very important item in the mineral wealth of this highly favored district, when railroads give it a free exit to the manufacturing world.

In Monongalia county, near Morgantown, is a stratum 30 feet thick, of a very soft sandstone that rapidly disintegrates on exposure to the atmosphere. and would make a good glass sand where absolute freedom from coloring matter was not a prerequisite. The same may be said of a deposit, of unknown size, in Morgan county, 1½ miles from Sir John's run, on the Balt. & Ohio R. R. In the same county, on Sandy ridge, are large deposits of a fine white sand, which are at present worked by a Philadelphia company for glass works in that city. The quarry is at Alpines, on the railroad, and while the sand is of good quality, it is not so pure as that at Blue's gap in Hampshire county.

OCHRE.

In Lewis county, on the land of Perry T. Smith, near Weston, is a deposit some 3 feet thick of an exceedingly fine yellow ochre, which in burning yields a pure rich red. It mines easily, can be ground to powder either raw or burnt, with the greatest facility, and, as it can go on the market at once, without further preparation, as a mineral paint of excellent quality, it will be of great value when railroads connect it with the commercial world.

In Hardy county a light yellow ochre—though not of so fine a quality as that from Lewis—has been observed in the South Branch valley about 6 miles south of Moorefield, as well as on Lost river near Harper's Mills, this latter being a delicate buff and very good. In Jefferson county, near Shepherdstown, ochre has been discovered, and the article is so pure that after washing, it already has been used as a pigment in oil paintings. Of a yellow color, this material also occurs at Clines Cross Roads, near Upper Tract in Pendleton county. In Cabell county on Guyandotte river is a very fine deposit several feet thick of a yellow ochre, and also in Wayne county near Ceredo.

BARYTES.

Is a heavy, white, mineral, used in cheap paints, and for the adulteration of white lead. Deposits occur in Jefferson county, 8 miles from the Baltimore & Ohio R. R., and 4 miles from the Winchester Branch of the same, but no tests have as yet been made, to show the size of the bed.

A very pure article has also been reported from Mercer county on the north side of East River mountain, but no information is obtainable as to the quantity present.

BLACK OXIDE OF MANGANESE.

Manganese is one of the important concomitants in the manufacture of steel by the Bessemer process, and the black oxide is used largely in bleaching and in printing cotton goods, and produces the purple color used in imprinting images on china ware.

It is also used by the flint glass manufacturer to correct the green tinge which his glass is apt to derive from the iron present in the sand he employs.

It will be found in the eastern counties of the State, associated with the strata that contain the Brown Oxide of Iron. A very pure article, though in what quantity is not yet known, is found on Anthony's creek, in Greenbrier county.

To make it marketable, from 60 to 70 per cent of the material mined should be pure mineral.

SALTPETRE

Is to be found mingled with the earth in many of the caves of the limestone region of Greenbrier, Monroe, and Pocahontas, and in the first named county, has been procured from time to time in considerable quantities from this source. This earth, or "petre-dirt," as it is called, is a sediment deposited from the waters formerly, or at the present time, found in these caves, and sometimes has a texture of such impalpable fineness as to indicate that the deposition took place while the liquid was in a very quiet state. Besides this, it also contains a large amount of nitrate of lime, which, by mingling the washings of common wood ashes with those of the petre-dirt, is, by direct chemical action, converted into saltpetre.

LEAD, ZINC, COPPER, GOLD, AND SILVER.

Lead.—In innumerable localities small pieces of Galena (Sulphide of Lead) are found, sometimes in a creek, and sometimes, in small nuggets or masses of several pounds weight, embedded in rock. These fragments have given rise to many traditions, handed down from Indian days, concerning vast deposits. They can be heard of in nearly every county in the State, but amount to traditions and traditions only, for nowhere within our borders is, or will, this metal be found in workable quantities, except, perhaps, in the extreme eastern counties, in some of the limestone formations, and even there it is doubtful.

Zinc and Copper.—Zinc is also found in several localities, but is not workable in a single one, and the same may be said in most emphatic terms of Copper.

As to *Gold and Silver*, many are the hopes that have been raised by old men's stories of money coined, and silver dollars *moulded* in the wild hollows of the State, and many a day's labor has been lost to the laboring man by "wild goose chases," induced by old traditions concerning the presence of these metals, when the geological structure of West Virginia does not, in a single locality, from north to south, or east to west, admit of their profitable presence. It would be far better for our general welfare if Nature had not put an ounce of Lead, Zinc or Copper within our borders, and that there were no shining yellow iron pyrites or silvery glittering scales of mica to tempt men off from profitable labor.

CHAPTER XIV.

MINERAL WATERS.

BY DR. J. J. MOORMAN,
OF THE GREENBRIER WHITE SULPHUR SPRINGS.

As a scientist might infer from the general geological character of West Va., and especially from the chemical character of her abounding minerals, numerous medicinal waters are found to exist in the State, some of which have been well and fully tested for many years, and are equal, or superior to any waters of their class, found in any portion of the world.

West Virginia comprises, within her southern and southeastern border, a large portion of the celebrated mineral spring plaza, long known as the "Spring Region of Virginia," and which, for the last 80 or 90 years, has been greatly resorted to by the seekers of health and pleasure, of every great section of the United States.

The springs of this State present considerable variety of chemical character, and therapeutic adaptation:—comprising various and differently compounded *sulphur* waters; the *Chalybeates*, simple, and compounded: the *Acidulous*. or *Carbonated*; the *Saline*: the *Aluminated Chalybeates;* with thermal waters, not of very high temperature.

Of these springs, the *sulphur* waters, so far as such springs have yet been developed, are found in greatest abundance, and in greater strength, on the southern border of the State, and on the western and northern slopes of the Alleghany mountains: The *Simple Chalybeates*, are found in every great section of the State, but in greatest strength, so far as they have been tested, along the course of the great Appalachian Ranges, extending from the northeastern to the southwestern extremities of the State,

The *Acidulous Carbonated* waters, as well as the *Aluminated Chalybeates*, are found in different parts of the State, but have been most developed on its southern border.

The most valuable mineral waters of the State, so far as they have been tested in the treatment of diseases, are the *sulphurous*,—the *alum* waters, as they are called commonly, and the *Compound Acidulated* waters. The latter especially, are generally found adjacent to faults in the strata, or where the rocks give evidence of displacement from their natural position, and near the junction of slates with limestone.

The alum waters, so far as I have ever known, are an infiltration through slate, which generally lies a few feet below the surface of the earth, but often cropping out considerably above it. I have examined numerous specimens of these waters, obtained from different sections, and found them all to possess the leading chemical characteristic of the springs of this class, which have been brought into popular use.

My observations are to the effect that the mineral waters of the State generally; and certainly those within the ranges of the disturbances of the rocks so common in the southern section of the State, are slightly thermal, compared with the temperature of the common springs in their vicinity, or of the earth through which they flow. The *decided thermal waters*, some of them running up as high as 107°, are found immediately on the eastern slopes of the Alleghany in Virginia, and within a few miles of the southern border of West Virginia.

In particularizing the leading, and long used mineral springs of the State,—and it is such only that I propose particularly to mention, I will first mention those on the extreme eastern border.

BERKELEY SPRINGS,

In the county Morgan, are the oldest in the State, or in the southern country, in public use. They were much visited in Colonial times, and long before the Revolutionary war. The land upon which they are situated, originally belonged to the Right Honorable Thomas Lord Fairfax. Building lots were laid off here by an act of the Legislature, in 1776, and among those who became owners of them and were the habitues of the springs, were Charles Carroll, of Carrollton, Gen. Horatio Gates, Gen. George Washington, and many others of note and distinction.

The bathing establishments are extensive and convenient. The ladies' bath house is an elegant structure, 90 feet long, containing nice private baths, and a plunge bath 30 by 16 feet, floored with white marble. The hotel accommodations are extensive and well gotten up.

The temperature of the water ranges from 72° to 74° Fahr., and remains the same at all seasons. It has never been carefully analyzed.

Medical Use.—While these waters possess considerable virtues when taken internally, they have been most celebrated as a *bath*. Thus used, they have been found beneficial in the whole class of *nervous disorders*, that are disconnected with a full plethoric habit, extreme debility, or decided organic derangements. In reduced habit, or debility, when sufficient power of reaction exists in the system, they prove useful. Persons who are suffering from a residence in a warm or damp climate, are generally much benefitted by these baths. In subacute rheumatism, they have a good reputation, and in many such cases have been advantageously employed.

As a *beverage*, they are serviceable in several of the mildly chronic, or subacute disorders; such as derangements of the digestion, unconnected with organic disease.

In the early stages of *calculus* diseases, attended with irritable bladder, their use internally and externally is often beneficial.

ORICH'S SULPHUR SPRINGS.

Situated three and a half miles from Berkeley, on the Warm Spring run, and near the road that leads to Hancock, is *Orich's Sulphur Spring*. It is a very pleasant water, of the temperature of 85° Fah. If properly improved, it will become a beneficial place for popular resort, and an important auxillary to Berkeley Springs.

SHANNONDALE SPRINGS.

The *Shannondale Springs* are in the county of Jefferson, and arise in a peninsula of the Shenandoah river, known as the "Horse Shoe." They are five and a half miles from Charlestown, the seat of justice for Jefferson county.

The springs are three in number, but one only is principally used. The temperature of the water is 55° Fah.

The Shannondale water seems to have some approximation, in its nature and effects, to the celebrated Bedford water. It may properly be classed as a *Saline Chalybeate*, and may be used with good effects, as a mild alterative tonic, in some forms of dyspepsia, nervous diseases, general debility unattended with serious organic derangements, chronic diseases of the mucous surfaces, such as gleet, leucorrhœa, etc., and in that class of female diseases requiring the aid of mineral tonics. The water acts generally as a *diuretic*, and very commonly has a noted aperient effect.

The late Dr. DeButts, of Baltimore, analyzed this water in 1821. One hundred grains of its solid contents afforded the following results:

Carbonate of Lime	10.5	grains
Sulphate of Lime	63 0	"
Sulphate of Magnesia	23.5	"
Chloride of Magnesium	1.0	"
Chloride of Sodium	1.0	"
Sulphate of Iron	0.3	"
Carbonate of Iron	0.7	"

Gaseous contents, sulphuretted hydrogen, quantity not ascertained; carbonic acid, quantity not ascertained.

The accommodations at Shannondale are not extensive, being perhaps adapted to 140 to 150 persons; but it is, admittedly a very delightful place, and the scenery is unsurpassed for its varied beauty and grandeur, exciting the admiration of all who behold it.

CAPON SPRINGS.

At the western base of North mountain, in the county of Hampshire, have been a favorite resort for those seeking recreation and health, for many years.

The improvements here are extensive, and comfortable; sufficient for the entertainment of seven or eight hundred persons. The bathing establishments are extensive and elegant.

The spring is bold, affording about 100 gallons of water per minute. The temperature of the water as it flows from the earth is 64°. A qualitative analysis shows that the water contains: Silicic acid, Soda, Magnesia, Bromine, Iodine, Carbonic acid.

Except in thermal character, this water cannot be closely

compared to any of the springs of the State. As a therapeutic agent it more resembles Berkeley, than any other.

Medical Uses.—Both as a *bath* and a *beverage* it will, when properly directed, be found very useful in a wide range of diseases, especially in idiopathic affections of the nervous system —dyspeptic depravities, chronic derangements of the mucous surfaces, etc.

It has acquired reputation, and I believe justly, as a remedy in *gravel*, and other derangements of the urinary organs. It is a valuable water, and like the Berkeley water, is destined to grow in public favor.

THE SWEET SPRING.

In the county of Monroe, next to Berkeley, is the oldest watering place in the South that has permanently kept up its visitations and maintained its reputation. The hotel accommodations are extensive and comfortable. The *bathing* facilities, for both sexes, are neat and well adapted to their purpose.

The temperature of the water of the spring and bath varies from 72° to 76° Fah. The analysis of the water by Professor Rogers, shows that it contains in 100 cubic inches, the following ingredients and proportions, viz:

1st. Solid matter procured by evaporation from 100 cubic inches of the water.................32.67 grains

2d. Quantity of each solid ingredient, estimated as perfectly free from water, in 100 cubic inches of water:

Sulphate of Lime	5.703 grains
Sulphate of Magnesia	4.067 "
Sulphate of Soda	2.746 "
Carbonate of Lime	13.012 "
Carbonate of Magnesia	0.357 "
Chloride of Sodium	0.060 "
Chloride of Magnesium	0.136 "
Chloride of Calcium	0.065 "
Peroxide of Iron	0.065 "
Silica	0.075 "
Earthy Phosphate	Trace.
Iodine	Trace.

3d. Volume of each of the gases contained in a free state, in 100 cubic inches of water:

Carbonic Acid	37.17 cubic inches
Nitrogen	1.87 " "
Sulphuretted Hydrogen	Trace.
Oxygen	Trace.

Therapeutic Effects.—Its first effects when drunk, due to its temperature and gaseous contents, are a feeling of warmth at the stomach, with a sensation of fullness of the head and some giddiness. Taken at intervals in moderate quantities, it produces a slight moisture of the skin, and an increase in the flow of urine. If the stomach be in a good condition, it increases the appetite, and imparts general vigor to the system. Its effects upon the bowels vary at first, but after some days use, it will be found to increase a costive habit.

As a tonic in pure debility, unaccompanied by congestion in the vital organs, it may be used both as a *beverage* and *bath*, to great advantage. In that form of dyspeptic depravity, accompained by *gastrodenia*, or spasm, with pains occurring at intervals, connected with heartburn, and generally with cold feet and topid skin, it is employed with decided advantage.

In chronic diarrhœa and dysentery, it is often highly beneficial.

In *sub-acute rheumatism*, in primary *neuralgia*, and for deli cate females, enervated by long nursing, it is employed with good effect. As might be supposed from its excess of carbonic acid, it is found useful in *calculus* and *nephritic* complaints.

As an exhilarating and tonic bath, this water is highly prized. It is advantageous in quite a large number of cases, for which baths of its temperature and chemical composition are adapted.

WHITE SULPHUR SPRINGS,

The White Sulphur Springs, so long famous among the mineral waters of the world, are in the county of Greenbrier, 5 miles west of the crest of the Alleghany mountains.

These springs have been known, and appreciated as mineral waters, for nearly 100 years, and for 75 of that period, have been held in high repute for their medicinal efficacy.

The improvements here are extensive, affording accommodations directly, and with their cottages, for from 1,500 to 2,000 persons. The altitude of the spring above the sea level is about 2,000 feet.

The spring is a bold one, yielding upwards of 30 gallons per minute, and is not influenced in its flow, or in the strength of the water, either by the season of the year, or by wet and dry weather. The temperature of the water is uniformly

62° Fah., which is 10° warmer than the neighboring surface springs, or the earth through which it flows.

The analysis of this water shows that 100 cubic inches, or 3½ pints, nearly, contain the following ingredients:

Sulphate of Lime,	31.680	grains.
" " Magnesia	8.241	"
" " Soda	4.050	"
" " Alumina	0.012	"
Protosulphate of Iron	0.069	"
Carbonate of Lime	1.520	"
" " Magnesia	1.071	"
Chloride of Calcium	0.010	"
" " Sodium	0.226	"
Earthy phosphates	a trace.	

Azotized organic matter, combined with a large amount of sulphur, about 005 grains.

Also some Iodine, combined with Sodium or Magnesium.

Volume of each of the gases, in a free state, estimated in 100 cubic inches of water:

Sulphuretted Hydrogen	0.66	cubic inches.
Nitrogen	0.66	"
Oxygen	0.19	"
Carbonic Acid	3.67	"

MEDICAL CHARACTER,

The distinctive medicinal influence of these waters upon the system are *cathartic*, *diuretic*, *sudorific*, and *alterative*. Some *cathartic* and *diuretic* effect, as well as a distinct determination to the skin by sweating, is induced by its use in the great majority that drink it; but *its most decidedly controlling effect* over diseased action, and that which, more than any other, gives it its highest and most valuable character as a remedy, is its *alterative* power, or that peculiar action by which it effects salutary changes, or alterations in the blood, in the various secretions, and in the tissues of the body generally.

The water has also the remarkable power of reducing the frequency of the pulse when unduly excited. This is not to be attributed to a direct sedative effect of the water upon the heart and arteries, but to its potent influence in abating general excitement, resolving inflammations, and removing obstructions, thus bringing back the system to its normal condition.

Experiment has abundantly established the fact of the *direct* and *positive* effect of these waters in controlling and eradicating many diseases. When properly used, their effect is to revive the languishing circulation, to give a new direction to the vital energies, re-establish the perspiratory action of the skin, bring back to their physiological type the vitiated or suppressed secretions, provoke salutory evacuations, either by urine or stool, or by transpiration; thus they bring about in the animal system, through their alterative power, an internal transmutation or *profound* change.

It is thus that they relieve chronic disordered action, and impart natural energy and elasticity to vessels that have been distended either by inflammation or congestion, while they communicate an energy to the muscular fibre and to the animal tissues generally, which is not witnessed from the administration of ordinary remedies. This is the *alterative* effect and the *profound* change to which I have alluded, and which gives to these waters their characteristic efficiency.

The White Sulphur water is used with good effect in most of the disorders of the *abdominal viscera*—such as *dyspepsia, chronic irritations of the mucous coat of the stomach and bowels, chronic liver complaint, jaundice,* and in long standing cases of *diarrhœa* and *dysentery,* when unattended by inflammatory action. In the various disorders of the *urinary organs,* and especially when such disorders depend upon *acid* predominance in the fluids it is useful. To *chronic rheumatism* and the various diseases of the *skin,* as *exema* and its kindred affections, it is most happily adapted.

A regular and marked effect of the free use of this water, is its potency in abating, or entirely overcoming, during the time of its use, the desire for drinking ardent spirits by those who have been habitually indulging in their use. During my long residence at the Springs, I have witnessed hundreds of cases justifying the above statement. This influence depends, first, on the action of the sulphuretted hydrogen in the water, which is an active nervine stimulant, and as such, supplies, for the time, the want the inebriate feels for his accustomed alcoholic stimulant; and secondly, on the alterative influence exerted by the waters on the organism, which brings the entire animal structure into harmoneous action, and produces an abatement of the *cerebral* and *nervous* irritation which prevails in the habitual drunkard. This enables him to exert a greater moral power than he could before, and at least gives him time for reflection, free from the craving for for alcoholic stimulants. Of course it is not meant that the waters are a sure cure for *absolute* or *threatened* inebriation, but that a proper and continuous use of them will be a valuable aid in returning to sobriety.

In that enfeebled, susceptible and very peculiar condition of the the system, often found to exist as the result of a long continued or injudicious use of *mercury*, and in what is commonly known as the *Secondary* form of *Venereal Disease*, the White Sulphur water, when carried to its full alterative effects, displays its highest curative powers. A long experience in the use of the water, in the peculiar forms of disease under consideration, causes me not to hesitate to name these as the diseases in which they are most certainly efficacious. The water in such cases, exerts a specific effect, and more certainly brings relief to the sufferer than any other agency. I have no hesitancy in saying to those who are so unfortunate as to be subjects of the disease in question, that they have in these waters, when *properly* and *fully used*, in connection with warm and hot sulphur baths, a reasonable hope of permanent cure, which they cannot have from the use of any other remedy known to the profession.

BATHS AT THE WHITE SULPHUR.

Warm and hot bathing, especially in highly medicated waters, is a remedy of leading importance, in a large number of the cases which resort to mineral waters for relief. The water used for bathing at the White Sulphur, flows from the spring from which the visitors drink, and no other waters in America, used for bathing, except the Washita Springs, in Arkansas, are more highly impregnated with mineral salts. These baths, in connection with the drinking of the sulphur waters, although not required in every case, are a matter of the utmost importance, in a large number of cases, in aiding to produce the best effects of the waters.

The *bathing-house* is large, affording ample accommodations for the bathers. The bathing-rooms are spacious, airy, and comfortable, and in addition to the usual *tub-baths*, they have erected *douche* baths, for the application of hot or warm water to local parts of the body, and have set apart rooms arranged for *sweating*-baths. The water is heated by steam in the vessel in which it is used, and the heat is never so great as to cause any precipitation, and loss of the solid contents. Hence they are left in their natural suspension in the water, to exert their specific effect upon the bather. Steam may also be let from time to time into the tub, so as to keep up the temperature during the entire period of bathing, a matter of no small importance.

THE RED SULPHUR SPRINGS,

In the county of Monroe 40 miles south from the White Sulphur, have been known and distinguished as a watering place for more than 60 years. The water of the spring is clear and cool, having the temperature of 54° Fah. The following is Prof. Rogers' analysis of this spring:

Gaseous contents in an Imperial Gallon:

Sulphuretted Hydrogen	4.54	cubic inches.
Carbonic Acid	8.75	"
Nitrogen	4.25	"

Solid contents in 32 *cubic inches of water*, 1.25 grains, consisting of sulphate of soda, lime, and magnesia, carbonate of lime, and chloride of sodium. Besides these ingredients, the water contains in considerable quantity, a peculiar organic substance, mingled with sulphur, which is deposited on the sides ef the spring, and seems to increase by a species of organie growth.

These springs have, for many years, had a high reputation in the treatment of various diseases of the *lungs*, as well as for many other diseases, for which the milder *sulphur* waters have been advantageously employed.

THE SALT SULPHUR SPIRNGS.

Near Union, in Monroe county, afford a valuable mineral water. They were largely visited for many years, especially by Southern people. The improvements here are large and comfortable, but for several years have not been opened to visitors. The following is the analysis of the water, furnished by Prof. Wm. B. Rogers:

Temperature, variable, from 49° to 56°.

Solid matter procured by evaporating 100 cubic inches of the water, and drying at 212°:—81.44 grains.

Quantity of each solid ingredient in 100 cubic inches, estimated as perfectly free from water:

Sulphate of Lime	36.755	grains.
" " Magnesia	7.883	"
" " Soda	9.682	"
Carbonate of Lime	4.445	"
" " Magnesia	1.434	"
Chloride of Magnesium	0.116	"
" " Sodium	0.683	"
" " Calcium	0.025	"
Peroxide of Iron from Protosulphate	0.042	"
Azotized Organic Matter	0.004	"
Earthy Phosphates	trace.	
Iodine	trace.	

Volume of each gas contained, in a free state, in 100 cubic inches:

Sulphuretted Hydrogen	1.10 to 1.50	cubic inches.
Nitrogen	2.05	"
Oxygen	0.27	"
Carbonic Acid	5.75	"

In addition to the springs already mentioned, there are in various parts of the State, indeed in every great section of it, mineral fountains that are well worthy of public attention. Among these are the *Blue Sulphur* springs in Greenbrier county, once a place of much resort and an excellent mineral water, and *Guinn's Spring*, in Fayette county, near the mouth of Lick creek. This has been but little tested, and not at all chemically. It is evidently a sulphur water of excellent promise. There is also a spring in the vicinity of Parkersburg, now attracting considerable attention, of which I know too little, either therapeutically or chemically, to attempt a description, but it is favorably regarded by many persons.

Besides the springs mentioned by Dr. Moorman, in the above paper, we may note here, two additional ones. The first of these is the *Hardy White Sulphur Spring*, situated at the east base of the South Branch mountain, 14 miles south of Moorefield. This is a white sulphur, forming a deposit of snowy whiteness. No analysis has been made of it, but carbonic acid escapes from it continually. The temperature in summer is 50° Fah., and in winter 48°. The flow is 65 gallons per hour,

It has been a place of resort for 45 years, and its medicinal qualities well established. It is anti-acid, and diuretic, and tonic, and in diseases arising from a disordered liver, its curative effects are well marked.—[Thos. Maslin.] The second spring to be noted, is the *Magnesia Spring*, on Howard's creek, near the White Sulphur in Greenbrier. The following analysis of it is by Dr. Aiken, of Baltimore, Md.

Solid contents in one imperial gallon:

Carbonate of Lime	22.367	grains
Carbonate of Magnesia	11.160	"
Carbonate of Iron	0.320	"
Sulphate of Lime	21.010	"
Sulphate of Magnesia	12.060	"
Sulphate of Potasium	1.460	"
Sulphate of Soda	1.201	"
Sulphate of Ammonia	0.179	"
Organic Matter	Trace.	
Chloride of Sodium	1.260	"
Chloride of Potasium	1.742	"
Silica	0.860	"
Iodine	Trace.	
Lithia	Trace.	
Bromine	Trace.	
Loss	0.43	"
Specific gravity	1.0004	

This is a new spring, and we have no report of its therapeutic effects.

The following analysis of the Parkersburg Mineral Wells was furnished by Rezin P. Davis, M. D., to the owner of the wells:

One quart of water contains:—

Carbonic acid gas	16	cubic inches
Sulphate of Magnesia	10	grains.
Sulphate of Soda	24	"
Sulphate of Iron	4	"
Chloride of Lime	41	"
Carbonate of Soda	4	"
Iodine	Trace.	

CHAPTER XV.

TRANSPORTATION.

BY M. F. MAURY.

With mineral riches of so vast an extent, with forests of such magnificent size, with soils of such fertility, and with so many other natural advantages as have been shown in the preceding chapters, the question naturally arises, Why, if these things be true, are the resources of West Virginia so little developed? The answer is readily given when we examine the lack of railroads within our borders.

Before the western country along the Ohio river sprang up, with its mighty power of population, manufactures and wealth the main markets of the Union were in the seaboard States, bordering the Atlantic, and all trade tended to them. Consequently the inauguration of public improvements were around these business centers, and, tending to bring them into closer communication, were made north and south, the western connections being built but slowly; so that 1861 saw but one company that had built an east and west line through West Virginia, and now, that, with its western feeders, does a heavier freight business than almost any road in the United States. Up to 1861, Old Virginia, which then stretched from the Atlantic to the Ohio, fostered the railroads centering around the eastern cities, and western connections, though projected, were not pushed, and the beginning of the war showed only the Baltimore and Ohio railroad, a foreign corporation, and one that carried trade to northern centers, and away from her seaports completed. During the sectional struggle of four years, no improvements were made, and it was not until 1872 that the southern portion of the State had any rail communication with markets.

There is another reason why we were passed over, viz.: Our population was comparatively small, and possessed nothing that was not found more or less abundantly elsewhere, and the Alleghany mountains on the eastern borders were generally looked upon as a very awkward barrier to be overcome in railroading. The knowledge concerning our mineral riches in the money centers, was vague and uncertain, and the existing lines in Pennsylvania passed through coal fields that could fill all demands. No north and south lines were built, simply because there were no great commercial cities to be connected by them, while the products along such lines would have gone into markets, with railroad charges on them, to compete with articles that already existed in great profusion around the termini.

But this state of things can no longer remain so. The trade of the west has become so great, and its surplus products, that find their best markets in Europe, and other portions of the world, have become so vast that they call for new routes to the seaports. The Alleghanies on our eastern border have been shown not to be the barrier supposed, for the Baltimore and Ohio railroad runs over their summits, and the Chesapeake and Ohio railroad passes them with grades of only 30 feet per mile, while other roads, already surveyed, show most practicable and feasible routes. Those now in operation have placed our coals in eastern markets, where they always equal, and sometimes outrank, the best of the United States; iron ores of good quality and in vast deposits have been well proven, while in every portion of the State streams have cut the roadbeds, so that lateral branches can be run up innumerable creeks to furnish a vast tonnage for the main trunk lines, and an enormous freight traffic can be looked for in local business in carrying coal to iron, and iron to coal, and then transporting the results of the manufacture.

In fact, though there can be no question that this lack of of transportation has been of great disadvantage in the past, and still is at the present, yet it has its compensatory advantages for the future, as it has left the riches of this State untouched, while all the country around was being developed and new markets constantly created—every year growing larger. Formerly we would, in common with the other States, have looked to the eastern trade alone, but now we are surrounded on the west, north, and east, by immense and ever consuming centres, that have been changed from producers and competitors into consumers and customers, and many an item of wealth that would, heretofore, on account of lack of demand or low price, have been used or prepared for market, in the most wasteful manner, and have been a positive loss to our ultimate prosperity, now becomes a source of revenue and wealth. Hence, West Virginia occupies the enviable position of being a "new country" with all the advantages of an "old one," in being surrounded with counsumers for every article that it can supply, and this fact alone should attract no little attention from the miner, lumberman, agriculturist, mechanic and laborer.

The following are the transportation companies now in operation:

Baltimore and Ohio Railroad—runs through the northern portion of the State, having Baltimore as its eastern terminus and passing through the counties of Jefferson, Berkley, Morgan, Hampshire, Mineral, Preston, Taylor, Marion, Wetzel, Marshall, and part of Ohio, connecting the towns of Harper's Ferry, Martinsburg, Keyser, Piedmont, Rowlesburg, Grafton, Fairmont, Moundsville and Wheeling. A branch leaves the main road at Grafton, in Taylor county, and passes through the counties of Harrison, Doddridge, Ritchie and Wood, to Parkersburg on the Ohio river. Besides its termini, the main towns on it are Clarksburg, West Union and Cairo.

Pennsboro & Harrisville Railroad, leaves the Parkersburg Branch of the Balt. & Ohio R. R. at Pennsboro, in Ritchie county, and runs about 14 miles to Harrisville, in same county. It was built to accommodate the timber interests of this section.

Chesapeake & Ohio Railroad.—In the southern part of the State with its eastern terminus on tide-water at Richmond, Va., and its western at Huntington, on the Ohio river. It passes through the counties of Greenbrier Monroe, Summers, Fayette, Kanawha, Putnam, and Cabell, having, as its principal stations, the White Sulphur Springs, Lewisburg, with

Ronceverte as the depot, 3 miles distant; Quinnimont Furnace, Kanawha Falls, Coalburg, Charleston, Saint Albans, Barboursville, and Huntington, whence it is 160 miles by the Ohio river to Cincinnati.

Martinsburg & Potomac Railroad.—In West Virginia this road is altogether in Berkeley county. It runs from the Baltimore and Ohio R. R., at Martinsburg, to Hagerstown in Maryland.

Pittsburgh, Cincinnati & St. Louis Railroad.—This road crosses the Ohio river at Steubenville and passes across the Panhandle in Brooke county, touching Hancock county at Holliday's Cove.

Pittsburgh, Wheeling & Baltimore Railroad.—Runs from Wheeling to Washington in Pennsylvania, where it has connections with Pittsburgh. In West Virginia it is altogether in Ohio county. When completed through to Baltimore, it will be shorter than of any existing line between Cincinnati and the seaboard, and will be used by the Balt. & Ohio R. R. as their quick passenger route.

Valley Railroad.—Passes from the Balt. & Ohio R. R. at Harper's Ferry, southward through Jefferson county, and into Virginia to the Chesapeake & Ohio R. R. at Staunton.

To show the interest that is being attracted to and manifested in the developement of this State, the following is a list of the charters that have been granted, and still exist, within our borders since 1867, though it is proper to remark, that the construction of some of the roads are in the distant future.

Blue Stone Mining Railroad Company.—To construct a railroad up the Blue Stone river in Summers and Mercer counties, for the development of the minerals.

Buckhannon Mineral Railroad Company.—To construct a railroad from some point on the Baltimore and Ohio Railroad, between Clarksburg and Grafton, to Buckhannon, in Upshur county.

Coal River Railroad Company.—To build a railroad from Saint Albans, in Kanawha county, up Coal river to the juncture of the Marsh and Clear Forks, in Raleigh county, to have a branch running up Little Coal river to Boone Court House. Objects: To develop the mineral and timber resources of Coal river.

Cumberland, Moorefield and Broadway Railroad Company.—To build a railroad from a point in Mineral county opposite Cumberland, to Moorefield, in Hardy county, thence to Petersburg, in Grant county, and thence to the State line near Monterey, in Highland county, Virginia.

Gauley River Railroad Company.—To build a railroad from the mouth to the head of Gauley river, passing through Fayette, Nicholas, and Webster, into Pocahontas. Objects: To develop the mineral and timber resources of Gauley river.

Guyandotte Railroad Company.—to build a railroad from the Chesapeake and Ohio Railroad, at Huntington, to Cabell Court House (Barboursville), and thence on up the Guyandotte river into Logan county. Objects: To develope the mineral and timber resources of the Guyandotte river.

Guyandotte and Ohio River Railroad, and Mineral Company.—To build a railroad from some point in Logan county, on Guyandotte river, above Dusenbury Mill, to the Ohio river, between the mouths of Four Pole and Seven Mile creeks. Objects: The same as the last.

Hartford, Mason and Clifton Railroad.—To extend along the Ohio river, in Mason county, to connect the three towns named in the title.

Iron Valley and Pennsylvania Line Railroad Company.—To build a railroad from where Big Sandy creek crosses the Pennsylvania line, via Brandonville, Bruceton Mills, Muddy Creek Furnace, valley of Green's Run, and Martin Iron Works, to a point on the Baltimore and Ohio Railroad. Altogether in Preston county.

Mud River Railroad Company.—To a build a railroad from Milton Station on the Chesapeake and Ohio Railroad, in Cabell county, up Mud river to the mouth of Upton creek, in Lincoln county, and thence crossing to Big Ugly creek, and down that stream to the Guyandotte river, in Logan county. Objects: To develop the mineral and timber resources along its line.

New River Railroad, Mining and Manufacturing Company.—To build a railroad from the Chesapeake and Ohio Railroad, at the mouth of Greenbrier river, up New river to the State line.

North Branch Railroad Company.—To build a railroad from a point on the Baltimore and Ohio Railroad, between Piedmont and Bloomington Ridge, south to a point on the Chesapeake and Ohio Railroad.

Northern and Southern West Virginia Railroad Company.—To build a railroad from the Pennsylvania line, in Monongalia county, via Morgantown, Fairmont, Clarksburg, Weston, and Charleston, to some point on the Kentucky line, in Wayne county. This is a most important line, being, as its name implies, a north and south one, and passing through the center of the State, developing enormous mineral and timber interests throughout its whole route.

Ohio River and Wayne County Mineral Railroad Company.—To build a railroad from any point on the Ohio river, in Wayne county, to the mineral lands in Wayne and Lincoln counties.

Paint Creek Railroad Company.—To build a railroad from the C. & O. R. R. at the mouth of Paint creek, up that stream, in Kanawha and Fayette counties. Objects: To develop the coal interests of Paint creek.

Pittsburgh, Wheeling and Kentucky Railroad.—To connect with the Pittsburgh, Cincinnati and St. Louis railroad, at Holliday's Cove, in Hancock county, and thence to pass down the Ohio river to Wheeling, and thence on to the Kentucky line, ultimately to connect with the Texas Pacific railroad. This is another very important north and south line, as it would develop all the Ohio river counties. The road bed is already graded as far south as Wheeling.

Potomac and Ohio Railroad Company.—To build a railroad from near Harper's Ferry, in Jefferson county, to the Ohio river, via the SouthBranch Valley, in Hampshire, Hardy and Grant counties.

Ripley and Ohio Narrow Gauge Railroad Company.—To build a railroad in Jackson county, from Ripley, down Mill creek to the Ohio.

Steer Creek Valley and Elk River Railroad Company.—To build a railroad from the mouth of Steer creek, in Calhoun county, to some point on Elk river, in Braxton county, between Little Otter and Duck creeks.

Shenandoah and Ohio Railroad Company.—To build a railroad from the Virginia line, in Pendleton county, on the east, to

Parkersburg, on the Ohio river, on the west. This will traverse the whole State through a most valuable mineral country.

South Branch Railroad Company.—To build a railroad in Hampshire county, from Romney to the Baltimore & Ohio Railroad. This is partially built.

Tug River Railroad Company.—To build a railroad from the Ohio river, up Big Sandy river and Tug Fork thereof, into Logan county, to a point opposite Lonsville, in Pike county, Kentucky. Object: to develop the mineral and timber resources of Big Sandy river.

Union and Greenbrier River Turnpike and Railroad Company.—To build a railroad from Union, in Monroe county, to some point on the C. & O. Railroad, on Greenbrier river.

Washington and Ohio Railroad Company.—This is a very important projected east and west line in the State, as it passes through the rich coal, iron, timber and agricultural region lying between the Baltimore & Ohio Railroad on the north, and the C. & O. Railroad on the south. It begins at Alexandria, in Virginia, on the Potomac, and the first 51¾ miles are completed. It will pass through Winchester, and enter West Virginia in Hampshire county, and thence, according to the route laid down on the map of West Virginia, will run through Hardy, Grant, Tucker, Randolph, Upshur, Lewis, Gilmer, Calhoun, Roane, Jackson, and Mason counties, to the Ohio river, at Point Pleasant.

West Virginia Railroad Company.—Beginning at or near the mouth of the Big Sandy river, in Wayne county, their railroad runs thence in an easterly direction to the Kanawha river, near St. Albans, in Kanawha county, thence to Charleston, at the mouth of Elk river, thence up that stream for 150 miles, thence northeasterly to the South Branch of the Potomac, and thence down the same to its mouth, passing through the counties of Wayne, Cabell, Putnam, Kanawha, Clay, Braxton, Webster, Randolph, Pendleton, Grant, Hardy, Hampshire and Morgan.

West Virginia Central Railroad Company.—From Charleston, their railroad runs up the Kanawha, thence up Gauley to its head, ad thence through Pocahontas county to Harrisonburg, in Virginia, passing through the counties of Kanawha, Fayette, Nicholas, Webster, and Pocahontas.

West Fork and Weston Railroad Company.—Their railroad runs from Weston, in Lewis county, to Clarksburg, in Harrison county.

West Virginia Division of the People's Freight Railroad Company.—Their railroad runs from the Ohio river, between Short and Buffalo creeks to where the State line crosses the latter, in Brooke county.

RIVERS.

The Ohio River forms the western boundary of the State for some 300 miles, and washes the counties of Hancock, Brooke, Ohio, Marshall, Wetzel, Tyler, Pleasants, Wood, Jackson, Mason, Cabell, and Wayne. Daily, weekly and tri-weekly steamers from Wheeling to Marietta, Parkersburg and Cincinnati, and mail boats from Parkersburg to Charleston, on the Kanawha, keep up constant communication between all the river landings in West Virginia, and the great markets in the adjoining States. There are also daily lines connecting with the C. & O. R. R., from Huntington to Cincinnati, and regular lines ply from Pittsburgh to Cincinnati, stopping at all West Virginia landings.

It is open to navigation, with but rare exceptions from ice and low water, all the year round.

Great Kanawha River—Is navigable all the year round, except in exceptional cases, when navigation is impeded by ice, from the Ohio to Brownstown, a distance of 70 miles. In a good stage of water we can go up to Loup creek, 22 miles higher. In low water only the smaller classes of boats can run. In order to give the enormous mineral interests of this stream, a free exit to the Ohio all the year, the United States Government is now locking and damming it so that 6 feet of water can always be expected. From Malden, 6 miles above Charleston, there is a weekly line of boats to Cincinnati, and a daily line to Gallipolis, on the Ohio, and tri-weekly connections with Parkersburg and Cincinnati packets.

Little Kanawha River—Is locked and dammed to Elizabeth, in Wirt county, and on good water steamboats pass up daily to Burning Springs, 38 miles from Parkersburg, on the Ohio river, and even to Grantsville, Calhoun county. The work is done by the Little Kanawha Navigation Company, and will tend much to foster the rich timber and oil resources, etc., of this important portion of our State.

The Mononghelia River, in Monongalia county, is navigable on good water to Morgantown, and in exceptional cases steamers have gone as far up as Fairmont, in Marion county. The United States Government are now locking and damming this stream as far as Morgantown, and steps are being taken for an appropriation to carry the work on to Fairmont, so as to give the important coal interests of Marion and southern Monongalia a cheap water exit to the western markets.

Big Coal River—In Kanawha and Boone counties, is improved by locks and dams by the Coal River Navigation Company to the Peytona Mines, 35 miles above its mouth. Many years ago Little Coal river, a branch of Big Coal, was locked and dammed for the first few miles for the accommodation of the Marae Mining Company, but the works have now gone to ruin, owing to the suspension of the mines. This stream could be improved as high as Boone court-house, which is some 40 miles from the Kanawha.

Big Sandy River—Which divides West Virginia from Kentucky, is usually navigable to Louisa, and in good water many miles above.

The Chesapeake & Ohio Canal.—Though this is nowhere within the borders of the State, yet, as it is largely used by the citizens of the eastern counties, it may be looked upon as one of the transportation lines of West Virginia. It extends from Cumberland to Georgetown, and follows the West Virginia line, on the opposite side of the Potomac river, from the first named place to Harper's Ferry, a distance of over 100 miles. The counties that are opposite to it are Mineral, Hampshire, Morgan, Berkely, and Jefferson. Before the completion of the Balt. & Ohio R. R., Cumberland was the great connecting point for all goods from the western country to the eastern markets and *vice versa*.

The following is a list of the other streams that have contemplated improvements, as shown by the charters to navigation companies.

Greenbrier River.—The St. Lawrence Boom and Manufacturing Company, whose boom and saw mills are at Ronceverte, Greenbrier county, have a charter to improve the navigation of this stream. The work so far done has been to remove the obstructions to the lumber business, so that logs can come down freely.

New River.—The Greenbrier, New, and Kanawha rivers, is the intended route for the James River and Kanawha Canal from Richmond, Va., to the Ohio river. The gap still left for completion, between this last point and Buchanan, on the James river in Virginia, is 207 miles. As regards its chances for completion, the following letter from Commodore M. F. Maury, who will readily be admitted as an authority of the highest standing, is very interesting.

VIRGINIA MILITARY INSTITUTE
LEXINGTON, 6th July, 1872.

COL. R. L. MAURY,

MY DEAR SIR:—You ask my opinion as to "the probabilities of completing the James River and Kanawha Canal." I think them not only reasonable but proximate, and any one who will make himself acquainted with that work, who will consider the rapidly increasing population and production, the growing wealth and political power of the West, and who will then consider what has been done with regard to it, will be very apt to come to a like conclusion.

That work was commenced more than a generation ago by the State of Virginia. After reaching the eastern base of the Allegheny mountains, the work, owing to difficulties of various sorts. and the absence of appropriations and the exigencies of war amongst them, was suspended.

During this long suspension, the public mind was withdrawn from this canal and given to things of more absorbing interest. But that attention was recalled to it by "*Report No.* 1. *Physical Survey of Virginia.*" * * * * *

Look at the map and you will see that Virginia is as the keystone to the arch of States that border on the Atlantic Ocean. She has the best harbor of the coast, is midway between the Northern and Southern extremes, and offers the shortest and best passage that can be found for commerce between the Atlantic seabord and the chief centres of the Mississippi Valley, such as Cincinnati, Louisville, St. Louis, St. Paul, and even Chicago, on the lakes; for, if you will take the the trouble to measure, you will see that by opening these routes, they will bring the Capes of Virginia and the sea, nearer to Chicago than Sandy Hook now is.

The Government in Washington, impresssd with these facts, sent out their corps of engineers to examine the ground and see if a practicable route for the canal can be found, and they have found it, for it was well known to exist. And in anticipation of this canal, Congress and the city of Richmond, as if to prepare for it have moved in the matter and are now spending large sums of money upon the improvement of James River. They aim ultimately to give this river 18 feet of water from the city to the sea, and by so doing to bring the seaport of the great West 100 miles up into the interior; and then by opening docks for its shipping, they expect to establish that port at Richmond. * * * *

For my part, content to wait and watch, I look upon a canal from the James river at Richmond to the "fairway" of the Kanawha River, as a thing that *must* be. There is no event of the future that falls not in the "order of nature." but which depends upon the accidents of time and circumstances, the coming of which I regard as more certain than the completion, sooner or later, of this canal. It is a work of transcendent importance and must be built.

Your truly,

M. F. MAURY.

Gauley River—In 1872 a charter was granted the Gauley River Improvement Manufacturing, Mining and Lumber Co. giving it the exclusive privilege of improving the river by removing obstructions to the navigation, and by constructing dams by cutting a canal or by sluices. So far the only work done has been to improve the navigation so that logs can come down freely from Peters creek, which is some 20 miles above the Kanawha.

Elk River.—The Elk River Navigation Company have put in one dam above Charleston, and the stream has been so improved that on a good stage of water a small steamboat can go up 70 miles to the furnace of the Elk River Iron and Coal Company. In this distance, according to the survey of the Northern and Southern West Virginia railroad, the fall of the River is 206 feet.

Guyandotte River.—Improvements were in progress before the war and dams built for some distance up, but neglected since, and finally destroyed.

Twelve Pole River.—A charter has been granted to the Twelve Pole River Mining and Navigation Company, an association "formed for the purpose of improving the navigation of Twelve Pole river and its tributaries by slack water dams and otherwise, and of mining and shipping coal and other products therefrom."

Steer Creek.—A charter has been granted to the Steer Creek Lumber, Boom and Navigation Company to improve the waters of that stream in Calhoun and Gilmer counties. Object: To develop the timber resources.

Middle Island Creek.—A charter was granted to the Middle Island Navigation Company, to improve the stream from its mouth throughout so much of its course as lies in Tyler and Pleasants counties.

Fishing Creek.—A branch of the Ohio river, in Wetzel county. Navigation to be improved by the Fishing Creek Lumber and Boom Company. Object: To develop the timber resources.

North Branch of the Potomac River.—A charter to the North Branch Lumber and Boom Company, to improve the navigation of Stony river and the North Branch to Cumberland. Object: Lumber shipping.

Shenandoah River.—In Jefferson county. The title of the improvement is the Shenandoah Navigation Company; to improve the navigation of the stream.

CHAPTER XVI.

EDUCATIONAL INTERESTS.

BY M. F. MAURY.

For much of the information in the following paper, I am indebted to a manuscript on this subject by Dr. J. G. Blair, Principal of the Branch of the State Normal School, at Fairmont.

FREE SCHOOLS.

The constitution of West Virginia requires the Legislature to provide by general law for a *thorough and efficient* system of Free Schools. To secure this end, "the existing permanent and invested school fund, and all moneys accruing to this State from forfeited, delinquent, waste, and unappropriated lands; from lands hitherto sold for taxes and purchased by the State of Virginia, if hereafter redeemed or sold to others than this State; all grants, bequests, or devises that may be made to this State for educational purposes; the State's just share of the literary fund of Virginia, whether paid over or otherwise liquidated; any sums of money, stocks or property which this State shall have a right to claim from the State of Virginia for educational purposes; the proceeds of the estates of persons who die without leaving a will or heir, and of all escheated lands; the proceeds of all taxes that may be levied on any corporation; all moneys that may be paid for exemption from military duty, and such sums as may be appropriated from time to time by the Legislature, shall be set apart as a school fund, and invested under such regulations as may be prescribed by law in the interest bearing securities of the United States, and of this State, or in such other solvent interest bearing securities as may be approved by the Governor, Superintendent of Free Schools, Auditor and Treasurer," who are constituted, "the Board of the School Fund, to manage the same under such regulations as may be prescribed by law, and the interest thereof shall be annually applied to the support of free schools throughout the State, and to no other purpose whatever. * * Any portion of said interest, remaining unexpended at the close of the fiscal year, shall be added to, and remain part of the capital of the school fund." The Legislature is required "to foster and encourage moral, intellectual, scientific and agricultural improvement, and when it may be practicable, to make suitable provision for the blind, mute, and insane, and organize such institutions of learning as the best interests of general education in the State may demand."

Under the Constitution of 1863, the Legislature put into efficient operation the Free School system of the State. The popular school law then adopted still retains its essential features, having only been changed in expedients, to give the schools greater advantages. This law, as re-enacted by the Legislature in 1873, compares favorably with the most liberal school legislation of other States.

For school purposes, each county is divided into districts (corresponding to townships in other States), and each of these into sub-districts. Each district is controlled by a "Board of Education," consisting of a President, and two Commissioners, and each sub-district, is under the management of one "Trustee." The officers are chosen by the electors of the district every two years.

In addition to the School Fund already alluded to, the School Law says: "For the support of the Primary Free Schools of their district, and in each independent school district, the Board of Education thereof shall annually levy by the authority of the people, such a tax on the property taxable in the district, as will, with the money received from the State for the support of Free Schools, be sufficient to keep such schools in operation at least four months in the year; provided, the said tax in any year shall not exceed the amount of 50 cents on every 100 dollars valuation." (School Laws, Sec 40.) The proceeds of this tax, together with the distributable State School Fund, constitute the "Teacher's Fund," which is to be used only in paying teachers' salaries.

Should any Board of Education fail to make this levy, after the people have voted to do so, the law requires that the county court shall compel them to do so, and every district rejecting said levy by a majority vote, shall not receive its pro rata of the State funds.

The School Law (Sec. 60) provides: "That for the support of Free Schools, there shall be a State tax, levied annually, of 10 cents on the 100 dollars valuation of all real and personal property of the State." This amount, combined with the interest accruing on the invested fund, makes up the annual appropriations by the State in aid of the "Teachers' Fund."

Section 38 of the School Law says: "To provide school houses and grounds, furniture, fixtures and appendages, and to keep the same in good order and repair, and to supply fuel and other things needed for comfort and convenience, the Board of Education shall annually levy a tax on the taxable property of each district, not to exceed in any single year 40 cents on the 100 dollars, valuation thereof, according to the latest assessment of the same for State and county taxation." This tax, together with the bequests and other revenues that may be for the purpose, constitute a "Building Fund," which is entirely distinct from the "Teachers' Fund."

The report for 1875 of the State Superintendent of Free Schools shows that the Permanent School Fund amounts to \$325,243 $\frac{34}{100}$; the Current Teachers' Fund to \$541,358 $\frac{83}{100}$; the Current Building Fund to \$255,233 $\frac{29}{100}$; and the aggregate amount expended for school purposes for that year to \$796,-592 $\frac{12}{100}$.

The school year begins on the 1st of September, and the District Boards hold their first meeting for this year on the 1st Monday of September, when they have to determine the number of months the schools shall be taught in each sub-district, the number of teachers to be employed, andtheir wages, which latter are graded according to the individual merits of the teachers, as shown by the certificates granted them by the County Board of Examiners. The trustee in each sub-district employs the teacher. He has discretionary power in minor matters relating to the comfort, order and success of the school.

At the time of electing the Trustees and District Boards, the people of each county elect a County Superintendent of Free Schools, who shall be, says the law: "a person of temperate habits, of literary acquirements, and of skill and experience in the art of teaching." This officer is charged with grave responsibilities, and by his efficiency contributes largely to school success. It is his duty to visit the schools of his county each year, to advise and direct the teachers in their work, to see that the school law is executed by all subordinate officers, to look after school finances, to act as Chairman of the County Board of Examiners, to examine into the condition of school-houses and property, to encourage and to aid in the organization of County Institutes, and, if need be, in the formation of Union Institutes between two or more counties, to distribute official blanks or papers relative to school work, and annually to report the exact condition of the schools in his district to the State Superintendent.

Two experienced teachers, appointed by the Presidents of the District Boards of each county, at a meeting held for that purpose in August of every year, constitute, with the County Superintendent, a County Examining Board," which issues teachers' licenses. These are granted for a period of not more than one year, and are of five grades, No. 1 being the highest. The examination fee is one dollar.

The Constitution provides for a State Superintendent of Free Schools, who is the highest officer known in the school law, and is elected by the people of the-State at large. His term of office is four years. The law provides that he shall be "of good moral character, of temperate habits, of literary acquirements, and skill, and experience in the art of teaching." His salary comes out of the general school fund. He has complete charge of all State educational matters, sees that the school funds are properly distributed, has to do everything that will lend energy and efficiency to his department at large, and makes an annual report to the Governor, as to the condition of the free schools of the State and their financial condition, with such suggestions for improvements in any of the departments, as may seem to him to concern their general welfare. This report is communicated by the Governor to the session of the Legislature at each biennial session thereafter.

The Code of West Virginia declares that "all teachers, Boards of Education, and all other school officers, are charged with the duty of providing that moral training for the youth of the State, which will contribute to securing good behavior and manners, and furnishing the State with exemplary citizens," (Sec. 32, chap. 123), and provides for three grades of of schools, viz.: Primary, Graded, and High.

The present free school system was inaugurated in the entire State in 1865, and speedily put into operation, though several counties adopted a similar system at a much earlier date.

In no State in the Union has the educational system been more cordially adopted, or met with less opposition, and the spirit of each Legislature has been in unison with the Constitution, in cherishing the State system of public instruction. From the first the schools have been of the most approved form that the funds would sanction. In 1865 there were 133 houses for free schools; in 1875, 2,959. The value of school property in 1865 was $52,856, while in 1875, it was $1,605,627. In 1875 the number of free schools, both high and sub-district, taught, was 3,231. In 1865 there were 387 teachers, of both sexes, engaged in teaching in the free schools, while in 1875, there were 3,461, which gives one teacher for about every 144 of our citizens. In Illinois, one of the first free school States of the country, the ratio is as 1 to 141.

The Free School work in West Virginia is shown with some degree of accuracy by the following official statistics, for the year beginning 1st September, from the office of the State Superintendent :

COUNTY.	Amount apportioned for the School year, 1874-5.	Enumeration of Youth for the School year, 1874-5, reported for apportionm't	Teachers' Certificates Granted.	COUNTY.	Amount apportioned for the School year, 1874-5.	Enumeration of Youth for the School year, 1874-5, reported for apportionm't	Teachers' Certificates Granted.
Barbour......	$ 4,706.74	3,942	75	Br't forward	....	....	......
Berkeley	5,892.39	4,935	81	Mineral.	$ 2,312 77	1,937	31
Boone..	2,078.75	1,741	32	Monongalia	5,907.91	4,948	46
Braxton......	3,420 81	2,865	70	Monroe......	3,884,08	3,253	67
Brooke.......	2,315.16	1,939	49	Morgan.......	1,796.97	1,505	29
Cabell	4,144.37	3,471	58	Nicholas..	2,350.98	1,969	44
Calhoun	1 732.49	1,451	24	Ohio..........	2,783.21	2,331	32
Clay,,.........	1,262.08	1,057	21	Pendleton ..	3,020.82	2,530	47
Doddridge...	3,633.34	3,043	69	Pleasants ...	1,798.16	1,506	29
Fayette	3,301.41	2,765	68	Pocahontas.	1,708.61	1,431	26
Gilmer	2,479.93	2,077	41	Preston.......	6,882.21	5,764	100
Grant..	1,905.62	1,596	35	Putnam.	3,806.47	3,188	52
Greenbrier..	4,884.65	4,091	85	Raleigh.......	2,622 02	2,196	54
Hampshire.	3,413.64	2,859	57	Randolph...	2,755.75	2,308	55
Hancock.....	1,993.98	1,670	44	Ritchie	4,481.08	3,753	89
Hardy........	2,390.38	2,002	48	Roane........	3,934.61	3,297	62
Harrison. ...	7,720.40	6,466	112	Summers ...	2,521.72	2,112	51
Jackson	5,475 68	4,586	104	Taylor........	4,152.73	3,478	......
Jefferson ...	5,469.71	4,581	44	Tucker	1,161.76	973	24
Kanawha....	11,052.94	9,260	105	Tyler,.........	4,022.58	3,369	66
Lewis..	4,602.87	3,855	70	Upshur......	3,755.13	3,145	71
Lincoln......	2,765.30	2,316	51	Wayne.......	4,701.97	3,938	62
Logan	2,330.68	1,952	21	Webster......	903.85	757	......
Marion	6.820.12	5,712	87	Wetzel	4,973.01	4,165	78
Marshall.....	7,203.40	6,033	85	Wirt	2,208 90	1,850	29
Mason........	8,183.68	6,854	......	Wood..	9,260.66	7,756	121
McDowell...	1,065.04	892	24	Wyoming...	1,583.24	1,326	26
Mercer	2,490.68	2,086	53	Wheel. City	10,763.91	9,015	73
					$214,791.32	179,897	2,993

During the present year the number of pupils who are studying all the branches of the free school course has been greatly increased. Each year is adding greatly to the elevation of the grades of study.

No text books books are used except those prescribed by the Legislature, which has provided most amply for all subjects taught in the best schools.

NORMAL SCHOOLS.

These were organized at an early period in the school work of West Virginia, to supply trained teachers for the rural districts and towns, and are therefore valuable adjuncts of the common school system.

They are under the direction of a Board of Regents, consisting of the Governor, Auditor, Treasurer, and Superintendent of Free Schools of the State, and one member from each Congressional district.

Section 88 of the School Law gives this Board the control of the property and conduct of the schools, and full authority to make such by-laws and regulations for the government of the same, as, in their opinion, will best subserve the purposes of their creation. They appoint the teachers, determine their compensation, prescribe the conditions upon which students shall be admitted, and the text books and general course of study, regulate the conditions of graduation, and prepare and confer normal diplomas, which, by a provision of law, are accepted throughout the State as teachers' certificates, and empower Boards of Education to employ such graduates as free school teachers, without further examination by County Boards. The object of this regulation was to encourage teachers to seek those higher qualifications for their work, which the Normal schools were designed to bestow.

In fulfilment of their duties the Board of Regents, on the 8th July, 1873, adopted the following regulations for the admission of pupils to these institutions:

The number of students which each county of the State shall be entitled to send to the Normal Department in the State Normal school and its branches, free of charge, for tuition, shall be as follows:

Barbour	9	Hancock	4	Monongalia	12	Roane	7
Berkeley	13	Hardy	5	Monroe	9	Summers	4
Boone	4	Harrison	15	Morgan	4	Taylor	8
Braxton	6	Jackson	9	McDowell	2	Tucker	2
Brooke	5	Jefferson	12	Nicholas	4	Tyler	7
Cabell	10	Kanawha	20	Ohio	26	Upshur	7
Calhoun	3	Lewis	9	Pendleton	6	Wayne	7
Clay	2	Lincoln	5	Pleasants	3	Webster	2
Doddriuge	6	Logan	5	Pocahontas	4	Wetzel	8
Fayette	6	Marion	13	Preston	13	Wirt	4
Gilmer	4	Marshall	13	Putnam	7	Wood	17
Grant	4	Mason	14	Raleigh	3	Wyoming	3
Greenbrier	9	Mercer	6	Randolph	5		
Hampshire	7	Mineral	6	Ritchie	8		

Applications for admission to the Normal Department of the State Normal School and its Branches, are made to the Superintendent of Free Schools of the county in which the applicant resides.

Male pupils must not be less than 15, and females not less than 13 years of age. No applicants can be selected unless they are of good moral character and found, upon examination, to be entitled to a No. 4 Teacher's certificate.

The county Superintendent shall require from each selected applicant, a written declaration, that they propose to become teachers in the State Free Schools and that they will, on the conpletion of their studies in the Normal School, teach for one year in the Free Schools, or upon failure to do so, to pay to the school, the usual amount of fees charged to other students. The Normal School, or any of its Branches, may admit paying students from any State (preference being given to those from West Virginia) whether they desire to become teachers or not. State students of any one of the Normal Schools may be transferred to another of said schools, only upon procuring a certificate of good deportment from the Principal of the school he has been attending or by permission of the Board of Regents, and the time he has so attended, shall be credited to him in course, by the Principal of the school to which he is transferred.

To all persons appointed in accordance with the foregoing provisions, tuition is free and students not qualified to enter the Junior class of the Normal course, may, if of proper age and otherwise qualified, receive one years preparatory instruction in the school.

The Normal course consists of two years—the Junior and the Senior.

The Junior Normal course shall embrace Reading, Spelling, Writing, Arithmetic, Geography, Algebra (commenced), English Grammar, Composition, and History of the United States.

The Senior Normal course shall embrace, Composition, Algebra (continued), Rhetoric, Physical Geography, Mental Science, General History, Geometry, and plain Trigonometry, School Economy, Method of Teaching, and Systematic Classification of pupils.

The Principal and assistants of any of the Normal Schools, are authorized to teach a classical and scientific course in addition to the Normal course; provided, the Normal course shall not be abridged or neglected in any manner, by the teaching of such scientific and classical course.

The rates of tuition for pay scholars are hereby fixed as follows:

For Junior Normal Course per year	$20 00
" Senior " " " "	24.00
Classical department per year	32 00

One-half of which shall be paid on entrance, and the residue, when half the year has elapsed.

The Board of Regents direct that the method of discipline in the Normal Schools shall be:

1st. Private admonition by the Instructor.

2d. Admonition by the Faculty.

3d. Admonition before the whole school.

4th. Suspension.

5th. Dismissal.

Striking in anger, any pupil or teacher, or the commission of any felony, is to be followed by expulsion, and any violation of the law of the State, is to be followed by suspension or expulsion, as the Executive Committee may direct.

The following Normal Schools have been provided for. A further increase in their number is prohibited by the Constitution, which says that "no appropriation shall hereafter be made to any State Normal School or branch thereof, except to those already established, or in operation, or now chartered."

WEST VIRGINIA STATE NORMAL SCHOOL, or, Marshall College. Has an admirable location on the Ohio, at Huntington, in Cabell county. As "Marshall Academy," it was aschool of high rank, before it was transferred to the State. On 27th February, 1867, an act of the Legislature established it a State Normal School. The main building of the college is 70 by 40 feet, with a wing 100 by 30 feet, both bebeing three stories high, and having accommodations for 100 boarders—60 male and 40 female. The institution has a small cabinet of minerals, a fair amount of chemical and philosophical apparatus, and a library—of much use to the students—of about 1,000 volumes of standard works. About 100 of its pupils are now teaching in the Free Schools. From 1870 to 1875, both inclusive, 47 students have graduated from the Normal School Department.

Fairmont Branch of the State Normal School, is situated at Fairmont, in Marion county. On the 8th March, 1868, the State purchased this property, consisting of a brick building 60 by 40 feet, two stories high, and created it a branch State Normal School. During the year, 1872–3, a substantial brick edifice three stories high, and 70 by 38 feet, was added to the former building, thus furnishing ample accommodation for 300 students. Nearly all the teachers who have graduated from this school, have been continuously engaged in teaching, and during the present year, about 160 of its pupils have been employed in the Free Schools. From 1872 to 1875, both inclusive, the number of graduates was 82. During the year, 1874-5, the number of pupils was 152.

Shepherd's College and Branch State Normal School, located at Shepherdstown, Jefferson county, has been in operation as a Normal School, since 8th September, 1873. The buildings are commodious and well arranged for school purposes. The main building is of brick, two stories high. To this are added two wings. The building occupies an eminence in the center of the town, and is surrounded by extensive and beautiful grounds. The property is valued at $40,000. The graduates of this school number 50, of which more than half, are now teaching in the State. The number of pupils in attendance the present year, is 135, of which 62 are in the Senior class.

Glenville Branch Normal School, located at Glenville, Gilmer county, has been conducted with success since its organization in March, 1873. The enrollment of pupils in 1875, was 105. The graduates have been 14 in all. This school is of great value to the State, as it is located in an interior county, where its educational influence is much appreciated.

The Branch Normal School at West Liberty, Ohio county, has been in operation since 1870. The buildings are very convenient for school purposes, and ample to accommodate from 100 to 150 pupils. The school began with 30 pupils, and at the end of 3 years had 110. Its graduates have nearly all become teachers in the State.

The Branch Normal School at Concord, in Mercer county, has been in operation only a short time, and has turned out no graduates.

WEST VIRGINIA UNIVERSITY.

This was designed to stand at the head of the literary institions of the State, and was located by the Legislature at Morgantown, in Monongalia county. The buildings are new, tasteful, spacious and well adapted to their purpose, consisting of a University Hall, an Armory, and new Central Hall. The surroundings are favorable for student life.

The origin of this institution began in the grant of lands, made several years ago, by the United States to most of the States of the Union, for the purpose of establishing agricultural colleges. The proceeds of the land script thus given to West Virginia were about $90,000. To this the State has since added about $20,000, thus furnishing the school a permanent fund of $110,000, the income from which goes to meet the current expenses of the college. In addition to this fund the Legislature has been accustomed to make special appropriation for its current expenses.

From the outset, the plan and scope of the college was made broad and liberal, assuming the features of a university. The departments of instruction embrace the literary, scientific, practical and experimental, agricultural and military. The United States furnishes arms and equipments, and also details an officer from the regular officer army to teach military science, &c.

The various departments, as at present arranged, are as follows:

1st. Philosophy and English Literature.

2d. Astronomy and Physics.

3d. Mathematics and Engineering.

4th. Military Science and Tactics.

5th. Modern Languages and Literature.

6th. History, Political Economy, and Belles Lettres.

7th. Chemistry, Natural History, and Agriculture.

The University is in possession of the apparatus, requisite for a thorough illustration of Chemistry and Physics, and its Museum contains extensive mineralogical, geological and conchological cabinets, together with many specimens in other departments of Natural History. Its laboratory of Practical Chemistry is in operation, the instruction at present being devoted chiefly to analysis, with its application to agriculture. Its library embraces about 4,000 volumes, which include not only valuable books of reference, but also standard works in the various departments of History, Biography, Theology, Agriculture, Arts, Sciences and General Literature.

In 1874-5 there were 150 students enrolled. This includes the preparatory class.

This institution is under the control of a Board of nine Regents, one from each judicial district of the State, who are appointed by the Board o the School Fund. The law provides that four cadets from each judicial district of the State may be appointed to the Military Department. These enjoy all the privileges of the college, have all their books furnished them, and are exempt from any charges for tuition.

STATE COLORED SCHOOLS.

When the number of colored youth in any sub-district of a county exceeds 25, the law requires the Trustee to provide a school for the class, or two or more sub-districts may unite in maintaining such a school. Accordingly there are well arranged, and conducted schools, in the cities of Wheeling, Parkersburg, Charleston, and Martinsburg, for this portion of the population of the State.

PRIVATE SCHOOLS.

In addition to the foregoing schools belonging to, and provided for, by the State, the youth of West Virginia have educational advantages in many private and denominational institutions, among which may be mentioned the following, as among the most conspicuous:

Bethany College, located at Bethany, in Brooke county, and under the control of the Christian Church, was organized by the renowned Rev. Alex. Campbell. It is a literary college of high grade, and offers a liberal training to its pupils. Its buildings and grounds are fine and ample; its library and apparatus extensive, and its students have become distinguished educators in this and other States.

Fleming College, at Flemington, Taylor county, was established as a "Free Will Baptist" College, in 1868. The course of study is largely of a normal character. During 1875, there were 70 pupils in attendance.

Stover College chartered in 1868, received its name from the late John Stover, of Maine, who gave $10,000 towards its endowment. It is situated at Harper's Ferry, in Jefferson county. It was the wish of the founder that it should be operated as a seminary and normal school, until its endowment should justify the establishment of a college course. Its catalogue says that a cardinal feature in its administration, is that "students shall be admitted without distinction, on account of race, color, sex or religious preferences." It is, however, only attended by colored pupils. Its buildings furnish a chapel, recitation rooms, library, printing office, reading room, and boarding hall for 70 male students, and the effort now is to erect a similar hall for girls. This has been begun, but is not completed. The school has an annual course of lectures on scientific, and other topics, and an excellent feature in its administration is, that instruction is given in *printing and industrial pursuits*. The course of study is academic and normal. The Board of Instruction consists of a principal and nine assistants. The aggregate number of pupils for the year ending June 1875, was 285.

Wheeling Female College, chartered in 1849, has been in excellent reputation for many years, and is the property of a joint stock company. The building occupies a commanding position in the centre of Wheeling, is well furnished, and can accommodate a large number of boarding pupils. At present it has an enrollment of 100 pupils, a large number of whom reside in Wheeling.

The Doddridge Music and Art School, located on 12th street, in Wheeling, was established in 1874. Instruction is given in oil painting, drawing and music. Number of pupils the present year, 69.

Morgantown Female Seminary, in Monongalia county, was organized in 1852, and has been in successful operation since that time, enjoying an excellent reputation. The want of statistics showing the extent of its work, is much to be regretted.

St. Albans Seminary, in Kanawha county, was begun a few years ago, under the care of the Baptist church, and has an excellent reputation. There is also an academy at French creek, in Upshur county. Also, a High School, at Buckhannon, in Upshur county, which bids fair to become very useful in the State.

St. Joseph's Academy, in Wheeling was opened 1st of September 1865, by the "Sisters of St. Joseph, for girls and boys under 12 years old. The present attendance is 115 of the former and 57 of the latter. German is taught gratis to children of German parentage. These Sisters also conduct *St. Joseph's Parish School* with 240 pupils; *St. Alphonsus* (German) with 300 pupils, and a *Parish and Orphan Asylum School*, with 260 pupils. Also in Grafton, Taylor county, they teach a parish school with 165 pupils; an academy at Clarksburg, Harrison county, with 122 pupils, and one at Charleston, Kanawha, with 88 pupils. Total number of pupils 1347. Number of teachers, including those engaged solely in teaching music and the languages, 46 In these schools the boys and girls are taught separately.

Mount de Chantel.—Near Wheeling, controlled by the "Sisters of the Visitation," has been in operation since 1864, and has done much valuable work. It is to be regretted that statistics showing the extent and progress of this institution, have not been furnished by those in charge.

Commercial Schools.—In Parkersburg, Charleston and Wheeling, business colleges have been organized, and are in successful operation. As a school of the highest type of its class in the State, may be named the National Business College in Wheeling. It is designed for the practical education of ladies, young men, and boys, in business affairs. It embraces instruction in all departments of Book-keeping, Penmanship, Arithmetic, Spelling, Commercial Law, Commercial Correspondence, Lectures and Practical Exercises.

PUBLIC SCHOOLS OF WHEELING.

Although the Free Schools of the State have been generally mentioned, yet those of Wheeling are so important that they merit a special notice.

The Free School system of this city was organized in 1849—many years before the formation of the State of West Virginia—and under it, they have been successfully conducted ever since, though the plans have been modified from time to time to meet the growth of the city, and the increasing needs of the youth. These schools are governed by a "Board of Education," consisting of 21 commissioners, elected to represent the eight wards of the city. There are seven large admirably constructed buildings, and one smaller one, suitably furnished for school purposes, and all conveniently located. Every school is under the charge of a Principal, assisted by teachers who each take charge of a room and class of pupils. In the highest grade the Principal gives instruction in Mathematics and various Physical Sciences. German is taught in all the grades, to such pupils as desire to study this language.

Colored Schools.—In accordance with the school law, before alluded to, a school for the colored youth of Wheeling was established in 1866. Since that date it has been taught 10 months in the year, under the control of Board of Education. It has a principal and one assitant, with an average daily attendance of 60 pupils. The building provides comfortable and ample room for the scholars.

The number of pupils in the Wheeling Public Schools in January, 1876, was 3,308. These were under the care of one Superintendent, one Secretary, nine Principals, and seventy-seven assistants.

TEACHERS' NORMAL INSTITUTES.

The school law of West Virginia makes it the duty of the State Superintendent of Schools, " to endeavor to render available to the people of the State, all such improvements in the system of Free Schools, and the methods of instruction, as may have been tested and proved by the experience of other communities." It enjoins upon the County School Superintendents "to encourage the formation of County Institutes, and to give such advice and instruction in regard to their management, as in his judgment may contribute to their greater efficiency." In obedience to this spirit, the State Teachers' Association was organized, soon after the establishment of the Free School system, and holds its meeting annually. The leading teachers of the State contribute liberally to the welfare and interest of these gatherings.

LITERARY CONTRIBUTIONS TO EDUCATION.

West Virginia teachers have not hitherto contributed largely to the general fund of text-books, &c., in circulation, but this is by no means an indication of their incompetency in this direction. Of those works that now exist, the following should be mentioned:

The Geography of West Virginia, by Miss A. C. Knote, embracing in simple and clear form, a complete view of the State, is especially adapted to use in the Primary Schools, and has been made one of the text books of our Free School system.

West Virginia Educational Monthly, a pamphlet of about 50 pages, is published in Parkersburg. Concerning it the following notice is clipped from the Wheeling *Register*, of the 22d of March, 1876: "This magazine of popular education and general literary intelligence, has been published in the interests of the educational work of the Free Schools, and literary institutions of West Virginia, for almost four years. During this time the 'Monthly' has done a good work for education in the State, by advocating and illustrating the best methods of instruction, by urging teachers to a higher degree of attainment, by stimulating them to study for the sake of their own culture, as well as for the benefit of their pupils, and by seeking to encourage every influence for good among the masses of the people. It contains items of intelligence connected with schools throughout the State, and affords to teachers and school officers, a medium for the interchange of ideas concerning the duties of the profession. In this way the 'Monthly' has been of great service in cultivating and developing laborers in our midst."

The Medical Student, a "monthly record of the progress of medicine, surgery, and the allied sciences," is published in Wheeling.

It is a matter of regret that the limits and scope of this volume on the resources of our State, will not permit a more detailed account of the history of the progress of its educational interests, but enough has been said to show that these advantuges are by no means narrow or limited, and it may be added that few States of the Union have made more ample or reliable provisions for popular education, or made schools more fully accessible to all the population.

CHAPTER XVII.

THE DESCRIPTION OF THE INDIVIDUAL COUNTIES.

The data given in the following account of the counties, so far as they relate to the topography, soil, productions, markets, &c., &c., were obtained from the answers to circulars, which, to the number of 4,000, were sent out into the State, and from such other sources as were available. It is to be regretted that the account is not, in all cases, as full and accurate as it might have been made, had the answers to the questions been more complete and satisfactory. The number of Public Schools was obtained from the Report of the Superintendent of Public Schools, for the year 1874, the number of Postoffices from the United States Official Postal Guide for October, 1875. The number of churches and the population were obtained from the United States Census for 1870, and the value of taxable property was gotten from the Auditor's Report for 1874.

BARBOUR COUNTY.

This county is hilly, and the hills in the east rise into the Laurel mountain range. The land is generally good, and a considerable amount of it is in a good state of cultivation. A large amount is in wood still, and the timber is very fine. The soil is mainly clay, or clay loam, which on the hills, is from 4 to 6 inches deep, and on the level lands about 12 inches. Corn, Wheat, Oats, and Rye are the crops best adapted to the soil in this county. The yields are: Corn, 25 to 50 bushels per acre; Wheat, 10 to 15 bushels; Rye, 20 to 25 bushels, and Oats, 30 to 50 bushels. The lower yields are on the hills, and the higher, on the levels and bottoms. No manures are used to produce these yields.

The value of the agricultural land varies from $12 to $40 per acre; of the mineral land, from $15 to $40; of timber land, $5 to $15. The value of the timber is about $1 per tree, standing, and $1 to $1.50 per hundred feet for lumber at the mills.

The principal industries are farming, grazing, and timber getting. The principal exports are cattle, wool, and forest products. The principal market is Grafton for the timber, where it is received and cut. Baltimore is the market for cattle. The minerals are, Coal, in abundance, in the hills and workable; Limestone, in quantities sufficient for building, and agricultural purposes; some Potters' Clay, some Iron. and Sandstone for building. No mines exist, except of coal for local use. Manufactures: One woolen factory, several saw and grist mills, one pottery, worked by Burley, Bennett & Lowry. Principal streams. Tygart's Valley river, navigable for canoes, and used largely in floating logs to Grafton. Improvements completed: Beverly turnpike and dirt roads; in contemplation: W. C. & St. L. Narrow Gauge railroad. Public Schools, 73; Postoffices, 16; Churches, 38. Population, 10,312. Value of taxable property, $2,020,800,98. County seat, Philippi. Newspapers, *Philippi Plaindealer* and *Barbour Jeffersonian*, both weekly, and published at Philippi.

BERKELEY COUNTY.

Berkeley, in the western part, is mountainous and broken, but in the eastern part, is smooth and undulating.

The soils are loams and clay; thinner and less productive in the west, but in the east there is a large amount of highly productive and improved calcareous lands, forming a part of the Great Valley of Virginia. Depth of soil not given, but varying from 4 inches to 2, on the hills, to 12 inches and more on the levels. The grains specially adapted to the lands, are Wheat, Corn, Oats, and Barley. All the cereals do well. Yield of Wheat, on hills, 8 to 10 bushels. On level, limestone lands, 12 to 15 bushels. The yields of the other grains are not reported. No manures are used to produce these yields. Value of land with limestome soil, $20 to $50 per acre. Mineral land, none sold.

Timber land, price according to the amount of wood; prices not reported. Timber, stumpage not reported; lumber at the mill, $1.50 to $2.00 per hundred. The principal industries are stock farming, and grain raising. The principal exports are Wheat, Corn, and Stock. The markets for stock and grain, Baltimore and Martinsburg. The minerals are some Anthracite coal, in the western part of the county, in Third Hill mountain, and its continuations, worked in a small way for local use. Iron Ore, in good quantities, is also found, of excellent quality, and is worked to some extent, and was shipped to Philadelphia. Limestone is abundant, and furnishes fine material for agricultural and building purposes, both when burnt for lime and quarried for building stone. Potter's Clay exists, and is manufactured into crocks, etc., at Martinsburg. Sandstone suitable for building, is also found. Mineral waters, sulphur and chalybeate exist. Manufactures, 4 cigar factories, producing 219,100 cigars; 2 small breweries, making 200 barrels of lager beer; 1 distillery, producing 253,914 gallons of spirits—value, $355,479.60. All these products are for 1875.

One woolen factory, one iron furnace, besides sawmills and other manufacturies, are established at Martinsburg, where the shops of the Baltimore and Ohio Railroad are located. Improvements, canal, turnpikes, Baltimore and Ohio Railroad, Martinsburg and Potomac Railroad; streams, the Potomac river, Opecquan, and Back creeks, are all navigable for good sized boats. Contemplated improvements: A railroad from Martinsburg to Bunker Hill. Schools: Two seminaries, and 53 public schools. Postoffices, 15. Churches, 39. Population, 14,900. Value of taxable property, $6,142,387. County Seat, Martinsburg, which is a wealthy and thriving town of some 3,500 inhabitants, and is situated on the B. & O. R. R. 101 miles from Baltimore. Newspapers, *Martinsburg Independent*, daily and weekly; *Martinsburg Statesman*, weekly, published at Martinsburg.

BOONE COUNTY.

This county, in most part, is very hilly and mountainous, with much of the hilly land too steep for profitable cultivation. Some good bottom land is found on Big and Little Coal rivers. The soil, even when the hills are steep, is usually quite deep and fertile, being on the hills, where they are cultivated, 5 to 6 inches deep, and on the levels, one to several feet. It is mainly a sandy or clay loam. Corn, Oats, Wheat Rye, and Tobacco grow well. The bottoms yield: Corn, 30 to 50 bushels; Wheat, 10 to 12 bushels; Oats, 30 bushels; Potatoes, 50 to 100 bushels. Hillsides: Corn, 25 bushels; Wheat, 12 bushels; Oats, 30 bushels. No manure is used for these yields. Principal industries, cattle raising, farming, lumber getting, and coal mining. Principal exports, cattle, lumber as staves, etc., and timber in Walnut. Poplar, etc., logs and Cannel coal from Peytona. Markets, neighboring counties for youngstock. The lumber goes to Cincinnati; also the Poplar timber. The Walnut timber is sent to New York. Minerals: Coals, Cannel of all kinds, Splint and Common Bituminous. Several seams of each kind of workable size are found in the hills above water level. See general chapter on Coals and Iron. Some little limestone. Excellent sandstone for building is found. Coal is mined extensively at Peytona, and shipped. Saw and grist mills exist; number not reported. Streams: Big and Little Coal rivers. Big Coal is locked and damed up to Peytona, and is navigable to that point, for small steamers and barges. Little Coal is navigable for canoes for some distance up. Improvements, are on Big Coal in the form of locks and dams. It is proposed to lock and dam Little Coal, and to build a railroad up Big Coal to the Forks of Coal, and up Little Coal to Madison. Public schools, 32. Postoffices, 8. Churches, 2. Population, 4,553. Value of taxable property, $595,732.46. County seat, Madison.

BRAXTON COUNTY.

Braxton is a hilly county, with some of the hills quite high, seven mountainous. The county is within the plateau region and hence although the streams are deeply sunken into the urface, and the hills along them are rough and broken, their summits are flat, and there is much rolling, and tolerably smooth surface in the uplands. The soils are red clay, and sandy loams, with a depth of 4 to 6 inches on the hillsides, and 10 to 12 and more, on the levels. Crops well adapted to the county are Corn, Oats, Wheat, and Grass, and Buckwheat. The yields are on the levels, Corn, 40 bushels: Wheat, 10 bushels; Hay two tons; on the hills, Corn, 30 bushels; Wheat 12 bushels; Rye, 20 bushels; Hay 1½ tons; Potatoes, 120 bushels. Value of the lands, agricultural, 5 to 15 dollars per acre; mineral land, 4 to 6 dollars per acre; of timber land, 3 to 5 dollars. Value of the timber; Stumpage, 50 cents; at the mill, 5 cents per cubic foot, or $1.00 per hundred, board measure. Principal industries; Farming, Cattle raising, Lumber getting, Principal exports, Stock and Lumber. Stock is raised and partly fattened, and then sold to parties who fatten farther, and send to eastern markets. The Lumber, goes to Charleston, where it is cut for home consumption, and for shipment to the markets on the Lower Ohio. Mineral: Coals, splint and soft bituminous, in workable seams, in the hills above water level, Iron in workable quantities is found, and worked by the Elk River Iron and Coal Company. Some limestone, and good sandstone for building. Two salt wells and furnaces are at Bull Creek near Sutton on Elk River. Besides the usual country grist and saw mills. the Messrs. Burns & Co., have a large 50 horse power steam saw mill at Lumberport, and the Elk River Iron and Coal Co., have erected a cold blast charcoal furnace, at Strange Creek, which went into blast in 1875. Elk River is the principal stream, and runs north and south 40 miles through the county. It is navigable for batteaux and light crafts 10 months in the year, and with some improvements, would be so for small Steamboats. Rich and Holly Rivers are tributaries of Elk in the county. No public improvements except the Weston and Gauley Bridge Turnpike. Slack water on the Elk is contemplated. Contemplated R. R.: The N. & S. & W. Va. R. R. Steer Creek Valley & Elk River R. R. and the W. Va. R. R. Public Schools 43; Post Offices, 15; Churches, 7; Population 6480. Value of taxable property $1.472,916,45, County seat, Sutton. Newspapers, "The Mountaineer," weekly, at Sutton.

BROOKE COUNTY.

Brooke county is hilly and rolling, the hills being quite high, but smooth, and capable of cultivation to their summits. The soils are clay, and calcareous loams, very fertile, and in a high state of cultivation. They have a depth on the hill sides of from 3 to 6 inches, and on the levels, of from 12 to 18 inches and over. Crops best adapted, are Corn, Oats, Wheat, Barley, Buckwheat, and Grass. Yields, on uplands and lowlands are about the same, viz: Corn, 40 to 60 bushels; Wheat 10 to 15 bushels; Oats, 30 to 45 bushels; Rye, 10 bushels; Grass, 1 to 2 tons. No manures are used for these yields. The farmers of this county, as well as of the adjoining ones of the Pan-Handle, by means of Timothy and Blue Grass, in rotation after grain crops, keep the land in a high state of productiveness. Value of the land, agricultural, from $40 to $100; mineral land, $25 to $100; timber land, $40 to $70 per acre. Principal industries, Farming, Cattle and Sheep raising, and Manufacturing. Principal exports, Sheep, Wool, Cattle and Grain. Markets, Pittsburgh, Wheeling, Baltimore, eastern cities, and points on the river. Minerals, Coal, bituminous. The Pittsburgh seam is above water level, and worked for local use. Some Sandstone, fit for building. Limestone is abundant. There are manufacturies of Mowing Machines, a Woolen Mill, a Paper Mill, one Brewery, making 127 barrels annually. Cigar factories, making 782,000 Cigars. An Iron Foundry, Machine Shops, &c., besides the ordinary Grist and Saw Mills. The Ohio river skirts the county, and is navigable for steamboats. Good roads exist. The West Virginia Division of the People's Freight Railroad is contemplated, and the Pittsburgh, Wheeling and Kentucky Railroad is partly completed. Schools and Colleges, Bethany College, and 27 Public Schools; Post-offices, 5; Churches, 13; Population, 5,464; value of taxable property, $2,739,772 94; County Seat, Wellsburg; Newspapers, *Panhandle News*, and *Wellsburg Herald*, both weekly.

CABELL COUNTY.

Cabell county is hilly, but the hills are low and easily cultivated. Wide flats are found along the Ohio river, and also on Mud river, and some on the lower Guyandotte river. These are all fine lands, with small exceptions. The uplands have generally a productive soil. The soil is clay and clay loam, sometimes quite stiff. The hills have a depth of soil of 4 to 6 inches, and the bottoms and levels a depth of 12 inches to many feet. The grains, &c., which do well are, Corn, Wheat, Oats, Tobacco, Rye, and Grasses. Corn, on bottoms, yields 40 to 50 bushel; Wheat, 10 bushels; Oats, 40 to 50 bushels. On uplands, Corn, 25 bushels; Wheat, 10 bushels; Oats, 15 to 20 bushels; Rye, 12 bushels; Tobacco, no estimate, but produces finely. Value of land, improved agricultural, hills, $5 to $20; bottoms, $40 to $100. Timber land, $2 to $9. Value of timber, stumpage, $1 per tree; at the mills, 10 to 12½ cents per cubic foot. Principal industries: farming and timber getting, markets for timber are down the Ohio river. Minerals: Coal, 4 feet seam of soft bituminous, above water level. Some Iron Ore, fine Yellow Ochre, good Fire and Potter's Clay, good Building Stones, of blue and grey sandstones, several Salt Wells, Magnesia, Sulphur, and Chalybeate Springs, Limestone in small amounts. Coal is worked for local use. Manufactures: Shops of the Ches. & Ohio R. R. at Huntington, also the Foundry of the Ensign Iron Works, for making Carwheels, &c.; Planing Mills, and Soap Factory. Near Huntington is a large Brush Factory at St. Cloud; at Guyandotte are a Woolen Factory and a large Saw Mill; at Milton is a Steam Saw and Grist Mill; at Barboursville a Tan-Yard and Grist Mill. Streams: The Ohio river skirts the county, and Guyandotte and Mud rivers, the latter both navigable for canoes and light crafts, and Guyandotte for "push-boats" some distance inland. Lines of Transportion: Ohio river, Ches. & Ohio R. R., Guyandotte and Mud rivers. Contemplated Improvements: The Locking and Damming of the Guyandotte river, also, of Mud. Railroads projected: Guyandotte R. R., Guyandotte & Ohio River R. R., Mud River R. R., The West Virginia R. R. Public Institutions: Marshall College, the State Normal School at Huntington, Public Schools, 49; Post Offices, 13; Churches, 13. Population, 6,429; Taxable Property, $2.902,466 39. County Seat, Barboursville; Newspapers: *Huntington Advertiser* and *Huntington Commercial*, both weekly.

CALHOUN COUNTY.

This county is hilly, and the land is generally good. Since a great deal deal of it is owned in very large tracts, there is not much land in cultivation. The soils are sandy and clayey loams, being about 15 inches deep in the bottoms and 6 to 8 inches on the hiils. The crop yields given in the reports for this county are so unsatisfactory that we cannot quote them. No manures are used.

The value of the agricultural land is: $5, to $20, per acre; of the timber land, $3 to $10; value of Timber, stumpage, 50 cents to $1 per tree, and at the mills 8 to 10 cents per cubic foot. The principal Industries are, Farming grazing, and lumbering. The principal export is Lumber; principal markets, Baltimore for Stock, and Pittsburgh, Baltimore, and Parkersburg. for Lnmber; principal minerals, Limestone for building and Agricultural purposes; good Sandstone for building, and Coal below water level, except in the southern part, where it will be fonnd in the hills; principal manufactures, 8 Grist Mills, worked mainly by steam, though the water power is good and extensive. The principal streams are the Little Kanawha and its tributaries; the former is navigable to Glenville on winter and spring tides, and to Burning Spring the whole year, per batteaux. In good water steamboats go to the latter place. Steer creek is navigable for batteaux as far as Stumptown. The means of transportation are the Little Kanawha river and county roads. The contemplated improvements are, the locking and damming of the Little Kanawha through the county, and the building of the Washington and Ohio R. R. Public Schools, 31; Post Offices, 6; Churches, 13. Population, 2939; value of taxable property, $513,972 00. County seat, Grantsville.

CLAY COUNTY.

Clay is an extremely hilly county, the hills being very high above the bottoms (800 to 1,000 feet), and having narrow tops. The valleys are very narrow, and the streams are deeply sunken below the surface. The land is mostly wild, and in very large tracts. The hills are usually too steep to cultivate to advantage, but have a pretty deep and fertile soil, it being 4 to 6 inches on the hills, and 12 inches or more on the level lands. The soil in some parts, is a stiff clay, and in others, a clay loam or sandy loam, which is naturally fertile. Grains adapted to the lands, are Corn, Wheat, Oats, Rye, &c. The yields on the hills and level lands do not differ much. Corn yields 25 bushels, Oats 20 bushels, Rye 10 bushels, Wheat 8 bushels, Potatoes 50 to 100 bushels, Turnips, 100 to 200 bushels. No manures are used for these yields. In general, the averages given for the grain yields in the counties, will be those obtained without manures. Value of land: Agricultural land is worth about $5 per acre, Mineral land the same, and timber land, $2 per acre. Timber is worth 10 to 20 cents per log, stumpage, and at the mills, 7 to 8 cents per cubic foot. The principal industry is lumbering and the principal exports are Saw-logs, Hoop-poles, Staves

&c., which all go to Charleston. Minerals: Coals, Splint, Cannel, and Soft Bituminous, all in workable quantities, in fine seams above water level. Iron Ore in workable beds is found. Some Limestone, and some good Sandstones for building. Streams: Elk river is the principal stream, and is navigable 70 miles from its mouth for small steamboats, and 100 miles, to Sutton, for batteaux. It is proposed to lock and dam Elk river in Braxton county. The same proposed railroads pass through Clay that penetrate Braxton. Public Schools 21, Postoffices, 6, Churches 2, Population 2,196. Value of taxable property, $399,879.50. County seat, Clay C. H.

DODDRIDGE COUNTY.

The surface of Doddridge is rolling and hilly, with average bottoms. The soil is loam and clay-loam, with a depth on the levels of 15 inches, and on the hills of 4 to 6 inches. A good deal of the land has fine timber on it. The grains best adapted to the soil, are Corn, Oats, Buckwheat, and Wheat. On the bottoms, the yields are: Corn, 30 to 50 bushels; Wheat, 10 to 15 bushels; Oats, 25 to 35 bushels; Rye, 20 bushels; Potatoes and Turnips, 100 bushels. On the hills, Corn, 25 bushels; wheat 8 to 10 bushels; Oats 20 bushels; Potatoes, 50 to 100 bushels. No manure used for these. The value of the agricultural land is $7 to $20; mineral lands, $10; timber lands, $5 to $15. The timber is worth $1 per tree stumpage, and lumber $12 50 per 1000 at the mills. The principal industries are, Farming, Lumbering and Grazing. The principal exports, are Timber and Stock. Market for stock, Baltimore; market for timber, Baltimore and other points east. Doddridge sends out a large amout of cooperage stuff, sawed lumber, and ship timber from Smithton, West Union and other points on the railroad, and down Middle Island creek. Coal in workable seams is found above water level. Some Limestone for building and agricultural purposes. Steam and water Grist and Saw Mills exist. The coal is mined only for local use. The only stream is Middle Island creek, navigable in winter, and in full stages of water, for rafts and flat boats. The lines of transportation are, the Baltimore and Ohio railroad, and the Middle Island railroad, a tram road 22 miles long, passing through the southern part of Doddridge, in order to develope the timber, &c., and several turnpikes. Public Schools, 59. Postoffices, 13; Churches, 28; Population,

7,076. Value of taxable property, $1,406,560 09. County Seat, West Union. Newspapers, *West Union Observer*, and the *Baptist Messenger*, both weekly.

FAYETTE COUNTY.

The surface of Fayette, is hilly, mountainous, and high tableland. The hills and mountains usually are not precipitous, and have a fertile soil, the soil is a rich light loam, and a sandy loam, which is well suited for the culture of Tobacco, There are some fine bottom lands on Meadow River, the soil is 6 inches deep on the hills, and 12 inches or more, on the levels. The grains and crops, especially suited to the lands, are, Corn, Oats, Wheat, Rye, Tobacco, and Grass. The principal exports are Coal, Timber, Tobacco, and Stock. Principal industries, are Coal, Mining, Farming, Lumbering, and Stock raising, Markets. The tobacco goes to Richmond, Stock to Baltimore, Timber to New York, and Cincinnati.

Minerals: Coal in large amounts, in fine workable seams, Soft bituminous, Splint, and Cannel, the two former are those mined and shipped. Some limestone, but poor. Fine sandstone for building purposes. The mineral waters are Alum, and Chalybeate. Several important Coal mines are in operation in this county, they are the Gauly Kanawha Coal Co. (limited), Longdale Coal and Iron Co; New River Car Co.; Nutallburg Mines; Coal Valley Coal Co. and a new Mine now being opened by George Straughan, besides these, there are several Mills and Factories, among which we may mention the Fayetteville Tobacco Factory, making 2568 pounds yearly Junction Saw Mill Co; Atlantic Barrel Co; Koontsman & Co's. Shook and Stave Factory; Kanawha Falls Lumber Co.

The principal streams, are the Gauley, New and Kanawha rivers. The Kanawha is navigable six months for steam boats, and 12 months for batteaux; Gauley, 8 months for batteaux, and 12 months for canoes for 12 miles; New river in the lower part is too rough for canoes even, in the upper part it is navigable for batteaux. The lines of transportation, are the rivers, and the Chesapeake & Ohio R. R., and the James river and Kanawha turnpike.

Contemplated improvements; locking and damming Kanawha and New Rivers, and the continuation of the James river and Kanawha canal, from its present eastern terminus.

Public Schools, 63; Post Offices, 23; Churches; 10. Population 6647. Value of taxable property $1.440,839,83. County seat, Fayetteville; Newspapers, *Fayetteville Enterprise*, weekly.

GILMER COUNTY.

Gilmer county is hilly, and has a rich soil. There are some fine bottoms with loam and sand. Red calcareous clay and sandy loams are found on the hills. On the levels the soil is 12 to 14 inches deep, on the level 6 to 8 inches. It is especially adapted to Corn and Grass. Wheat does best on the hills. The county has fine forrest range for cattle.

Some of the level land grows 80 to 105 bushels of corn. The average yields are, on the bottoms, Corn, 40 bushels; Oats, 15 to 25; Turnips, 150. On the hills, Corn yields 20 bushels; Wheat, 10 to 15; Oats, 10 to 25; Turnips, 100. The Tobacco grown on the hills is large, bright, and very fine; on the bottoms, it is large and heavy. Little or no attention is paid to manures.

The value of agricultural land, slightly improved, is $5 to $10 per acre; of the improved, $10 to $25; of the timber land, $2 to 5. The principal industries are farming, stock-raising, and lumbering. The principal exports are timber and stock. The markets are, for stock, Baltimore and eastern cities; for timber, Parkersburg and Pittsburgh. Principal Minerals: Coal, and Sandstone for building purposes. The principal manufactures are two steam saw mills on Tanner's Fork, and one at Troy, as well as various grist mills, both steam and water. The means of transportation are, by the Little Kanawha, which is navigable for batteaux and rafts 9 months of the year, and by various county roads and turnpikes. The principal stream is the Little Kanawha, on which, on rare occasions, steamboats have been as far as Glenville. The contemplated improvements are: The locking and damming of the Little Kanawha to Glenville, and the building of the Washington and Ohio railroad. Schools, &c.: Glenville Normal School, at Glenville; Public Schools, 40; Postoffices, 13; Churches, 14. Population, 4,338. Value of taxable property, $856,174.00. County seat, Glenville.

GRANT COUNTY.

Grant county is rolling table land, and mountainous, with fine broad bottoms on the streams. Much of the county is in the original forest, and the land is in both small and large tracts. The soil along the streams, is exceedingly fertile, and much of the rolling table land has a very productive soil, as is shown by the exceedingly fine timber which covers it. The soil of the bottoms is a deep loam, of the uplands, sandy loam. It is slaty and thin, on some of the hills and mountains. Depth on hills, 0 to 4 inches, on bottoms, 12 inches to many feet. Crops best adapted, are: Corn, Wheat, Oats, Rye, Grass. Corn yields, on bottoms, 50 to 80 bushels; Wheat 10 to 25 bushels; Oats, 30 to 50 bushels; Potatoes, 75 to 200 bushels. On uplands, Corn 25 to 40 bushels; Wheat 8 to 10 bushels. The principal industries are farming and grazing. Principal exports, Cattle, Sheep, Hogs, Grain. No development has been made of the timber of this county. The vast amount of Hemlock and Black Spruce, &c., on the west face of the Alleghany, points to this as an important source of future revenue. The markets for Cattle, are Baltimore and Philaaelphia, and New York for the best cattle. This county, with the others of the "South Branch District," is emphatically a cattle and grain producing region. Bottom lands are worth $35 to $100; hill lands, $5 to $10 per acre. There is no market for timber except the home ones. At the mills plank is worth $12 to $20 per 1000. Minerals: Coal, in large and workable seams above water level; Iron in abundance, both red fossiliferous and brown häematite; Limestone in large amounts, good for agricultural and building purposes; some Hydraulic Limestone. Mineral Springs, white sulphur and chalybeate. Principal stream, South Branch of the Potomac. This was used for boating flour and grain, before the completion of the Baltimore & Ohio Railroad. The present lines of transportation are, the Baltimore & Ohio Railroad, and various mud pikes leading to it. Contemplated lines: Washington & O. Railroad, Cumberland, Moorefield & Broadway Railroad, North Branch Railroad, Potomac & Ohio Railroad. Public Schools, 41; Postoffices, 10; Churches, 12; Population, 4,467; value of taxable property, $1,835,533 21; County Seat, Grant C. H. Three small Woolen Factories exist in the county, and it is intended to establish an Agricultural Fair next year, (1877.)

GREENBRIER COUNTY.

This county, on the eastern and western sides, is mountainous, the western mountains rising high above the sea, but not so much in proportion above their bases. They are not too rugged for cultivation in parts, or for grazing. The central portion is a rolling plateau, embracing very fertile and highly cultivated grass and grain lands. The soil on the eastern and western sides is a red clay, or clay loam. In the central portion, over the limestone, the soil is yellowish, red clayey, and calcareous loams. The depths on the hills is 4 to 6 inches; on the levels, 12 to 18 inches. The crops best adapted to the land, are Corn, Wheat, Oats, Buckwheat, Grass. Corn produces on the levels, 20 to 40 bushels; Wheat, 15 bushels; Oats, 30; Buckwheat, 30; Potatoes, 100; on the hills corn produces 10 to 15 bushels; Oats 15; Wheat, 8; Buckwheat, 35; Potatoes, 75. No manures used for these yields. The value of the land is: Best Agricultural, $20 to $50; second-class and rougher land, with less improvements, but some subsoil, $2 to $10; Timber lands, $1.50 to $6; Iron and Coal lands are worth from $2.50 up to $100, according to distance from railroad and richness of deposit. In the N. part, near the Greenbrier river, is a good deal of valuable timber, especially White Pine.

Timber is worth, stumpage, $1.25 per 1,000 feet; at the mill, $6 to $7.50. The principal industries are farming and stock-raising. The principal exports are grass-fed Cattle, Sheep, Horses, Wool, &c. The county is emphatically a grazing one.

The market for stock is Baltimore; some goes to Richmond. Surplus grain is fed to shipping stock. Horses go to North Carolina and East Virginia. For timber, Baltimore, and other eastern cities. In the western part, some workable seams of Coal; fine workable Iron Ores on Anthony's and Howard's creeks, and elsewhere; Limestone in abundance, of all qualities for agricultural, building, and hydraulic lime; Clays suitable for rough crocks are found, and these were made, for years, at Lewisburg. Excellent grit for grindstones is found. Mineral Springs: White Sulphur, Blue Sulphur, and Alum. Many Chalybeate springs. Coal was formerly worked on Little Sewell, and hauled 22 miles to Lewisburg, now discontinued, on account of more ready transport on the C. & O. railroad, for the coals further west. Manufactories: four Carding Mills, three Woolen Mills, one Tan Yard, exporting leather, and several smaller ones, St. Lawrence Boom and Manufacturing Company. The Greenbrier river is the principal stream, and is navigable for canoes and batteaux on rises. Means of transportation, Chesapeake and Ohio railroad, and turnpikes.

Contemplated lines, the Pittsburgh, Virginia and Charleston railroad. Schools, Lewisburg Female Institute, High School at Frankford, and 68 Public Schools; Postoffices, 22; Churches, 35. Population, 11,417. Taxable property, $4,524,562.59. County seat, Lewsburg. Newspaper, *Greenbrier Independent*, weekly.

HAMPSHIRE COUNTY.

Hampshire county is composed of mountains, rolling hills, and bottom lands, in the proportion of two-fifths mountains, two-fifths hills, and one-fifth bottom land. Soil on the uplands, 4 to 8 inches, of a light loamy character. On the hills, the soil is sandy and clayey, 5 to 10 inches deep, and is especially adapted to grazing and small grain. In the bottoms, the soil is a black and sandy loam, 3 to 15 feet deep, and brings immense crops of Corn, Wheat, Potatoes, Hay, etc., without rotation or fertilizers. The grains especially adapted to the county are, Corn, Wheat, Oats, Rye, and Buckwheat. The yields on the bottoms are on an average, Corn, 50 bushels; Wheat, 20 bushels; Oats, 40 bushels; Potatoes, 100 bushels; Hay, 2 tons. On the uplands, Corn produces 25 bushels; Wheat, 12 bushels; Oats, 25 bushels; Buckwheat, 25 bushels. A little barn yard manure is sometimes used on the uplands. No Fair is held in the counties of the South Branch district. They are represented at the Fairs held at Winchester, Virginia. The bottom lands sell for $100 per acre, and upwards. Clay and hill land from $5 to $30. Timber lands from 50 cents to $10 per acre. There is no fixed price for mineral lands, of which there are large areas. Hardly anything is done in timber, except for home consumption. Price on stump, 25 cents per hundred. At the mill, $12 50 to $15.00 per thousand. The principal industries are farming and stock raising. The principal exports, are Cattle, Horses, Hogs, Wheat, etc. Of these, cattle are by far the most important, since all the counties of this district, make the fattening of Cattle their main business. The heavy Cattle go to New York, and the lighter to Baltimore and Philadelphia, these latter cities not having a sufficient demand for the finer grades. The cattle are grazed on the uplands and mountains, in summer, and fed on corn in winter.

Hence all the corn raised is consumed at home. Wheat, Oats, Rye, and small marketing find sale in Cumberland and the mines around. Excellent Iron ores, both red fossiliferous and brown hæmatite, are found in workable deposits in the county, and are smelted at the Bloomery Furnace. Good limestone for building and agricultural purposes is found, and some potters clay, which is worked by a pottery on North river. One at Glencoe has suspended operations. Good sandstones for building are found, and a deposit of fine glass sand also. The celebrated Capon Mineral Springs are found in this county. The iron ore is worked in the vicinity of the Bloomery Furnace. Besides this last, there are among the manufactories, three woolen factories. The Big Capon and South Branch run through the county, and are navigable for batteaux in seasons of full water in winter and spring. The North Branch of the Potomac skirts it on the north, to which the same remarks apply. The present lines of transportation are the Baltimore and Ohio Railroad, which runs through the northern part, and the county roads and pikes. Contemplated lines are: The Washington and Ohio Railroad, the South Branch Railroad, the West Virginia Railroad, the Potomac and Ohio Railroad. The Deaf and Dumb Asylum is at Romney. Public schools, 51. Postoffices, 22. Churches, 15. Population, 7,643. Value of taxable property, $2,542,408.82. County seat, Romney, with 600 inhabitants. Newspapers, *South Branch Intelligencer*, weekly.

HANCOCK COUNTY.

This is the most northerly county in the State. It is hilly and somewhat broken, with the hills quite high, and valleys narrow. The soil is the usual calcareous and clayey loam of the Pan-Handle counties. The depth on the hillsides is from 5 to 7 inches, being deeper, as is usual in the counties of this part of the State, on the north sides of the hills. On the levels and bottoms, it is from 12 inches, to many feet. The crops best adapted to them, are Corn, Oats, Barley, Wheat, and especially grain. All the calcareous lands of the Pan-Handle, bring fine Blue Grass, Timothy, Clover, etc., while the height of the hills make them well adapted to the pasturage of sheep. The hills and levels produce equally well. Corn yields 50 to 75 bushels; Oats, 40 bushels; Wheat, 15 bushels; Pototoes, 100 to 200 bushels; Hay, 1½ to 2½ tons. No manures are used for these yields. Value of improved agricultural lands, $50 to

$90 per acre, and over. Mineral lands: Coal, $50. Timber land, $30. No timber sold except for home use. Principal industries, Sheep and Wool growing, Farming, and manufacturing of Fire Clay. Principal exports, Sheep, Wool, various products of the manufacture of Fire Clay, such as bricks, drainage pipes, etc. Markets: For grain, etc., home; for Sheep, Wool, etc, eastern cities. Minerals: Good Coal, in workable beds above water level. Good sandstone, for building. Limestone in abundance for building and agricultural purposes. Large deposits of excellent fire clay, which is largely manufactured. Principal stream, the Ohio river, which is navigable for good sized steamers. Manufactories: One woolen mill, several flouring mills, and about 20 companies engaged in mining and manufacturing fire clay, brick, etc., affording employment to from 200 to 300 hands. Public schools, 21. Churches, 7. Postoffices, 6. Population, 4,363. Taxable property, $2,052,676.11. County seat, Fairview. Newspaper, *Hancock Courier*, weekly.

HARDY COUNTY.

The same remarks apply to the topography and soil, crops, yields, value of land and timber, principal industries, markets, and exports of Hardy, that were made concerning these points in connection with Hampshire. The deposits of Iron in Hardy are larger than those in Hampshire. They are worked at the Capon Iron Works. Hardy has a great number of Mineral Springs, Alum, Sulphur and Chalybeate, none of which are improved. The Hardy White Sulphur Springs are considered by some equal to the Greenbrier White Sulphur. Near Moorefield good fire clay is found, also pipe and potter's clay, which last has been worked to some extent. Good lime for building and agricultural purposes, and the fluxing of iron exists. Good sandstone for building are also found. Iron is mined for Capon Furnace. The principal streams are, the South Branch of the Potomac and Capon river, both navigable for batteaux and canoes one-half of the year. Transportation is to the Balt. & Ohio R. R. by county roads, and to the Valley R. R. in Virginia. Contemplated lines are, the Washington & Ohio R. R., the Cumberland, Moorefield & Broadway R. R., Potomac & Ohio R. R., the West Virginia R. R. Schools: High School for males and Seminary for girls, at Moorefield, and 36 Public Schools; Post-Offices, 11; Churches, 9. Population 5,518; value of taxable property, $2,312,194 37. County seat, Moofield, a thriving village with 850 inhabitants. Newspapers, *Moorefield Courier and Advertiser* and *Moorfield Weekly Examiner*, both weekly.

HARRISON COUNTY.

The surface in Harrison is rolling and hilly. The hills are broad and low, comparatively speaking, and the valleys wide.

The county has much improved land with good soil, and is well cultivated. The soil is mainly clay loam and calcareous loam, 6 to 8 inches deep on the hills and from 12 inches to 18 inches on the levels. Crops best suited are Corn, Oats, Wheat, Rye, and especially grass. The Blue Grass sods over the land spontaneously. The county is pre-eminently a grazing one. Hills and levels yield about alike. Corn, 30 to 60 bushels; Wheat, 10 to 15 bushels; Oats, 15 to 25 bushels; Rye, 15 to 25 bushels. The Central Agricultural and Mechanical Society holds an annual Fair at Clarksburg, where $1,550 (about) are distributed in premiums. The prices of improved agricultural land is $25 to $50 per acre, of mineral land (Coal), $75 to $100 per acre, of timber land, $10 to $15 per acre. The timber of Harrison is not so abundant as that in the counties farther west, though still considerable in amount. Price, stumpage, $2,50 per 1,000 feet; after sawing $10 to $12 50 per 1,000 feet, The principal industries are Stock raising, Farming, and Coal mining. Principal exports, Stock, Coal and Lumber. Markets for Stock, Baltimore; for Grain and General Produce, Clarksburg and other home markets; Coal is sent, for gas making, to the eastern cities; Timber goes to Pittsburgh, mainly White Oak and Poplar logs, Lumber as cooperage stuff, and sawed stuff goes east. Minerals: Coal in large quantites above water level; Limestone, both for agricultural and building purposes; Potter's Clay exists, and has been worked: Sandstone of good quality for building is found; several mines of Coal are worked on a large scale for gas making; among them are the Despard Coal Company, The Murphy's Run Coal Company, Harrison County Coal Company, Wakeman Mines, Monongahela Gas Coal Company, &c., Harrison county is well supplied with mills and manufactories. They are as follows: Three Cheese Factories, 1 Pottery, 8 Tanneries, 16 Grist and Saw Mills, 7 Flour and Saw Mills, 4 Saw Mills (3 portable), 3 Grist Mills, 2 Flour Mills, 1 Flour Mill with Saw and Carding, 1 Flour Mill and Woolen Factory, 1 Portable Saw Mill and Machine Shop, making doors, sash, &c., 1 Flour Mill with wood-working machinery, 1 Saw Mill with wood working machinery, 1 Planing Mill with machinery for making doors, sash, &c., 1 Foundry and Machine Shop and Manufacture of Saw-Mill Truck Cars. 1 Foundry with machinery for making Portable Grist and Saw Mills, Truck Cars, Portable Engines, &c., &c. The principal stream is the West Fork of the Monongahela, navigable for rafts and batteaux during high water. Means of transportation are, the Balt. & Ohio R. R. and turnpikes. Contemplated lines are, The Buckhannon Mineral R. R., Northern & Southern West Virginia R. R., The Weston and W. Fork R. R. Schools: Academy at Clarksburg, and 101 Public Schools; Post-Offices, 25; Churches, 57. Population, 16,714; value of taxable property $7,331,486 48. County Seat, Clarksburg, a thriving town, with a population of about 1,600 inhabitants. Newspapers *Clarksburg Telegram* and *The News*, both weekly.

JACKSON COUNTY.

The surface of the county is hilly and rolling, the hills to the eastward becoming quite high. All are somewhat rough. Considerable flats are found on the Ohio river, which skirts the county for 30 miles. Along this, the bottoms avere age ½ mile. The bottoms on Mill and Sandy creeks, averag 200 yards. These are, as is usual in this part of the State, very productive. The soils vary a good deal, being a heavy clay, calcareous loam, and sandy loam, in different locations. About ⅞ of the county is in timber, some being very fine. The depth of soil on the hills is 6 to 8 inches; on the levels and bottoms, 1 foot to many. On the bottoms Corn yields 40 to 60 bushels; Wheat, 12 to 15 bushels; Oats, 40 to 50 bushels; Potatoes, 100 to 150 bushels; Hay, 1 to 2 tons. These are the crops, along with Tobacco, best suited to the lands. On the hills, Corn yields 25 to 30 bushels; Wheat 10 to 12 bushels; Oats, 25 bushels; Potatoes, 75 to 100 bushels. No manures are used for these yields. It is proposed to establish an Agricultural Fair at Ripley, the county seat, under the auspices of the Patrons of Husbandry. Price of improved bottom lands, from $40 to $70; Upland Farming land, $5 to $20; Timber land, $4 to $8. The timber is worth, stumpage, $1 per tree; sawed at the mills, $5 to $12.50 per 1,000. The principal industries are, farming, cattle-raising, and lumbering. The principal exports are, Timber, Stock, and Grain, and Tobacco. The markets for the Timber are down the Ohio river; for grain, along the Ohio; for stock, Baltimore. Minerals: Coal in small seams, enough for local use, above water level; some Iron Ore in workable quantities; excellent sandstone for building purposes; a considerable amount of Limestone in the northern part of the county, which will make good agricultural and building lime; Iron Ore is worked on Mill creek, by Mr. Melville for the Bellaire Iron Works. Manufactories: One Tobacco factory, making 4,808 pounds; one cigar factory, making 5,300 cigars; Woolen Mill, at Ripley; Wagon Factory; Flour Mill, and Barrel Factories at Ravenswood; Flour Mill, and Saw Mill, at Sandyville and Cottageville, and several movable steam Saw Mills. Principal streams: The Ohio, along the west border; Mill and Sandy creeks penetrate the county, and are navigable 10 to 20 miles from the Ohio, by rafts and canoes, on high waters. Means of transportation: Ohio river and turnpikes; contemplated ones: W. C. & St. L. Narrow Gauge railroad; Pittsburgh, Wheeling and Kentucky railroad; Ripley and Ohio Narrow Gauge railroad; Washington and Ohio railroad. Public Schools, 69; Churches, 21; Postoffices, 20. Population, 10,300. Value of taxable property, $2,342,559.19. County seat, Ripley. Newspapers, *Jackson County News*, weekly, at Ravenswood.

JEFFERSON COUNTY.

This county has a rolling and hilly surface, except in the eastern part, where it is bounded by the Blue Ridge mountains. The soil is mainly calcareous loams and clays. The depth on the hills varies from 2 to 8 inches, and in the valleys, from one to many feet. Crops adapted to the soils, are Wheat, Corn, Oats, Rye, and Grass especially. Crops yield on the hills, Wheat, 10 bushels; Corn, 30 bushels; Rye, 15 bushels; Potatoes, 100 bushels; Oats, 30 bushels. On the bottoms, the yields are one-third to one-half more. These are all for the improved calcareous agricultural lands. The value of the agricultural land, which embraces all the county is from $30 to $60 per acre, according to location and amount of improvement. Not much is done in timber. The principal industries, are farming, manufacturing and stock raising. The principal exports are grain and stock of various kinds, manufactured articles, and some Poplar and Walnut. Markets for timber, Baltimore and home. For grain, Baltimore and eastern cities. For stock, Baltimore and Philadelphia. Minerals: Iron ore is found in several localities. On the Potomac, near Antiotam creek, it is worked for the Antietam Iron Works. Other localities where it is in workable quantities are near Bolivar Heights, and on the Shanandoah river, at Mulby's Ore Bank, which is now worked. A fine deposit of hydraulic limestone is worked at Shepherdstown, and furnishes a cement of well known good quality. Limestone for building stone, is quarried of good quality, and sent down the canal. Limestone for burning, of good quality is abundant.

Some of the limestones approach marble in grain, and occasionally yield a stone of good color and taking a good polish. A good quarry of grey marble might be obtained at Shepherdstown. Chalybeate and sulphur springs exist. Some potters clay is found. Manufactories: 4 cigar factories, making 329,-350 cigars; 3 wool factories, 20 flour mills, 2 hardwood factories, 4 or 5 portable steam saw mills, 2 paper mills, 1 planing mill and sash factory, agricultural implement factory and foundry, 1 cement mill, and 1 pottery. The county is skirted by the Potomac and Shenandoah, the latter being navigable on full waters by flat boats. Means of transportation are by Baltimore and Ohio Railroad, Chesapeake and Ohio Canal, and Valley Railroad. Contemplated improvements: The Shenandoah Valley Railroad, Potomac and Ohio Railroad, and the improvement of the Shenandoah river. Public institutions: State Normal School at Shepherdstown, schools, etc.; Stover College, for colored persons, at Harper's Ferry, and 32 public schools. Churches, 27. Postoffices, 11. Value of taxable property, $7,434,309.63. Population, 13,219. County seat, Shepherdstown, with a population of about 2,200. Newspapers, *Charlestown Spirit of Jefferson*, *Shepherdstown Register*, and *Virginia Free Press*, all weekly.

KANAWHA COUNTY.

The topography of this county is hilly and mountainous. The

hills in the west are comparatively low; in the middle portion they become quite high, and in the western part, they become mountainous. Much of the surface is quite rough and broken. The valleys are usually narrow. The soil is naturally productive, and is quite deep. On the hills, it varies from 4 to 12 inches, and on the levels from 12 inches to many feet. The crops suited to the lands are Corn, Wheat, Oats, Rye, and Tobacco. On the bottoms, as those along the Kanawha, the yields are high. Corn produces 40 to 60 bushels; Oats, 30 to 40 bushels; Wheat, 10 to 15 bushels; Tobacco, 1,000 to 1,400 pounds. On the hills, Corn produces 20 to 50 bushels; Oats, 20 to 25 bushels; Wheat, 8 to 10 bushels; Tobacco, 800 to 1,000 pounds. Value of improved lands, $5 to $50; of mineral lands, coal, $10 to $100, according to location and deposits. Timber lands, $5 to $20; value of timber, stumpage, 2 to 3 cents; at mill, 8 to 10 cents, per cubic foot. Principal industries, farming, lumbering, coal mining, and the manufacture of salt. Principal exports, Coal, Salt, Timber, Grain, and Tobacco. Markets for timber, Ohio river and eastern cities; for grain and farm produce, Charleston and home. Stock goes east, as does some of the timber. The coal goes down the Ohio, and to the eastern cities. The principal minerals are Coal, Iron, and Salt. The iron is siderite, and blackband; the former has been worked somewhat. Large exports of salt are made, mainly down the Ohio, and to Richmond. Fire clay was worked, and shipped to Cincinnati. Sandstone for building can be obtained, of good quality. There are: 1 tobacco manufactory, manufacturing 648 pounds; 3 cigar manufactories, making 51,100 cigars; 1 brewery, making 722 barrels; 1 bromine works. Mines: These are exclusively of coal, which is common bituminous, splint and cannel. The mines now in operation are Bibby's mine, Pioneer Coal Company, Campbell's Creek Coal Company, J. B. Lewis & Co., Coalmont Coal Company, Houston Mining and Manufacturing Company, Kanawha and Ohio Coal Company, Hampton Mines, Blacksburg mines, Blackberry mines, Enterprise Coal and Iron Company, Kanawha Semi-Cannel Coal Company, Gordon & Seal, Cannelton Coal Company, and various mines to supply the salt companies. Salt companies are: Brook's Furnace, Lorena Furnace, Snow Hill Furnace, Campbell's Creek Furnace, Pioneer Furnace, a furnace a short distance above Malden; now building at Charleston, the Kanawha Coal and Iron Furnace. Lines of transportation now used: Kanawha river, navigable by steamboats and barges; Elk, navigable for batteaux, in all stages, and for rafts in full water, and also for small steamers, 10 miles. Big Coal is locked and damed to Peytona, and used by small steamers and barges. Rafts are sent out of Pocatalico in full stages. Contemplated improvements: The locking and daming of Elk, extension of the James river and Kanawha canal, Coal River Railroad, Northern and Southern West Virginia Central Railroad, Paint Creek Railroad, West Virginia Railroad, the West Virginia Central Railroad. Public schools, 125. Churches, 37. Postoffices, 24. Population, 22,349. Value of taxable property, $6,430,051. County seat, Charleston, with a population of 5,000. It has one woolen mill, two barrel factories, 10 steam saw mills in and near Charleston, 1 brewery, 1 foundry, 2 tanneries. One steam saw mill is at St. Albans, and another at Coalburg. Newspapers: *Charleston Courier*, tri-weekly; *Kanawha Chronicle*, weekly; *West Virginia Journal*, weekly; *all* at Charleston.

LEWIS COUNTY.

The surface of Lewis is rolling and hilly. The soil is uniformly fertile, being clay and clayey loam, sometimes calcareous. It produces grass well. Depth on hills 3 to 12 inches, and on the levels, 12 to 18 inches. Crops suited to the lands, are Corn, Wheat, Oats, and the grasses; yields on the levels, Corn, 40 to 60 bushels; Wheat, 10 to 12 bushels; Oats, 25 to 40 bushels; on the hills, Corn, 25 to 30 bushels; Wheat, 8 to 10 bushels; Oats, 20 to 25 bushels. The Lewis County Agricultural and Mechanical Association hold an annual Fair near Weston. The usual sum distributed in premiums per annum is $2,000. The price of Agricultural land is from $5 to $25; Timber land, from $2 to $6. Timber is worth, stumpage, $1 per average tree; at the mills, sawed, $10 per 1,000.

The principal industries are farming and stock-raising. The county is mainly a grazing one. The principal exports for stock are Baltimore and eastern cities. Some timber is exported to Pittsburgh and Brownsville, Pa. Minerals are coal, ordinary bituminous in large seams, and of good quality; Limestone is found for cement, and Agricultural purposes; Potters' Clay is found and worked by Parker & Co.; Sandstones for building, of excellent quality, and very handsome, exist. The Insane Asylum, at Weston, is built of a handsome sandstone, quarried on the spot. A fine Ochre, of a rich orange color is found, and used in painting in the vicinity. The West Fork of the Monongahela is the principal stream, and is used in high stages of water for running rafts out. But for the dams it could be navigated by canoes. The means of transportation at present are pikes and dirt roads alone. Contemplated improvements are, the Weston and West Fork railroad, and the Washington and Ohio railroad, the Northern and Southern West Virginia railroad, Shenandoah and Ohio railroad. The Insane Asylum is at Weston. Manufactories are, Cigar factories, making 78,000 cigars; Weston Woolen Mills, Weston Flouring Mills, Weston Iron Foundry, for castings and hollow ware, Furniture factories, &c. Public Schools, 72; Churches, 36; Postoffices, 14. Population, 10,175. Taxable property, $2,616,650.00. County seat, Weston, a growing town with about 1,200 inhabitants. Newspaper, *Weston Democrat*, weekly.

LINCOLN COUNTY.

The surface of Lincoln is hilly, with hills generally of a considerable elevation, in some cases rising almost into mountains. The slope is usually sufficient for cultivation Only about one-fifth of the land is cleared, and much of the uncleared land is in large tracts, up to 100,000 acres. There is some fine bottom land along the Guyandotte river, but the hills on the Guyandotte and Coal rivers are high and rough. On Mud river, the soils are clay, elsewhere they are Sandy loams, all generally deep and very fertile. The crops best suited to the lands, are Corn, Oats, Wheat, Rye, Buckwheat, and Tobacco. Lincoln is one of the most extensive Tobacco raising conntıes in the State, and the soils are especially adapted to this crop. The grasses also do finely. Lincoln produces large amounts of ginseng. The soils are from 7 to 10 inches deep on the hills, and 12 to 14 inches on the levels. The hilis and levels produce about alike. Corn yields 30 to 40 bushels; Wheat, 10; Rye, 12; Oats, 20. Land in large tracts is worth, when con taining fine coal, as much of it does, $5 to $10, which is also about the value of the farming land. The timber is in large amounts, and of the finest quality. Coal and timber land can also be purchased at from $1 to $1.50. Timber is worth 50 cents per tree, stumpage, and at tne mills 6 to 10 cents per cubic foot. Principal industries, farming, lumbering, and stock raising. The stock is very good. Principal exports, timber, lumber, tobacco, forest products, and stock. Markets: The timber is sold at the stump, and rafted down to markets on the Ohio river, as is the lumber. The tobacco and stock are sent to Cincinnati. Minerals: Coal in great quantity; splint, common bituminous, and cannel; fine sandstones for building, Manufactories: Three or more large grist and saw mills, on Mud river, one on Guyandotte river, and several steam saw mills, two tan-yards, at Hamlin. The principal streams are Guyandotte and Mud rivers. The former is navigable several months of the year for "push boats," and timber may be floated down it on full water. Mud and Little Coal are navigable for canoes and rafts in full stages. Means of transportion at present, are the above streams, and county mud roads, to the Chesapeake and Ohio railroad. Contemplated improvements: Coal River railroad, the branch running up Little Coal; Guyandotte railroad, Guyandotte and Ohio River railroad, Mud River railroad, Ohio River and Wayne County Mineral railroad. Public Schools, 50; Churches, 6; Postoffices, 7. Population, 5.053. Value of taxable property, $1,073.901.45. County seat, Hamlin.

LOGAN COUNTY.

This county is quite broken, the hills which occupy most of the surface are very high, attaining the dignity of mountains in places. The valleys are narrow, with, as a rule, little bottom land. On the Guyandotte there is a good deal of gently rolling and bottom lands. A considerable amount of gently sloping land is also found on Pigeon and Island creeks, while near and below the court-house is fine farming land. The soil is loam, more or less sandy or clayey, quite productive, and yielding grass and grain well. The crops are Corn, Wheat, Oats, Rye, Buckwheat and Tobacco. All yield well, $\frac{7}{8}$ of the land is in timber, which grows to enormous size. Some of the largest trees in the State, especially of Poplar and Oak, are reported here. The land is in large tracts and mostly has the timber untouched. The soil is deeper on the northwest side of the hills, and is usually on the uplands from 4 to 15 inches; on the bottoms 12 inches to several feet. The yields on the hills, where cultivated, which is only in patches, are the same as the bottoms: Corn produces 30 to 60 bushels; Oats, 20 to 40 bushels; Wheat, 10; Rye, 12. Not much farming on a large scale is done. Grass grows luxuriantly, and the winters are mild. Some stock is raised. The land in large tracts may be bought at from $1 to $10. The timber and wild lands mainly at the former price. Value of timber, stumpage, 50 cents to $1 per tree, and $2 on the river. For logs in the river, 8 to 10 cents per cubic foot. Principal industries, Farming and Lumbering. Principal exports, Timber in Logs, and forest products. Logan, as well as Lincoln, exports a large amount of Ginseng, the collecting of which form a considerable business with the inhabitants, as they go long distances for it. The markets for all products are down the Ohio. Minerals: Coal, Splint, Cannel, and ordinary Bituminous, in fine workable seams; Sandstone for building is abundant; Salt water is found in some localities. There are several Saw and Grist Mills on Guyandotte river. The people manufacture at home a good deal of the minor articles for household use. The present means of transportation are the Big Sandy and Guyandotte rivers. The former stream is navigable for steamers, barges, and timber rafts, several months in the year, as is the Guyandotte for canoes and timber rafts. Contemplated improvements: Improvement of the navigation of the Guyandotte river, which was in progress before the war; Tug River R. R.; Mud River R. R.; Guyandotte & Ohio R. R.; Guyandotte R. R. Public Schools, 43; Churches, 8; Post-offices, 9; Value of taxable property, $604,851 14. Population, 5,124. County Seat, Logan Court-House.

MARION COUNTY.

The surface of the county is rolling and hilly, the hills being often quite high, and the valleys narrow. The soil is usually pretty deep, and naturally fertile. It is a loam, clayey, sandy, or calcareous, from 6 to 8 inches deep on the hills, and 10 to 12 inches on the levels. The land is well adapted to the production of Grass, Corn, Wheat, Oats, Rye, Potatoes, and Buckwheat. There is little difference between the yields on the hills and levels. The average without manures is as follows: Corn, 30 to 40 bushels; Wheat, 12 bushels; Oats, 30 bushels; Potatoes, 75 to 100 bushels; Rye. 15 bushels. An annual Fair is held at Fairmont; the amounts given out in premiums are not reported. Principal industries, farming, stock-raising, coal mining, and lumbering. Principal exports, stock, farm products, lumber and coal. Large amounts of sawed and cooperage stuff are sent from along the line of the railroad, and large exports of excellent gas coal are made from the vicinity of Fairmont. Markets for stock, Baltimore; for timber, Baltimore, eastern cities, &c.; for coal, eastern cities. Minerals: A large and fine seam of Gas Coal, and other workable seams; good Limestone for agricultural and building purposes; good Sandstones for building; good Potter's Clay, manufactured at Palatine; Clay near Paltine suitable for Potter's slip; excellent Tin Clay, mined and manufactured at Nuzum's Mills, by the Glade Tin Brick Company. The following coal mines are in operation: The Gaston mines of the Fairmont Gas Coal Company, the West Fairmont mines, of the West Fairmont Gas Coal Company; the Palatine mines, of the O'Donnell's; the Central mines, of O. Jackson. Manufactories: These have not been fully reported, and we cannot give them in any detail. There are ten cigar factories in the county, making 242,100 cigars in 1875; a pottery in Palatine; a fine brick manufactory at Nuzum's Mills; at Fairmont, Palatine and other points, there are 9 steam Flouring mills, most of them have saw attachments; 9 Water mills; Furniture shops; a Foundry and Machine shops; Agricultural Machine manufactory, &c.; Flouring mills, &c., &c; at Valley Falls, is a Saw mill and Shook factory; at Farmington, Flour and Grist mills, a Tannery, &c.; at Mannington, a good deal of lumber and shooks are shipped; there are here Flouring, Grist, and Saw mills, a Planing mill, a Wagon Factory, a Foundry, &c., &c. Principal streams are, the West Fork, Tygart's Valley, and Monongahela, all navigable for timber rafts and batteaux in full stages. Good sized steamers have several times been up as high as Fairmont in very high stages of water. The present lines of transportation are, the Baltimore and Ohio railroad and turnpike roads; in contemplation, are the improvement of the Monongahela river, the Northern and Southern West

Virginia railroad. The Fairmont Normal school is at Fairmont. Public schools, 94 , Churches, 37; Postoffices, 21. Population, 12,107. Value of taxable property, $4,169,099.06. County seat, Fairmont, a thriving town on the Monongahela river. Newspapers, *Fairmont Index*, *Fairmont West Virginian*, *Mannington Ventilator*, and *Golden Rule*.

MARSHALL COUNTY.

The topography of this county is much like that of Ohio county. The amount of bottom land along the Ohio river and Grave creek is considerable, and of excellent character. The hills are high, but not rocky, and the slopes are not too steep for grazing and cultivation; they have narrow valleys between. The soil is very fertile, being calcareous clay loam, or sandy loam. The depth on the hills is 7 to 8 inches, and on the levels 1 to many feet. The crops adapted to the lands are Corn, Oats, Wheat, Barley, and especially Grass. The hills and levels produce about alike. Corn produces 40 to 70 bushels; Oats, 30 to 40 bushels; Wheat, 6 to 15 bushels. No manures are used for these yields. Agricultural improved land is worth $50 to $300 per acre; Mineral land (Coal) $1,000 to $1,500; Timber land, $35 to $40. Timber is worth $2 per cord, stumpage, and $4 per cord at the mill. Principal industries: Farming, Stock raising and Manufacturing. Principal exports: Stock, such as Hogs, Sheep, and Cattle, also, Grain. Markets for Stock, the East; for Grain and general produce, Wheeling, also, for Timber. Minerals: Coal, in good seams above water level; Limestone for agricultural and building purposes, &c., are found; a Sandstone for building is obtained; Coal is mined at Moundsville and up the river for consumption in the vicinity. Manufactories: Two Rolling Mills, Cigar Factories making 454,000 cigars, 1 Blast Furnace, Saw Mill at Bellton and Moundsville, Flouring Mills, Saddlery, Wagon Manufactories, Brick Yards, &c., &c. We may state here, that the reports made to us of the manufactories in the several counties, are very imperfect, and our lists cannot pretend to be complete. The principal stream is the Ohio river. Means of transportation are the Ohio river and the Balt. & Ohio R. R. Contemplated: The Pittsburgh, Wheeling & Kentucky R. R. The State Penitentiary is at Moundsville. Public Schools, 88, Churches, 13; Post-Offices, 21. Population, 14,941. Value of taxable property is $4,363,713 35. County seat, Moundsville, a considerable village. Newspapers, *Moundsville National*, *Moundsville Reporter*, and *New State Gazette.*

MASON COUNTY.

The surface of this county is gently rolling and hilly, with much flat land along the Ohio and Great Kanawha. The hills are low and gently sloping, comparatively speaking, and the valleys are wide. The Ohio skirts the county for 50 miles, and the Kanawha passes through its center. The county has 75,000 acres of river bottoms. The soil on the flats is a rich loam very deep. Clay loams, clays, and calcareous loams, are found on the hills. More than half of the land is in cultivation, and the rest contains a great deal of fine heavy timber. The levels have a soil from one to many feet deep, while on the hills it is from 8 to 12 inches. The crops raised are Corn, Wheat, Oats, Rye, and the Grasses, which do finely. The yields on the bottoms are Wheat, 15 to 20 bushels; Corn, 40 to 50; Oats, 30 to 40; Rye, 30. On the uplands, Corn yields about 30 to 35 bushels; Wheat, 10; Oats, 25 to 30, etc. No manures used for these yields. Corn has been produced on the flats, at the rate of 106 bushels in a 30 acre field. The Mason County Agricultural and Mechanical Association holds an annual Fair at Point Pleasant. Value of premiums distributed, $1,000. The bottom lands sell for $80 to $100 per acre; the uplands for from $5 to $20; mineral land (coal), $200 to $400; timber, stumpage, is worth $1 per tree; at the mill, $10. The principal industries are farming, stock raising, lumbering, salt manufacturing, mining, etc. Mason pays a good deal of attention to stock and the introduction of improved breeds, for the raising of which its fine grass lands afford many advantages. The principal exports are Coal, 5,000,000 bushels; salt, 2,500,000 bushel; Wheat, Cattle, Bromine, Nails, Glass, Wool, Hogs, Lumber, etc. Markets: The agricultural products and stock, go to eastern cities; others down the river. Minerals: Coal, in a seam from 5 to 6 feet, is exposed above water level for 7 miles in the northern edge of the county. Salt water is furnished from wells 1,000 to 1,200 feet deep, in the northern part of the county. Clay, for tile making, is found and worked. Sandstone of good quality abounds in the county. Mines: Coal is mined at nine different openings from Camden to New Haven City. They send 5,000,000 bushels down the Ohio, and use half that amount in making salt.—[I. W. C. Davis.] This is soft bituminous coal. Manufactories: Mason county has one brewery, making 126 barrels of beer per annum. Salt is manufactured by 11 companies, with 13 furnaces. These, with the coal mines, and other manufactories, make a continuous village along the Ohio for six miles. There are bromine works at Clifton, Mason City, and Valley City, and two at Hartford City. One nail factory and rolling mill, of large size, at Clifton, 2 glass factories at Mason City, 2 stove factories at Hartford City; also 2 steam saw mills at Mason City, 1 steam saw mill and 1 keg factory at Clifton, 1 tile factory opposite Point Pleasant, 1 flour, 1 lumber and planing mill at Point Pleasant, 1 flour mill at New Haven City, 3 saw mills along the Ohio above Point Pleasant, and 1 floating dock at that place. Principal streams: The Ohio and Kanawha, both navigable for large steamers. Present means of transportation: The Ohio and Kanawha rivers. Improvements contemplated: The improvement of the navigation of the Kanawha, the Washington and Ohio Railroad, the W., C. & St. L. Narrow Gauge Railroad, the Pittsburgh, Wheeling and Kentucky Railroad, Hartford, Mason and Clifton Railroad. Public schools, 96. Churches, 29. Postoffices, 22. Population, 15,978. Value of taxable property, $6,207,710.49. County seat, Point Pleasant. Newspapers: *The Weekly Register*, *The Mason County Journal*, both weekly.

M'DOWELL COUNTY.

McDowell is a hilly and mountainous county, much of it broken and rough. Most of the land is in the original forest, and very little cultivation is carried on, except in patches. The land is generally held in large tracts. The county is very inaccessible, as may be gathered from the fact that not a single answer has been obtained to fifty circulars sent into it, asking for information. In consequence of this, we cannot give any detailed account of it. The topography, soil, industries, etc., are like those of Wyoming, except that the land is rougher, and less cultivated. The soil is naturally fertile, the winters mild, and the timber very fine. There are no public improvements, and no means of transportation, except down the Big Sandy and rough roads. The improved land is worth $5 to

$10 per acre, and the unimproved wild lands, in large tracts, 50 cents to $1. The crops, industries, and exports are the same as those of Wyoming and Logan. Good coal, in workable seams, exists. Public schools, 14. Churches, 8. Post-offices, 4. Value of taxable property, $303,878.43. Population, 1,952. County seat, Perrysville.

MERCER COUNTY.

This county is flanked on the east by the East River mountains, and on the west by the Flat-Top mountains. It consists chiefly of hilly or rolling plateau land, with some mountains. The soil is fertile, being a clay, sandy loam, and calcareous loam. The soil on the hills is 6 to 8 inches deep, but thinner near the mountains; on the levels, 10 to 12 inches and more. The crops raised are, Corn, Oats, Wheat, Tobacco, and Grass, for which latter much of the soil is especially adapted, making this essentially a grazing country The yields on the levels are, Corn, 30 to 40 bushels; Wheat, 15 to 20 bushels; Oats, 40 to 50 bushels; Tobacco, 1,200 pounds; on the hills, Corn, 15 to 25 bushels; Wheat, 7 to 9 bushels; Oats, 20 to 30 bushels; Tobacco, 900 pounds. These are without manures. The agricultural land is worth from $8 to $50 per acre; timber land, from $2 to $5, and mineral land (coal and iron), the same. Timber is worth, stumpage, 25 cents per tree, and at the mills, $10 to $12.50 per 1,000 feet. The principal industries are, stock-raising and farming. Principal exports, stock, wheat, and tobacco. Markets for tobacco and grain, Richmond, Virginia; for stock, Baltimore and Philadelphia. *Minerals*, good Coal (ordinary bituminous), in workable seams above water level; abundance of Limestone, suitable for building and agricultural purposes; good Potters' Clay is obtained and worked; large deposits of good brown haematite are found. The manufactories are not definitely reported; one Pottery exists on East river, making crockery and pipes, and one or more woolen factories are in the county. The principal streams are Blue Stone and New rivers. The former is navigable for canoes, and the latter for batteaux and canoes. Present means of transportation, are by these rivers and the county roads. Contemplated improvements, improvement of the navigation of New river, the New River railroad, Blue Stone Mining railroad. The Mercer county Normal school is at Concord. Public schools, 38; Churches, 11; Postoffices, 12. Population, 7,064. Value of taxable property, $660,895.06. County seat, Princeton.

MINERAL COUNTY.

Mineral county is mountainous, with long valleys along the streams. What was said of the soil, products, &c., &c., of Grant and Hampshire counties applies to Mineral, with the important exception that this county has a large amount of fine Coal and not so much Iron. The soil along the broad bottoms is extremely fertile, and brings fine Grass and Grain crops. The soil on the hills and mountains is sandy and sandy loam. Depth on highlands, 0 to 10 inches; on the bottoms many feet. Crops: Corn, Wheat, Oats, Rye, Grass. In the bottoms, Corn yields 30 to 50 bushels; Wheat, 10 to 15 bushels; Rye, 10 to 15 bushels; Oats, 25 to 35 bushels. On the hills, Corn, 20 bushels; Wheat, 8 bushels; Oats, 10 to 15 bushels; Rye, 10 bushels; Buckwheat, 20 bushels. Value of land, (agricultural, bottom), $20, to $100; uplands, $5 to $20; Timber land $1 to $5; Mineral lands, $50 to $150, per acre. Timber is worth, stumpage, $1,25 to $3 per 1,000; at the mills, sawed $15 per 1,000. The principal industries are Farming, Grazing, and Coal mining. Principal exports: Cattle, Timber, Coal; Timber is sold to Balt. & Ohio R. R. and eastern cities; Cattle goes to Baltimore and eastern cities; Coal goes east for steam making. Minerals: Soft Bituminous, in large workable beds. Knobby mountain contains an abundance of Limestone, good for agricutural and building purposes; good Sandstone for building purposes exists. The Virginia Coal Company, and the Baltimore and Hampshire Coal Company, are mining and shipping it from this county. The Manufactories have not been reported from this county. The Balt. & Ohio R. R. Machine Shops are located at New Creek or Keyser City, as it is now called. The principal streams are the North Branch of the Potomac and Patterson's creek, both navigable for small boats and timber rafts in high water. The present means of transportation are the Ches. & Ohio Canal, and the Balt. & Ohio R. R. and county roads. Contemplated: The improvement of the North Branch of the Potomac; The Cumberland, Moorefield & Broadway R. R.; North Branch R. R. Public Schools, 28; Churches, 21; Post-Offices, 9. Population,

6,332; Value of taxable property, $2,463,434 96. County Seat, Keyser. Newspapers: *West Virginia Tribune*, and *The Piedmont Independent*, both weekly.

MONONGALIA COUNTY.

The surface is very hilly, with many of the hills quite high, but none too steep for grazing and agricultural purposes. Many of the hills have broad tops, on which a good deal undulating land is afforded. Laurel hill on the east rises into a low range of mountains. The soil is a loam, varying from sandy to clayey, with some calcareous lands. All is naturally productive and well suited for grass. The depth on the hills is from 6 to 15 inches, deepest on the northwest sides; on the levels, from 1 to several feet. The crops are Corn, Oats, Wheat, and Grass. There is not much difference in the product of the hills and levels. Average yields are, Corn, 30 to 40 bushels; Oats, 25 to 35 bushels; Wheat, when succeeding, 10 to 12 bushels; Potatoes, 75 to 150 bushels. The Monongahela Agricultural and Mechanical Association holds an annual Fair at Morgantown, where about $1,400 in premiums are distributed. Value of land (Agricultural), from $10 to $75; no Mineral or Timber land is sold as such. Timber is worth, stumpage, 3 to 4 cents per cubic foot, and sawed lumber at the mills, $1,50 per hundred. The principal industries are Farming and Stock raising. Principal exports, Farm Produce, Stock, and some White Oak Timber. The market for Timber is Pittsburgh and down the river; for Stock, Baltimore; for Farm Products, Pittsburgh. Minerals: Good Coal in numerous workable beds above water level, all common bituminous; Limestone in large amounts, in the east, of fine quality for agricultural and building purposes; large amounts along the river; Iron Ore in workable quantities; excellent Sandstone for building; good Glass Sand; good Fire Clay, from which bricks have been made Manufacturers: One Cigar Factory, making 71,600 cigars; Carriage Factory and Planing Mill at Morgantown; Cabinet and Furniture Factory, and several large Steam Saw and Grist Mills. The principal streams are the Monongahela and Cheat rivers; the latter navigable for small boats, and the former for steamers on full water. Present means of transportation: The Monongahela river and dirt pikes. Contemplated and in progress: The improvement of the Monongahela by locks and dams, also, the Northern and Southern West Va. R. R. Public institutions: West Virginia University at Morgantown; Schools, &c.: The Morgantown Female Seminary, and 79 Public Schools; Churches, 39; Postoffices, 27. Population, 13,547. Value of taxable property, $4,597,207. County seat, Morgantown. Newspapers, *Morgantown Post* and *The New Dominion*, both weekly, at Morgantown.

MONROE COUNTY.

What was said of the topography, soil, products, etc., etc., of Greenbrier, applies, in great part, to Monroe. The surface is hilly and undulating, rising suddenly at some points into pretty high mountains. The soil is loam, clay, and calcareous clayey loam, producing fine farming and grazing lands. Depth on hills, 4 to 10 inches; on levels, 12 to 18 inches. Crops are Corn, Oats, Wheat, Grass, and Tobacco. Corn yields on the level lands, 30 to 40 bushels; Wheat, 15; Oats, 25 to 30. On the hills: Corn, 10 to 15; Wheat, 8 to 10; Oats, 15. Value of the land, which is mainly agricultural, $10 to $50; timber land, $5 to $20. Value of the timber, stumpage, 50 cents per tree; at the mill, $8 to $15. Principal industries: Farming and grazing. Principal exports: Stock of all kinds, and farm produce, tobacco, etc. Markets for grain and tobacco, Richmond; for stock, Baltimore. Minerals: Iron in workable quantities (brown hæmatite). Limestone in abundance, for building and agricultural purposes. Several celebrated mineral springs exist in this county, viz: "The Red Sweet," "Salt Sulphur," etc. The manufactories are not reported. One cigar factory is worked, making 3,000 cigars. Principal streams, New and Greenbrier rivers. Present means of transportation, Chesapeake and Ohio railroad, and turnpike roads. Contemplated: The New River railroad, the improvement of New river, and the extension of the James River and Kanawha canal. Schools: 1 high school, 1 female seminary, and 69 public sehools. Churches, 32. Postoffices, 15. Population, 11,123. Value of taxable property, $2,891,953.20. County seat, Union. Newspapers: *Border Watchman* and *Monroe Register*, both weekly.

MORGAN COUNTY.

Morgan county is a mountainous one, with numerous rocky

ridges, many of which are too steep, and the soil too thin, for ordinary cultivation. There is some fine bottom land along the Potomac, and good farming land along the Great Cacapon and Sleepy creek. The soil is loam and sandy, from 0 to 4 inches on the highlands, and 4 to 8 inches on the levels. The crops are Wheat, Corn, Oats, Tobacco, and Buckwheat. The yields on the cultivated lands, which are mainly the levels, are: Corn, 15 to 25 bushels; Oats, 10 to 20 bushels; Buckwheat, 15 to 30 bushels; Wheat, 8 to 15. The value of agricultural land is from $4 to $20; of timber land, on an average, $3 to $4. Price of timber, stumpage, $1 per tree; of lumber sawed at the mills, $10 per 1,000 feet. The principal industries are farming and lumbering. The principal exports are forest products, such as crossties, shingles, staves, hoop-poles, straps, tanbark and sawed lumber, mainly Yellow Pine. The markets are the Baltimore and Ohio railroad, and eastern cities. Minerals: Iron ore of fair quality on Sandy ridge. Large deposits of white sand on Sandy ridge, now used by a Philadelphia company. Some potters clay, which was formerly worked, at Hancock station. The Berkeley Mineral springs have long been celebrated, and much resorted to. Manufactures, etc: 2 large tanneries, 1 small woolen factory, 1 broom factory, 4 steam saw mills, and 14 grist and saw mills moved by water. The principal streams are the Potomac, Sleepy creek, and Great Cacapon, all navigable for rafts and canoes, 4 months in the year. Present means of transportation: Baltimore and Ohio railroad, and Chesapeake and Ohio canal. Contemplated: Improvement of the navigation of the Great Cacapon, the Potomac and Ohio railroad, the West Virginia railroad. Public schools, 25. Churches, 14. Postoffices, 11. Population, 4,315. Value of taxable property, $1,082,354.80. County seat, Berkeley Springs. Newspaper, *Morgan Mercury.*

NICHOLAS COUNTY.

The surface is hilly, mountainous, and platoau, or glade. The soil is generally good. Much of it is held in large tracts, and is unimproved, or in the original forest. The soil is loam, sandy, and sandy loam; depth on hills, 4 to 8 inches; on the bottoms, 8 to 20 inches. Crops raised are Corn, Oats, Wheat, Rye, Irish and Sweet Potatoes. Corn brings on the levels 30 to 40 bushels; Wheat, 10 to 12 bushels; Rye, 15 to 20 bushels; Potatoes, 100 to 150. On the hills: Corn, 15 to 25 bushels; Wheat, 8 to 10 bushels; Rye, 10 to 15 bushels; Potatoes, 50 to 75 bushels. The unimproved land is worth from $1 to $3 per acre, and the improved, $5 to $15. Timber is worth, stumpage, about $1 per tree; at the mill, $7.50 to $12. Principal exports, farming, grazing, and lumbering. For want of means of transportation, but little is sent out of the county, and this is mainly timber and stock. Market for stock, Baltimore; for timber, mouth of Gauley, where it is sawed up. Minerals: Coal; bituminous (ordinary), splint and cannel, in workable seams above water level. Good sandstone for building; also, millstone and grindstone grits. Brine has been found in the county. Principal stream, Gauley, navigable for rafts and single logs, on full tides. Present means of transportation, county roads. Contemplated improvements: Improvement of the navigation of the Gauley, Gauley River railroad. Public schools, 49. Churches, 11. Postoffices, 8. Population, 4,458. Value of taxable property, $990,847. County seat, Summersville.

OHIO COUNTY.

This county is very hilly, many of the hills being quite high, but they are fertile, and may be cultivated to their summits. It has a large amount of splendid bottom land on the Ohio and the creeks. The soil is excellent everywhere, and is mainly well cultivated. The soils of the bottoms are sandy loams, of the uplands, clay and sandy loams, usually like the other counties of the Panhandle, with a large amount of calcareous matter. On the levels the soil is from 12 inches to many feet deep; on the hills from 5 to 7 inches, being deeper and better on the north sides. All the cereals and root crops, grow well, and grass flourishes. The yields on the hills and bottoms are nearly alike; Grass produces 2 to 3 tons of Hay; Corn, 60 to 75 bushels; Oats, 40 to 50; Wheat, 15 to 20; Rye, 20 to 30; Potatoes, 100 to 200 bushels. No manures are used. Grapes do well, and in good seasons, produce as much as 1,000 gallons of wine per acre. Value of agricultural land, from $50 to $100 per acre. Good land can be rented for from $5 to $10 per acre per annum. The principal industries are farming grazing, mining coal, and manufacturing. Principal exports, farm products, stock, wool, and manufactured articles. Markets for produce, stock, wool, &c., Wheeling, Pittsburgh, and eastern cities. The minerals are coal, in large quantities, limestone for agricultural purposes and hydraulic cement. The principal river is the Ohio, which is navigable for steamers during the greater part of the year. The means of transportation are the Ohio river, the Baltimore and Ohio railroad, Pittsburgh, Baltimore and Wheeling railroad; contemplated railroads are the Pittsburgh, Wheeling and Kentucky railroad, partly completed from Steubenville to Wheeling. Public institutions, State Capitol, Custom House, Branch of the State Normal School. Schools, &c., are, Catholic Female Seminary, Commercial College, and 33 Public Schools; Postoffices, 8; Churches, 36. Population, 40,831. Value of taxable property, $15,104,740.00. Newspapers, *Standard*, daily and weekly; *Intelligencer*, daily and weekly; *Register*, daily, tri-weekly and weekly; *Sunday Leader*, weekly; *Arbiter Freund*, German, weekly; *The Medical Student*, monthly, all published at the county seat, *Wheeling*, which is the principal city of the county and State, being the State Capital.

THE CITY OF WHEELING.

This is both the principal town and Capital of the State. Its population, according to the latest data, is a little over 30,000. Its principal industry is manufacturing, and in this it is surpassed by few, if any, cities of its size in the Union. For the purpose of manufacturing, and bringing the completed articles to market with smallcost, it has unexceptionable advantages.

A large seam of good coal crops out in the hills around, and almost overhangs the furnaces consuming it. The Ohio river and Wheeling creek, furnish an abundance of water, while the Ohio river and railroad connections give easy and cheap access to all parts of the country.

Within the limits of this article we can only notice the leading manufactures. These are, the production of cigars, malt liquors, glass, and various manufactured forms of iron. For information concerning the manufacture of tobacco and liquors, we are indebted to Thos. J. Blair, Deputy Collector Internal Revenue, who has kindly furnished the statistics which follow.

Manufacture of Cigars.—Mr. Blair says: "The manufacture of cigars in the city of Wheeling, has been quite extensive for many years, to my knowledge, say 25 years, and what are known as 'Wheeling Stogies' have had a *national* reputation for at least that period. They are made of what is known as 'Kentucky Leaf Tobacco' and weigh, on an average, about 12 pounds to the 1,000, and were sold in the year 1875, at from $10 to $12 per 1,000, the United States revenue tax being, for two months of said year, $5 per 1,000, and for the remaining part of the year, $6 per 1,000.

"Other cigars of finer grades, ranging in value from $15 to $30, per 1,000, have also been produced to some extent, but are not to be compared in numbers to the 'Stogies' above referred to.

"I believe from examination, that during the year, 1872, there were more cigars manufactured in the city of Wheeling than in any previous year, and also, perhaps, outside of the city, and within the First District of West Virginia, viz.:

"Manufactured in the city of Wheeling, in 1872	31,000,000
"Manufactured outside of the city of Wheeling, in 1872	5,000,000
"Making a total production of	36,000,000

"The number of cigars manufactured in the city of Wheeling during 1875, was 22,783,000, and the total sales in the city were 22,765,000, while the number of cigar factories in that year was 52. The number of hands employed in the city in 1875, in the manufacture of cigars, was, on an average, 260.

"The manufacture of Tobacco for the year 1875 shows a falling off, as compared with previous years. The production of smoking tobacco during the year 1875, was, from three factories, about 38,000 pounds, taxed by the government at the rate of 24 cents per pound.

Malt Liquors.—The production of Ale, Beer, and Porter, in the city of Wheeling, has been for many years quite large, and is increasing every year, that of Beer especially. The following is the number of barrels manufactured in 1875:

"Ale and Porter, 2 breweries, barrels	3,760
"Beer, 8 breweries, barrels	21,606
"Total	25,366

"Taxed by the government at the rate of $1 per barrel."

The following facts concerning the manufacture of glass, were kindly furnished by Mr. Joseph Bell, President of the Excelsior Glass Company:

Manufacture of Glass in Wheeling.—The first manufacture of window glass in this State was undertaken in Wheeling about 1820. The commencement of this branch of business, and the subsequent change to the manufacture of *flint glass* are described in the following extracts from a letter written by Col. Redick McKee. He says:

"Up to 1817 or 1818, Wellsburg, then called Charlestown, was the principal town in the Pan-Handle, but the approaching completion of the "National Road" caused business men from other places to move into Wheeling, and changed the relative position of the two places. However, the immigrants brought, as a general thing, but little active capital, and the former inhabitants, though many of them were wealthy, had their money mainly locked up in lands, town lots, &c. Hence, new enterprises, such as the building of factories, steam mills, &c., were left to new-comers.

"About 1820 or 1821, Mr. George Carothers of Brownsville, Pa., came to Wheeling and proposed the building of a Window Glass Factory. Aided by Wheeling capital, he erected the necessary buildings for an eight-pot furnace, annealing ovens, &c. Owing to accidents the first attempt at glass making in this furnace failed, and the works were finally bought by Knox & McKee, who employed Carothers as superintendent, and in the latter part of 1821, or early in 1822, commenced successfully the manufacture of *cylinder glass*, packing mainly in half boxes (50 feet), with the brand, "Virginia Works, Knox & McKee, Wheeling."

"We," says Col. McKee, "continued the business satisfactorily for several years, turning out, I think, annually, some 3,000 or 4,000 boxes of all sizes, from 6x8 to 14x20, together with large quantities of green hollow-ware; gallon, half gallon, and quart bottles; oil and porter bottles; and pint bottles innumerable. Our 6x8 and 7x9 glass was sent to Boston; for other sizes the west and south furnished a market. Our No. 1 glass was in high repute, and bore transportation to distant points, even going to the trading posts in New Mexico.

"As factories multipled, and blowers became more numerous and skillful, prices declined, and finally ceased to pay. We followed them down from $12 to $3,50, and then changed the concern into a White Flint Hollow-Ware Factory, under the firm of Wheat, Price & Co."

The glass works spoken of above by Col. McKee, occupied the square on which now stands the Fourth Ward School House.

"In 1829 a Flint Glass House was erected in Wheeling by John and Craig Ritchie, located on the side of the hill, east of the Second Ward Market House. This establishment was operated for several years with great activity and success, and had a wide spread reputation for the manufacture of fine cut glass-ware.

"This success, and the unrivalled advantages for procuring cheap fuel at Wheeling, encouraged other firms to embark in the business, and in 1835 the Messrs. Sweeney put a large 'Flint Glass Works' into operation, in the northern part of the town, which was followed in the course of the next few years, by the erection of another large establishment at the extreme south end, built by Plunkett & Miller. The establishment built by the Messrs. Sweeney, was operated actively for more than 35 years, in Wheeling, until, in the changes of business, its proprietors found it to their advantage to move it across the river, where it is now known as the 'Excelsior Glass Works.'" These works, though on the Ohio side, are operated by Wheeling capital, and have the company incorporated under the laws of West Virginia. Hence, as it is in fact a Wheeling enterprise, it should be mentioned here. Mr. J. Bell, the President of the company, has kindly furnished us with the following statistics:

"The goods manufactured are known as crystal glassware made up into table, lamp, and bar goods, such as goblets tumblers, pitchers, bowls, dishes, beer glasses, lamps, lamp-chimneys, &c. About 150 persons are employed, of whom 10 to 15 are females. The annual product is about $115,000."

Returning to the establishments within the limits of the city of Wheeling, we quote still further from Mr. Bell's description of them:

"The works built at the south end of the city by Plunkett

& Miller, are now owned and operated by Hobbs, Brockunier & Co. The establishment has grown to be one of the most extensive in the country, and its products deservedly have a national reputation for excellence of quality.

"Another extensive and noted establishment located in the city of Wheeling, is known as the 'Central Glass Works,' making flint glassware. This has been in existence about fourteen years. It commenced with one small furnace, and now has three large furnaces, producing large quantities of common and fine cut glassware, and enjoys a reputation equal to any in the country.

"The increase in the number of establishments does not fully represent the growth of glass production in Wheeling, for it is safe to say that any one of the works now operating makes ten times the quantity produced by any one running in Wheeling forty years ago. The improvement in quality, and the cheapening of the cost of production have been equally marked. Articles of great beauty of design, excellence of finish, and unsurpassed in purity of metal, are of every day manufacture, and are sold at prices so low as to excite surprise. It is safe to say that nowhere is glassware of equal quality made more cheaply than in Wheeling."

IRON INTERESTS OF WHEELING.

BY A. W. CAMPBELL, ESQ.

Wheeling is chiefly known as the centre of a large iron industry, particularly for Cut Nails. The city and vicinity constitute the largest Nail market in the world. The growth of this business, as indeed of all the manufactures of Wheeling, is due to the abundance of cheap fuel (stone coal) in the hills around the city, and to the facilities for reaching all the markets of the country, either by rail or water, at low rates for freight.

The iron out of which these nails is made is produced on the spot, mostly from mixtures of Missouri and Lake Superior ores, and when made is immediately in market, without cost for transportation. There are now, at Wheeling and Steubenville, nine blast furnaces for the manufacture of iron, as follows: On the Wheeling side of the river, the "Top Mill" furnace, the "Belmont," and the "Riverside." On the

Ohio side, the "Bellaire" furnace, the "Benwood," the "Mingo," the two "Jefferson" furnaces, and the "Stony Hollow." These furnaces have mostly 16 feet boshes and 60 feet stacks. The "Top Mill" has an 18 foot bosh, and the Benwood a 13 foot. They produce mostly "Red Short" irons, such as are used for Nails. At this time iron is made as low as $19 per ton, worth in the market say $22, on four months' time. The connection now being made, via the Hempfield Short-line, between Wheeling and Connellsville, will so reduce the price of coke as to give Wheeling a further margin in its manufacture of iron.

The Nail mills at Wheeling and vicinity are as follows: The "Riverside" works, running 126 machines, including, also, a separate Bar and Rail mill belonging to the same company. Their blast furnace is three miles below their mills, with which they connect by rail and water.

The "Top Mill," running 106 machines, situated in the north part of the city, on the line of the Pittsburgh, Wheeling and Kentucky railroad—a new road not yet completed. Their blast furnace immediately adjoins their mill, and iron can be handled at a minimum cost through all its processes.

The "Belmont Nail Works," situated in Center Wheeling, running 110 machines. This mill has turned out as high as 8,155 kegs of nails in one week, on an extraordinary run. Its blast furnace immediately adjoins the mill. It has also a large cooper shop, whereat all its kegs are made.

The La Belle Nail Works, running 85 machines, but is one of two mills owned by the same company. The other is the Jefferson, situated at Steubenville, and it also runs 85 machines, and has two blast furnaces. Together they form a large and wealthy company, which was originally started as a practical workingmen's organization.

The Benwood Nail Works, running 112 machines, four miles below the city. The company owns some 80 tenement houses, and has built up the suburb of "Benwood." The Mill has a cooper establishment connected with it. Its blast furnace is on the opposite side of the river, in the suburb of Martin's Ferry.

The Bellaire Nail Works, situated immediately opposite Benwood, on the Ohio side, runs 100 machines, and has a blast furnace on its premises. Is a large and valuable property.

The Ohio City Nail Works, situated in the suburb of Martin's Ferry, a town lying opposite the north end of the city of Wheeling. This is a new mill, and only runs 50 machines. On a double turn it can produce 2,500 kegs of Nails per week.

During the years 1871, '72 and '73, the mills above named, except the Ohio City, produced 2,995,509 kegs of Nails. In those years Wheeling manufactured about one-fourth of all the Nails made in the United States.

Nails can be shipped at the following low rates of freight: To New Orleans, 20 cents per keg; to St. Louis, 10 cents; to Chicago, 22 cents; to Cincinnati, 7 cents.

The other principal iron manufactories of Wheeling and vicinity, are as follows:

The Wheeling Hinge Company, now in the 12th year of its existence, has steadily grown from a small affair to be a large concern. It owns the patent for the Dunning hinge—an article intended to supersede, to a certain extent, the old screw and strap hinge.

The Superior Machine Works, a large concern organized for the manufacture of the Superior Reaping and Mowing Machines, and where also engines and other machinery are built.

The Centripetal Power Company Works, organized for the manufacture of portable machinery for the use (principally) of farmers, whereby important advantages are claimed in overcoming friction, and in the retention of speed and momentum.

The Crescent Rail and Sheet Mills—situated on the south bank of Wheeling creek—connected by a bridge across said creek with the 4th ward of the city, and directly opposite the works of the Wheeling Hinge Co. A large concern, owned by the Whitakers, well known iron men. Is principally run now on sheet iron.

The Ætna Iron Works, situated in the suburb of Ætnaville, a new village just growing up opposite the city, midway between Bridgeport and Martin's Ferry. Manufactures bar and sheet iron, and also small rails for coal banks and light roads.

The Norway Tack Factory, situated in the 4th ward of the city; started in 1865—owned by Jones, Heald & Phinney—manufactures all varieties of tacks and a fine three-penny nail.

The Arlington Stove Works and Foundry of Joseph Bell &

Co.; the Star Stove Works and Foundry of Benjamin Fisher; the Boiler Works of Moorehead & Son; the Foundry, Machine and Repair Works of A. J. Sweeney & Son; the Foundry, Machine and Repair Works of Cecil, Hobbs & Co.; the Bellaire Implement Factory; the Stove Works and Foundry of Spence, Baggs & Co., at Martin's Ferry; the Ohio Valley Machine Works of L. Spence & Co., (same place,) whereat were built the engines of the Belmont Blast Furnace, and where also are made Threshers and Cleaners, and other machinery; the large Foundry of Culbertson, Wiley & Co., (same place,) where was cast the heavy iron work of the Ætna Mill.

The foregoing are the principal iron establishments in and around Wheeling. Quite a number of them are of recent origin, either in whole or part. Just previous to the panic of 1873, an important impetus had been given to the development of the iron business of this vicinity, growing out, as we have said, of the abundance of cheap fuel and the facilities for shipment. It is hoped that these advantages will, at an early day, re-assert themselves, and go on, as in the years '72 and '73, increasing the number of our manufactories.

Tanneries.—The business of tanning has long been important in Wheeling. Hides and bark are obtained in the vicinity. The following data are given by one knowing the facts: 2 large steam tanneries and 5 small ones, employ 100 workmen, use yearly 4,700 cords of bark, 25,000 hides, and make 725,000 lbs. of harness, sole and upper leather; the principal part being harness leather, of a quality second to none in the country, which is sold to all parts of the Union, from Main to Wisconsin, Kansas and Texas. These tanneries also dress 8,000 calf skins, and 60.000 to 70,000 sheep skins a year. Large numbers of saddles, harness, collars, &c., are made in the city. 2 glue factories make 75,000 lbs. of glue yearly.

Lumber.—This trade is extensive. 5 large steam planing mills make flooring, doors, sash, boxes, &c. Steamboat building, and the making of wagons, carriages, barrels, kegs and other articles composed in whole or part of wood, deserve mention. Furniture is made in several factories.

Miscellaneous.—Six factories are engaged in making candy. The amount made yearly, exceeds 350,000 lbs. 1 woolen factory uses from 60,000 to 80,000 lbs. of wool, making 6,000 yards of flannel a month, also knitting yarn. 2 factories make soap and candles. The supply of clay for brick is good, abundant, and largely worked. The manufacture of flour, paper, drugs and medicines, paper boxes, blank books, printed caliço, gloves, brushes, willow ware, shoe nails, and wrought trace chains, while not as extensive as the interests before named, should not be overlooked. It may be added that Wheeling manufactures enjoy the reputation of being exceedingly well made.

PENDLETON COUNTY.

Pendleton county in position, topography, and soil, belongs to the South Branch group of counties, and much that was said of Hampshire and Hardy may be said of it. The amount of mountain land is larger, however, and the elevations are greater, the surface rougher, and the amount of cultivation less than in the counties to the north of it. The mountains of this county form some of the highest, if not the very highest, land in the State. The soils are sandy, sandy loams, clayey loams, with some calcareous soil. The crops are Wheat, Corn, Rye, Oats, Buckwheat, and Grass, which latter is the staple. The grains are raised only for home consumption. The depth of soil on the highlands is 0 to 12 inches; on the levels, 4 to 12 inches. Yields of grain on the bottom lands, are Corn, 20 to 50 bushels; Wheat, 12 to 15 bushels; Oats and Buckwheat, 25 to 40 bushels. On improved uplands, not much less. The mountainous lands are not cultivated. Value of land: The South Branch agricultural land is worth from $5 to $100 per acre; timber land is worth from $5 to $10. Timber is worth on the stump, 35 to 50 cents per cord; at the mills, $10 to $12.50 per 1,000. The principal industries are farming and stock raising. The principal exports, cattle, sheep, horses and wool. The principal market for stock is Baltimore. Minerals: Iron, in workable quantities (brown and red hæmatite, and fossil ore). Limestone in abundance for agricultural and building purposes. Some potters' clay, that has been worked with success. Good limestone and sandstone for building. Mineral waters: White Sulphur, Alum, and Chalybeate. One woolen factory exists. Principal streams: Headwaters of the South Branch of the Potomac; these are not navigable. Present means of transportation, county roads. Contemplated: The Cumberland, Moorefield and Broadway railroad, Potomac and Ohio railroad, Shenandoah and Ohio railroad, W., C. &

St. L. Narrow Gauge railroad. Public schools, 63. Churches, 13. Postoffices, 15. Value of taxable property, $1,559,435.51. Population, 6,455. County seat, Franklin. Newspaper, *Pendleton News*, weekly.

PLEASANTS COUNTY.

This county is hilly, like the others along the Ohio river, and has a good deal of flat land along the Ohio, and the numerous creeks which empty into it. On the bottoms, the soil is a sandy loam; on the hills, clayey loam, with some calcareous land. The first Ohio bottoms have 3 feet and more of soil; the second bottoms and valleys, 1 foot and more; the hills, 6 to 8 inches. Crops are Corn, Oats, Wheat, Rye, Potatoes, and Grass. On the bottoms Corn yields 40 to 60 bushels; Wheat, 15 to 30; Oats, 20 to 30; Rye, 20. Hills yield of Corn, 20 to 25 bushels; Wheat, 10; Oats, 15; Rye, 10. No manures used for these yields. The value of the land is: Ohio bottoms, $80 to $100; creek bottoms, $40 to $50; hill land, $15 to 20; timber land, $10 to 20. Timber is worth, stumpage, 2 cents per linear foot; at the mill, 10 cents per cubic foot. Principal industries, farming, stock raising, and lumbering. Principal exports, grain, cattle, wool, lumber, cooperage stuff, etc. Market for stock, Baltimore; for grain, lumber, etc., points down the Ohio river. Minerals: Thin coal seams above water level. Some good sandstone for building. Petroleum and salt water are found. The petroleum is worked and exported. Several tanneries, barrel and shingle factories, saw mills, etc., exist, but are not definitely reported. The principal streams are the Ohio river and Middle Island creek. Middle Island is navigable for flatboats, rafts, etc., when high. Present means of transportation: The Ohio river, Baltimore and Ohio railroad, and Middle Island. Contemplated: Slack water navigation for Middle Island, the Pittsburgh, Wheeling and Kentucky railroad. Public schools, 25. Churches, 15. Postoffices, 6. Population, 3,012. Value of taxable property, $784,841.86. County seat, Saint Marys.

POCAHONTAS COUNTY.

This county has a considerable variety of surface. Much of the land is in high mountains, which are rough and broken. The county has a good deal of the smoothly undulating limestone land, found in Greenbrier and Monroe, which is of the finest character. The soils are calcareous clays, or loams, or sandy loams. On the levels, the depth is 18 inches and more; on the hills and highlands, 0 to 6 inches. Crops are Corn, Wheat, Oats, Rye, Buckwheat, and Grass. Yields on the bottoms, Corn, 35 to 40 bushels; Wheat, 15 to 20; Oats, 30 to 40; Rye, 20 to 30; Buckwheat, 20 to 30 bushels; on the uplands, when cultivated, Corn, 20 to 25; Wheat, 8 to 10; Oats, 25 to 30; Rye, 20 to 25; Buckwheat, 30 to 40 bushels. No manures used with these yields. Value of best agricultural land, $40 to $75 per acre; of ordinary $5 to 20; of timber land, $1 to $8. Timber, stumpage, is sold by the acre at $1.50 to $2 per acre; at the saw mills lumber is worth $12,50 per 1,000. The principal industries are farming and grazing. The principal exports are, cattle, sheep, timber, and farm produce. Market for farm produce, Staunton; for cattle, Baltimore and New York; timber, mainly white pine, is sent down the Greenbrier river to Ronceverte. Minerals, limestone in abundance for agricultural and building purposes; good sandstone for building; also grits for grindstones and whetstones; iron ore of good quality and in workable seams. Mineral waters, sulphur and chalybeate. Principal stream, Greenbrier river, navigable for rafts and small boats in high water. Present means of transportation, the turnpike and dirt roads to the Chesapeake and Ohio railroad. Contemplated: Improvement of the Greenbrier river, the W. C. & St. L. Narrow Gauge railroad, North Branch railroad, West Virginia railroad. Public Schools, 35; Churches, 9; Postoffices, 16. Population, 4,069. Value of taxable property, $1,405,462.69. County seat, Huntersville.

PRESTON COUNTY.

The surface of Preston county shows a good deal of variety, it being mountainous, hilly and rolling, and "glady," or with a rolling plateau character. The soil varies a good deal also, being sandy, sandy loam, clay loam, and calcareous loam. The limestone appears in the hills, and gives the strongest soil. The "glade land" has a deep, black, unctious soil, often several feet deep, and sometimes needs ditching. Crops are Corn, Wheat, Oats, Rye, and Buckwheat. The depth of soil on the levels is 12 to 15 inches; on the hills, 4 to 6 inches. Yields of grain, Corn, 25 to 40; Oats, 15 to 25; Buckwheat,

20 to 25; Rye, 12 to 15 bushels. These are on improved agricultural lands. Value of land, best agricultural, $25 to $40; common, from $10 to $20; timber land, $5 to $10; mineral land, $5 to $40. Value of timber, stumpage, $1 per tree; at the mills, $10 to $15 per 1,000. Principal industries, farming, grazing and lumbering. Principal exports, stock, lumber, and coal. Markets for all these are in the eastern cities. The minerals are coal (common bituminous), in several good workable seams; iron (siderite), in workable quantities; an abunance of excellent limestone, for building and agricultural purposes; good sandstone, for building purposes; potters' clay of good quality is found and worked. Manufactures and mines, the Newburg Orrell Coal Company, and the Austin mines, both ship a good deal of coal. Besides these, there are many openings for local use. Manufactures, &c., are, two iron furnaces, one foundry, four woolen factories, besides various saw and grist mills; one cigar factory, making 105,400 cigars; stave factories, &c., &c., the number and kind not being definitely reported. The principal stream is Cheat, navigable in its lower portion for rafts and flat boats. Present means of transportation, Baltimore and Ohio railroad and several good turnpike roads. Contemplated improvements, Iron Valley and Pennsylvania Line railroad. Public Schools, 110; Churches, 38; Postoffices, 30. Population, 14,555. Value of taxable property, $3,106,778.00. County seat, Kingwood, with about 900 inhabitants. Newspapers, *Preston County Journal* and *Preston County Herald*, both weekly.

PUTNAM COUNTY.

This county is generally hilly and rolling. It has a good deal of bottom land of considerable fertility on the Kanawha and the numerous creeks. These bottoms are a mile wide on the Kanawha, and have a deep loam. On the hills the soil is clay, and calcareous clayey loam, of considerable productiveness. The county is wooded over five-sixths of its area. The crops are Corn, Wheat, Oats, Buckwheat, and Tobacco. Yields of Corn on the bottoms are 50 to 80 bushels; Wheat, 12 to 15 bushels; Oats, 25 to 30 bushels; while on the hills Corn produces 20 to 30 bushels; Wheat, 8 to 10 The soil on the bottoms is many feet deep, and on the hills 12 to 18 inches, producing fine grass and tobacco.

Value of land: Kanawha bottoms bring $100, other lands from $1 to $20, according to location and condition. Timber, stumpage, is worth about $1 per tree; at the mills, $13. Principal industries: Farming and Lumbering. Principal exports, Lumber, Cooperage Stuff, Grain, and Coal. Staves, &c, go to England; Farm Produce, to Richmond and Cincinnati; Timber, in logs, and Coal are sent down the river to Cincinnati, &c. Minerals: Coal of fine quality, and workable in quantity, is above water level; some good Limestone, and Sandstone suitable for building occurs. Mines: Raymond Coal Co., shipping annually from 1,300,000 to 1,400,000 bushels. Oak Ridge Colliery has just commenced operations. Manufactories, &c.: A large Flour Mill at Buffalo, Flour and Saw Mill at Winfield, Saw Mill at Hurricane, and at Raymond City, all driven by steam. Principal streams, Kanawha, navigable for steamers; Pocatalico, navigable for batteaux and rafts in good water. Present means of transportation, Kanawha river and Ches. & Ohio railroad. Contemplated: Improvement of the Kanawha river, now going on, and the West Va. R. R. Public Schools, 48; Churches, 14; Postoffices, 11. Population, 7,794. Value of taxable property, $1,823,624 00. County seat, Winfield. Newspaper, *Winfield Independent*, weekly.

RALEIGH COUNTY.

The surface of Raleigh is hilly and mountainous, with a large proportion of plateau land, covered with undulating and rolling hills. The rivers cut deeply into the plane of the country, and the roughest land lies in the sides of the hills facing them. The soil is a loam, or sandy loam, 4 to 6 inches deep on the hills, and 6 to 10 inches, or more, on the levels. The hills and levels produce about alike. The crops are Corn, Wheat, Oats, Buckwheat, and Potatoes. Yields are Corn, 20 to 40 bushels; Oats, 20 to 25; Wheat, 10; Rye, 15 to 25; Potatoes, 100 to 150. Price of agricultural land, $5 to $15; of timber and coal lands, from $1 to $5. Timber is worth 50 cents to $1 per tree, according to kind and location; at the mills, $10 per 1,000. Principal industries, farming and stock raising. Principal exports, cattle. Market: Cattle go to Baltimore. Manufactures, etc.: Several steam saw mills, besides the usual grist and saw mills on streams. Minerals: Coal, in workable seams of good quality; iron, in workable quantities;

sandstone of good quality for building; good millstone grit. Principal streams: New river, navigable for batteaux; Piney river, for logs, in full water. Present means of transportation: Chesapeake and Ohio railroad and county roads. Contemplated: The improvement of New river, and the Coal River railroad. Public schools, 47. Churches, 4. Postoffices, 10. Population, 3,673. Value of taxable property, $730,862.19. County seat, Raleigh C. H.

RANDOLPH COUNTY.

This county is quite mountainous, with a large proportion of rolling plateau, or glade land, and a good deal of fertile bottom land along the streams. It has a great amount of heavily timbered forests, and a considerable proportion is owned in large tracts. The bottoms are loam, and sandy loam; the uplands and glades, sandy loam, and some calcareous land. On the hills the depth is 3 to 10 inches; on the bottoms, from one to many feet. Crops are Corn, Wheat, Oats, Rye, Buckwheat and fine Grass. Corn produces on the levels, 25 to 70 bushels; Wheat, 10 to 15; Oats, 25 to 40. On the hills, Corn, 15 to 25; Wheat, 8 to 10; Oats, 20; Buckwheat, 20. Value of improved land, bottoms, $50 to $100; mountain, or glade land, $4 to $10; timber land, in large tracts, from $1 to $2.50 per acre. Value of timber, stumpage, $1 per tree. After sawing at the mills, $10 to $12.50 per 1,000. Principal industries, farming and stock raising. Principal exports: Stock and wool. The stock goes to eastern markets. Minerals: Coal, in workable beds in the western part; limestone, suitable for building and agricultural purposes; good sandstone for building. Tygart's Valley is the principal stream; navigable for small boats in full water. Present means of transportation: Turnpikes and good county roads. Contemplated improvements: Washington and Ohio railroad, Potomac and Ohio railroad, W., C. & St. L. Narrow Gauge railroad, Shenandoah and Ohio railroad, and West Va. railroad. Public schools, 70. Churches, 14. Postoffices, 17. Population, 5,563. Value of taxable property, $1,561,101.23. County seat, Beverly. Newspaper, *Randolph Enterprise*, weekly.

RITCHIE COUNTY.

This county is for the most part very hilly, and some of the hills are quite high, rising 600 feet above their valleys. There are fine bottom lands along the streams. The soils are clayey and sandy loams, on the levels, 12 to 18 inches deep, and on the hills, 4 to 6 inches. The crops adapted to these soils are, Corn, Oats, and Grass. But little wheat is sown, and most of the flour used comes from the State of Ohio. The crops average, per acre, on the levels, Corn, 40 to 50 bushels; Oats, 20 to 25; Potatoes, 75 to 100; Grass, 2 tons, and 1 ton on the hills. The hill crops of the grains are often as good as those on the levels. No manures are used for these yields. The value of the agricultural land is $10 to $20 per acre, and of the timber land from $4 to $6, according to location and amount of timber. Value of timber, stumpage, $1 per tree, and at the mills, 8 to 10 cents per cubic foot. Principal industries, farming, grazing, lumbering, and oil production. Principal exports, timber, lumber, cooperage stuff, on a large scale, stock, oil, and building stone. Principal markets, Parkersburg, Cincinnati, Baltimore, and eastern cities. The minerals are, petroleum, building stone of fine quality, and small seams of coal above water level. Manufactures, &c., stave factory at Pennsboro, one at Petroleum, and four mills on the North Fork of Hughes' river, five mills on the South Fork, and several steam and water mills in other parts of the county; cigar factories making 77,000 cigars. The Baltimore and Ohio Railroad Company works a large and valuable quarry of superior building stone. The Ritchie Asphaltum mines formerly carried on extensive operations, but the deposit has now given out. The principal streams are the North and South Forks of Hughes' river. They are navigable for rafts, batteaux, and canoes, on a full stage of water. The means of transportation are, Parkersburg Branch of the Baltimore and Ohio railroad, Pennsboro and Harrisville railroad, and county roads. Public Schools, 78; Postoffices, 21; Churches, 35. Population, 9,055. Value of taxable property, $1,981,650.00. Newspaper, *Ritchie Gazette*, weekly, published at Harrisville, the county seat.

ROANE COUNTY.

The surface of this county is hilly and rolling. The hills are lower than those on the Kanawha river, and have broad tops, with gentle slopes and valleys of considerable width between them. The soil is clay, and clay loam, usually with calcareous matter, and very fertile. The depth on the hills and levels is nearly the same, viz.: 8 to 12 inches. Crops are, Corn, Wheat, Oats, Tobacco and Grass. The bottoms yield, of Corn, 40 to 50 bushels; Wheat, 15 to 20 bushels; Oats, 30 to 40. On the hills, Corn produces 25 to 30; Wheat 10 to 15; Oats, 20 to 25. Value of agricultural land, $10 to $20; of timber land $5. The timber of Roane is very fine. European ship builders have agents getting out material for exportation. Timber is worth 75 cents to $1 per tree, stumpage, and at the mills, $10 to $14 per 1,000. Principal industries, farming stock raising, and lumbering. Principal exports, cattle, tobacco, forest and orchard products. Market for farm produce, Charleston and home; for stock, Baltimore; for tobacco, Parkersburg; for timber, Parkersburg and points on the Ohio. Minerals, coal, in a good seam above water level; good sandstone for building. The county has flouring and other mills, and woolen factories, but as they have not been reported we cannot say anything definitely about them. Pocatalico is the principal stream, and is navigable in high water for flatboats and rafts. Present means of transportation, county roads. Contemplated improvements, Washington and Ohio railroad, and W. C. & St. L. Narrow Gauge railroad. Public Schools, 72; Churches, 6; Postoffices, 16. Population, 7,232. Value of taxable property, $1,022,767.00. County seat, Spencer.

SUMMERS COUNTY.

This county has some high mountains and a large proportion of rolling, or gently undulating plateau land. The soil is sandy or loam, and clay loam, with calcareous matter in some parts. On the hills it is 3 to 6 inches deep; on the bottoms, 6 to 12. The crops are Corn, Wheat, Oats, Rye, Tobacco and Grass. Corn yields, on the levels, 30 to 35 bushels; Wheat, 15 to 18; Rye, 15; Oats, 35. On the hills, Wheat and Rye, 10 bushels; Corn and Oats, 25; Tobacco, 600 pounds. Value of agricultural land, from $10 to $40 per acre; of timber land, $1 to $5. Timber, stumpage, is worth 50 cents to $1 per tree; at the mills, pine and poplar, are worth $15 per 1,000. Principal industries, farming, lumbering and stock raising. Principal exports: Stock, tobacco, and timber. Market for stock, Baltimore; for tobacco, etc., Richmond and Cincinnati; for timber, eastern cities. Minerals. Coal, in probably workable seams; sandstone, for building purposes; good limestone, for building and agricultural purposes. Alum, Chalybeate and Sulphur Springs. Manufactures: Hinton lumber mills, Burk's and Clark's lumber mills, 3 or more flouring mills, 1 tobacco factory, producing 1,250 pounds, etc. Principal streams: New and Blue Stone rivers, navigable for canoes. Present means of transportation: Chesapeake and Ohio railroad. Contemplated improvements: Improvement of New river, Blue Stone Mining railroad, and New River railroad. Public schools, 28. Postoffices, 17. Value of taxable property, $752,711. County seat, Hinton. Newspaper, *Mountain Herald*, weekly.

TAYLOR COUNTY.

The surface of this county is very hilly, many of the hills being quite high. Laurel Hill range passes through this county, but flattens out so as to be nothing more than a high range of hills. The land is mostly quite fertile, and most of it is arable. The soils are sandy loam, calcareous, and clay loams. On the hills they are 4 to 12 inches; on the bottoms, 6 to 15 inches deep. The hills are about as productive as the levels. The crops are Corn, Wheat, Oats, and Grass. Corn produces 25 to 50 bushels; Wheat, 8 to 15 bushels; Oats, 15 to 25 bushels. The Taylor County Agricultural and Mechanical Society holds an annual Fair at Grafton, and distributes about $3,000 in premiums. The value of the agricultural land, when improved, is $20 to $60; of timber land, $12 to $25. For the privilege of mining the 7 foot gas coal seam, without the surface land, average price $100 per acre; for the same privilege for the 5 foot seam, $20; for the 4 foot seam, $10, etc. Price of timber, stumpage, good Oak and Poplar, $4 per tree; Walnut, $5; other trees, $2; at the mills, $7 per 1,000. Principal industries: farming, stock raising, and lumbering. Principal exports: horses, cattle, timber, lumber, cooperage stuff, and coal. Markets: for timber, the mills in the county, where it is manufactured into plank, shooks, etc., and sent east. Some logs sent down the Monongahela to Pittsburgh. For stock, the markets are eastern cities; for grain and general produce, the villages of the county. Minerals: abundance of good coal in large seams; iron, in workable quantities; good limestone, for agricultural and building purposes; excellent sandstones, for building; good fire clay. Mines: Coal—Tyrconnell mines,

Flemington mines, Claysville mines, Pruntytown mines; the latter two for local use. Manufactures: Webster woolen factory, 2 steam furniture mills at Grafton, 2 steam furniture mills at Fetterman, 1 steam excelsior mattress factory at Grafton, where there are also 1 foundry and machine shop, the Baltimore and Ohio repair shops, 1 wood pump factory, 3 shook factories, 2 steam planing, sash and door factories, 1 cigar factory, making 596,400 cigars annually. Besides these there are in the county 12 steam saw mills, 6 steam flouring mills, 11 water grist mills, on Tygart's Valley river, and its tributaries; 6 tanneries. There are 6 water mills in Taylor county, on the river, within a distance of 15 miles.

The principal stream is Tygart's Valley, which has, at Grafton, a large boom. It is capable of floating rafts, and is navigable for batteaux and canoes all the year. Present means of transportation: Baltimore and Ohio railroad (main stem) and Parkersburg Branch, Tygart's Valley river, and two principal turnpike roads. In contemplation: Slack water of Tygart's Valley river, and Buckhannon Mineral railroad. Schools: West Virginia College at Flemington, High School at Grafton, and 46 public schools. Churches, 3. Postoffices, 11. Population, 9,367. Value of taxable property, $4,058,763.27. County seat, Pruntytown, with a population of about 800. Newspaper, *Grafton Sentinel*, weekly.

TUCKER COUNTY.

Tucker is a mountainous county, mostly in wild land. There is, however, a good deal of rolling plateau country, and the soil is very fertile in many places. The timber is very fine in amount, size, and kinds. The soil is sandy loam, and clayey loam; on the levels 3 to 12 inches deep; on the hills 2 to 6 inches. Corn, Oats, Rye, and Buckwheat are the crops. Corn produces 20 to 30 bushels; Oats, 20 to 25 bushels; Rye, 8 bushels, on the hills or plateau. On the levels or bottoms, Corn produces 40 bushels; Rye 12 bushels; Oats 25 to 30 bushels; Buckwheat, on levels, 30 bushels; on the hills 35 bushels. Value of land: Agricultural, $5 to $10; Wild Timber lands in large tracts, $1 to $5. Value of Timber, stumpage, $1 per tree; at the mills, $6,25 to $10 per 1,000. Principal industry: Farming. Principal exports: but little is exported from the county. A few Cattle and some Forest Products, Ginseng, &c., are sent out, and some little Lumber. The markets are along the Balt. & Ohio R. R. and in eastern cities. Minerals . Good Limestone for building and agricultural purposes, and sandstone for building. There are some Saw and Grist Mills in the county. Principal stream, Cheat river. Public Schools, 18; Churches, 9; Post offices, 9. Population, 1,917. Value of taxable property, $377,111 24. County seat, Saint George.

TYLER COUNTY.

The surface of the county, back from the river and creeks is hilly; however the hills are not rough, but are arable and fertile. There is a large amount of fine bottom land along the Ohio river, and Middle Island and other creeks. The soil is sandy loam, loam, and clayey loam, or clay, usually deep and mellow. On the levels it is from one to many feet deep; on the hills 8 to 12 inches. Crops are, Corn, Wheat, Oats, Tobacco, and Grass. On the bottoms, Corn yields 50 to 65 bushels; Wheat, 10 to 12 bushels; Oats, 30 to 40 bushels; on the hills, Corn brings 35 to 40 bushels; Wheat, 8 to 10 bushels; Oats, 25 to 30 bushels; Tobacco, 800 to 1,000 pounds. Value of land: Agricultural bottom lands, $40 to $100; Upland, $20 to $30; Timber land, $10 to $20. Value of timber, stumpage, 3 to 4 cents per cubic foot; at the mills, 5 to 10 cents per cubic foot. Principal industries: Farming, Stock raising, and Lumbering. Principal exports: Tobacco, Grain, Stock, Sawed Lumber, and Cooperage Stuff. Markets for timber, points on the Ohio river; for Tobacco, Cincinnati; for Stock, Baltimore and Philadelphia. Minerals: Small Coal seams above water level; some Iron and Limestone, and good Sandstone for building. Manufactures: Two Woolen Mills, and several Saw and Grist Mills, not definitely reported. The principal streams are the Ohio river and Middle Island creek; the latter is navigable for rafts and flat boats on full water. Present means of transportation: The Ohio river and Balt. & Ohio R. R. Improvements contemplated: The improvement of the navigation of Middle Island creek, The Pittsburgh, Wheeling & Kentucky R. R. Public schools, 67; Churches, 22; Postoffices, 15. Population, 7,832. Value of taxable property, $1,838,126. County seat, Middlebourne, with a population of about 500 inhabitants.

UPSHUR COUNTY.

This county has a very diversified surface; a portion is rough; most of it hilly, with a good deal of undulating and table land. The soil is sandy, clay, and loam; depth on the levels, 8 to 10 inches; on the hills, 4 to 6 inches. Crops, Corn, Wheat, Oats, and Grass. The hills produce nearly as well as the levels. Corn yields from 25 to 40 bushels; Wheat, 5 to 15; Oats, 20 to 30. Value of land: agricultural, $5 to $30; timber land, $1 to $5. Value of timber: stumpage, $1 per tree; at the river, delivered in the stream, $1 to $2 per log; sawed at the mills, $5 to $7.50 per 1,000. Principal industries: farming, stock raising, and lumbering. Principal exports: stock, tobacco, lumber, timber, and forest products. Cattle go to eastern cities, timber to Grafton. Coal in workable seams, some iron, good sandstone for building. Manufactures, mills, &c., not reported. Principal stream, Buckhannon river, navigable for canoes. Present means of transportation, turnpike and county roads. Improvements contemplated: Buckhannon Mineral railroad, Shenandoah and Ohio railroad, and Washington and Ohio railroad. Schools, &c., Buckhannon Normal Academy, Frenchton Academy, Public Schools, 58; Churches, 31; Postoffices, 15. Population, 8,023. Value of taxable property, $2,353,008.54. County seat, Buckhannon. Newspaper, *Buckhannon Delta*, weekly.

WAYNE COUNTY.

The surface of this county is hilly, the hills being comparatively low on the Ohio, and rising higher back in the country. There is a good deal of fine bottom land on the Ohio river (the bottoms are about half a mile wide), and on the other streams and creeks. These bottoms, and the sloping hills near the water-courses, form all the cleared land, most of the county being in forest. This county yields some of the finest timber in the State. The soil is mainly loam, very deep on the levels, and lying 6 to 8 inches thick on the hills. The land is usually very fertile, and produces fine Corn, Wheat, Oats, Tobacco and Grass. Some acres of Ohio bottoms have produced 110 bushels of Corn. The yields are, on the bottoms, of Corn, 50 to 70 bushels; Wheat, 10 to 15; Oats, 25 to 40; on the hills, Corn, 30 to 50 bushels; Oats, 20 to 30; Wheat, 8 to 10. Value of Ohio bottoms, $80 to $100; other bottom land,

$10 to $20; hill mineral, and timber land, $5 to $10 per acre. Value of timber, stumpage, $1 per tree; at the mills, 8 to 10 cents per cubic foot. Principal industries, farming and lumbering. Principal exports, grain, young cattle, tobacco, timber. The markets for all are down the Ohio, except for the young cattle, which are sold to inland counties. Minerals: Wayne has abundant supplies of the finest splint, cannel, and common bituminous coal, in large seams above water level; iron ore in workable quantities; fine potters' clay and good sandstone for building; yellow ochre; salt water is found at Warfield, Kentucky, just beyond the south corner of the county; 250 bushels of salt per day are made. Manufactures, At Ceredo, two extensive saw and planing mills; steam saw and grist mills at Cassville, Trout Hill, and other points, along Sandy and Twelve-Pole rivers. The principal streams are the Ohio, Big Sandy and Tug Fork. The two latter are navigable for from 5 to 10 months of the year, by steamers and heavy barges. Rafts are floated down Twelve-Pole, in freshets. Present means of transportation, Ohio river and Big Sandy. Improvements contemplated: Improvement of the navigation of the Big Sandy, and of Twelve-Pole, the Northern and Southern West Virginia railroad, Ohio River and Wayne County Mineral railroad, Pittsburgh, Wheeling and Kentucky railroad, and Tug River railroad. Public Schools, 66; Churches, 10; Postoffices, 18. Population, 7,832. Value of taxable property, $1,965,714.46. County seat, Wayne C. H. Newspaper, *Wayne Advocate*, weekly.

WEBSTER COUNTY.

The southern portion of this county, next to Nicholas, is rolling and hilly plateau land, which is also the character of the northern part. The central and eastern portions, making up a large part of the county, are exceedingly rocky and rough, with very high mountains. Much of this land is too rough for cultivation, the soil being also thin and obstructed with stones. In our remarks, we will deal only with the arable plateau lands. The soil is sandy and loam, from 4 to 6 inches deep on the hills, and on the levels 8 to 12 inches. The crops are Corn, Wheat, Oats, Rye and Grass. The yields on the levels and hills are about the same; Corn 25 to 35 bushels; Wheat 8 to 10; Oats 25. Value of farming land, $2 to $5;

wild lands in large tracts sell for 25 cents to $1 per acre. Value of timber not reported, but there is no sale for it, and it is used only for home consumption. The principal industry is farming and stock raising. Principal exports: Cattle and Sheep, which find their way through intermediate points to the eastern cities. Minerals: thin Coal seams in the hills; Limestone for agricultural and building purposes; excellent Sandstone.

Most of the county is covered with heavy forests, and is very inaccessible. The only means of transportation is by dirt roads. The principal stream is Elk river, by which some logs are floated out from the western part of the county. Contemplated improvements: the West Virginia Central railroad, the West Virginia railroad, and the Gauley River railroad. Public Schools 10; Churches, 3; Postoffices, 7; Population, 1,730; value of taxable property, $543,192 39; County Seat, Webster C. H.

WETZEL COUNTY.

Wetzel county has a good deal of fine bottom land along the Ohio river and Fishing creek, which resembles the usual bottoms along this river and its affluent creeks, being noted for fertility. Most of the county is occupied by hills with narrow valleys. The hills along the Ohio are quite high, and rise to a very considerable height towards the western side of the county, where they have narrow backs and steep slopes. Though so hilly, the land is not rocky or rough usually, but has a fine depth of fertile soil. However, the slopes of the hillsides are too steep to render frequent ploughing advisable. The soil is a loam, or sandy loam. The depth on the hills is 6 to 10 inches, and on the levels from one foot to many. The crops are Corn, Oats, Wheat, and Potatoes. The hills produce as well as the upland levels. The yields are, Corn, 40 to 50 bushels; Oats, 30 to 40, Wheat, 10 to 12; Potatoes, 100 to 150. The value of the Ohio bottoms, as usual, is from $75 to $100; other arable lands, $10 to $25; timber land, $10 to $12. The timber has a higher value, according to its proximity to the Ohio river and the railroad. Value, stumpage, is $1 to $2.50 per tree; at the mills, $10 to $12 per 1,000. Principal industries, farming, stock-raising, and lumbering. Principal exports, stock, timber and lumber. Markets for stock and farm produce, Baltimore and Wheeling; for timber, &c., Baltimore; Wheeling, and other points on the Ohio. Minerals, coal in workable seams above water level; good sandstone for building; some limestone for agricultural and building purposes. Manufactures, 3 woolen mills, and various saw mills, not reported definitely. The principal streams are the Ohio river and Fishing creek. Fishing creek is navigable for rafts and flat boats in high water. Present means of transportation: Baltimore and Ohio railroad and Ohio river. In contemplation, Narrow Gauge road from New Martinsville to the Forks of Fishing creek, improvement of the navigation of Fishing creek, and the Pittsburgh, Wheeling and Kentucky railroad. Public Schools, 61; Churches, 12; Postoffices, 14. Population, 8,595. Value of taxable property, $1,633,764.43. County seat, New Martinsville. Newspaper, *Labor Vindicator*, weekly.

WIRT COUNTY.

This county is hilly, and in some parts rough. It has good bottom lands on the rivers and creeks. The soils are clay, or clay loam, 18 inches deep on the level lands, and averaging 8 inches on the hills, being deepest and best on the north sides. The crops adapted to the soils are, Corn, Wheat, Oats, Potatoes, and Tobacco. The yields are, on the bottoms, Corn, 30 to 40; Wheat, 15 to 20; Oats, 25 to 30; Potatoes, 100 to 150 bushels; Tobacco, 1,000 to 1,200 pounds; on the hills, Corn, 30 to 35; Wheat, 10 to 15; Potatoes, 100; Tobacco, 1,200 to 1,500 pounds. No manures are used for these crops. Value of improved agricultural land, from $10 to $100 per acre; of oil land, $100 to $1,000; of timber land, $2.50 to $25. Principal industries: farming, grazing, oil-raising, and lumbering. Principal exports: lumber, hoop-poles, tan-bark, petroleum, and stock. The general markets for timber are Parkersburg and points on the Ohio river. Value of the timber, stumpage, is $1 per tree, and 8 to 12 cents per cubic foot at the mills. The principal minerals are, limestone for building and agricultural purposes, sandstone for building, whetstone, potters' clay, and oil; coal is above water level in small seams. Manufactures are, one woolen factory at Elizabeth, six steam lumber mills, one flouring mill at Elizabeth, and two on Hughes' river, as well as various grist mills. Means of transportation: steamers on the Little Kanawha, and county roads. Contemplated improvements: the further improvement of the Little Kanawha. Public Schools, 43; Postoffices, 6; Churches, 8. Population, 4,804. Value of taxable property, $1,035,798.00. County seat, Elizabeth. Newspaper, the *Wirt County Mentor*, weekly, published at Elizabeth.

WOOD COUNTY.

The general surface of Wood county is hilly, with some quite high hills and rough land. There are extensive flats on the Ohio and Little Kanawha, and the hills near these streams are comparatively low and smooth. About one-third of the county is cleared. It has fine timber in the southern part, where the soil is calcareous. The soil is loam, sandy, clayey and calcareous in different portions of the county. The best upland soil is in the south, where limestone is displayed among the strata. The crops are Corn, Wheat, Oats, Tobacco and Grass. On the ordinary uplands Corn produces 20 to 25 bushels; Wheat, 6 to 8 bushels; Oats, 15 to 20 bushels; on the bottoms Corn produces 40 to 80 bushels; Wheat, 12 to 15 bushels; Oats, 20 to 30 bushels. Soil on the hills often thin, from 1 to 4 inches; on the bottoms, one foot to many. An annual Fair is held at Parkersburg, where about $6,000 are distributed in premiums. Value of Ohio bottoms, $60 to $100, other bottoms, $20 to $50; hill land from $1 to $15, according to the character of the soil; timber land from $2 to $15. Value of timber, not reported. Principal industries: farming, stock raising, manufacturing, oil raising, and lumbering. Principal exports: Oils of various kinds, manufactured articles, lumber, stock, and grain. Markets for stock and farm produce, eastern cities; for oils, east and west; for timber, Parkersburg, and points on the Ohio. Minerals: small coal seams; petroleum, pumped from over 200 wells; good pipe and potters' clay; good sandstone, for building; limestone, in the southern part, good for agricultural and building purposes; mineral water (magnesium). Manufactures, etc.: 2 breweries, producing 2,206 barrels; 4 tobacco factories, producing 44,918 pounds; — cigar factories, producing 831,000 cigars; 6 oil refineries at Parkersburg and one at Volcano; one pottery; Baltimore and Ohio railroad machine shops at Parkersburg; one large cooper shop and several smaller ones at Parkersburg and Belleville; brick works at Parkersburg; besides numerous flour, saw and planing mills and tanneries at Parkersburg, Rockport, Wadeville, and other points. This list is not complete, as we have very imperfect reports of the manufactories. The principal streams are the Ohio river and Little Kanawha, both navigable the year round for steamers and barges. Present means of transportation: these streams and the Baltimore and Ohio railroad. Contemplated: Pittsburgh, Wheeling and Kentucky railroad. Public institutions, United States Custom House. Public schools, 99, Churches, 49. Postoffices, 23. Population, 19,000. Value of taxable property, $6,959,-263. County seat, Parkersburg, a thriving town of about 8,000 inhabitants. Newspapers: *Daily and Weekly Times, State Journal, Sentinel, Inquirer,* (last three weekly), and the *West Virginia Educational Monthly.*

WYOMING COUNTY.

This county has a good deal of rough, broken land. Its surface is hilly, the hills rising into high mountains. Nearly all of the land is in the original forest. The climate is quite mild. The soil is a loam, or sandy loam, very deep and rich on the bottoms. There is a good deal of wide bottoms near the Court House, where the land is very productive. The soil on the hills, is from 4 to 6 inches deep, and very fertile. There is very little cultivation carried on in the county generally. The crops are Corn, Wheat, Rye, Oats, Buckwheat, Tobacco, and Grass. The hills and bottoms yield about alike. Corn produces 30 to 50 bushels; Wheat, 10 to 15; Buckwheat, 25 to 30; Oats, 25 to 30. Principal industries: stock raising and lumbering. Principal exports: stock, timber, ginseng, and skins of wild animals. Markets: animals are driven eastward, timber is rafted down to points on the Ohio, other produce is transported to the Chesapeake and Ohio railroad. Corn is imported into this county from Ohio at $1 per bushel (January, 1876). Minerals: Coal is in fine workable seams; fine building stone (sandstone). Principal stream, Guyandotte river; it will float logs in high water. Present means of transportation: rough county roads. Public schools, 29. Churches, 2. Postoffices, 10. Population, 2,861. Taxable property, $955,-377.63. County seat, Oceana.

FINIS.

INDEX.

www.ingramcontent.com/pod-product-compliance
Lightning Source LLC
LaVergne TN
LVHW021139110826
845150LV00005B/1066

* 9 7 8 1 4 2 5 5 4 8 4 6 9 *